SHOPPING IN EXCITING AUSTRALIA & PAPUA NEW GUINEA

Ronald L. Krannich
Caryl Rae Krannich
Bruce Bennett

IMPACT PUBLICATIONS
Manassas, VA

SHOPPING IN EXCITING AUSTRALIA AND PAPUA NEW GUINEA: Your Passport to the Unique and Exotic

Copyright © 1989 by Ronald L. Krannich and Caryl Rae Krannich

Library of Congress Cataloging-in-Publication Data

Krannich, Ronald L.
    Shopping in exciting Australia and Papua New Guinea: your passport to the unique and exotic / Ronald L. Krannich, Caryl Rae Krannich, Bruce Bennett.
      p. cm.
    Includes index.
    1. Shopping--Australia--Guide-books. 2. Shopping--Papua New Guinea--Description and Travel--Guide-books. 3. Australia--Description and travel--Guide-Books. I. Krannich, Caryl Rae. II. Bennett, Bruce, 1951-. III. Title.
TX337.A8K73 1989   380.1'45'0002594--dc20   89-7475
ISBN 0-942710-22-3 $13.95

Cover designed by Orion Studios, 1608 20th St., NW, Washington, DC 20009

For information on distribution or quantity discount rates, call 703/361-7300 or write to: Sales Department, IMPACT PUBLICATIONS, 10655 Big Oak Circle, Manassas, VA 22111-3040. Distributed to the trade by National Book Network, 4720 Boston Way, Suite A, Lanham, MD 20706, 301/459-8696.

TABLE OF CONTENTS

PART III
SECRETS OF EXOTIC
PAPUA NEW GUINEA

PREFACE

Exciting Australia and Papua New Guinea offer some of the most unique and exotic shopping adventures in the world for those who know what to look for, where to go, and how to shop these two South Pacific countries properly. For in our visits to these two unique countries we have discovered some extremely interesting and rewarding shopping centers, arcades, department stores, shops, factory outlets, emporiums, markets, and villages that yield some truly lovely treasures.

Australia and Papua New Guinea offer many shopping opportunities for clothes, jewelry, arts, antiques, handicrafts, tribal artifacts, and home decorative items. From our visits to these countries we return home with unique and quality items to enhance our home and wardrobes. If approached properly, we believe Australia and Papua New Guinea may well become two of your favorite travel and shopping destinations.

The chapters that follow present a particular perspective on traveling and shopping in Australia and Papua New Guinea. Like other volumes in our *Shopping in Exotic Places* series, we purposefully decided to write more than just another descriptive travel guide primarily focusing on hotels, restaurants, and sightseeing and with only a few pages on shopping. Our primary focus is on shopping, and we do more than describe just the "whats" and "wheres" of shopping in these two countries.

Our experience convinces us that there is a need for a book that outlines the "how-tos" of shopping in Australia and Papua New Guinea along with the "whats" and "wheres". Such a book should both educate and guide you through the shopping maze in these two countries. Consequently, this book focuses on the **shopping process** as well as provides you with the necessary **details** for making informed shopping choices in specific shopping areas, arcades, centers, department stores, markets, shops, and villages.

Rather than just describe the "what" and "where" of travel and shopping, we include the critical **"how"** -- what to do before you depart on your trip as well as while you are in Australia and Papua New Guinea. We believe you and others are best served with a book which leads to both **understanding and action.** Therefore, you will find little in these pages about the general history, culture, economics, and politics of Australia and Papua New Guinea; these topics are covered well in other travel books. However interesting, such topics are not of particular importance to enhancing your shopping experience.

The perspective we develop throughout this book is based on our belief that traveling should be more than just another adventure in eating, sleeping, sightseeing, and taking pictures of unfamiliar places. Whenever possible, we attempt to bring to life the fact that Australia and Papua New Guinea are important centers of talented artists, craftspeople, traders, and entrepreneurs who offer you some wonderful opportunities to participate in their societies through their shopping processes. When you leave these countries, you will take with you not only some unique experiences and memories but also quality products that you will appreciate for years to come.

We have not hesitated to make qualitative judgments about shopping in Australia and Papua New Guinea. If we just presented you with shopping information, we would do you a disservice by not sharing our discoveries, both good and bad. While we know that our judgments may not be valid for everyone, we offer them as **reference points** from which you can make your own decisions. Our major emphasis throughout this book is on **quality shopping.** We look for shops which offer excellent quality and styles which we think are appropriate for Western homes and wardrobes. If you share our concern for quality shopping, you will find many of our recommendations useful to your own shopping.

Buying quality items does not mean you must spend a great deal of money on shopping. It means that you have taste, you are selective, you buy what fits into your wardrobe and home. If you shop in the right places, you will find quality products. If you understand the shopping process, you will get good value for your money. While shopping for quality may not be cheap, it need not be expensive. But most important, shopping for quality in Australia and Papua New Guinea is fun and it results in lovely items which can be enjoyed for years to come! Throughout this book we have included "tried and tested" shopping information. We make judgments based upon our experience and research approach: visited many shops, talked with numerous people, and simply shopped.

We wish to thank the many individuals and organizations that made this trip possible. Three excellent airlines, Qantas, Ansett Airlines, and Air Niugini, took us safely to, from, and around Australia and Papua New Guinea. Special thanks goes to Leif Stubkjaer who was a gracious host and friend who welcomed Bruce aboard his 50-foot Danish sailing ketch "Feen" for a unique adventure to the Trobriand Islands. We also appreciated Ron Grant's assistance with navigating the streets of Port Moresby as well as better understanding current developments in PNG.

Australian Tourism and the Melanesian Tourist Services were extremely helpful in ensuring that this project be completed in a timely manner. Throughout this book we include contact information on the local tourist offices in Australia as well as the tour services in Papua New Guinea who can assist you with every phase of your journey. We urge you to contact these offices before you leave as well as visit them once you arrive at your destinations. You will find they offer many informative maps, booklets, and services, and their personnel can answer many of your questions concerning local shopping, sightseeing, and touring opportunities.

We wish you well in your travel and shopping adventure to Australia and Papua New Guinea. The book is designed to be **used** on the streets and on the waters of these two countries. If you **plan your journey** according to the first three chapters, **handle the shopping process** according to the introductory chapters of each country section, and **navigate the streets** of Australia and Papua New Guinea based on the detailed information for each city and country, you should have a marvelous time. You'll discover some unique and exotic places, acquire some choice items, and return home with fond memories of these exciting places. If you put this book to use, it will become your passport to shopping in exciting Australia and Papua New Guinea!

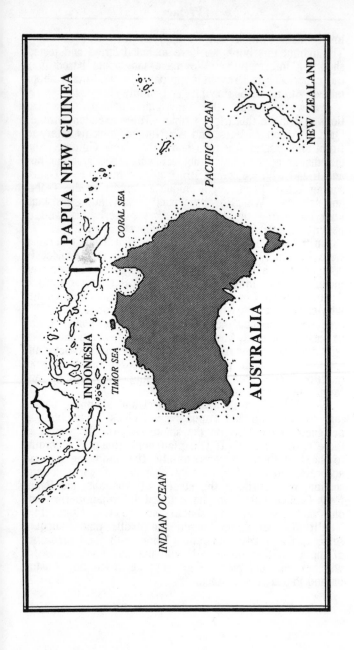

Chapter One

SHOPPING IN UNIQUE AND EXOTIC PLACES

Welcome to two of the South Pacific's most unique and exotic shopping places. Somewhat isolated from the rest of the world, large in area, small in population, and exhibiting beautiful beaches, idyllic islands, unusual landscapes, and fascinating peoples, Australia and Papua New Guinea offer some of the world's most exciting travel and shopping adventures largely unknown to most tourists and travelers to this part of the world.

From the chic boutiques, department stores, shopping centers, factory outlets, and markets of Sydney, Melbourne, Brisbane, and Adelaide to the Aboriginal art and craft shops of the Northern Territory and the tribal artifact emporiums, markets, and villages of Papua New Guinea, let us take you on a shopping adventure of a lifetime as we fly, drive, cruise, and sail to some of the world's most exciting shopping places. Come with us and we will show you an Australia and Papua New Guinea largely absent in tourist brochures, travel books, and advertisements aimed at bringing you to a different world Downunder!

1

AN EXCITING WORLD OF SHOPPING SURPRISES

Few people ever think of the South Pacific as a shopper's paradise. The South Pacific is an area of beautiful islands and beaches, emerald seas, majestic volcanic mountains, outdoor sports, and friendly peoples. Indeed, Australia has masterfully managed to create a travel image, complete with cliches, of a unique country offering surf, sun, hedonism, and adventure. If one reads the literature and listens to the advertisements, Australia is all about beaches, fishing, sailing, pubs, the Outback (Australia's desolate interior), underdogs, rugged individualism, and egalitarianism -- images reinforced by such major international events as the America's Cup Race and the arrival of *Crocodile Dundee* and other Australian films to packed movie houses and video stores around the world. Papua New Guinea, less involved with projecting a unique international image, is a colorful world of primitive peoples who dress and behave in exotic ways.

While there is much truth to such images and stereotypes that entice visitors to the shores of Australia and Papua New Guinea, there is also a great deal of hype and exaggerated claims to fame visitors should take with a smile. These are relatively new and provincial nations, lacking both glorious histories and homogeneous populations, in search of a unique national identity and an international role that would set them apart from other nations in the Pacific, Asia, Europe, and North America. Historically a dumping ground for European prisoners, geographically both an Asian and Pacific nation, culturally and linguistically European, and socially and artistically North American, Australians continue in search of the "real" Australian character which would allow them to define who they really are to themselves as well as to the rest of the world.

There are also many other Australias and Papua New Guineas that deserve equal time. Indeed, we discovered a very different Australia and Papua New Guinea unknown to most travelers -- as well as to many local residents -- who are primarily oriented toward the Outback, pubs, beaches, reefs, and exotic peoples of these two countries. These are countries of extremely talented and artistic peoples who create some of the finest arts and crafts in the world, who extend their creative and artistic talents into an exciting world of fashion and design.

For us, Australia and Papua New Guinea are prime shopping places for unique and exotic locally-produced items largely unavailable outside these countries. It's a world of outstanding arts and crafts, intriguing tribal artifacts, creative fashion clothes, unique jewelry, and fabulous contemporary art found in some of the world's most unique shopping centers, department stores, hotel shopping arcades, small shops, markets, towns, and villages throughout Australia and Papua New Guinea. Our advice: *get there soon to buy quality items and to experience a true shopping and travel adventure before shopping becomes discovered by too many tourists!*

SURPRISING CITIES, TOWNS, AND VILLAGES

Shopping in Australia and Papua New Guinea takes place in a variety of interesting locations and amongst truly interesting and talented peoples. Australia, for example, is primarily an urban nation clinging to the ocean and nearby hills with two very large cities -- Sydney and Melbourne -- several intermediate cities, and numerous small towns that dot Australia's colorful coastlines, hills, and Outback. Shopping opportunities abound throughout this vast country of talented artists, craftsmen, and designers consisting of an amalgam of local-born whites, European and Asian immigrants, and Australia's original inhabitants, the black Aboriginals. Visit the shopping centers, hotel shopping arcades, department stores, boutiques, small city shops, and factory outlets to indulge your shopping fancies, but don't forget to also venture into markets, small craft towns, and a few Aboriginal communities. There you will have an opportunity to meet artists and craftsmen as well as discover products closely tied to the cultures and lifestyles of urban artists, eccentric craftsmen dwelling in the hills, and intriguing Aboriginals representing their "Dreamtime" culture in abstract designs on bark, canvas, and wood.

While close to Australia and Indonesia, **Papua New Guinea** -- or PNG to its residents and seasoned visitors -- is unlike any other country in the world. Quickly emerging from a near Stone Age existence in the space of only 50 years, this is perhaps the world's most incredible travel and shopping adventure. Here is a mysterious but beautiful country of dense and steaming jungles, remote and rugged mountains, wild and muddy rivers, quaint trading towns, former headhunters, colorful tribespeople, dedicated missionaries, enterprising merchants and tour operators, and assorted expatriates in search of meaningful lifestyles in the midst of muggings, murders, and mischief. Remembering that many primitive tribesman became acquainted with the wheel only when a Cessna plane first landed in the Highlands during the 1930s, you participate in a true-life frontier adventure by flying into remote areas, exploring tribal villages, and sailing on to idyllic islands for one of the most exhilarating shopping and travel experiences of a lifetime!

Australia's city and towns are surprising shopping centers for some of the world's most interesting and high quality arts, crafts, and fashion clothes. Each city and area has its own unique character and a range of shopping strengths that differ from other cities and areas in Australia. To shop Australia properly, you must visit its many cities and towns as well as have an appreciation for a broad range of unique Australian and imported products, from designer clothes, accessories, and souvenirs to antiques, arts, crafts, artifacts, and home decorative items produced by and Australians, Aborigines, tribal peoples of Papua New Guinea, Asians, and Europeans. Indeed, Australia is a shopper's paradise for a fascinating range of excellent quality products.

Brisbane, capital of the East Coast state of Queensland, surprises many visitors who expected a small and provincial city. This is one of Australia's largest and most cosmopolitan, enterprising, and friendly cities which boasts great weather, a fine performing arts and cultural center, a strong crafts tradition, and the ability to attract millions of visitors to its downtown, suburban, hill, and coastal areas. Walk through its downtown pedestrian mall, explore its colorful suburban communities, or shop in its nearby hill towns and coastal communities and you will quickly discover a Brisbane which offers a wide range of resortwear, designer clothes, antiques, arts, crafts, and Aboriginal art and artifacts.

Sydney, the country's largest and most cosmopolitan city, is a wonderful place to visit and shop. Nestled on a charming harbour, Sydney boasts a dynamic central business district, adventuresome architecture, fine hotels and restaurants, and numerous cultural, entertainment, and recreational opportunities. Sunny Sydney is a brash, enterprising, fast-paced city which offers some of the best shopping opportunities in all of Australia. It has the country's most interesting shopping centers (Strand Arcade and Queen Victoria Building) and its most exclusive department store (David Jones) and suburban shopping area (Double Bay). If you're looking for clothes, jewelry, antiques, arts, crafts, and souvenirs, the shops and markets of Sydney have something for everyone. The shopping emphasis here is on clothes, accessories, jewelry, opals, souvenirs, art, and imported antiques (England) of special appeal to Sydney's cosmopolitan and up-market population as well as to the millions of tourists who come to discover this extremely liveable city.

Melbourne, the country's second largest city and elegant competitor to Sydney, is the most European of Australia's cities. It retains much of its old world charm. Its charming street cars, European architecture, parks, large immigrant communities, and ethnic restaurants set this city apart from other cities in Australia. The fashion center of Australia, conservative Melbourne is a shopper's paradise for clothes and accessories. Here you will find the latest in Australian designer clothes in downtown and suburban boutiques, department stores, and factory outlets. The arts and crafts are particularly well and alive in Melbourne. Antique and art lovers find many treasures in Melbourne's numerous antique shops and galleries. And many of Melbourne's factory outlets compete favorably with the highly overrated factory outlets of Hong Kong!

Adelaide is a pleasant surprise to many visitors who normally end their visit to Australia in Sydney and Melbourne or on the beaches of Queensland. A charming and festive city of beautiful architecture, spacious parks, and an inviting countryside, this is one of Australia's major arts and crafts centers. Shop its downtown pedestrian mall, suburban shops, and craft towns and you will surely leave with some lovely handcrafted items from South Australia.

Alice Springs is Australia's true Outback, a vast, harsh land of sand, heat, and flies. Situated in the Red Centre of the country, Alice Springs is a small but surprising frontier city which plays a major role in opening the Outback of Ayers Rock, desert, wilderness, and Australia's fascinating Aboriginals to thousands of visitors each year. Here the fashion clothes, antiques, arts, and crafts of Brisbane, Sydney, Melbourne, and Adelaide disappear as a whole new shopping experience emerges relating to the Outback environment and culture. Shopping in Alice Springs takes on a different character altogether as you are introduced to the culture of Australia's original inhabitants, the desert Aborigines, who create some of the world's most unusual art -- acrylic sand paintings representing elements of Aboriginal "Dreamtime" stories, woodcarvings, and silk screen fabrics.

Darwin, Australia's relatively isolated Top End city, faces the Timor Sea and Southeast Asia's most populous country -- Indonesia. A city with a remarkable history of survival and revival from repeated disasters brought on by Japanese bombings of World War II and periodic hurricanes, Darwin is a tropic city with intentions of becoming a major resort destination. A cosmopolitan city with a large Asian minority, Darwin is a shopper's delight for a broad range of central and coastal Aboriginal art, Australian arts and crafts, and tropical resortwear. Aboriginal art and artifact shops offer excellent prices on sand paintings, bark paintings, musical instruments, woodcarvings, and clothes produced by the Aborigines from nearby Arnhem Land and Bathurst Island as well as from the central desert near Alice Springs. Here you can buy direct from Australia's unique and enterprising Aboriginals -- the Tiwi people -- who make their home on Bathurst and Melville islands, just off the coast from Darwin. They produce Tiwi designed clothes, carved burial (*pukamani*) poles, and colorful bark baskets with abstract motifs. You can also purchase bark paintings with "Dreamtime" stories represented in the unique x-ray paintings of the Aborigines in Arnhem Land.

Cairns, Australia's gateway city to Papua New Guinea and the South Pacific, offers surprising shopping opportunities for visitors who primarily come here to soak up the sun, explore the Great Barrier Reef, and go sport fishing. A rapidly developing city similar in size to Darwin, the once sleepy Cairns has awakened to the realities of becoming a major tropical resort destination for over one million visitors each year. Boasting new resort hotels, shopping centers, a bustling downtown shopping mall, and nearby craft and resort towns, Cairns is a great place to shop for tribal art from Papua New Guinea, resortwear, contemporary art, and unique handcrafted items.

Papua New Guinea is a totally different world from the urban and cosmopolitan centers of Australia. Here you enter into the fascinating world of over 700 different ethnic and linguistic groups that primarily live in remote areas along rivers and in the heavily jungled interior. But most important for many visitors to this unique and colorful country, Papua New Guinea is a shopper's paradise for woodcarved tribal artifacts that are continuously produced in response to local tribal ceremonial traditions as well as to the steady foreign demand for primitive art and home decorative items. Indeed, this is a living museum of talented craftsmen who produce some of the world's most striking primitive art. At the same time, contemporary art -- expressed in the form of oil paintings, prints, sculptures, and textiles -- is emerging in the urban centers as new and exciting art and craft movements that provide additional shopping opportunities for visitors. In Papua New Guinea one's shopping locations include such cities and towns as Port Moresby, Lae, Madang, Wewak, and Rabaul as well as towns and villages in the Highlands, along the Sepik River, and in the Trobriand Islands.

SELECTING AND ORDERING YOUR PLACES

The cities and towns appearing in this book are in the

sequence in which we visited them in our most recent trip to Australia and Papua New Guinea. The decision to do Brisbane first and then Sydney, Melbourne, Adelaide, Alice Springs, Darwin, Cairns, Port Moresby, the Highlands, the Sepik River, and the Trobriand Islands was purposeful given scheduling and shipping considerations.

Brisbane is a good entry point to Australia. From there you can proceed south to Sydney, west to Melbourne and Adelaide, north to Alice Springs and Darwin, and complete the circle at Cairns on the northeast coast. Since Cairns is the gateway city to Papua New Guinea, it is a good place to relax and survey excellent quality Papua New Guinea artifacts after a fast-paced Australian adventure. Throughout Australia we used one shipping consolidation point in Brisbane. All large items purchased in other cities were shipped to our Brisbane contact where all items were combined in a single sea freight shipment. If you have a different sequence of cities, we recommend that your first city where you make a bulky purchase become your central shipping consolidation point. Therefore, it is best to pick a large East Coast city such as Brisbane or Sydney.

In Papua New Guinea it is best to spend at least two days in Port Moresby surveying your shopping options and making contacts with potential shippers prior to venturing on to the Sepik River and towns outside Port Moresby. If you fail to do this, you may end up with a very expensive shipping bill with separate shipments coming out of different locations, going into Port Moresby, and leaving as separate shipments. You will want to consolidate all your shipments with a Port Moresby-based shipper who knows the business well and can coordinate the logistics of consolidating large items you left in towns outside the capital to be brought into his central packing and shipping warehouse in Port Moresby.

Consequently, you will also want to return to Port Moresby for a day or two at the end of your journey to do any last minute shopping as well as finalize all shipping arrangements with your Port Moresby shipper. This includes providing the shipper with the list of items and prices, identifying the port to receive your goods, prepaying for the shipment, and completing the documentation work. Since you will need at least a half-day to finalize these shipping arrangements, and you will probably want to spend another half-day doing last minute shopping in Port Moresby's two artifact emporiums, be sure to leave sufficient time at the end of your trip to do such shopping and make final shipping arrangements.

FOCUS ON QUALITY AND UNIQUE ITEMS

Shopping in Exciting Australia and Papua New Guinea is designed to provide you with the necessary **knowledge and skills** to become an effective shopper in these two countries. We especially designed the book with two major considerations in mind:

- Focus on quality shopping
- Emphasis on finding unique items

Throughout this book we attempt to identify the **best quality shopping** in both Australia and Papua New Guinea. This does not mean we have discovered the cheapest shopping or best bargains, although we have attempted to do so when opportunities for comparative shopping arose within and between communities. Our focus is primarily on shopping for **unique and quality items** that will retain their value in the long run and can be appreciated for years to come. This means many of our recommended shops may initially appear expensive. But they offer top value that you will not find in many other shops. For example, when we discover the unique jewelry designs of Robert Clerc in Sydney, we acknowledge the fact that his work is expensive, but it is very beautiful and unique, so much so that you quickly forget his prices after you acquire and continue to admire his outstanding work. When we examine tribal art from Papua New Guinea, we identify key shops in Port Moresby and Cairns that offer good quality items. While more expensive than items found along the Sepik River, many of the artifacts found in these shops are one-of-a-kind pieces you cannot find elsewhere. The same is true for a few art, antique, and home decorative shops we discovered in Brisbane and Adelaide that offer artifacts from Papua New Guinea which were once part of private collections. These items may initially seem expensive, but some are museum quality which cannot be purchased elsewhere at any price.

On the other hand, we also identify what we consider to be the best buys for quality items. For example, while you will find excellent quality Aboriginal bark and acrylic paintings in Brisbane, Sydney, Melbourne, and Adelaide, you can discover similar quality Aboriginal paintings at half of the big city prices in Alice Springs and Darwin. And even in Darwin, the best buys for Tiwi art are found in the Aboriginal shops on nearby Bathurst Island where you will pay one-half of the price for the same items available in the shops of Darwin. If you are interested in clothes, some of your best buys are found in the factory outlets of Melbourne where you can buy, for example, a A$180 Rob Paynter sweater for A$70! And your best buys on opals come when you know the differences in the types and quality of opals and look for deep discounts on these stones or shop for antique opal jewelry.

APPROACHING THE SUBJECT

The chapters that follow take you on a whirlwind shopping adventure of Australia and Papua New Guinea. Our choice of cities may seem unusual, with some curious absences, to many readers. While we would have preferred to cover all cities in Australia, including Perth, Hobart, and Canberra as well as more craft towns in the hills and along the coasts of Sydney, Melbourne, and Adelaide, we had to make choices given the time limits and logistics in getting this rather ambitious project literally off the ground and running. We quickly learned, for example, Canberra and Hobart offered some -- but by no means extensive shopping -- and Perth a great deal more shopping for clothes, jewelry, arts, and crafts. But these places are not as much in Australia's central shopping loop for clothes, arts, crafts, and Aboriginal arts and artifacts as are cities and towns surrounding Brisbane, Sydney, Melbourne, Adelaide, Alice Springs, Darwin, and Cairns.

We hope to include Perth, Hobart, Canberra, and additional craft and resort towns in subsequent editions of this book. In the meantime, do visit these places and look for shopping opportunities in the central business districts, suburbs, and nearby towns.

The same holds true for our choice of shopping towns, islands, and villages in Papua New Guinea. Time only permitted us to initially focus in-depth on what we learned were the major shopping areas. However, we hope future editions of this book will take you into other potentially rewarding shopping areas of Papua New Guinea -- the Blackwater River, Lae, Wewak, and New Ireland -- and of course the continually evolving contemporary art and textile movements centered in Port Moresby.

We've given a great deal of attention to constructing a complete user-friendly book that focuses on the shopping process, offers extensive details on the "how", "what", and "where" of shopping, and includes a sufficient level of redundancy to be informative, useful, and usable. The chapters, for example, are organized like one would organize and implement a travel and shopping adventure to these two countries. Each chapter incorporates sufficient details, including names and addresses, to get you started in some of the best shopping areas and shops in each city, town, or village. We purposefully include what we call a functional level of redundancy, where the same shops appear in both "Where To Shop" and "What To Buy" sections, so the reader can easily cross-reference the important "where" of shopping.

Indexes and table of contents are especially important to us and others who believe a travel book is first and foremost a guide to unfamiliar places. Therefore, our index includes both subjects and shops, with shops printed in bold for ease of reference; the table of contents is elaborated in detail so it, too, can be used as another handy reference index for subjects and products. If, for example, you are interested in "what to buy" or "where to shop" in Melbourne, the best reference will be the table of contents. If you are interested in factory outlets in Melbourne, look under "Factory outlets" in the index. And if you are interested in learning if and where you can find a Country Road clothing store in Adelaide -- just in case you passed up a lovely item in one of their stores in Sydney or Melbourne -- then look under "**Country Road**" in the index. By using the table of contents and index together, you can access most any information from this book.

The remainder of this book is divided into three parts and 15 additional chapters which look at both the process and content of shopping in our unique and exotic places. Part I -- **"Traveling Smart"** -- assists you in preparing for your Australia and Papua New Guinea shopping adventures by focusing on the how-to of traveling and shopping in these two places. Chapter Two, "Know Before You Go", takes you through the basics of getting to and enjoying your stay in each country, including international and domestic transportation and the promises and pitfalls of local travel. Chapter Three, "Plan and Manage Your Adventure", examines how to best prepare for your trip to Australia and Papua New Guinea, including what best to pack as well as how to best manage your money, identify your shopping needs, and ship your purchases home with ease.

Eight chapters in Part II -- **"Secrets of Exciting Australia"** -- examine the how, what, and where of shopping in seven of Australia's major shopping destinations: Brisbane, Sydney, Melbourne, Adelaide, Alice Springs, Darwin, and Cairns. Here we identify major shopping strengths of each city; detail the how, what, and where of shopping; and share information on some of the best hotels, restaurants, and sights for each community and surrounding area.

The five chapters in Part III -- **"Papua New Guinea"** -- examine the how, what, and where of shopping in Papua New Guinea. It includes separate chapters on products, places, and shopping procedures.

RECOMMENDED SHOPS

We hesitate to recommend specific shops since we know the pitfalls of doing so. Shops that offered excellent products and service during one of our visits, for example, may change ownership, personnel, and policies from one year to another. In addition, our shopping preferences may not be the same as your preferences.

Our major concern is to outline your shopping options in Australia and Papua New Guinea, show you where to locate the best shopping areas, and share some useful shopping strategies that you can use anywhere in Australia and Papua New Guinea, regardless of particular shops we or others may recommend. Armed with this knowledge and some basic shopping skills, you will be better prepared to locate your own shops and determine which ones offer the best products and service in relation to your own shopping and travel goals.

However, we also recognize the "need to know" when shopping in unfamiliar places. Therefore, throughout this book we list the names and locations of various shops we have found to offer good quality products. In some cases we have purchased items in these shops and can also recommend them for service and reliability. But in most cases we surveyed shops to determine the quality of products offered without making purchases. To buy in every shop would be beyond our budget, as well as our home storage capabilities! Whatever you do, treat our names and addresses as **orientation points** from which to identify your own products and shops. If you rely solely on our listings, you will miss out on one of the great adventures of shopping in Australia and Papua New Guinea -- discovering your own special shops that offer unique items and exceptional value and service.

EXPECT A REWARDING ADVENTURE

Whatever you do, enjoy your shopping and travel adventure to Australia and Papua New Guinea. These are two very interesting and special countries. They offer many unique items that can be purchased and integrated well into many homes and wardrobes outside these countries.

So arrange your flights and accommodations, pack your credit cards and traveler's checks, and head for two of the South Pacific's most delightful shopping and travel destinations. Three to four weeks later you should return home with much more than a set of photos and travel brochures. You will have some wonderful purchases and shopping tales that can be enjoyed and relived for a lifetime.

Shopping our unique and exotic places only takes time, money, and a sense of adventure. Take the time, be willing to part with some of your money, and open yourself to a whole new world of shopping. If you are like us, your shopping adventure will introduce you to an exciting world of quality products, friendly people, and interesting places that you might have otherwise missed had you just passed through these places to eat, sleep, see sights, and take pictures. When you go shopping in unique and exotic places, you are not just another tourist. You are a special kind of international traveler who discovers quality and learns about these places through the people and products that define their urban and rural cultures.

PART I

TRAVELING SMART

Chapter Two

KNOW BEFORE YOU GO

Australia and Papua New Guinea are not on major international routes nor are they well known to many outsiders. Most visitors have some idea of what to expect in Australia. At least they have heard about such cities as Sydney and Melbourne, and perhaps Brisbane, Darwin, and Perth. But few travelers have ever heard of Cairns and Port Moresby or such exotic places as Mt. Hagen, Ambunti, the Sepik River, Madang, and the Trobriand Islands. Such questions as *"How do I get there?"* and *"What can I expect in terms of local transportation, food, accommodations, weather, and potential problems?"* are concerns for many people planning to make a trip to this unique and exotic part of the world.

LOCATION AND CLIMATE

Australia and Papua New Guinea are located in the southwest corner of the South Pacific island group. Australia lies west of New Zealand and south of Indonesia. Papua New Guinea is found just northeast of Australia, directly east of Indonesia, south of the Philippines, and west of the Solomon Islands. Australia is the largest island continent in the world; Papua New Guinea occupies the eastern half of the world's second largest island, New Guinea.

Papua New Guinea lies just south of the equator whereas Australia stretches over both tropical and temperate zones. While Papua New Guinea's location and climate is decidedly equatorial -- both hot and humid -- its mountains and high elevations mediate the worst effects the heat and humidity. Depending on where you travel, much of Papua New Guinea's weather can be pleasant, with mild days and cool evenings. On the other hand, Australia's weather varies greatly: a tropical climate embracing Darwin and Cairns in the north and northeast; extremely hot and bitter cold weather in Alice Springs; beautiful clear skies and warm temperatures in Brisbane; bright but sometimes chilly Sydney; often dreary and wet Melbourne; and unpredictable in Adelaide. Since Australia is in the Southern Hemisphere, remember her seasons are just the opposite of those in the Northern Hemisphere.

The best time to visit Australia and Papua New Guinea depends on where you plan to visit. If you include all the places outlined in this book, June to August would be the best months for many places. However, since this is Australia's winter, you might find Sydney chilly at times and Adelaide and Melbourne very wet, dreary, and cold. But Alice Springs, Darwin, Cairns, and most parts of Papua New Guinea can be very pleasant at this time of year. On the other hand, if you plan to primarily confine your visit to Sydney and Melbourne, the best time to visit would be during their Spring and Fall -- the Northern Hemisphere's Fall and Spring.

WHAT TO PACK AND WEAR

Packing clothes for a combined trip to these countries can be problem, especially if you arrive in the midst of Australia's winter. We recommend taking light-weight clothes and packing light in anticipation of filling your bags with purchases along the way. If you will be in Australia during the winter, take a medium-weight jacket, wool sweater, and a pair of gloves. Chances are you might encounter a mild winter. If not, you can always buy another sweater in Australia -- preferably one made from the fine Australian wools or an inexpensive import from China -- and layer your clothes. We do not recommend taking many heavy bulky clothes, although on a bitter cold day or night you may wish you had! We prefer taking the minimum amount of outer wear and take our chances with the cold winter. The worst thing that can happen is that you must go shopping for warmer clothes. If this happens, the best place to buy inexpensive clothes will be some of the markets and factory outlets in Sydney and Melbourne. As you will see later, Australian-made clothes, especially those found in department stores and shopping centers, tend to be expensive.

Both Australia and Papua New Guinea are very casual countries. You can wear casual shirts, blouses, and slacks most everywhere.

THE PEOPLES

Australia and Papua New Guinea have very diverse populations. While most of Australia's 17 million population are white, with European immigrant roots, Australia also has a sizeable black Aboriginal population and a large number of Asian immigrants. Most Australians and Asians live in cities and a few Outback communities. Many Aborigines inhabit the harsh interior, although some, such as the Tiwi, live on Bathurst and Melville islands and the fertile coastal and Arnhem Land areas of the north. This population diversity gives Australia a unique character. Darwin, for example, has an interesting mix of whites, Aboriginals, and Asians. It's numerous ethnic restaurants testify to the fact that Darwin's European and Asian immigrants still prefer their ethnic foods.

The peoples of Papua New Guinea are strikingly different from Australians. Papuans are Melanesian peoples. While black, they should not be confused with the black Aboriginals in Australia who are not of Melanesian stock. Altogether, there are over 700 different ethnic and linguistic groups among these Melanesian peoples. Papua New Guinea also has a sizeable Australian, European, and North American expatriate community primarily involved in mining operations, shipping, commerce, government administration, education, and missionary work. As might be expected from their close proximity to and colonial involvement in Papua New Guinea, the Australians make up the largest expatriate community. Most expatriates are found in the larger urban centers. The Papuans largely live in rural villages where they continue to practice their traditional, sometimes near Stone Age, customs. Many, however, have migrated to the towns and cities where they are involved in education and government work, are laborers, or remain unemployed as well as involved in mischief. You will also find some Chinese who run local businesses in the cities and towns.

GETTING THERE

Several international airlines service Australia, but fewer fly into Papua New Guinea. PNG's national carrier, Air Niugini, and Australia's Qantas Airline are the major carriers for these two countries.

You can take international flights into most major cities in Australia -- Sydney, Melbourne, Adelaide, Canberra, Brisbane, Cairns, Darwin, and Perth. The national carrier, Qantas, is the major international carrier servicing most large coastal cities in Australia. Other major airlines, such as Air New Zealand, United, Continental, Canadian Airlines, UTA French Airlines, British Air, Air India, Lufthansa, KLM, and Singapore Airlines, also fly to Australia.

We flew to Brisbane on **Qantas** from San Francisco in the United States via Honolulu and Cairns. Qantas lived up to its reputation as a very good airline, with excellent service; flights normally depart and arrive within 15 to 30 minutes of the stated times. Qantas' real strengths are its informative pilots and videos that keep passengers abreast of flight conditions, arrival times, and transportation from airport to the city and baggage handling which is efficient and treated with care.

Australia's major domestic airlines are Ansett Airlines of Australia, Australian Airlines, and East West Airlines. In addition, you will find several regional airlines, such as Kendell Airlines, Sunstate Airlines, and Air Queensland, servicing the states. All of the cities included in this book are serviced by Ansett Airlines and Australian Airlines. Both of these airlines tend to depart and arrive at the same destinations within a few minutes of each other, so neither has a scheduling advantage over the other. All of our domestic flights were on **Ansett Airlines.** Similar to Qantas, Ansett has excellent service and flights generally depart and arrive on time. Ansett also is a full service travel organization that offers several travel services. Be sure to book and reconfirm your flights in plenty of time. During certain times of the year both Ansett and Australian Airlines may be fully booked if you wait until the last minute.

All Australian airlines have some of the most restrictive cabin luggage restrictions in the world -- one small bag (22 x 15 x 8) not weighting more than 11 pounds. While we are not sure of the reason for such an extreme restriction, it is the rule nonetheless, and airline personnel are extremely bureaucratic in enforcing this restriction to the letter. For shoppers who are used to being permitted by other airlines to carry some of their delicate purchases on board, these restrictions will require you to pack such purchases well and send them through with your luggage. Luckily, Australian baggage handlers take good care of luggage.

Since many places in Papua New Guinea are remote locations not serviced by roads, this is a flying country. **Air Niugini** services Sydney, Brisbane, Cairns, and Townsville from Port Moresby as well as flies to and from Singapore, Hong Kong, Manila, Honiara, Port Vila, and Jayapura. It also flies between the major towns in Papua New Guinea. Except for a small chartered Talair flight from Port Moresby to Ambunti, all of our domestic flights were on Air Niugini. This is young, pioneering, and friendly airline with excellent service and safety records. For our international flight we flew from Cairns to Port Moresby and then back Cairns. This flight departs three times a week and only takes about one and a half hours. When booking your flights, keep in mind that Air Niugini offers a special domestic rate. The cost of domestic Air Niugini flights is reduced by 40%, if you book them as part of your international ticketing, arrive and depart Papua New Guinea on Air Niugini, and have purchased an all inclusive local tour package. Contact your travel agent or an Air Niugini office in the U.S., Frankfurt, Tokyo, Hong Kong, Singapore, Manila, Honiara, or Australia for information on this special rate.

GETTING AROUND WITH EASE

It is fairly easy to get around Australia. Not only are all of its major cities and towns serviced by airlines, it also has an extensive all weather road system linking these communities by bus, car, and truck.

It is relatively easy to drive in Australia. Maps are good and roads are usually well marked, although a street with one name often changes to another name unexpectedly. However, keep in mind that this is a very big country to drive, and driving in the Outback can be dangerous should you have a breakdown. For people with limited time, we recommend flying to the major cities, using local transportation within the city, and renting a car to visit outlying areas.

Australia also has a rail system that links Cairns to Brisbane, Sydney, Canberra, Melbourne, Adelaide, and Perth as well as the famous Ghan line connecting Adelaide with Alice Springs.

Getting around in Papua New Guinea is another story altogether. You will most likely fly into most towns by jet on Air Niugini or by prop planes on such small airlines as Talair, MAF, Douglas Airways, Bougair, and Provincial

Air Services. We do not recommend renting a car under any circumstances. It is very dangerous to drive in Papua New Guinea because of the potential for violence should you be in an accident. Indeed, if you are involved in an accident, regardless of whose fault it is, you should immediately flee the area and head for the nearest police station for protection. Accidents invariably lead to some form of on-the-spot "pay-back"; a serious pay-back could very well cost you your life! Many locals do not understand such concepts as insurance, police investigations, and court justice -- only making things even, which is the payback. Our best recommendation is to fly into communities, take public transportation -- a taxi when available -- or rent a car with an experienced driver. Taxis and cars with drivers may cost more, but they are safer than the local buses (PMVs). Taxis in Port Moresby are reasonable though not cheap given the long distances between areas, but in the Trobriand Islands our car with driver cost K1.25 per mile. We discovered one of the reasons for such expensive charges was the high cost of local maintenance. If a tire had to be changed, it had to be air-freighted for service in Port Moresby!

Since this is not a convenient do-it-yourself travel country, the best way to see Papua New Guinea is to arrive in Port Moresby on your own and then connect to a pre-booked tour of the Highlands, Sepik River, or the islands. Alternatively, you can arrive in Papua New Guinea as part of a package tour to Australia or an all inclusive tour of Papua New Guinea. However you approach it, do make in-country tour reservations in plenty of time, especially if you plan to visit from June to August, since many of the tours may be fully booked. On the other hand, if you decide to travel on short notice, you may be able to book at the last minute depending on booking levels and unexpected cancellations.

FOOD AND ACCOMMODATIONS

Food and accommodations can be expensive in both Australia and Papua New Guinea if you insist on staying at deluxe and first-class hotels and eating at major restaurants. A deluxe hotel, for example, can cost A$250 or more a night in Sydney. While Papua New Guinea does not have deluxe hotels on the same level as those in Australia, their good first-class hotels can cost over US$100 a night. However, both countries also have a range of inexpensive accommodations.

You will find plenty to eat in Australia. It has excellent restaurants and take-away food shops offering a good range of ethnic, but by no means inexpensive, foods. On the other hand, Papua New Guinea has few restaurants, selections are limited, and finding good and inexpensive food outside hotels may not be your idea of a good time. It's good to pack some extra snacks and drinks; department stores in Port Moresby have grocery sections with a good range of foodstuffs. If you book an all inclusive tour in Papua New Guinea, your meals will be included in the tour package.

PROMISES AND POTENTIAL PITFALLS

Traveling and shopping in Australia and Papua New Guinea is relatively easy if you approach these countries right. We find Australia very clean, comfortable, and convenient to get around; health and sanitation standards are some of the best in the world; the people are generally friendly and helpful; many Australians display an interesting character -- a creative, innovative, analytical, independent, and entrepreneurial *"give it a go"* streak; the sights are both interesting and unusual; and the shopping is often marvelous. It's such an easy country to navigate that one sometimes forgets that this is not home. It's only when you see the unusual landscape, encounter the Aborigines, drive on the left side of the road, or have difficulty with some of the Australian English words and phases (French dressing in Australia is Italian dressing and visa versa; the ground floor is our first floor; entrees are appetizers and main courses are entrees; sauce is catsup; jumpers are sweaters; Manchester is linens) that you feel you are in a foreign country after all.

The downside of Australia is very minor but there nonetheless. Except for a few sections of Sydney, the interior countryside is not particularly attractive; most cities are architecturally unattractive; street signs are often missing or streets change their names unexpectedly; large companies, businesses, and officials tend to be overly bureaucratic and obsessed with rules and regulations rather than with getting things done; except among Asian immigrants, Australian service and the work ethnic leave much to be desired; products and services tend to be overpriced; many Australians have an irritating habit -- in part indicative of a young, insecure nation in search of a national identity and in part due to their relative unfamiliarity with the rest of the world -- of overstating they are or they possess the "biggest" and "best" in comparison to other cities and countries; the sight and plight of Australia's Aborigines as well as public debates on Asian immigrants and Papua New Guinea that challenge the dominant image of an easy going, caring, tolerant, and classless Australia.

Papua New Guinea also has its upsides and downsides. Its major attractions are its natural beauty -- mountains, beaches, islands -- interesting peoples, fabulous tribal arts, and convenient airlines and tours. Its downsides tend to be its inconvenience in getting around; the general lack of travel amenities; questionable service; overpriced products and services; mosquitos; rudimentary health and sanitation facilities; and potential threats of crime and violence.

But let's be fair to Papua New Guinea. This is a Third World country, a new, struggling, and proud nation in the midst of major social and cultural changes. Except for a few tour companies that largely define this country's tourism industry, Papua New Guinea is not organized to handle large numbers of tourists who expect the very best travel amenities. You may have to rough it for US$100-300 a day, but it's well worth the expense and potential irritations -- both of which may become humorous "war stories" in the years ahead.

To really enjoy PNG, one should expect some inconveniences, be tolerant of the people and services, and be open to that wonderful experience of serendipity. In the end, we should always put such places in comparative perspective. Port Moresby, for example, is not nearly as crime-ridden or violence-prone as Washington, DC, New York City, Detroit, or Los Angeles. If you can be open-minded and keep everything in comparative perspective, the downside of Papua New Guinea will quickly disappear as you experience one of the most thrilling travel and shopping adventures of a lifetime!

Chapter Three

PLAN AND MANAGE YOUR ADVENTURE

Preparation is one of the most important ingredients to ensuring a successful trip to Australia and Papua New Guinea. But it involves much more than just examining maps, reading travel literature, making airline and hotel reservations, or booking tours. Preparation, at the very least, is a process of minimizing uncertainty by learning how to develop a shopping plan, manage your money, determine the value of products, handle Customs, pack for the occasion, and ship with ease. It involves knowing **what** products are good deals to buy **where** in Australia and Papua New Guinea. Most important of all, preparation helps organize and ensure the success of all aspects of a shopping adventure.

ANTICIPATE COSTS

Traveling and shopping in Australia and Papua New Guinea can be as inexpensive or expensive as you want them to be. In general, however, these are expensive places to visit, especially if you are used to traveling and shopping next door in inexpensive Southeast Asia. Indeed,

23

many Australians prefer doing their shopping in Singapore, Bangkok, and Hong Kong. But Australia and PNG are no more expensive than visiting or shopping in many parts of Europe.

The major problem with cost and value is the very high cost but low productivity of Australian labor. Australian unions are politically powerful, exacting major hour, wage, and benefit concessions from both management and government. The minimum wage in Australia, for example, is $A6 -- including dishwashers and maids. Such costs are passed on to consumers in the form of high restaurant and hotel bills. Moreover, you will find many restaurants and shops close on the weekend, because they cannot afford to pay time-and-a-half which is mandated by law for most such establishments staying open on Saturday afternoons and Sundays. Restaurants even include a weekend surcharge on your bill because of this time-and-a-half pay requirement.

Many of the high costs in Papua New Guinea are influenced by the dominant economic role played by Australia in this country as well as by the high costs of imported foods and consumer goods.

One of your least expensive trip costs will be your international air transportation. It is still relatively inexpensive compared to costs 10 or 20 years ago or current costs of domestic airfares in the U.S. or international airfares from the U.S. to Europe. For example, depending on what time of year you go and how far in advance you book and pay your fare, you can fly roundtrip from the U.S. West Coast to Cairns, Brisbane, Melbourne, or Sydney for around US$1000. Many excellent package tours will include 10 days of hotels and some ground arrangements for under US$2000. Some 7-day packages from New York City and Washington, DC to Australia go for as little as US$1200!

Hotels and local transportation in Australia and Papua New Guinea can be very expensive. Deluxe hotels in Sydney, for example, can cost more than US$200 per day; first-class hotels in Port Moresby, Mt. Hagen, and Madang can cost more than US$100 a day. However, Australia has a range of medium to inexpensive accommodations, especially motels, ranging from US$30 to US$60 a night. You can also find similarly priced accommodations in Papau New Guinea. Domestic air transportation can be expensive in Australia if you fly to all of our destinations. Australia is simply a big country that requires one to three hour flights between many destinations.

Food is also relatively expensive in Australia and Papua New Guinea. It is difficult to eat at a good restaurant in

Australia for under US$25 per person; don't be surprised if your bill approaches US$50 per person, excluding drinks. And with weekend surcharges at most restaurants, the bill can seem quite high for what you get. The best buys on food are the fast-food chain restaurants and take-away food establishments. Indeed, we consistently found the take-away places, especially those offering Asian cuisine, to have the best and least expensive food in Australia. While tipping is not an acceptable practice in both countries, the taxes, surcharges, and high costs of labor reflected in your restaurant tab more than off-set any price advantages suggested by the no-tipping rule.

Your unexpected traveling costs will most likely be the cost of shopping for local products. Here, we cannot give you specific guidelines other than the general observation that you should take enough cash, personal checks, and traveler's checks as well as sufficient credit limits on your credit cards in anticipation of finding plenty of treasures in these two countries. If you are a serious shopper for antiques, arts, crafts, tribal artifacts, jewelry, and clothes, you may quickly find you've spent more than you expected given the large number of quality items you will probably want to buy in both Australia and Papua New Guinea. Even here the prices seem high compared to similar items in other countries. The best buys will be on locally produced arts and crafts which do not reflect the overall high costs of local union labor nor international transportation costs and import duties incurred on the many imported goods found in Australia and Papua New Guinea.

DEVELOP AN ACTION PLAN

Time is money when traveling abroad. The better you plan and use your time, the more time you will have to enjoy your trip. If you want to use your time wisely and literally hit the ground running, you should plan a detailed, yet tentative, schedule for each day. Begin by:

- Identifying each city and area you plan to visit.
- Block out the number of days you will spend in each area.
- List those places you feel you must visit during your stay.
- Leave extra time each day for new discoveries.

Keep this plan with you and revise it in light of new information.

If you decide to join one of the excellent tours in Papua New Guinea, all planning will be taken care of for you during the duration of the tour. However, most tours also offer some flexibility to accommodate individual interests. When you sign up for one of the tours, keep in mind that you might be able to make some changes in your tour itinerary.

WELCOME SERENDIPITY AND GOOD LUCK

Planning is fine, but don't overdo it and thus ruin your trip by accumulating a list of unfulfilled expectations. Planning needs to be adapted to certain realities which often become the major highlights of one's travel and shopping experiences. This is especially true of surprising Australia and Papua New Guinea. Good luck is a function of good planning: you place yourself in many different places to take advantage of new opportunities. You should be open to unexpected events which may well become the major highlights of your travel and shopping experiences.

If you want to have good luck, then plan to be in many different places to take advantage of new opportunities. Expect to alter your initial plans once you begin discovering new and unexpected realities. Serendipity -- those chance occurrences that often evolve into memorable and rewarding experiences -- frequently interferes with the best-laid travel and shopping plans. Welcome serendipity by altering your plans to accommodate the unexpected. You can do this by revising your plans each day as you go. A good time to summarize the day's events and accomplishments and plan tomorrow's schedule is just before you go to bed each night.

Keep in mind that your plan should be a means to an end -- experiencing exciting travel and shopping - and not the end itself. If you plan well, you will surely experience good luck on the road to a successful trip!

CONDUCT RESEARCH AND
NETWORK FOR INFORMATION

Do as much research as possible before you depart on your Australia and Papua New Guinea adventures. A good starting place is the periodical section of your local library. Here you may find several magazine and newspaper articles on travel and shopping in Australia and Papua New Guinea.

You should also write, call, or fax the Australian Tourist Commission and Air Niugini for information on their countries. The Australian Tourist Commission (in the U.S.

call 415/865-5126 or write to Tourism Australia, 1150 Marina Village Parkway, Suite 104, Alameda, CA 94501), for example, puts together an excellent trip planning book entitled *The Aussie Holiday Book* which is free for the asking. Air Niugini (in the U.S. call 714/752-5440 or write to Air Niugini, 5000 Birch St., Suite 3000, Newport Beach, CA 92660) provides information on travel to Papua New Guinea. Names, addresses, and information on individual tour operators are found in the information packets distributed by the Australian Tourist Commission and Air Niugini.

We also recommend **networking for information and advice**. You'll find many people, including relatives, friends, and acquaintances, who have traveled to Australia and Papua New Guinea and are eager to share their experiences and discoveries with you. They may recommend certain shops where you will find excellent products, service, and prices. Ask them basic who, what, where, why, and how questions:

- What shops did you particularly like?
- What do they sell?
- How much discount could I expect?
- Whom should I talk to?
- Where is the shop located?
- How do I get what I want?

Once you arrive in Australia, be sure to contact the local tourist offices in each city. Most Australian cities have two tourist information offices -- a state tourism office affiliated with the Australian Tourism Commission and a city convention and information office. The state tourism office is usually the most helpful since it is also organized to help individuals in scheduling hotel reservations and tours. You will not find similar offices in Papua New Guinea since the government is not actively promoting tourism through its own information office. This function is primarily performed by private companies -- Air Niugini and the local tour operators.

CHECK CUSTOMS REGULATIONS

It's always good to know Customs regulations before leaving home. If you are a U.S. citizen planning to return to the U.S. from Australia and Papua New Guinea, the U. S. Customs Service provides several helpful publications which are available free of charge from your nearest U.S. Customs Office, or write P.O. Box 7407, Washington, D.C. 20044.

- *Know Before You Go* (Publication #512): outlines facts about exemptions, mailing gifts, duty-free articles, and prohibited and restricted articles.

- *International Mail Imports* answers many travelers' questions regarding mailing items from foreign countries back to the US. The U.S. Postal Service sends all packages to Customs for examination and assessment of duty before it is delivered to the addressee. Some items are free of duty and some are dutiable. The rules have recently changed on mail imports, so do check on this before you leave the U.S.

- *GSP and the Traveler* itemizes goods from particular countries that can enter the U.S. duty-free. GSP regulations, which are designed to promote the economic development of certain Third World countries, permit many products, especially arts and handicrafts, to enter the United States duty-free. Most of your purchases from PNG should be allowed to enter duty-free. However, most purchases from Australia, will be dutiable.

MANAGE YOUR MONEY WELL

It is best to carry traveler's checks, two or more major credit cards with sufficient credit limits, U.S. dollars, and a few personal checks. Our basic money rule is to take enough money and sufficient credit limits so you don't run short. How much you take is entirely up to you, but it's better to have too much than not enough when shopping in Australia and Papua New Guinea.

We prefer using credit cards to pay for hotels and restaurants and for major purchases as well as for unanticipated expenses incurred when shopping. Most major hotels and stores in Australia honor MasterCard, Visa, American Express, and Diner's cards. It is a good idea to take one or two bank cards and an American Express card. Most places in Papua New Guinea that do accept credit cards only accept an American Express card. Take plenty of **traveler's checks** in U.S. denominations of $50 and $100. Smaller denominations are often more trouble than they are worth, but you may want a few. Most major banks, hotels, restaurants, and shops accept traveler's checks, and they usually give you a better exchange rate on traveler's checks than on cash. Banks will give you the best exchange rates, but at times you'll find hotels to be more convenient because of their close proximity and better hours.

Personal checks can be used to obtain traveler's checks with an American Express card or to pay for goods to be shipped later -- after your check has cleared your bank. Some shops in both Australia and Papua New Guinea will accept personal checks. Remember to keep one personal check aside to pay Customs should you have dutiable goods when you return home.

Use you own judgment concerning how much **cash** you should carry with you. Contrary to some fearful ads, cash is awfully nice to have in moderate amounts to supplement your traveler's checks and credit cards. Some US$20 bills are good when you need to change money before leaving a country and don't want to convert much money back to your own currency on departure. But of course you must be very careful where and how you carry cash. Since traveler's checks are widely accepted in Australia and Papua New Guinea and you get the best exchange rates on them, you may choose to put most of your cash into traveler's checks. Most shops in Australia and Papua New Guinea accept U.S. dollars along with traveler's checks. However, outside Port Moresby -- especially along the Sepik River -- only local currency is accepted. Take small denominations since many villagers do not, or claim not to, have change for large bills.

USE CREDIT CARDS WISELY

Credit and charge cards can be a shopper's blessing. They are your tickets to serendipity, convenience, good exchange rates, and a useful form of insurance. Widely accepted throughout Australia and in tourist hotels and shops in Papua New Guinea (primarily American Express card in PNG), they enable you to draw on credit reserves for purchasing many wonderful items you did not anticipate finding when you initially planned your adventure. In addition to being convenient, you usually will get good exchange rates once the local currency amount appearing on your credit slip is converted by the bank at the official rate into your home currency. Credit cards also allow you to float your expenses into the following month or two without paying interest charges. Most important, should you have a problem with a purchase, your credit card company can assist you in recovering your money and returning the goods. Once you discover your problem, contact the credit card company with your complaint and refuse to pay the amount while the matter is in dispute. Businesses accepting these cards must maintain a certain standard of honesty and integrity. In this sense, credit cards are an excellent and inexpensive form of insurance against possible fraud and damaged goods when shopping abroad. If you rely only on cash or traveler's checks, you have no such institutional recourse for recovering your money.

SECURE YOUR VALUABLES

Australia is a relatively safe country to travel in if you take the normal precautions. Australians in general tend to be a very honest people. On the other hand, Papua New Guinea has numerous theft problems, so be very cautious about taking valuables with you, don't leave them out in the open or advertise your wealth. We have never had a problem with thieves or pickpockets but neither have we encouraged such individuals to meet us. If you take a few basic precautions in securing your valuables, you should have a worry-free trip.

Be sure to keep your traveler's checks, credit cards, and cash in a safe place along with your travel documents and other valuables. While money belts do provide good security for valuables, the typical 4" x 8" nylon belts can be uncomfortable in Papua New Guinea's hot and humid weather. Our best advice is for women to carry money and documents in a leather shoulder bag that can be held firmly and which should be kept with you at all times, however inconvenient, even when passing through buffet lines. Choose a purse with a strap long enough to sling around your neck bandolier style.

For men, keep your money and credit cards in your wallet, but always carry your wallet in a front pocket. If you keep it in a rear pocket, as you may do at home, you invite pickpockets to demonstrate their varied talents in relieving you of your money, and possibly venting your trousers in the process. If your front pocket is an uncomfortable location, you probably need to clean out your wallet so it will fit better.

You may also want to use the free hotel safety deposit boxes for your cash and other valuables. If one is not provided in your room, ask the cashier to assign you a private box in their vault. Under no circumstances should you leave your money and valuables unattended in your hotel room, at restaurant tables, or in dressing rooms. You may want to leave your expensive jewelry at home so as not to be as likely a target of theft.

If you get robbed, chances are it will be in part your

own fault, because you invited someone to take advantage
by not being more cautious in securing your valuables.

TAKE ALL NECESSARY
SHOPPING INFORMATION

We recommend that you take more than just a copy of
this book to Australia and Papua New Guinea. At the
very least you should take:

- A prioritized "wish list" of items you think
  would make nice additions to your wardrobe,
  home decor, collections, and gift giving.

- Measurements of floor space, walls, tables,
  and beds in your home in anticipation of
  purchasing some lovely home furnishings.

- Photographs of particular rooms that could
  become candidates for home decorative items.
  These come in handy when you find something you think -- but are not sure -- may fit
  into your colors schemes, furnishings, and
  decorating patterns.

- Take an inventory of your closets and identify particular colors, fabrics, and designs you
  wish to acquire to complement and enlarge
  your present wardrobe.

DO COMPARATIVE SHOPPING

Since most of what you are likely to buy in Australia
and Papua New Guinea are unique locally-produced items,
you need not do much comparative shopping before you
arrive in Australia and Papua New Guinea. However, if
you plan to purchase opals in Australia, you will feel more
comfortable with your purchases if you first look for shops
at home selling opals to see what is available and learn
about quality and pricing. In the United States, for example, only the white opal is widely available.

Our general rule of thumb for buying tribal artifacts outside Papua New Guinea is that they will cost you from 3
to 5 times more in Australia and from 10 to 20 times more
in Europe and North America. Most middlemen and
dealers double and triple their prices. Consequently, a
tribal artifact reaching New York City, Frankfurt, or London may have passed through the hands of three or four
middlemen who each doubled and tripled their prices

before the New York, Frankfurt, or London dealer doubled or tripled them again, although many such dealers multiply by five in arriving at their retail prices. At the same time, items from the Sepik River and Trobriand Islands purchased in Port Moresby will cost you three to five times more than what you would pay along the river. However, don't expect to find the same items along the river and in the islands as you will find in the artifact emporiums of Port Moresby. Many of the shop offerings are unique, hard-to-find items that are well worth the asking prices.

You may want to do comparative shopping in Australia, but it does take valuable shopping time to do so. In general, expect to find your least expensive prices in places with the least overhead costs. Weekend markets, shops in small craft towns, and state subsidized arts and crafts centers (Jam Factories and Meat Markets) have the least overhead and thus usually the best prices for similar items found in shopping centers, hotel shopping arcades, and street shops.

However, since many arts and crafts are unique items, comparative shopping may be a waste of time. Many of the best quality arts and crafts will be found in high rent districts, such as in The Rocks in Sydney and along Collins Street in Melbourne. In the case of clothes, expect department stores and small boutiques to have the highest prices. The best prices on clothes will be found in the factory outlets of Melbourne and Sydney, although many of the clothes may be seconds or end of season styles.

PACK RIGHT AND LIGHT

Packing and unpacking are two great travel challenges. Trying to get everything you think you need into one or two bags can be frustrating. You either take too much with you, and thus transport unnecessary weight around the world, or you find you took too little.

We've learned over the years to err on the side of taking too little with us. If we start with less, we will have room for more. Your goal should be to avoid lugging an extensive wardrobe, cosmetics, library, and household goods around the world! Make this your guiding principle for deciding how and what to pack: *"When in doubt, leave it out"*.

Above all, you want to return home loaded down with wonderful new purchases without paying extra weight charges. Hence, pack for the future rather than load yourself down with the past. To do this you need to wisely select the proper mix of colors, fabrics, styles, and accessories.

You should initially pack as lightly as possible. Remember, much of the climate in Australia and Papua New Guinea is mild, hot, and humid. Since you will do a great deal of walking in Australia and Papua New Guinea, we recommend taking at least one pair of comfortable walking shoes. Break these shoes in before you take them on this trip. Wearing new shoes for lengthy periods of time can become quite uncomfortable.

CHOOSE SENSIBLE LUGGAGE

Whatever you do, avoid being a slave to your luggage. Luggage should be both **expandable and expendible**. Flexibility is the key to making it work. Get ready to pack and repack, acquire new bags along the way, and replace luggage if necessary.

Your choice of luggage is very important for enjoying your shopping experience and for managing airports, airplanes, and Customs. While you may normally travel with two suitcases and a carry-on, your specific choice of luggage for shopping purposes may be different. We recommend taking two large suitcases with wheels -- it's best when one can fit into another; one large carry-on bag; one nylon backpack; and one collapsible nylon bag.

If you decide to take hard-sided luggage, make sure it has no middle divider. With no divider you can pack some of your bulkier purchases. This type of luggage may appear safer than soft-sided luggage, but it is heavy, limited in space, and not necessarily more secure. A good soft-sided piece should be adequately reinforced.

Your **carry-on bag** should be convenient -- lightweight and with separate compartments and pockets -- for taking short trips outside major cities. Since Australian airlines have very restrictive carry-on regulations, be prepared to check through most of your large purchases. Be sure to pack delicate items very well.

We also recommend taking a small nylon **backpack** in lieu of a camera bag. This is a wonderfully convenient bag, because it can be used as a comfortable shoulder bag as well as a backpack. It holds our cameras, film, travel books, windbreakers, umbrella, drinks and snacks and still has room for carrying small purchases. We take this bag with us everywhere. When we find our hands filled with purchases, our versatile backpack goes on our back so our hands are free for other items.

A collapsible **nylon bag** also is a useful item to pack. Many of these bags fold into a small 6" x 8" zipped pouch. You may wish to keep this bag in your backpack or carry-on for use when shopping.

SHIPPING WITH EASE

One of the worst nightmares of shopping abroad is to return home after a wonderful time to find your goods have been lost, stolen, or damaged in transit. This happens frequently to people who do not know how to ensure against such problems. Failing to pack properly or pick the right shipper, they suffer accordingly. This should not happen to you in Australia and Papua New Guinea.

On the other hand, you should not pass up buying lovely items because you feel reluctant to ship them home. Indeed, some travelers only buy items that will fit into their suitcase because they are reluctant to ship larger items home. But you can easily ship from Australia and Papua New Guinea and expect to receive your goods in good condition within 12-16 weeks. We seldom let shipping considerations affect our buying decisions. We know we can always get our purchases home with little difficulty. For us, *shipping is one of those things that must be arranged*. You have numerous alternatives from which to choose, from hiring a professional shipping company to hand carrying your goods on board the plane. Shipping may or may not be costly, depending on how much you plan to ship and by which means.

Before leaving home you should identify the best point of entry for goods returning home by air or sea. Once you are in Australia and Papua New Guinea, you generally have five alternatives for shipping goods home:

- Take everything with you.
- Do your own packing and shipping through the local post office (for small packages only).
- Have each shop ship your purchases.
- Arrange to have one shop consolidate all of your purchases into a single shipment.
- Hire a local shipper to make all shipping arrangements.

Taking everything with you is fine if you don't have much and you don't mind absorbing excess baggage charges. If you are overweight, ask about the difference between "Excess Baggage" and "Unaccompanied Baggage". Excess baggage is very expensive while unaccompanied baggage is less expensive, although by no means cheap.

If items are small enough and we don't mind waiting six to eight weeks, we may send them through the local post office by parcel post; depending on the weight, sometimes air mail is relatively inexpensive through local post offices.

Doing your own packing and shipping may be cheaper, but it is a pain and thus no savings in the long run. You waste valuable shopping time waiting in lines and trying to figure out the local rules and regulations concerning permits, packing, materials, sizes, and weights.

On the other hand, most major shops are skilled at shipping goods for customers. They often pack the items free and only charge you for the actual postage or freight. Many of these shops use excellent shippers who are known for reasonable charges, good packing, and reliability. If you choose to have a shop ship for you, insist on a receipt specifying they will ship the item. Also, stress the importance of packing the item well to avoid possible damage. If they cannot insure the item against breakage or loss, do not ship through them. Invariably a version of Murphy's Law operates when shipping: *"If it is not insured and has the potential to break or get lost, it will surely break or get lost!"* At this point, seek some alternative means of shipping. If you are shipping only one or two items, it is best to let a reputable shop take care of your shipping.

If you have several large purchases -- at least one cubic meter -- consider using local shippers since it is cheaper and safer to consolidate many separate purchases into one shipment which is well packed and insured. Sea freight charges are usually figured by volume or the container. There is a minimum charge -- usually you will pay for at least one cubic meter whether you are shipping that much or less. Air freight is calculated using both weight and volume and usually there is no minimum. You pay only for the actual amount you ship. One normally does not air freight large, heavy items, but for a small light shipment, air freight could actually cost you less and you'll get your items much faster. When using air freight, use an established and reliable airline. In the case of sea freight, choose a local company which has an excellent reputation among expatriates for shipping goods. It is relatively easy to get this information. Consult the Yellow Pages under the heading "Shipping" or "Removers". In each city you will find numerous shippers listed, many with familiar names. However, you will be taking pot luck if you randomly choose one from this list. Instead, you should do some quick research. If you are staying at a good hotel, ask the concierge about reliable shippers. He should be able to help you. Personnel at the local embassy or international school know which companies are best. Call a few expatriates and ask for their best recommendations. For small shipments, try to have charges computed both ways -- for sea and for air freight. Sea shipments incur port charges that can further add to your charges. If you have figures for both means of shipping, you can make an informed choice.

We have tried all five shipping alternatives with various results. Indeed, we tend to use these alternatives in combination. For example, we take everything we can with us until we reach the point where the inconvenience and cost of excess baggage requires some other shipping arrangements. In Australia, we consolidate our shipments with one key shop early in our trip and have shipments from other cities sent to that shop for consolidation. In Papua New Guinea we make shipping arrangements with a major shipper in Port Moresby. This company coordinates the consolidation of our shipments from other parts of Papua New Guinea.

When you use a shipper, be sure to examine alternative shipping arrangements and prices. The type of delivery you specify at your end can make a significant difference in the overall shipping price. If you don't specify the type of delivery you want, you may be charged the all-inclusive first-class rate. For example, if you choose door-to-door delivery with unpacking services, you will pay a premium to have your shipment clear Customs, moved through the port, transported to your door, and unpacked by local movers. On the other hand, it is cheaper for you to designate port to port. When the shipment arrives, you arrange for a broker to clear the shipment through Customs and arrange for transport to your home. You do your own unpacking and dispose of the trash. It will take a little more of your time to make the arrangements and unpack.

We simply cannot over-stress the importance of finding and establishing a personal relationship with a good local shipper who will provide you with services which may go beyond your immediate shipping needs. A good local shipping contact will enable you to continue shopping in Australia and Papua New Guinea even after returning home!

PART II

SECRETS OF
EXCITING AUSTRALIA

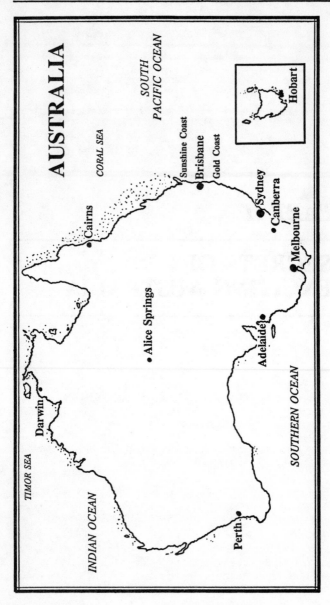

Chapter Four

WELCOME TO AUSTRALIA

Welcome to the "Land Downunder", a land of nearly 17 million people who live in one of the world's most unique and interesting lands. Located south of Indonesia and west of New Zealand, this is a vast island continent approximately the size of the United States. Over 80 percent of its population clings to the coastal cities and towns that are primarily found in the southeast (Brisbane, Sydney, Canberra, Melbourne, Adelaide, and Hobart) but also in the southwest (Perth) and north (Darwin).

SURPRISING AUSTRALIA

Australia is a land of great diversity, surprises, and monotony. Its regions, cities, and towns each have their own particular character that sets them apart from the rest of Australia. Projecting an image of an earthy, rugged, friendly, unpretentious, classless, sports-minded, and beach-oriented people, surprising Australia is also a very talented, cultured, creative, artistic, provincial, and sometimes insecure, bureaucratic, contentious, and opinionated nation in search of its own national identity. The people are a diverse mix of European and Asian immigrants as well as

39

Aboriginals, many of whom still wander harsh reserved interior lands. Its flora and fauna, including the Great Barrier Reef, rainforests, deserts, canyons, kangaroos, koalas, emu, wallabies, wombats, platypus, and cockatoos, accent the unusual and surprising in Australia. Its vast and varied landscape of hills, mountains, deserts, canyons, and the stark and monotonous Outback often gives way to miles and miles of gorgeous beaches.

THE BASICS

Location and Geography

Situated in the Southern Hemisphere with its nearest neighbors being Papua New Guinea, Indonesia, and New Zealand, Australia is a geographical anomaly. It is not what you would normally expect to encounter in an Asian or Pacific country. In terms of location it is both Asian and Pacific, but in terms of its geography and people it is neither.

Australia is the world's oldest continent which has been physcially isolated from the rest of the world for nearly 60 million years. It's age and isolation are partly responsible for its unique flora, fauna, and unusual looking and heavily worn landscape. Uninviting and uninspiring to many explorers, Australia has always been a frontier country with most people living on its urban and coastal fringes with their faces to the sea and their backs turned on an empty and inhospitable interior.

But Australia also has its moments of beauty, be it the rainforests and beaches of the East Coast, Kakadu National Park in the Northern Territory, the Blue Mountains of New South Wales, the Barossa Valley of South Australia, or Sydney's harbor and Opera House.

The country is divided into six states (Queensland, New South Wales, Victoria, South Australia, Tasmania, and Western Australia), the Northern Territory, and the National Capital area of Canberra. The majority of the population lives in the Southeast region in and around the cities of Brisbane, Sydney, Canberra, Melbourne, and Adelaide. Perth in Western Australia, Alice Springs in the Outback, and Darwin in the North are relatively isolated cities that have developed their own character.

Most tourists visit the East Coast to enjoy the beaches and visit the Great Barrier Reef, one of the great wonders of the world with its massive coral reefs and idyllic islands. They also tend to venture on to Sydney, Canberra, perhaps Melbourne. Visitors determined to see most of the country also venture on to Adelaide, Alice Springs, Darwin, Perth, and Hobart. To see it all, however, takes a great deal of time. But one should try to see as much as possible in Australia because it is a very special place with some exciting sights, inviting cities, wonderful beaches, and intriguing shopping.

Climate, Seasons, and When To Go

Australia's climate varies depending on one's location on this continent. The north and northeast of Darwin, Cape York, Cairns, and Townsville are tropical areas with hot, humid, and mild temperatures year-round, similar to many parts of the Caribbean and Southeast Asia. The most heavily populated Southeast region, encompassing Brisbane, Sydney, Canberra, Hobart, Melbourne, and Adelaide, has distinct seasons which tend to be very hot in the summer and cool in the winter. While it seldom snows, except in the mountains, the weather can turn bitter cold during the winter in Sydney, Canberra, Melbourne, Adelaide, and Hobart.

Given the seasonal and climatic diversity of Australia, almost any time is a good time to visit this country, depending where you go. The summer months of November to March, for example, in the center and the north can be very hot -- even torrid -- and dry. The winter months, June through August, can become bitter cold in the far south. The East Coast usually manages to have decent weather year-round, although it rains a lot there during January and February. In general, the best time to travel to Australia will be the spring and fall, but summer and winter can also be very pleasant times.

Documents

Be sure to apply for a visa before departing on your journey to Australia. You will need a Visitors Visa and a valid passport to enter Australia as well as an ongoing ticket out of the country for stays of up to six months. Visitors Visas are issued free of charge and should be applied for through the nearest Australian Embassy or Consulate. If you get a copy of the Tourism Commission of Australia's *The Aussie Holiday Book*, you will find a Visitors Visa form in the book.

Travelers from the U.S. and Canada do not need vaccinations. However, if you arrive from an endemic zone or a Yellow Fever, Smallpox, Cholera, or Typhoid infected area, you will need an international health certificate verifying you have the proper innoculations.

Currency and Credit Cards

The Australian dollar comes in bills of $100, $50, $20, $10, $5, and $2 denominations. Coins are minted in $1, 50c, 20c, 10c, 5c, and 1c denominations. At present the Australian dollar is equivalent to US$.82.

You will normally receive a higher exchange rate on traveler's checks than on bank notes. The US dollar is often accepted in shops when making large purchases. It is best to exchange your money at airports or city banks. City banks are open from 9:30am to 4pm, Monday through Friday.

Most hotels, restaurants, and businesses accept major credit cards: Visa, MasterCard, American Express, Diners Club, and Access.

Tipping

Australians have an aversion to the common Western practice of paying gratuities, and hotels and restaurants do not add service charges onto their bills. In general, you are not expected to give tips. Given generous minimum wage laws and the high cost of labor in Australia, most service workers are well paid for their labor. However, as more visitors come to Australia and tip service workers, the practice of giving gratuities is becoming more acceptable. Our recommendation: When in Australia, do like the Australians.

Business Hours

Most businesses remain open from 9am to 5pm, Monday through Friday. Shopping hours are normally from 9am to 5:30pm, Monday through Friday, and from 9am to 12 noon on Saturday. Most downtown and suburban shopping centers and shops remain open until 9pm on either Thursday or Friday night, depending on the particular city. But most shopping comes to a halt at 12 noon on Saturday as well as all day Sunday.

Two exceptions to this weekend closing rule are the arts and crafts shops and weekend markets. Artists and craftsmen operate shops seven days a week. Markets will generally be open Saturday or Sunday, or both days. Knowing this, it's a good idea to do all your other shopping during the week, keep Thursday or Friday nights open for suburban shopping, and concentrate on shopping for arts and crafts on the weekends.

Transportation

As we outlined in Chapter Two, Australia is serviced by several international and domestic transportation companies. Given limited time, our preference is to fly between major cities. However, within each city we use a combination of public transportation and private car. In large cities such as Brisbane, Sydney, Melbourne, and Adelaide where parking can become a problem, we prefer using buses and taxis to get around to the various shopping areas.

One can also enjoy the convenience and comfort of renting cars in Australia. It can make shopping much easier and traveling more interesting. You will need an international driver's license. In addition, if you possess an American Express Card, you need not make the large deposits or take the expensive insurance required by the rental agencies. The American Express Card gives you coverage. Indeed, the annual fee charge for an American Express Card will quickly pay for itself if you rent many cars in Australia.

We normally rent a car when we want to shop outside the central city, such as in hill towns and coastal communities. In the cases of Darwin and Cairns, renting a car is very convenient for getting around the city and outlying areas. Alice Springs is such a small town that you can easily walk to all the downtown shops and shopping centers. We do not recommend driving a car in the Outback; breakdowns in the heat of the Outback can quickly endanger one's life.

You will find several rental car companies in every city. The major rental agencies usually have desks at the airports -- Hertz, Avis, Budget, and Thrifty. Less expensive local car rental agencies are located near the airports or in the downtown areas. Renting a car is not cheap, nor need it be expensive. If you shop around, you can find a few car rental agencies that rent cars for A$25 or less a day with 200 to 300 free kilometers -- more than enough to cover most shopping areas in, around, and outside most cities.

Electricity, Water, and Drinks

Electricity in Australia is 240/250 volts, AC 50HZ. If you bring 110 volt appliances with you, be sure to bring a voltage converter. Most hotels use the Australian 3-pin power outlet. Chances are if you have an international set of socket adapters, you have a 2-prong plug that will fit. The third prong is for grounding the appliance. Some hotels can loan you an adapter but many do not have them available or they are in short supply. Our advice: purchase an international travel converter and adapter kit before you leave home which will have the proper adapter plugs for Australia -- as well as Papua New Guinea.

Tap water is normally safe to drink. You will find most international soft drinks as well as good teas, beers, and fruit juices in local supermarkets.

Health

Australia is a very clean and health conscious country, moreso than most countries in the world. You need not worry about potential health problems other than lying in the sun too long or being stranded in the Outback! Health facilities are excellent should you become ill. We do recommend taking with you a sufficient supply of any special medications you require even though you are likely to find what you need in local pharmacies. Australia is one of the few countries where rabies has never occurred. This is largely due to the very restrictive and vigilant policies against the importation of diseased animals. Expect to have your cabin sprayed as your international flight comes in for a landing. This, too, is indicative of Australia's obsession with keeping its country free of any foreign pests. So far they have been remarkably successful.

Resources

In preparation for your Australian adventure you will find a great deal written on Australia. More and more travel books, which primarily outline the same hotels, restaurants, and sights, are being published. You might, for example, look at the APA Insight Guide *Australia*. This is another attractive volume in a series noted for its lovely photos and well written text. This volume provides an overview of the history, society, and culture of Australia. It also includes a useful travel section which you may want to photocopy and take with you. Leave the rest of the book at home since it is big and heavy -- not our idea of a good travel companion.

Five other excellent guide books to Australia include Robert Bone's *The Maverick Guide to Australia*, Fodor's *Australia, New Zealand, and the South Pacific*; Frommer's *Australia on $25 a Day*; Charles and Babette Jacobs' *South Pacific Travel Digest*; and *The American Express Pocket Guide to Australia*. The American Express volume is an excellent travel companion given its small size and abbreviated listings of the best hotels, restaurants, and sights.

Once you arrive in Australia, be sure to visit the local bookstores. There you will find numerous additional travel guides and detailed maps on Australia as a whole as well as on individual cities. We especially like the *Out and About in...* guides to Sydney, Melbourne, and Perth. You will also find a few shopping guides to Sydney and Melbourne which we identify in the appropriate chapters on these cities.

If you are interested in the history, society, and culture of Australia, you might want to read Robert Hughes' *The Fatal Shore*, a popular but somewhat depressing, overbearing, and tiring history of Australia's checkered founding; it's perhaps best to read this book after you return from Australia! Also, look at Ross Terrill's *The Australians*; and Linda Christmas' *The Ribbon and the Ragged Square*.

MAJOR SHOPPING CHOICES

Australia offers a wide variety of shopping choices from the latest in fashion clothes to exquisite Australian, Aboriginal, and tribal arts and crafts. Australia's major shopping strengths are arts, crafts, clothes, jewelry, antiques, and souvenirs. The arts and crafts -- both Australian and Aboriginal -- are some of the best quality and most unique items we have found anywhere in the world. The Aboriginal art is especially striking and expressive of the unique Aboriginal culture. Australian clothes are unique in two aspects: for the use of lovely Australian wools and the large number of Australian designers creating fashionable garments, from formal wear to resort wear. Opal jewelry as well as uniquely crafted gold and silver jewelry are especially attractive purchases in Australia.

WHAT TO BUY

Many travelers do not think of Australia as a shopper's paradise. This stereotype is true only if you equate a shopping paradise with bargain prices and an abundance of shops selling the latest in electronic gadgetry. Australia is not Hong Kong, but there is no need for apologies on her part either. Australia has plenty to keep most shoppers happy and ready to return to her shores for yet another shopping experience.

Few things in Australia are good buys for individuals who expect to find bargain prices. Lacking inexpensive products, shops in Australia tend to offer many unique and high quality handcrafted products. Therefore, *a good buy in Australia is something you love that you can not find elsewhere.* These might include, for example, a lovely handcrafted item not available outside Adelaide, a one-of-a-kind antique chest, an opulent opal with a glorious play of colors, a wonderful designer dress, an Aboriginal bark painting or a *tambuan* (woven ceremonial figure) from neighboring Papua New Guinea.   Such good buys will each become wonderful continuing reminders of the great time you had on your trip to the "wonder down under".

GEMS AND JEWELRY

It is nearly impossible to think of Australian gems without thinking about opals. And you certainly can't be in any city in Australia for long without being bombarded with the outlets selling unset opals, opal jewelry, and opal decorating accessories as well as offering films showing the opal mining process and an on-the-spot demonstration of the opal cutting and polishing process.

If you are used to seeing the milky white opals most frequently sold in shops in the U.S., you are in for a surprise in the shops of Australia. The "white" or "milk" opals are mined in Coober Pedy in South Australia. This is by far the largest opal mine field in Australia and that is why you primarily see the White Opal in stores overseas. However, the scarcer -- and hence more valuable -- opals tend to have far more color and beauty. These are known as the Boulder Opal and the Black Opal. The Boulder Opal has an overall white background but splashed with a play of colors that in both range and intensity are much greater than the colors seen in the White Opal. The Black Opal, as its name suggests, is formed by a background that appears black or dark gray/blue, and also displays a range of vibrant colors across its face.

The price of opals varies with a number of factors besides the obvious one of size. There are three different types of opals and the most valuable is a solid opal. If you are making a purchase of an opal as an investment you probably won't consider any other type. However, if you want the beauty of an opal but without paying as high a price as you would pay for the solid opal you may consider a doublet or a triplet. A doublet is made by glueing thin slices or veneers of precious opal to a "common" opal backing with a black epoxy resin. The dark backing intensifies the colors of the opal making the stone appear to have better color. The triplet is made by adding a clear cap of quartz, perspex or glass to the top of a doublet and all else being equal is usually the least expensive of the three types. Each type of opal has its niche in filling various consumer's needs. You may decide to buy a solid opal for yourself and a doublet or a triplet as a gift for a relative back home. The important thing is that you are aware of the differences and make your purchase carefully so that you do not pay solid opal prices only to get home and find you purchased a doublet!

Another thing to look for when purchasing an opal is the play of color. The extent and overall completeness of color adds to the value of the stone. The number of colors as well as the actual colors also play a part in determining an opal's value. The highest valued opal includes all the colors of the spectrum -- especially red and violet/purple which are rare.

The opal is not crystalline like other gems, but a hydrated silica. Although its hardness (about 5 1/2 to 7 on MOH's hardness scale) is about the same as an emerald, it is a more delicate stone. Before you buy, check to make sure your opal is free from cracks and flaws -- major flaws can be seen with the naked eye. An opal with a crack or flawline is more susceptible to breaking if you should hit it against something by accident. An opal that is set in a surrounding bezel is less vulnerable to breaking than one that is in a prong setting; however, it is more difficult to spot a doublet or triplet in a bezel setting.

Be sure to carry your passport and airline ticket with you when shopping for opals or any gold or silver jewelry. You can purchase on a tax-free basis because as an overseas visitor you do not have to pay Australian sales tax. This is essentially a value-added tax and is already included in the price of the goods. With your passport and airline departure ticket in hand you can often save 30% on the marked price of the goods. The actual amount varies from one store to another. In most of the duty-free shops the tax savings is about 30% but in various jewelry stores the percentage varied from about 8% to 30%. There is no duty on opals because they come from Australia, so since you are buying tax-free rather than duty-free, you can take the item with you. If you are buying jewelry that has been imported and has duty-free status you will be required to pick up your purchase at the airport as you depart the country.

The outlets for opal jewelry -- both jewelry stores and "duty-free" -- shops abound all over Australia. The larger cities such as Sydney, Melbourne and Brisbane have the greatest number of outlets for opal jewelry, but you will find a good selection of opals available in every city in Australia.

Diamonds may not seem to be uniquely Australian, but Australia has its own unique diamonds -- Argyle diamonds. Although there are the classic whites we're all familiar with, Argyle's are found in an incredible range of colors:

deep cognac, champagne, light yellows, peach, beige, green, blue and exotic pinks. Pink has become synonymous with Argyle -- one of the most beautiful varieties of natural colored diamonds and rarely found anywhere else in the world -- it is both rare and expensive. So rare are the Argyle pinks that at a recent sale in Geneva, all 82 stones varying from rose to burgandy, were snapped up by one dealer. Argyle diamonds are even laser inscribed with a code visible under magnification as a mark of authenticity.

If you are interested in viewing or buying Argyle diamonds in Sydney try Percy Marks, Hardy Brothers or Bruce and Walsh; in Melbourne stop by Paul Bram or Hardy Brothers; in Adelaide try Chez Jewels or Wendts; in Brisbane look for Hardy Brothers or Bruce Robinson Diamonds; in Perth look for Charles Edward, Mazzucchelli's, Linney's or Kalli Brinkhaus; in Hobart it's Diamond World and if in Port Douglas look for Hardy Brothers.

There are outstanding jewelers working in gold and silver who are crafting **jewelry** in **unique Australian designs.** Robert Clerc located on the ground floor in the Strand Arcade in Sydney fashions innovative designs in gold. His Aboriginal collection features jewelry intricately carved on both sides: traditional Aboriginal artwork on one side and a stylized design on the reverse. Some of the pieces in this collection feature Australian opals. Also elegant and often set with stones is his Egyptian collection. In Darwin, The Opal House at Paspalis Centrepoint has created a stunning range of jewelry depicting the unique animals, birds and legends of Australia. The Australian Collection consists of over one hundred pieces hand-finished in sterling silver or gold.

Visit Chibnall of Cairns on Abbott Street for a look at more uniquely Australian themes in silver jewelry. This shop has designed two popular collections -- The Aboriginal Collection and the Marine and Rainforest Collection -- using local themes in handcrafted jewelry.

A wonderful surprise for most first-time visitors to Australia are the handicrafts found in and around the major cities. The range and quality of handicrafts found in other product areas is also available in **craft jewelry.** In fact, the work is often so lovely and so professionally crafted that it almost seems a misnomer to consider it a handicraft, but that really is the category to which it belongs. From handcrafted gold or silver items to ceramic or textile fashioned earrings, brooches, bracelets and bolo ties these pieces are truly works of art. Although you will find good quality jewelry represented in most of the shops that show handicrafts, no doubt the overall best quality of the craft jewelry is to be found at Makers Mark in Melbourne.

DESIGNER CLOTHING

One of Australia's major shopping strengths are its fashion clothes. While you will find some imported clothes and boutiques from such noted designers as Diane Freis and Laura Ashley, most fashion clothes are creations of Australian designers. Hundreds of creative fashion designers, primarily based in Melbourne and Sydney but also found in Adelaide, Brisbane, and Canberra, turn out uniquely designed clothes ranging from high fashion to resort wear and using Australian wools, cottons, and imported silks and polyesters.

Australian fashion design is very much a cottage industry related to local artistic and entrepreneurial traditions. Designers such as John Cavill, Lou Wiseman, Jenny Kee, Liz Davenport, Jill Fitzsimon, Walter Kristensen, Adele Palmer, Angela Padula, Ken Done, Rob Paynter Teena Varigos, Stunning, Lizzie Collins, Carla Zampatti, Shephards, and Anthea Crawford, create some truly unique fashion clothes that largely define the world of Australian high fashion at home and abroad. While many of these designers have their own boutiques in Melbourne, Sydney, and elsewhere, others sell their creations through department stores, clothing stores, and factory outlets. Other Australian designers produce a medium range of clothing which appeals to a larger and less affluent audience of clothing and department store buyers: Country Road, Sportsgirl, Rodney Clark, R. M. Williams, Morrisons, and Brian Rochford.

Shopping for Australian designed clothes is a shopping adventure in and of itself. You discover young struggling designers in Melbourne; acquaint yourself with fashionable boutiques in shopping centers, hotel shopping arcades, and department stores; and learn about one of Australia's most creative and artistic cottage industries which is beginning to make its mark on the international fashion scene. Most of the major designers are well represented in the boutiques and department stores of Melbourne, Sydney, and Adelaide. Sydney's fashion centers are Double Bay, Strand Arcade, and the Queen Victoria Building. In Melbourne one must visit the Shop of Shops (Collins Street), Toorak Road, and numerous factory outlets to discover why Melbourne is indeed known as Australia's fashion center. In Adelaide the shops along King William and Unley roads are this city's fashion center.

Australian clothes can be expensive, so don't expect to do bargain shopping for uniquely designed clothes. The best deals are found during sales or at factory outlets. Garments produced in limited designs and quantities, such as fine wool knits requiring extensive hand work, are also good buys compared to similar quality garments found in the boutiques of Europe. Some Australian designers and clothing stores, such as Shepherds, Carla Zampatti, and Country Road, have now opened boutiques and shops abroad in such places as New York City and Washington, DC. If you are in these areas before arriving in Australia, you may want to sample their creations and compare prices.

AUSTRALIANA

Merchandise we characterize as Australiana, ranges from marvelous puzzles made in part from precious metals and stones beautifully displayed in suede lined leather boxes to printed T-shirts sporting local animals, scenery, or Aboriginal designs. Hence Australiana products run the gamut from relatively inexpensive items that make great gifts for friends back home to really exquisite pieces with price tags to match.

Some small shops tend to stock only Australiana, and most department stores will have a section devoted to Australiana goods. Most of these shops feature Aboriginal arts and crafts. Boomerangs and didgeridoos are available although these are of a different quality than those discussed under traditional Aborigine arts. Although they are often made by Aborigines, the boomerangs are generally smaller than the traditional boomerangs, are the returning type boomerang, and sport anything from a drawing of a kangaroo to a picture of the Sydney bridge.

Cuddly stuffed animals of all sizes are available depicting the unique animals of Australia. Koalas are a favorite with many, while others may prefer a kangaroo, platypus or opossum. While a stuffed furry animal may be great for the kids, adults may prefer the beautiful bronze animals. These lovely animals -- available in other metals as well -- depict unique animals from the frill neck lizzard to the platypus.

Placemats and coasters feature Aboriginal designs, native animals and birds, as well as local scenes. There are soaps, bath oils and drawer liners -- all with the scent of Australian native flowers. If you want to try growing your own flowers, packaged seeds of native flowers are available. Old-fashioned Australian health remedies and goods such as eucalyptus and ti tree oil and Billy tea can be bought as can notecards, stationery and gift wrap in Australian designs.

Leather wallets stamped with local designs, neckties with tasteful small kangaroo designs, scarves with local motifs are all available alongside sterling silver jewelry and spoons as well as fun and fashion jewelry. Some shops carry Australiana gear -- often referred to as citified outback clothing. Drizabone coats, Akubra hats, Snowy River hats, serious slouch hats or swagman humorous hats, moleskin pants, shearer's shirts and wool jumpers -- everything that you've ever seen in the movies that brings to mind Australian clothing -- is on sale for you to buy and take home.

Although they're not easy to carry home, one of our favorite Australiana products are the wood frame animals covered with sheepskin that children can ride. Most glide back and forth rather than rock, but if you're shipping other things back home anyway, these make great gifts for the kids on your list.

HANDCRAFTED PRODUCTS

Perhaps the greatest surprise of our shopping "research" in Australia was to find the marvelous arts and crafts that are available there. Both the quantity and the quality are excellent. The real renaissance in the arts and crafts has taken place within the past five years. At present it is alive and well and appears to be gaining momentum.

The craftspeople work in almost any medium and the outcome ranges from just cute or interesting to superb. The preponderance of work seems to be in **ceramics and pottery**. All size pieces are available from small vases that can easily be packed in a suitcase to large pieces or sets of dishes that would need to be shipped. Designs range from country-cute to sophisticated modernistic pieces.

We also saw some beautiful **wood** pieces. Bowls, vases, and covered boxes of some of the most beautiful burl woods you have ever seen. One of our favorite styles combined a small wood covered box in interesting shapes set off by one or two lovely silver spiders -- and we never thought we would use "lovely" to describe a spider! Even the bowls were beautiful in their simplicity of style contrasting with the interesting grains of the wood itself. We even found some lovely baby rattles and teething rings being made out of special Australian woods.

There are wonderful selections of **jewelry** handcrafted by talented artisans. Craftspeople are working in gold and silver as well as copper fashioning beautiful contemporary styled earrings, pins, rings, necklaces and bracelets. Whether they have worked in the metal alone or combined metal with semi-precious stones, many of the designs are stunning. There are also artisans who are combining metal and ceramics to produce some unique and attractive jewelry.

Many artists are working in **stained glass** and producing everything from pieces to hang in front of windows to lamps. Some are small enough to pack easily and carry home in a suitcase.

Fiber artists are producing an array of marvelous **textiles**. Silk, cotton and of course, the great wools that Australia is famous for can all be found being worked by the craftspeople into beautiful garmets as well as works of art for home decorating. Whether woven or handprinted fabrics, these are special works of art.

We also found some craftspeople working in **metals** -- silver alloys and copper alloys were especially prevalent for fashioning into plates, bowls or even clocks as well as the popular fountains. Everywhere you look you will find marvelous works of art being made by the craftspeople of Australia. Much of what you will see is museum quality work. Expect to be pleasantly surprised by the profusion and quality of the work you will encounter. Even if you have never been interested in arts and crafts before, we predict that the Australians will win you over.

TRADITIONAL ABORIGINAL WORKS

The original Australians, the Aborigines, have experienced a history somewhat like the American Indians. As the early inhabitants of the land and without undue competition for its resources, they were free to wander unrestrained by things like cities or roads and fences. Everything they needed they were able to take from the earth, yet without destroying the balance of nature that would allow earth and man to live in harmony. Once "civilization" arrived on the scene however, things began to change. Little by little the space left for the Aboriginals was taken over by agriculture or herding or given over to cities and towns. Traversing the "*songlines*" was no longer always possible. The old existence was gone and yet many could not or chose not to adapt to the new ways of life that were absorbing the countryside. After a somewhat turbulent period, the Australians have come to accept the Aboriginal way of life, though different, as one that should be protected and preserved. That is fortunate for those shoppers who have an interest in collecting ethnic art and artifacts from various parts of the world. It is unlikely that the traveler will find for sale any truly antique pieces of Aboriginal art -- most of that fragile work that has survived is already in museums or in private collections. However, there are some truly beautiful pieces that are being produced today.

Perhaps the art that most first time travelers to Australia are most familiar with are the **bark paintings**. Some of these are still painted in the traditional way using bark fibers rather than a brush to apply the colors. Other Aboriginal artists use a brush. The colors are usually a combination of ochre, black and white, but yellow is often included. The X-ray style that is often used depicts the major organs inside the animal's body. The bark paintings are most attractive as decorative pieces if they are put on top of a frame or encased in a frame of lucite against a black or ochre backdrop. If you like the bark paintings but aren't sure how to best display one, look around at what some of the better shops are doing to display the ones they have on sale. You may decide to purchase one from a less expensive source and take it home and have your local framer help you suitably display your bark painting. You can also find bark baskets produced in a similar way to the paintings. These baskets can be especially attractive if dried flowers are displayed in them. We found the very best quality bark paintings, with prices to match, in galleries in Sydney. However, we found some very good quality bark paintings at a fraction of the price in Darwin. You will be able to find some bark paintings in all the major cities.

More contemporary and a bit easier to carry home with you are the Papunya paintings being done northwest of Alice Springs. These are called **sand paintings**, but don't expect anything like the sand paintings being done by the Southwest American Indians. A more accurate way to describe them is to call them **acrylic dot paintings**. Acrylic based paints are applied to canvas and most are heavily comprised of dots to form the pattern. Although you will see many of these already framed, most are not yet framed or can be taken out of the frame and rolled carefully and placed in a tube for ease of carrying home. These pictures use the patterns of the ancient sand paintings and tell stories to the Aborigine. Central Australian Aborigines traditionally drew in sand the stories of the dreaming -- the time when, according to Aboriginal belief, the world and all it contains came into being. These intricate patterns disappeared with the wind and the rain. But the stories and the designs were passed by memory from one generation to the next. Outsiders are often told the basics of the stories behind a particular painting, but don't expect to ever be told the full meaning. We found the largest selection of acrylic paintings at the best prices

Springs. That should come as no surprise since they are produced in that area. However, you will find examples of this work in all the major cities.

You will also see **carved wood animals, bowls**, and **boomerangs**. The animals and bowls are of wood and look as if they have had designs woodburned upon them. This type of design is made by the Aborigines of central Australia and a good variety at good prices can be found in Alice Springs. The boomerangs are often painted with the designs of the dreamtime, and have a decidedly different look about them than the touristy ones found in the Australiana shops. They also tend to be larger in size. You will also see wood carved animals painted in black, white, yellow or ochre as well as the *pukamani* or **burial poles**. These items come from the Tiwi people of Melville and Bathurst islands and the best buys are found in Darwin or can be purchased at their source if you take the tour offered by Tiwi Tours.

One thing you will find is that the good pieces are expensive. We saw beautiful bark paintings in Sydney that we liked that ranged from about A$3000 to A$5000. We decided we could live without one and kept looking. In Darwin we finally found one we liked as well as the ones in Sydney for A$300. No doubt the expensive ones we saw in Sydney were by artists with more established reputations. You will have to decide whether you are buying for investment and are willing (and able) to pay the price for the noted artists or whether you simply want a piece you love to decorate your home.

You can also find Aboriginal prints on silk and cotton scarves in many shops. Most of these are not actually made by Aboriginal artists. If this makes a difference to you be sure to ask if it is not marked on the item. Another interesting item you are sure to see are the ostrich eggs with Aboriginal designs painted on them. These may seem a bit delicate to pack in your luggage, but many shops indicate they can pack them well for travel.

PAPUA NEW GUINEA ARTIFACTS

It may seem strange to some to find a segment in the Australian goods section devoted to artifacts from Papua New Guinea. But if you have an interest in PNG artifacts, you will want to know what you are likely to find in Australia since this is one of the prime locations to buy PNG art. If, for example, you are interested in museum quality or old pieces of PNG art, head as soon as possible for Australia. Old PNG artifacts are rarely seen outside museums or private collections in PNG. Those pieces that are still in villages have most likely been declared "National Cultural Property"; whether they have been declared so or not, it is illegal to export old pieces without permission of the National Museum in Port Moresby.

Because of Australia's proximity and close association with PNG many valuable old pieces were taken out of Papua New Guinea to Australia many years ago. At times a collector loses interest in part of his collection or when an individual dies the benefactors of her estate may not have an interest in keeping these specialized items. In either case, the items are likely to wind up for sale in an antique furniture or art gallery. We came across shops in both Brisbane and Adelaide that happened to have some unique old PNG pieces for sale. However, this could happen in any city. So if you have an interest in these items be on the lookout as you travel around Australia.

We also found many shops selling more recent acquisitions from PNG. Almost every city has shops that specialize in PNG art. The best shops are found in Cairns (Gallery Primitive and Asian Connection) and Sydney (New Guinea Primitive Art, Ethnographics, and Duk Duk).

ARTS AND ANTIQUES

Australia is a paradise for fine art and antique lovers. Sydney, Melbourne, and Brisbane abound with art and antique shops that offer everything from oils, watercolors, and lithographs to Australian and European furniture and collectibles. You could literally spend weeks in Australia just shopping for art and antiques.

Australia's fine art market is booming and prices can be very high. You will find numerous galleries in Sydney, Melbourne, and Brisbane offering works of local portrait and landscape artists who capture the unique Australian character and colored landscape. Many of the small towns within a few hours drive of these and other cities offer excellent selections of Australian art. Indeed, no visit to Australia for Australian art would be complete without focusing your shopping on many of these towns.

One of the curious aspects of the antique business in Australia is its regular resupply of antiques from Europe. Since Australia is still a relatively new country whose antiques are seldom more than 100 years old, many antique shops must regularly import containers of antiques from England and France to satisfy the insatiable appetite for period furniture and collectibles.

You will find the largest concentration of antique shops along Queen Street in Sydney, High and Melvern streets in Melbourne, Paddington Circle in Brisbane, and numerous suburbs that surround these and other cities. Don't forget to also visit small craft towns which have numerous antique shops offering all kinds of unique items discovered in the antiques and basements of Australians living in the hills and Outback.

Chapter Five

BRISBANE

Welcome to Australia's center for sun, surf, and hedonism! Here you will find beautiful beaches, along with the world famous Great Barrier Reef, all within just a few hours drive from downtown Brisbane. Here's where 60% of all tourists to Australia come to relax, shop, and party. It's an area of many travel surprises and shopping delights.

A CITY AND ITS HINTERLAND

Brisbane, Australia's third largest city, is strategically located along the east coast in the southern section of Queensland State, Australia's second largest state and most rapidly growing economy. A bustling city of 1.2 million, Brisbane boasts an enviable hinterland of beautiful beaches and mountains stretching for hundreds of miles to the north and south. Known as the Sunshine Capital, for its attractive east coast and sunny recreational climate, Brisbane is also the gateway city to the country's most rapidly developing region. The city and its hinterland are magnets for some of the country's most spectacular commercial investments, real estate development, tourism, and recreation.

Above all, Brisbane and its surrounding areas are a shopper's delight!

SURPRISING BRISBANE

Brisbane is an unusually pleasant, casual, sophisticated, cosmopolitan, progressive, entrepreneurial, and delightfully livable city. It comes as a surprise to many visitors who primarily pass through this city on their way to Queensland's three great sun and surf playgrounds to the north and south -- the Great Barrier Reef, Sunshine Coast, and Gold Coast.

Brisbane is a city with a unique entrepreneurial flair for taking big risks that frequently result in big payoffs. In recent years Brisbane has experienced a level of economic development and dynamism that would be the envy of many cities throughout the world. It's impressive skyline of newly constructed high-rise commercial buildings and numerous first-class and deluxe hotels testify to the fact that Brisbane is on the move as the premier financial and business center for Queensland. The new Cultural Centre, resting on the south bank of the lazy Brisbane River, emphasizes Brisbane's commitment to preserving culture and promoting the finest in arts and entertainment for its citizenry and guests. Its ability to host the Commonwealth Games in 1982 and the World Expo in 1988 as well as attract the world's largest gathering of conventioneers in 1991 -- 50,000 Lions International Congress delegates -- clearly demonstrates its cosmopolitan and international character. And its numerous shopping malls and arcades in close proximity to the city center, as well as quaint arts and crafts towns to the north of the city, offer visitors an excellent mix of travel and shopping opportunities normally associated with cities much larger than Brisbane.

MORE THAN SUN, SURF, AND HEDONISM

Queensland is best known as Australia's seaside recreational capital. For years visitors have flocked to the East Coast to enjoy some of the world's finest beaches. From Port Douglas in the north to Coolangatta in the south, the East Coast has grown into a mecca for deep sea fishing, reef walking, scuba diving, boating, and beach bumming. It is to Australia what Miami Beach, Ft. Lauderdale, and Daytona Beach are to the United States -- minus the urban problems and traffic congestion. It is Australia's version of the French Riviera and Costa del Sol all rolled up into one.

Serving as the capital for the State of Queensland, Brisbane for years was content at playing the roles of state bureaucrat, banker, and broker as thousands of Australian and international tourists merely passed through the city on their way to the towns and beach resorts dotting the gorgeous coastline. But no longer do visitors just pass through this terminus to the coast. In recent years Brisbane has transformed itself into a major tourist attraction offering excellent shopping, sightseeing, entertainment, cultural, and recreational opportunities. It's a city worthy of a trip alone to enjoy its many and varied pleasures or at least a three day stop-over in transit to the popular beach and island reef resorts to the north and south. If you love to shop, this city will both surprise and delight you with its pleasant shopping malls, arcades, department stores, and markets offering everything from the latest in fashion to unique Australiana and tribal arts and crafts.

GETTING TO KNOW YOU

Here's a city you will quickly learn to like and feel at ease in navigating. Juxtiposing the old and the new, Brisbane is bright, brash, and assertive. From the moment you step off the airplane into its sunny climate, you will feel at home in this city. Nestled along the meandering Brisbane River, spread over charming hills, and sprouting new buildings left and right, this is a big city with a friendly, inviting, small town atmosphere.

Brisbane is a convenience city for visitors. Its relatively compact downtown area, centered around a pleasant and vibrant pedestrian mall, houses most of the city's major shopping arcades, department stores, specialty shops, commercial buildings, and hotels. All are within easy walking distance of one another as well as in close proximity to the city's showpiece for art and culture, the Cultural Centre. The public transportation system converges both above and below ground at Brisbane's most spectacular downtown shopping center, the Myer Centre. A special bus service, the 80-kilometer Great Circle Line, is organized to take shoppers to both downtown and suburban shopping centers. Major suburban shopping areas of interest to visitors, such as Paddington Circle and Fortitude Valley, are within three kilometers of downtown Brisbane, an easy five-minute bus ride. Other suburban shopping malls of primary interest to locals, such as Toowong Village and Westfield Indooroopilly Shoppingtown, are conveniently reached by regular bus service. And plans are proceeding to construct additional shopping centers along the banks of the Brisbane River.

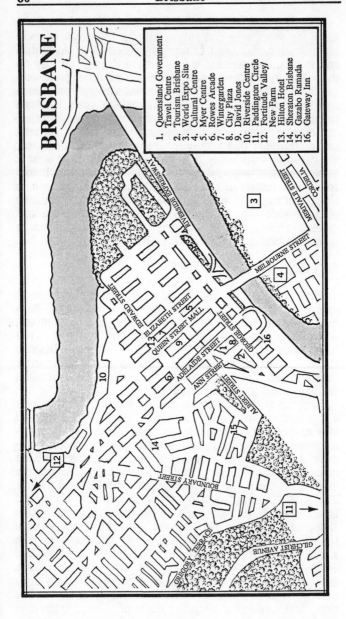

BRISBANE

1. Queensland Government Travel Centre
2. Tourism Brisbane
3. World Expo Site
4. Cultural Centre
5. Myer Centre
6. Rowes Arcade
7. Wintergarden
8. City Plaza
9. David Jones
10. Riverside Centre
11. Paddington Circle
12. Fortitude Valley/ New Farm
13. Hilton Hotel
14. Sheraton Brisbane
15. Gazabo Ramada
16. Gateway Inn

While Brisbane's shopping is not as sophisticated nor diverse as shopping in Sydney or Melbourne, you will nonetheless find plenty of unique shopping opportunities here. You will discover, for example, some of Australia's best beachwear in Brisbane as well as fashionable clothes designed by some of Brisbane's and Australia's leading designers. You will not find the haute couture of Sydney's Double Bay or Melbourne's Toorak Village shops, but you will discover some fine fashion shops in Brisbane's Rowes Arcade. Brisbane may not have Sydney's Queen Victoria Building nor Melbourne's Myer Department Store, but it has the specialty shops of Myer Centre along with a unique entertainment and market center (Top's) perched on its two top floors. If you are interested in tribal arts and crafts, you will be pleasantly surprised to find two shops that offer unique collections of items not found elsewhere in Australia. And if your interests include Australian arts and crafts, you will enjoy taking a one-day trip to the pleasant craft towns in the hills north of Brisbane.

Best of all, you will get to know this city very quickly. You can easily walk its streets, climb its hills, and cruise its river. The local tourist associations can assist you with literature and advice on all aspects of visiting Brisbane, from arranging tours outside the city to navigating its rail and bus systems. If you are just passing through this city on your way to the beach resorts, you may well want to return to Brisbane to enjoy its many urban and suburban pleasures.

THE STREETS OF BRISBANE

The city of Brisbane is located on both the north and south sides of the Brisbane River. However, you will find most shopping opportunities centered on the north side in downtown Brisbane as well as in the suburbs of Paddington, Red Hill, and Fortitude Valley.

Downtown Brisbane is a relatively compact area where shops and shopping centers are concentrated within easy walking distance of each other. The major shopping area is bordered by George, Elizabeth, Edward, and Ann streets. Here you will find Brisbane's major department stores, shopping arcades, specialty shops, hotels, restaurants, banks, and an information booth and tourist offices ready to handle all your travel and shopping questions. Within this area, Queen Street Mall is the major center for shopping. Located between Edward and George streets, this pleasant pedestrian mall is a shopper's paradise. You will enjoy strolling down its wide traffic-free walkway, browsing through the many shops and arcades that front on the mall, eating at one of the many indoor or outdoor restaurants and small eateries, or just watching the steady flow of shoppers from 8:15am to 9pm each weekday, and from 8:15am to 5:30pm on weekdays. Adjacent George, Elizabeth, Adelaide, Ann, Albert, and Edward streets yield numerous additional shops and arcades to make this downtown area Bribane's shopping mecca.

Plan to walk the major shopping streets of downtown Brisbane. Since all the department stores, shopping arcades, and specialty shops are in such close proximity to one another, you can easily cover the downtown area on foot. You will find plenty of taxis and buses stopping along these streets, but you only need such transportation when leaving downtown for suburban shopping areas.

Outside the downtown area -- within five minutes by taxi, car, or bus -- you will find several suburban shopping streets and centers. **Paddington Circle**, a commercial designation for an area encompassing the main streets of suburban Paddington (Given Terrace and Latrobe Terrace) and Red Hill (Musgrave Road), is one of Brisbane's major suburban shopping and historical areas. Consisting of numerous restored cottages, quaint specialty shops, and markets, as well as newly constructed shopping centers, Paddington Circle is to Brisbane what Toorak Road and High Street are to Melbourne and what Paddington's Oxford Street is to Sydney. The streets are lined with specialty shops selling everything from high fashion clothes to gifts and antiques. If you are interested in exploring this area, be sure to pick up a copy of *"The Paddington Circle Inc."* guide map which is available at the downtown tourist information booth in the center of Queen Street Mall or at the Brisbane Information Centre in City Hall just above and behind the City Plaza Shopping Centre on Ann Street. This handy brochure includes a detailed map of the area along with information on 43 of the shops and restaurants that line the major streets of Paddington Circle. Since the map is not drawn to scale, you will quickly discover the area is much more spread out and walking distances much lengthier than might otherwise be suggested.

The best way to get to Paddington Circle from downtown Brisbane is to take a taxi or a number 144 bus from Adelaide Street to Caxton Given Terrace, Caxton Street, and Latrobe Terrace or a number 146 or 172 bus from Adelaide Street to Musgrave Road in Red Hill. Better still, you may want to rent a car for the day so you have the convenience of driving from one section of this area to another. A good plan would be to rent a car for the day. Drive to Paddington Circle in the morning, preferably during the weekday since Paddington Circle can be very crowded on weekends. Arrive around 10am and spend three hours shopping the main streets of this area. Use the car in the afternoon to explore other suburban areas, such as nearby Fortitude Valley. Since it is easy to drive in Brisbane, you will find the car to be very convenient for shopping in these areas.

One reason we recommend renting a car is that the Paddington Circle area is not easy to walk. You can find buses along the main streets and an occasional taxi or you can call a taxi from a shop. But going from Paddington into Red Hill can be inconvenient. This whole area is spread out over one very long street which runs from Caxton Street in the south to Given Terrace and Latrobe Terrace in the north and along a small street to the east, Musgrave Road. If you plan to walk this area, be sure you have a good pair of walking shoes and a great deal of time and perseverance. This is a very hilly area. The streets running north progressively go up hill. And the east-west streets linking Red Hill's Musgrave Road to Paddington's main street go up and down steep grades.

If you do not have a car, we recommend that you begin shopping this area by taking a bus or taxi to the top of the hill at Latrobe Terrace. Get off at the bus stop on Latrobe Terrace, opposite Gilday Street or shop number 43 on Latrobe Terrace, just before Latrobe Terrace turns into MacGregor Terrace. From here you will be walking down hill as you explore the many shops on both sides of Latrobe Terrace which also becomes Given Terrace. This is a long walk, so expect to spend a good two to three hours walking the length of the street. In many sections of this street you will find few shops, but other sections will have several shops next to each other.

To go from Given Terrace in Paddington to Musgrave Road in Red Hill is a major walking effort. Take George Street from Given Terrace to walk east to Musgrave Road. Despite what your map might indicate, this is more than just a little walk. It may take you 30 minutes as you huff and puff up steep inclines to get to the intersection of Great George Street and Musgrave Road. Depending on how much you like exercise, you may elect to take a taxi from Paddington to Red Hill. Start at the intersection of Great George Street and Musgrave Road so you will be walking downhill along Musgrave Road.

Riverside Centre, located to the north of the city center and on the west bank of the Brisbane River, includes some shops and a popular Sunday market. A long walk from the central city, this area is best reached by taxi or bus.

The adjacent suburban areas of **Fortitude Valley, New Farm,** and **Newstead** are located to the north and east of the city center. Fortitude Valley is noted for the famous Potters' Gallery (483 Brunswick Street) which offers the largest collection of handcrafted pottery in Queensland. Fortitude Valley also is noted for its colorful Chinatown Mall, a replica of an Imperial Chinese Village. New Form is famous for Paddy's Markets whereas Newstead is noted for the Pierots Arts and Crafts Centre. Located within five kilometers of downtown Brisbane, you can easily get to these three areas by taking a bus or taxi.

If you are interested in seeing where and how the locals shop as well as touring the Greater Brisbane area at your own pace, take a bus tour of Brisbane's **eight major suburban shopping centers.** The Great Circle Line, operated by the Brisbane City Council on weekdays (Tel. 225-4444 for the exact timetable) is conveniently organized to take you to these shopping centers. Departing every half hour and stopping every 10 minutes, the bus makes 11 stops along this 80-kilometer route. In addition to stopping at the eight major shopping complexes, the Great Circle Line passes by the Mt. Coot-tha Botanic Gardens, two public hospitals, primary and secondary schools, a TAFE college, and Griffith University. All you need to do is buy a full day River ticket ($4 from the bus driver or $3 from newsagents; a Concession Rover ticket designed for pensioners and children is only $2 from the bus driver and $1.50 from newsagents) and get on and off at your leisure. Plan to spend a full-day covering the eight shopping centers and other sites along with way.

Time permitting, you may want to spend a day or two exploring shopping opportunities outside Brisbane. Three major areas, each offering distinct shopping opportunities, are within a few hours drive of downtown Brisbane: the craft towns of Maleny, Montville, and Mapleton in the northeastern hill country; the Sunshine Coast, from Coloundra in the south to Noosa Heads in the north; and the Gold Coast in and around Surfers Paradise in the south.

We especially recommend renting a car for the day and taking the scenic drive north to the **craft towns of Maleny, Montville, and Mapleton** and then returning to Brisbane by way of the Sunshine Coast. Take Bruce Highway north of Brisbane for about 50 kilometers and turn left onto Old Bruce Highway at the sign for Beerburrum. The road will take you into some lovely hill country. You will initially pass by a few craft shops, such as De Maine Pottery Studio Workshop (Maleny Road, Landsborough) and Yoorooga Australian Craft (at the intersection of Maleny and Mt. Mellum Road, 3.5 kilometers from Landsborough). The first major craft town you will come to is the small town of Maleny. Here you will find a few art, craft, and antique shops. Returning to the main highway, take a left and drive on to Montville, approximately 15 kilometers north of Maleny. Here you will discover a large concentration of nice quality arts, crafts, and antique shops as well as a few delightful restaurants that make this trip well worth while. From Montville, continue north for another five kilometers until you come to the small town of Mapleton. Not much here compared to Montville, but the drive is nice.

From Mapleton go east a few kilometers until you come to the main highway at Nambour which will take you back to Brisbane if you go south or to the Sunshine Coast if you go east or northeast. The major **Sunshine Coast** town is Noosa Heads, a 45-minute drive northeast of Mapleton. Along the way you will pass through Yandina -- noted for its Ginger Factory -- Eumundi, and Noosaville. Noosa Heads is a typical beachside resort with lots of sun and surf. You will find several shops near the beach along Hastings Street (Bay Village) selling beachwear and a couple of local shopping centers (The Junction and Ocean Breeze) offering goods for local residents. Other than that, this is not a noted shopping area. Go here primarily to see the beachside resorts and the lovely beaches. From Noosa Heads, drive south along the David Low Highway on your way back to Brisbane. You will see many lovely beaches along the way from Noosa Heads to Caloundra -- but little or no shopping worth stopping for. After Caloundra it's back to the interior Bruce Highway for a less interesting return drive to Brisbane. Since the whole trip from Brisbane into the craft towns and on to the Sunshine Coast will take a full day, be sure to leave Brisbane by 8am so you will have plenty of time to enjoy the areas. If you shop the towns and keep moving quickly from one area to another, you should return to Brisbane by 6pm.

To the south of Brisbane is the famous **Gold Coast,** a one to two-hour drive from downtown Brisbane. This is Queensland's Miami Beach with numerous high-rise condominiums, beachfront resorts, and shops. Most commercial and recreational activities center around the booming city of Surfers Paradise. Here you will find numerous shops and chic boutiques selling everything from beachwear and Australiana to fine jewelry, art, and clothes. Many shops from Sydney and Melbourne have opened branch shops in Surfers Paradise. The best way to shop this area is to pick up a free copy of the Gold Coast tourist guide, *Point Out.* It's filled with ads as well as detailed beachfront maps identifying the major hotels, restaurants, and shops and shopping centers, such as Centrepoint Arcade, Centre Arcade, Dolphin Arcade, The Mark Shopping

Complex, Holiday City Galleria, and numerous shops along Orchard Avenue and Elkhorn Avenue.

WHAT TO BUY

Opals and Jewelry

Like other cities in Australia, Brisbane has its own stores offering a wide selection of opals and jewelry. Most of these shops are concentrated in the downtown section in and around Queen Street Mall. Shops offering a wide selection of fine opals include **Opal World** (315 Wintergarden shopping arcade, Queen Street Mall), **Quilpie Opals** (Lennons Plaza Building, 68 Queen Street), **Endors Opal Gallery** (Rowes Arcade, 235 Edward Street), **The Rock Shop** (193 Adelaide Street), **Darrell James** (260 Adelaide Street), as well as several of the duty-free shops. Local jewelers include **Wallace Bishop** (King George Square at the corner of Adelaide and Albert streets; and Queen Street Mall at the corner of Edward Street), **Robert White Jewellers** (Shop 11, Brisbane Arcade, Queen Street), and **Citigold Jewellery** (223 George Street). Look for other opal and jewelry shops, such as **Prouds, Anita Jewellery, De Lisle Jewellers, Van Wyk Jewellers, Goldmark Jewellers,** and **Strand Watches & Jewellery,** in The Myer Centre and Wintergarden shopping arcades.

Fine Arts and Antiques

Brisbane and its surrounding area have several art and antique shops offering very good quality oils, prints, lithographs, and European and Australian antiques. We recommend that you start your fine art and antique shopping by visiting the art gallery and museum at the **Queensland Cultural Centre,** on the south bank of the Brisbane River directly opposite the downtown area. Their art and historical collections will give you a good overview of the artistic talent and history of Queensland. The Cultural Centre also has an excellent shop offering a good collection of books on all facets of Australian arts, crafts, and culture. Also stop at the **City Hall Art Gallery and Museum** (King George Square) to see their collection of historical materials, ceramics, and fine arts.

You will discover art and antique shops throughout the greater Brisbane area. Unlike Sydney's Paddington and Queens Street or Melbourne's High street, Brisbane's art and antique shops are not concentrated in one particular section of the city or suburbs. In Brisbane you must know what shops are located where and then travel from one shop to another in different parts of the city and suburbs.

In downtown Brisbane you will find **Eilisha's Antiques** and **Antiquarian Print Gallery** (The Mansions, 40 George Street), **Kellies Antiques** (Shop 21 T&G Arcade, corner of Queen and Albert Streets), **Dimensions Art Gallery** (101 Adelaide Street), **Adrian Slinger Galleries** (230 Edward Street), and **The Town Gallery and Japan Room** (4th floor, Dunstan House, 236 Elizabeth Street). In nearby South Brisbane look for **Cordelia Street Antique and Art Centre** (housed in a church building on the corner of Cordelia and Glenelg Streets).

Outside the downtown area you will find several art and antique shops in nearby suburbs of Paddington, Red Hill, Fortitude Valley, New Farm, Bardon, Milton, Clayfield, Annerley, Hawthorn, Sherwood, Windsor, Taringa, Mt. Gravatt, and Greenslopes all located within a few minutes drive from downtown Brisbane. And don't forget to visit the small towns of Maleny and Montville to the north of Brisbane. Montville is the most interesting and important center for arts and antiques. If you are a dedicated art and antique collector, then a one-day excursion to Montville should be a "must" on your travel and shopping agenda.

You will find two excellent quality **art shops in Paddington.** Both are found in the northern Latrobe Terrace section of Paddington. **Grahame Galleries** (181 Latrobe Terrace) offers a good selection of contemporary Australian and international paintings as well as presents exhibits of major artists. **Latrobe Gallery** (199 Latrobe Terrace) specializes in contemporary French art, offering an interesting selection of originial watercolors, oils, prints, etchings, engravings, mezzotints, and woodcuts.

The **antique shops of Paddington** are primarily concentrated under one roof at the **Paddington Antique Centre** (167 Latrobe Terrace), Brisbane's second largest antique center. Here you will find 58 dealers offering a wide range of collectibles. Browse through its narrow pathways and you may discover a unique piece of porcelain, glass, jewelry, Australiana, toys, dolls, and furniture. If you are interested in good quality pine and country furniture from England, Europe, and Australia, be sure to visit **Country Charm** (201 Latrobe Terrace). For colonial furniture visit **Jupiter Antiques** (173 Latrobe Terrace).

Fortitude Valley and **New Farm,** suburbs adjacent to downtown Brisbane, have a few art and antique shops worth visiting. Fortitude Valley's antique center, **Wickham Street Antique Galleries** (400 Wickham Street -- next to the Valley pool and on the road to the airport), has one of the best collections of Victorian and Georgian antique furniture, jewelry, and collectibles. **Philip Bacon**

Galleries (2 Arthur Street, New Farm) offers a wide selection of fine art produced by many of Australia's leading artists.

Clayfield, a suburb located five kilometers north of downtown Brisbane along Sandgate Road, is home for one of Brisbane's largest antique centers. Here you will want to visit the **Brisbane Antique Market** (791 Sandgate Road). Open seven days a week, this antique emporium displays the offerings of 40 dealers. Nearby you will find **Noble Antiques** (685 Sandgate Road).

You will find a few art and antique shops in other suburbs within five to 10 minutes from downtown Brisbane: **Rick Everingham Studio Gallery** (12 Victoria Street, Spring Hill), **Red Hill Gallery** (61 Musgrave Road, Red Hill), **Hang Ups Distinctive Art** (99 Musgrave Road, Red Hill), **Claudia Connolly Antiques** (208 Musgrave Road, Red Hill), **Southside Antique Centre** (484 Ipswich Road, Annerley), **Philip Bacon Galleries** (2 Arthur Street, New Farm), **And Woven Cane** (194 Boundary Road, Bardon), **Cintra Galleries** (40 Park Road, Milton), **Chantilly Antiques** (corner of Junction and Sandgate Roads, Clayfield), **Annie's Old Things** 9209 Wynnum Road, Hawthorn), **Turn O'the Century** (377 Oxley Road, Sherwood), **Discovery Corner** (236 Lutwyche Road, Windsor), **Hinds Antiques** (143 Moggill Road, Taringa), **Millar and Allan Antiques** (238 Newnham Road, Mt. Gravatt), and **Collector's Corner Antiques** (540 Logan Road, Greenslopes).

Fine arts and antiques are well and alive in the hills of Maleny and Montville. Rent a car for the day to make this two hour drive from downtown Brisbane. You will discover one of Australia's most rewarding country art and antique centers. The small town of **Maleny** has only two art and antique shops. **Patrina** (32 Maple Street) alone is well worth a visit to Maleny. Here you will find a wide selection of fine art, antiques, and jewelry ranging in price from $1 to $100,000. This shop is a good place to go if you are interested in buying home decorative items. Look for the owner's fine art gallery which will open soon a few doors away at the old fire station. This "by appointment only" shop (071/94-2283) will offer investment quality paintings. If you are looking for a more traditional antique shop offering furniture and collectibles, visit **Steve Lidbury's Antiques** (38 Maple Street).

Nearby **Montville** is a treasure-trove of fine art and antique shops. It's easy to find all the shops in Montville since they are spread over a one-kilometer stretch of Main Street, the highway that passes through the center of town. Coming in from Maleny, you will initially see a pottery factory on your right and a few cottages on your left selling arts and crafts. As you go further into town you will find the major concentration of fine art and antique shops in an area called The Village Green. Here you will find **Rainbird Gallery** and **The Courtyard Gallery**, small galleries selling quality oils produced by some of Australia's leading artists. Across the street is **The De'Lisle Gallery** (The Village Green), a large gallery offering investment quality oils by major artists from all over Australia; this gallery charges a nominal admissions fee -- 30c for adults and 10c for children.

You will find several antique shops along Main Street in Montville selling everything from European and Australian furniture to African artifacts and antiques. If you like antique furniture, colonial wares, and estate jewelry, be sure to visit **Montville Antiques.** For a selection of African arts and antiques, stop at **Sallanger's.**

Australian Arts and Crafts

Like many other Australian cities, Brisbane is a center for many Australian artists and craftsmen who produce exquisite arts and crafts found in numerous shops and galleries throughout the Brisbane area. Both the city and the state of Queensland actively promote the arts and crafts through the Queensland Cultural Centre, the Brisbane City Hall Art Gallery and Museum, and the Crafts Council of Queensland.

Other than visiting the Queensland Cultural Centre and the Brisbane City Hall Art Gallery and Museum, you will find few arts and crafts shops in downtown Brisbane. Most are located in and around the Queen Street Mall and The Myer Centre. For example, look for **Margaret Francey Australian Fine Crafts** (Balcony Shop 18, Brisbane Arcade, Queen Street Mall), **The Handmade Shop** (Level 2, Shop 232, The Myer Centre), **The Wilderness Shop and Gallery** (Shop 12, Adelaide Street, Mace Arcade), **Wood Family Cottage Crafts** (Shop 418 "Top" Myer Centre) as well as a few Australiana shops selling arts and crafts.

Most arts and crafts shops are found a few kilometers outside the city center as well as in the northern hill towns of Maleny and Montville. For good quality pottery, be sure to visit **The Potters Gallery** (483 Brunswick Street) in Fortitude Valley. Operated by the Queensland Potters' Association, The Potters Gallery displays and sells the works of members as well as guest potters. For one of the largest collections of Australian arts and crafts, including craftsmen and artists, visit the **Pierrot Arts & Crafts**

Centre (251 Arthur Street) in Newstead. **Nakina Fine Arts** (185 Days Road) in The Grange offers a comprehensive range of paintings, pottery, and crafts. The **Australian Woolshed** (148 Samford Road) in Ferny Hills has an award-winning craftshop and loft gallery.

You will find a few arts and crafts shops in the **Paddington and Red Hill** (Paddington Circle area). For elegant glassware, contemporary handsculpted glass, and unique glass art produced by several Australian craftsmen, visit **Lucence** (Shop 2, Paddington Central, corner of Latrobe Terrace and Warmington Streets). A few home decorative and gift shops also offer arts and crafts: **Majors** (2 Latrobe Terrace), **Merryl Ducat Interiors** (11 Latrobe Terrace), and **Break of Day Gift Shop** (Shop 50, 283 Given Terrace). In nearby Red Hill stop at the **Red Hill Gallery** (61 Musgrave Road) to browse for pottery, jewelry, paintings, and crafts produced by some of Queensland's leading artists and craftsmen.

In the nearby suburb of **Chelmer**, you will find **Plumridge Fine Craft Gallery** (123 Oxley Road) which also sells a wide selection of arts and crafts produced by leading Queensland craftsmen and artists. Look for quality gifts and collectibles made from glass, clay, wood, leather, and stone.

One of the largest concentrations of arts and crafts shops is found outside the Greater Brisbane area in and around the small hill towns of **Maleny** and **Montville** north of Brisbane. On the road to Maleny and Montville, just after passing through the town of **Landsborough** via Bruce Highway and Maleny Road, you will find two craft shops worth visiting: **De Maine Pottery Studio Workshop** (Maleny Road, Landsborough, Tel. 071/94-1458) and **Yoorooga** (corner of Maleny and Mt. Mellum Roads, Tel. 071/94-1771).

Amongst the many art and antique shops on the main streets of Maleny and Montville, you will find many craft shops selling a wide selection of items produced by Queensland craftsmen. In **Maleny** a "must stop" is **Patrina** (32 Maple Street), with its fine selection of arts and crafts that make nice gifts as well as home decorative items. A small shop selling country crafts produced by members of the Maleny Arts and Crafts Group and sold on consignment is **The Elizabeth McDonald Workshop** (Maple Street).

Montville is one of the largest arts and crafts centers in the state of Queensland. Approaching the town from Maleny, you will initially come to a pottery factory on your right (**Montville Pottery**) and country craft shops on the left (**The Herb Garden**). As you go further along

Main Street you will find several arts and crafts shops selling everything from traditional country crafts to imported arts and crafts. **Sunshine Coast Crafts**, a co-operative shop staffed by volunteers, offers a wide selection of items produced by local craftsmen -- textiles, pottery, ceramics, leatherwork, jewelry -- as well as pickles and jams. Also, look for **Cadman Cottage, Comphor Cottage, Spring Cottage, Melba's of Montville, The Irish Shop,** and **Gallery D** (Gallery D, The Dome).

Aboriginal, Tribal, and International Arts and Crafts

While Brisbane is not considered to be a major center for acquiring quality Aboriginal arts and crafts, it does have an excellent collection on exhibit at the **Queensland Cultural Centre**. Two shops in the Centre offer Aboriginal arts, crafts, and books. The first shop is located just outside the Aboriginal exhibit. You will find several Aboriginal souvenirs here, including postcards, stationery, placemats, coasters, acrylic paintings, didjeridoos, and clap sticks. Another shop is located on the ground floor adjacent to the art gallery. This shop has Brisbane's best collection of books on Aboriginal arts and crafts.

Although the best shopping for Aboriginal arts and crafts is found in Darwin, Alice Springs, Melbourne, and Sydney, you will find a few shops in Brisbane offering limited selections of bark paintings, didjeridoos, clap sticks, boomerangs, weapons, place mats, coasters, music, and books. A popular tourist quality shop run by Aboriginals is the **Queensland Aboriginal Creations** (135 George Street). A shop that offers some of the best quality and most expensive Aboriginal bark paintings and carvings is located behind the Town Hall on George Street. Also look for **Wiumulli** (121 Melbourne Street) in South Brisbane, one block from the Queensland Cultural Centre and directly across from the 1988 Expo site.

Brisbane has three of Australia's best shops offering international arts and crafts, with particular emphasis on Papua New Guinea and several countries in Asia. Across from the Myer Centre in downtown Brisbane, be sure to visit Ian Thomson's **Decorators Gallery** (57 Elizabeth Street). This is the best international decorative arts and crafts shop we found in all of Australia. It's the ideal place for collectors, decorators, and gift seekers alike. You'll find arts and crafts from over 30 countries including Korean chests, Japanese kimonos, Indian carvings and paintings, Thai and Burmese figurines and tapestries, Louvre Museum replicas, Egyptian jewelry as well as tribal arts from Papua New Guinea, Africa, and Indonesia. Best of all, you will discover excellent quality items at very reasonable prices here. A second **Decorators Gallery** (93 Musgrave Road) is located in the Red Hill section of Paddington Circle. We recommend visiting both shops since they do not carry the same items, and you will enjoy browsing through two shops that have their own distinctive character.

Another excellent shop to visit is **Karavan** (34 Latrobe Terrace) in Paddington. This shop has a unique collection of traditional arts from Southeast Asia, Papua New Guinea, and the Middle East. Collectors and decorators alike will discover numerous treasures here. You will find furniture, carpets, woodcarvings, pottery, tribal jewelry, and textiles at Karavan. This is the only shop in Australia that we found offering Philippine colonial furniture and intricate woodcarvings from the island of New Ireland in Papua New Guinea.

If your interests include Latin American arts and crafts, visit the **South American Art and Craft Gallery** (543 Milton Road) in nearby Toowong. This shop offers arts and crafts, including jewelry and clothing, from Central and South America.

Clothes and Accessories

While Brisbane does have a few local designers, most clothes are brought into Brisbane shops from Melbourne and Sydney or imported from abroad. Several shops stock popular Australian designer labels, such as Ken Done. You will also find in Brisbane branches of popular clothing stores and designer boutiques which are primarily based in Melbourne, Sydney, and Adelaide: Carla Zampatti, Walter Kristensen, Shepherds, Country Road, Cherry Lane, Designer Savings, Jeanswest, Just Jeans, R. M. Williams, and Settlers & Co.

Although Brisbane is not a noted fashion center, you will find plenty of shopping for fashionable clothes in this city. Brisbane's major clothing strength, however, is its good quality **sports** and **beachwear**, especially distinctively designed swimsuits and clothes using **tropical weight cotton fabrics**, which are not available in many other Australian cities.

Most clothing stores and boutiques in downtown Brisbane are found in and around the Queen Street Mall: Rowes Arcade, Wintergarden, The Myer Center, David Jones Department Store, and Myer in the City department store. Shops offering the closest thing to haute couture are found in the small but elegant **Rowes Arcade**. Here is where many of Brisbane's rich and famous -- and those with both good taste and plenty of money -- come to shop. **Alla Mode** (Shop F7, Rowes Arcade, Plaza Level, 217 Adelaide Street), offers an exquisite collection of imported European fabrics from which they will make garments to your specifications. You can select your favorite outfit from their many patterns and magazine photos, and they will ship abroad. **Fashion House of Helena Kaye** (Shop 5, Rowes Arcade, Edward Street) is a small but exclusive boutique selling dresses made in South Australia using Spinelli wool from Italy. **Shepherds** also has a shop in Rowes Arcade offering distinctive and colorful women's fashion. **J. B. Conlan** (Gallery Level, Rowes Arcade) offers quality menswear.

For a good selection of quality cotton clothes designed for tropical living, visit **Gauguin Tropical Fashions** (Pavilion Arcade, corner of Queen and Albert streets). **Canterbury** in the Wintergarden shopping arcade has an excellent selection of cotton leisurewear. **Barneys of Brisbane** (corner of Edward and Elizabeth streets) is noted for good quality menswear.

You will find several women's clothing and accessory stores in **The Myer Centre** (Queen Street Mall). Some are local stores but many are branches of chain stores based in Melbourne and Sydney: **Canterbury, Centrefold Clothing, Cherry Lane, Country Road, Designer Savings, Fiona's Clothes Horse, Jeanswest, Jill's Designer Collection, Just Jeans, Kilroy Klothing Kompany, Laura Ashley, Tokyo Boutique,** and **Vincci.** Menswear in The Myer Centre can be found at **Boxer Rebellion, Frenz Mens, Gauci Menswear, Lenard Charles Menswear, Lowes Menswear, Roger David,** and **Tom Browns Menswear.**

Wintergarden shopping arcade (Queen Street Mall opposite David Jones Department Store and adjacent to the Hilton Hotel) is also filled with clothing and accessory stores. For women's clothes and accessories, look for **Ambition Clothing Co., Australian Designer Art, Carla Zampatti, Country Road, Covers, Cue, Designer Savings, Events, Fionas Clothes Horse, Maggie T., Nik Nik, Pucci, Remartchi,** and **Walter Kristensen.** Men should look for **Bjorn Borg Menswear Collection, Country Road Mens, Elio, Frendz Menz, Frenzi-Leather Forever, MacArthur Menswear, Palmer & Palmer, R. M. Williams, Signatures By Fletcher Jones,** and **Tony Barlow.**

Brisbane's two major up-market department stores located on the Queen Street Mall -- **Myer in the City** and **David Jones** -- have a wide range of designer label clothes catering to a large range of tastes and prices.

Settlers & Co., on the second floor of the Myer in the City department store, has a good selection of Australian leather clothes. Here you will find good quality and selections of the famous Australian Akubra hats.

Paddington Circle has a few unique boutiques. **Joonz** (47 Arthur Terrace, Red Hill) offers a wide range of original designs produced by over 30 of Australia's designers. Here you will find applique wear, leather accessories, screen-printed resort gear, elegant evening wear, tops, and jackets. Other shops in Paddington selling unique fashion clothes, swimwear, and accessories include **Jootsies Boutique** (102 Latrobe Terrace), **Thai Boutique** (corner of Given and Latrobe Terrace), **Lyn Hadley Clothes** (Shop 46, 283 Given Terrace), and **Timbuctoo** (Shop 9 and 10, Paddington Market, 261-265 Given Terrace).

Brisbane's famous sportswear and beachwear will be found in the downtown department stores (Myers and David Jones) and shopping arcades (The Myer Centre and Wintergarden) as well as in many shops along the Sunshine Coast (Noosa Heads) and Gold Coast (Surfers Paradise). You will find unique patterns and designs made from nice lightweight cotton fabrics.

Wools, Furs, and Leather Products

You will find a few shops offering wools, furs, and leather products. **Baa Baa Black Sheep** (Shop 17, Balcony Level, Brisbane Arcade, corner of Queen and Adelaide streets) has a good selection of quality handmade Australian wool products. **M. E. Humfress & Co.** (26 Market Street) stocks a large range of kangaroo fur and leather coats, bags, and purses as well as sheepskin vests, jackets, coats, hats, slippers, boots, and mittens. If you want to see a program complete with trained rams, sheep shearing, spinning, and sheepdog demonstrations as well as purchase wool products, be sure to visit the **Australian Woodshed** (148 Samford Road) in Ferny Hills, located about 20 minutes from downtown Brisbane. You'll find an award-winning craftshop and loft gallery at Australian Woodshed.

Brisbane's major furrier is **J. Jackson** (Shop 245, The Myer Centre, Shop 245, Queen Street) in downtown Brisbane. You will find a large range of furs and leather clothes which are duty-free purchases for international tourists.

Several leather shops sell both Australian and imported leather products. **Settlers & Co.** (second floor of Myer in the City department store) and **R. M. Williams** (Wintergarden shopping arcade) both offer Australian outback leather clothes including the famous Australian Akubra

hats and fashionable coats and jackets. Stores selling
leather shoes, handbags, briefcases, and accessories abound
in **The Myer Centre** and **Wintergarden** shopping arcades.
Many of these products are imported from Europe. In **The
Myer Centre** look for **Bagfashion, Bagstop, Dundee
Country, Handbags International, Kay's Bags, Strand-
bags, The Leather Shop,** and **The Leather Baggery.** In
Wintergarden you will find **Bagstop, Chaps, Florsheim,
International Shoes and Accessories, Handbags International, Hunt Leather, Oroton,** and **Standbags.** Be forewarned, however, that prices on most imported leather
products will be very expensive. Expect, for example, to
pay over A$200 for good quality leather shoes and hand-
bags. Don't be surprised to find imported briefcases starting at A$350. For some of the best quality imported
leather products, visit the chain store **Oroton** in Wintergarden shopping arcade.

Household Furnishings and Accessories

A few shops in and around Brisbane offer good selections of home furnishings and accessories for individuals
interested in home decorating. We especially like Canberra-based **The Australian East India Company** in The
Myer Centre (ground floor, Elizabeth Street entrance).
This is a home decorator's warehouse, somewhat similar to
Pier I stores in the United States but more up-market and
service-oriented. The tasteful selections in this large shop
include nicely designed furniture, rattan furnishings, living
room accessories, tableware, and kitchenware. It's a delightful store to browse through or just stop for a cup of
coffee. The service here is some of the best we found in
all of Australia. You will also find the **Designer Shop**
(248, Level Two) in The Myer Centre.

A few of the arts and crafts shops in **Paddington** and
Red Hill specialize in home decorative items. Look for
Majors (2 Latrobe Terrace, Paddington), **Meeryl Ducat
Interiors** (11 Latrobe Terrace, Paddington), **Aero Designs**
(285 Given Terrace, Paddington), and **Red Hill Gallery**
(61 Musgrave Road, Red Hill). Other arts and crafts
shops in the city, suburbs, and in the hill towns of **Maleny**
and **Montville** offer interesting home decorative items.

If your home decorating tastes include the exotic, especially unique tribal and Asian furnishings, we highly recommend stopping at Ian Thomson's two **Decorators
Gallery** shops (57 Elizabeth Street, downtown Brisbane,
across from The Myer Centre; and 93A Musgrave Road,
Red Hill) as well as **Karavan** (34 Latrobe Terrace, Paddington). We made some of our nicest purchases in all of

Australia at these three shops.

Australiana, Souvenirs, and Gifts

Like other cities in Australia, Brisbane has its share of Australiana, souvenir, and gift shops offering everything from tourist kitsch to quality arts and crafts. T-shirts and stuffed koala bears are popular items offered by many such shops. Look for several such shops in downtown Brisbane: **The Proud Australian** (Shop 3, The Pavilion, corner of Queen and Alberts streets), **Francis Nixon Souvenirs** (Shop 15, Brisbane Arcade, Queen Street), **Arunga Gifts** (195 Adelaide Street), **Koalamania** (Queen Street Mall; and Albert Street), **Gift Shop** (The Mansions, George Street), **Shops 12** (T&G Arcade, corner of Queen and Albert streets), and **M. E. Humfress & Co.** (26 Market Street). At Riverside Centre and Paddington, look for the **Down Under House** (Shop 6, 123 Eagle Street, Riverside Centre; and 213A Given Terrace, Paddington) for original T-shirts, sweat shirts, and scarves in distinctive Australian designs as well as beachwear, housewares, calendars, and cards.

You'll find several nice gift shops in The Myer Centre and Wintergarden shopping arcade. The Myer Centre has **Living and Giving** (Shop 41), **Portofino** (Shop 114), **The Handmade Shops** (Shop 232), and **The Treasure House** (Shop 82A). At the Wintergarden shopping arcade, look for **Everything Australian** (Shop 217) and **Focus on Gifts** (Shop 306). Several jewelry and opal shops, such as **Prouds** and **Opal World**, offer a good selection of quality gifts.

The beach resort cities of **Noosa Heads** on the Sunshine Coast and **Surfers Paradise** on the Gold Coast have numerous shops selling Australiana, souvenirs, and gifts, with a heavy emphasis on T-shirts and beachwear.

Sports Equipment

Brisbane is one of Australia's major sports centers. You will find several shops in downtown Brisbane offering the latest in sports equipment and clothes: **Bill Brown's Sportscene** (City Plaza, corner of George and Adelaide Streets; and Mayfair Arcade, 124 Adelaide Street), **Golf World** (85 Elizabeth Street), and **Amart All Sports** (32 Burnett Lane). Amart All Sports has five additional branches in the suburbs as well as one branch along the Gold Coast and Sunshine Coast.

Duty-Free Shopping

Brisbane has its share of duty-free shops offering the usual selection of liquor, tobacco, cosmetics, perfumes, fashion, opals, jewelry, watches, cameras, audio and video equipment, macadamia nuts, sports equipment, handbags, leather goods, and Australian souvenirs. Most of these shops are part of large duty-free chains found in several other Australian cities. In downtown Brisbane look for **Downtown Duty Free** (Macarthur Chambers, corner of Edward and Queen streets), **Orbit Duty Free** (136 Queen Street Mall), **Darrell James** (260 Adelaide Street), and **City International Duty Free** (86 Queen Street; and corner of Adelaide and Creet streets). The airport also has a duty-free shop.

Books and Music

You will discover several good bookstores and music shops in the downtown area. One of our favorites is the bookstore at the museum shop in the **Queensland Cultural Centre**. **Brashs** (Wintergarden, Queen Street Mall), has one of Brisbane's largest selections of music.

WHERE TO SHOP

The pattern of shopping in Brisbane is very similar to that found in other Australian cities. You will find the typical pedestrian mall located in the heart of the central business district. This is where most of Brisbane's shopping action is centered around numerous shopping arcades, department stores, and specialty shops. Within only a few minutes of the downtown area you will come to several suburban shopping areas. Some of these areas cater to tourists but most are popular with locals who live in the suburbs. Further outside the city you will discover arts and crafts towns as well as large and small resort towns along the Sunshine Coast to the north and the Gold Coast to the south.

Shopping Approach

We recommend that you begin your shopping in downtown Brisbane along the Queen Street Mall. A compact, high density area, you can easily spend a good day or two exploring the many arcades and shops along this and adjacent streets. All the shops in the downtown area are within easy walking distance. After completing your downtown shopping, head for a few nearby suburban areas, especially Paddington, Red Hill, Fortitude Valley, and New Farm -- all within a five to 10-minute bus or taxi ride from the city center. If you want to see where the locals shop, buy a bus ticket for the Great Circle Line which will take you to eight major suburban shopping centers. If you plan to go out of town to shop in the arts and crafts towns or visit the Sunshine Coast and Gold Coast, it's best to rent a car and drive to these areas.

Downtown Shopping Mall, Arcades, Shops

Brisbane's major shopping is centered in and around the **Queen Street Mall.** A pleasant pedestrian mall running between Edward and George streets, this is a shopper's paradise crammed with arcades, department stores, boutiques, restaurants, hotels, and banks. Open from 8:15am to 5:30pm each day, Queen Street Mall should be your very first shopping destination. Here you will find Brisbane's three major shopping arcades which are "must see" shopping stops for anyone visiting downtown Brisbane:

—— MAJOR SHOPPING ARCADES ——

- **The Myer Centre and Top's:** The Myer Centre Brisbane's newest (1988) and most up-market shopping center. Located on Queen Street Mall as well as along Elizabeth and Albert streets, The Myer Centre is attached to Brisbane's largest and most elegant department store--Myer on the Mall--as well as a unique recreation and food center on its top two floors appropriately called "The Top's", The Myer Centre consists of over 230 specialty shops, 8 theaters, and numerous fast food establishments. In addition to the unique fantasy and leisure center on the top two floors, The Myer Centre also boasts Australia's largest underground bus interchange on the bottom floor. From here you can connect with buses to other parts of the city and to several suburban areas. The specialty shops run the gamut from fashion clothes and accessories to jewelry and housewares shops. Several of Australia's major clothing stores (**Cherry Lane, Country Road, Designer Savings, Fletcher Jones, Just Jeans, Laura Ashley,** and **Shepherds**) have branch stores in this complex. Look for numerous shops selling shoes, handbags, and leather goods as well as jewelry, Australiana, gifts, and home decorative items. If you are interested in furs, **J. Jackson Fine Furs and Leather** has a shop here (Level 2, Shop 245). We especially like **Country Road** (Level 1, Shop 191) for women's fashion clothes, **Angus & Coote** (Queen Street, Shop 122) and **Prouds** (Queen Street, Shop 138) for jewelry and gifts, and **The Australian East India Co.** (Elizabeth Street, Shop 90) for home decorative items and housewares.

• **Wintergarden:** This used to be Brisbane's top shopping center until The Myer Centre opened in 1988. Completed in 1982 and expanded in 1986, Wintergarden is considered Brisbane's major fashion center. You will find numerous famous men's and women's apparel shops in this complex. Located on the Queen Street Mall and attached to the Hilton Hotel on Elizabeth Street, this is a three level shopping complex housing 123 specialty stores, boutiques, and restaurants. Watergarden has similar types of shops as found in The Myer Centre -- clothes, accessories, jewelry, and gift. Here you will find boutiques of two of Australia's top designers --- **Carla Zampatti** and **Walter Kristensen.** **Country Road, Cue, Designer Savings, Just Jeans, Maggie T., Palmer & Palmer,** and **Pucci** have branch shops in this complex. Men will appreciate the fashionable clothes offered by **Bjorn Borg, Country Road Mens, Palmer & Palmer, R. M. Williams,** and **Tony Barlow.** For fine imported leather goods, visit **Oroton** (Shop 71). If you're looking for Australiana, **Everything Australian** (Shop 217) should have what you want. If opals are on your shopping agenda, be sure to stop at **Classique** (Shop 243) and **Opal World** (Shop 315). **Prouds** (Shop 230) also has a branch jewelry and gift shop in this shopping complex.

• **Rowes Arcade:** Compared to The Myer Centre and Wintergarden, this is a very small but extremely elegant shopping arcade. Located at 235 Edward Street, Rowes Arcade has entrances on both Edward and Adelaide streets as well as from the Post Office Square. A nicely restored building with stained glass, mosaic tiles, and cedar panelling, here is where many of Brisbane's rich and famous choose to shop for clothes and accessories. Two levels of shops offer some of Australia's finest quality clothes and accessories. **Alla Mode** (Level 2, Shop F7) offers gorgeous European fabrics and provides in-house design and tailoring services for women interested in elegant hand-made garments. **Fashion House of Helena Kaye** (Level 1, Shop 5) specializes in elegant women's knitwear using fine Spinelli wool from Italy as well as a line of cotton dresses with designs from Fiji. The famous **Shepherds** (Level 1) presents women's apparel in distinctive designs and colors. **J. B. Conlan** (Level 1) specializes in quality menswear.

You will discover several additional shopping arcades in and around Queen Street Mall. Most are small arcades filled with all types of specialty shops and boutiques offering a large range of goods of varying quality. Look for these arcades in downtown Brisbane:

- **City Plaza Shopping Centre:** Located behind City Hall and with entrances from Ann, George, and Adelaide streets. Has 57 specialty shops offering everything from fashion, jewelry, gifts, and kitchenware to candy. Includes coffee and snack shops.

- **T&G Arcade:** Across the street from The Myer Centre and on the corner of Queen and Albert streets. Entrances on both Queen Street Mall and Albert streets. Includes 21 specialty shops offering men's and women's fashion clothes, accessories, jewelry, gifts, flowers, and photo services.

- **Brisbane Arcade:** Located in the center of Queen Street Mall, connected to Adelaide Street, and opposite the King George car park. Includes 15 specialty shops offering women's fashion and accessories, jewelry, gifts, and souvenirs as well as a Kentucky

Fried Chicken on the lower level.

- **Post Office Square:** Opposite Anzac Square and between Adelaide and Queen streets. Has several specialty shops along with coffee shops and delicatessens. Heavily trafficked by downtown workers.

- **The Pavilion:** On the corner of Queen and Albert streets. Two levels of shops selling clothes and accessories, sheepskin and leather goods, and Australiana.

- **The Mansions:** Located on George Street at the corner of Margaret Street. An elegantly restored building with only four shops. Look for antiques, prints, books, and the National Trust gift shop.

- **City Centre Arcade:** Small shopping arcade on Adelaide street, between Albert and Edward streets.

- **Piccadily Arcade:** Small shopping arcade on Adelaide Street, between Wharf and Creek streets.

- **Riverside Centre:** Brisbane's newest waterfront commercial development with restaurants and shops. Best to shop here on Sunday when its weekend market is open.

Outside these major shopping centers you will also find many interesting shops along the streets in downtown Brisbane. We especially like Ian Thomson's **Decorators Gallery** (57 Elizabeth Street) for lovely arts, antiques, and home decorative items from over 30 countries. You will also find two Aboriginal art and craft shops along George Street: **Queensland Aboriginal Creations** (135 George Street) and a shop behind the Town Hall. The famous designer **Carla Zampatti** also has a shop along George Street. If you just explore George, Elizabeth, Queen, Adelaide, Albert, and Edward streets, you will discover numerous interesting shops offering everything from fashion clothes to sporting goods.

Department Stores

Brisbane's three major department stores are located on the Queen Street Mall. **Myer in the City** is Brisbane's newest and most elegant department store. The second largest Myer department store in the country -- next to the enormous Myer Department Store in Melbourne -- Myer in the City anchors The Myer Centre. Spacious, modern, and inviting, this five-level store offers everything from the latest fashion clothes and travel goods to Australian gifts and souvenirs. On Level 2, for example, you will find a small up-market Australiana shop operated by **Settlers & Co.** Before exploring this store it's best to stop at the Information Centre on Level Q (Queen Street Level) to pick up a brochure and map of the store.

David Jones Department Store is also located on the Queen Street Mall. Recently refurbished, this is another elegant branch of the David Jones Department Store chain. This store offers good quality mens' and womens' clothes as well as the usual assortment of household goods.

Coles Department Store is located two doors north of David Jones Department Store on the Queen Street Mall. This is Australia's answer to America's Kmart and F. W. Woolworths. An older and congested store, shop here for inexpensive items from toys to toiletries. Coles also has a grocery section.

Queensland Cultural Centre and the Southside

While South Brisbane offers few shopping opportunities, you should at least spend a couple of hours touring the impressive **Queensland Cultural Centre** and browsing through a few nearby shops. From downtown Brisbane you can easily get to the Centre by walking across the Victoria Bridge at Queen Street. Resting on the banks of the Brisbane River, the Cultural Centre houses a museum, art gallery, and performing arts center. It's a big complex well worth visiting early during your stay in Brisbane. Art and antique lovers who browse through the Centre will get some idea of possible shopping choices in the area. The museum, for example, has an excellent collection of arts and crafts from Papua New Guinea and the South Pacific Islands as well as memorabilia on the history of Queensland. The art gallery has permanent as well as traveling exhibits. You will find an excellent collection of Aboriginal art and paintings by many of Australia's famous artists.

While visiting the Cultural Centre, don't forget to stop at the Centre's two shops. Just outside the Aboriginal art exhibit you will find a small shop selling Aboriginal arts and crafts, including postcards, stationery, placemats, coasters, didjeridoos, acrylic paintings, and clap sticks; most items are of tourist quality. The second shop is located on the ground floor adjacent to the fine arts gallery. This shop primarily sells art books and posters. We found this shop to have one of the best selections of books on Aboriginal arts and crafts as well as on Australian artists.

You will find a few art and antique shops in South Brisbane within a five minute walk from the Cultural Centre. **Wiumulli** (121 Melbourne Street) has a good collection of Aboriginal arts and crafts. The **Cordelia Street Antique and Art Centre** (corner of Cordelia and Glenelg streets) offers a large assortment of antiques and collectibles, including gold and silver jewelry.

Paddington Circle

Paddington Circle actually consists of two adjacent suburban shopping areas -- Paddington and Red Hill -- tied together by a merchants' association called Paddington Circle Inc. A five minute bus ride from downtown Brisbane (#144, 147, 172), the historical Paddington Circle area is filled with galleries, antique shops, arts and crafts stores, boutiques, home decorative shops, and restaurants and cafes. Paddington's main street -- which changes its name three times from Caxton Street to Given Terrace to Latrobe Terrace -- is a long and hilly walk. Since most of the shops are concentrated along the Latrobe Terrace section of this street, you may want to start your shopping here. If you don't have a car, we suggest you begin your shopping excursion at the top of the hill near the corner of Gilday Street and Latrobe Terrace. Look for **Country Charm** (201 Latrobe Terrace), a nice antique pine and country furniture shop, which is the very last shop along the upper end of Latrobe Terrace. You'll find a bus stop directly across the street from this shop. From here you can walk south -- and downhill -- along Latrobe Terrace. You will want to explore the shops on both sides of the street.

Several shops are worth visiting in Paddington. We especially like **Latrobe Gallery** (199 Latrobe Terrace) for good quality art -- prints, etchings, engravings, woodcuts, watercolors, and oils; **Karavan** (34 Latrobe Terrace) for tribal arts and crafts; **Paddington Antique Centre** (167 Latrobe Terrace) for antiques and collectibles; **Majors** (2 Labrobe Terrace) for home decorative items; **Lucence** (Shop 2, Paddington Central, corner of Latrobe Terrace and Warmington streets); **Merryl Ducat Interiors** (11 Latrobe

Terrace); **Break of Day Gift Shop** (Shop 50, 283 Given Terrace); and **Lyn Hadley Clothes** and **Timbuctoo** (Shops 9, 10, and 46, Paddington Market, 261-265 Given Terrace) for unique clothes.

The adjacent Red Hill area also has a few shops worth visiting. We especially enjoy Ian Thomson's **Decorator's Gallery** 93A Musgrave Road) for a unique collection of attractive ethnic arts, antiques, and home decorative items. Also look for **Hang Ups Distinctive Art** (99 Musgrave Road) and **Red Hill Gallery** (61 Musgrave Road).

Fortitude Valley, New Farm, Newstead, Riverside Centre

Three of Brisbane's major suburban shopping areas are located within five minutes from the central business district. Fortitude Valley, New Farm, Newstead, and Riverside Centre are located adjacent to each other on the north side of the city. **Fortitude Valley** is well known for one shop -- **Potters' Gallery** at 483 Brunswick Street. Housed in an old historic church, Potters' Gallery is the gallery shop of The Queensland Potters' Association. It offers the largest collection of handcrafted pottery in Queensland. Potters' Gallery includes two galleries -- one selling members' pottery and another with exhibits of guest potters which changes every three weeks. Fortitude Valley also houses the colorful **Chinatown Mall**, a replica of an Imperial Chinese Village, bordered by Brunswick, Wickham, and Ann streets. In addition to offering excellent Oriental restaurants, Chinatown Mall also has a market where you can purchase numerous handcrafted items, gifts, and souvenirs from vendor stalls. Also look for **Wickham Street Antique Galleries** at 400 Wickham Street for a good selection of Victorian and Georgian antique furniture, jewelry, and collectibles.

New Farm is famous for the colorful **Paddy's Markets** (corner of Macquarie and Florence streets), a five acre five-story covered shopping complex with numerous stalls selling everything from furniture to ribbons. Open seven days a week, Paddy's Markets hosts a Flea Market on Saturdays and Sundays at the rear of the ground floor. Also look for **Philip Bacon Galleries** at 2 Arthur Street for good quality paintings by many of Australia's leading artists, such as Boyd, Daws, Crooke, Friend, Fullbrook, Nolan, Sawrye, and Whiteley.

Newstead is home to **Pierrot Arts and Craft Centre** (251 Arthur Street), a market offering one the largest collections of Australian arts and crafts in the Brisbane area.

Riverside Centre is Brisbane's new riverside development housing offices, restaurants, and shops. While still part of the city of Brisbane, Riverside Centre is located on the banks of the Brisbane River adjacent to Fortitude Valley and New Farm. The best time to visit here is on Sunday when Riverside Centre becomes a popular outdoor market selling local arts and crafts.

Suburban Brisbane

Brisbane has several suburban shopping centers, such as Toowong Village and Westfield Indooroopilly Shoppingtown, which primarily cater to local residents. You can easily tour the eight major shopping centers by taking the special bus service -- the Great Circle Line -- which stops on the hour at each of the suburban shopping centers on its 80-kilometer route. The bus leaves from a stop on Adelaide Street in downtown Brisbane. Telephone 225-4444 for information on this service.

The Markets

Brisbane has three major markets primarily offering arts and crafts. **Paddy's Markets** (Tel. 52-7211) is located at the corner of Macquarie and Florence streets in New Farm. Open seven days a week from 9am to 3pm, this huge five acre complex also has a flea market on Saturdays and Sundays.

Pierrots Arts and Crafts Centre (Tel. 252-1015), located at 251 Arthur Street in Newstead, has one of the largest collections of Australian arts and crafts in Brisbane. This market is open seven days a week from 10am to 5pm.

The new **Riverside Centre**, located next to the suburbs of New Farm, Fortitude Valley, and Newstead and adjacent to the Brisbane River, becomes a lively arts and craft market on Sundays from 10am to 4pm. This is a delightful area to enjoy the river view and restaurants while shopping for arts and crafts.

Northern Craft Towns

Within a two to three hour drive northeast of Brisbane are several small hill towns offering some of the best arts and crafts in Queensland: Maleny, Montville, and Mapleton. Take Bruce Highway north of Brisbane for approximately 50 kilometers and turn left at the sign for Beerburrum which is the Old Bruce Highway. You will initially go through the small town of Landsborough and continue on Maleny Road to the first major craft town of Maleny. Before arriving at this town you will come to a nice pottery shop located 3.5 kilometers outside Landsborough -- **De Maine Pottery Studio Workshop**. Further along this road, at the intersection of Maleny and Mt. Mellum roads is a quaint little shop offering a nice collection of local arts and crafts -- **Yoorooga Australian Craft**.

Maleny has a few good arts and crafts shops. One of best shops in the whole northeastern area is **Patrina** at 32 Maple Street. This shop offers excellent quality fine art as well as unique handcrafted items from Queensland. Two other shops in Maleny offer antiques and arts and crafts: **Steve Lidbury's Antiques** (38 Maple Street) and **Maleny Arts and Crafts** (The Elizabeth McDonald Workshop also on Maple Street).

Montville is the largest arts and crafts town in this area. Indeed, you can easily spend half a day browsing through its many interesting shops which offer fine arts, crafts, and antiques. All of the shops are located on the one main street that runs through this charming little town. For fine art, visit **The De'Lisle Gallery**, **Rainbird Gallery**, and **The Courtyard Gallery**. These galleries offer excellent oils and watercolors by some of Queenland's best artists as well as artists from other parts of Australia. For antiques, browse through **Montville Antiques**. You will even find an African arts and antiques shop here -- **Sallanger's**. For handcrafted items, visit **Montville Pottery**, **The Herb Garden**, **Sunshine Coast Crafts**, **Cadman Cottage**, **Comphor Cottage**, **Spring Cottage**, **Melba's of Montville**, **The Irish Shops**, and **Gallery D**.

Sunshine and Gold Coasts

The Sunshine Coast and Gold Coast are Brisbane's two major sun and surf resort areas. Located within two hours drive north and south of Brisbane respectively, these are two major destinations for visitors who come to this part of Queensland. The **Sunshine Coast** is the smaller and quieter of these two resort areas. Centered at the peninsular town of Noosa Heads, a 45-minute drive northeast of the arts and crafts hill town of Mapleton, this area has a few shops selling the usual type of beach resort goods -- clothes, swimwear, T-shirts, and souvenirs. Most shops are located along **Hastings Street** (Bay Village) and in two local shopping centers -- **The Junction** and **Ocean Breeze**. We found nothing particularly distinctive in this area -- just the usual beach resort-type shops.

The **Gold Coast** is the major resort area in Queensland. Centered at the town of Surfers Paradise, this is a booming resort area of deluxe hotels, elegant restaurants, condominiums, and shopping centers. You will find several typical beach resort-type clothing and souvenir shops as well as nice quality arts, crafts, and jewelry stores catering to the upmarket clientele that stay at Surfers Paradise. Indeed, several shops in Sydney and Melbourne have opened branch shops here in Surfers Paradise. Most of the shops are found in and around the major shopping centers and commercial streets of Surfers Paradise: **Centrepoint Arcade, Centre Arcade, Dolphin Arcade, The Market Shopping Complex, Holiday City Galleria, Orchard Avenue**, and **Elkhorn Avenue**.

ENJOYING YOUR STAY

If you stay in Brisbane, the best and most expensive hotels are the **Sheraton Brisbane** (249 Turbot St., Tel. 835-3535), **Hilton International Brisbane** (190 Elizabeth Street, Tel. 224-9740), **Brisbane Parkroyal** (Alice and Albert streets, Tel. 221-3411), **Gazebo Ramada** (345 Wickham Terrace, Tel. 831-6177), **Mayfair Crest** (King George Square, Tel. 229-9111), **Gateway** (85 North Quay, Tel. 221-0211), and **Brisbane City TraveLodge** (Roma Street, Tel. 238-2222).

Cosmopolitan Brisbane has numerous restaurants appealing to many tastes -- Australian, French, Italian, Lebanese, Chinese, Japanese, Indian, Thai, Korean, Malaysian, Vietnamese, and Mongolian. Be sure to pick up a free copy of *Dining Out in Brisbane* which is available in most hotels and tourist information booths and offices. Some of Brisbane's best restaurants include **Michael's on the Mall** (64 Queen Street Mall, Tel. 229-4911), **Michael's Riverside** (Riverside Centre, 123 Eagle Street, Tel. 832-5522), **David's** (157 Elizabeth St., Tel. 229-9033), **The Drawing Room** (Brisbane City TraveLodge, Roma Street, Tel. 238-2288), **Barrier Reef Seafood Restaurant** (138 Albert Street, Tel. 221-9366), and **Milano Restaurant Italiano** (78 Queen Street, Tel. 221-5972). You will find several fast-food restaurants, food halls, and outdoor cafes on Queen Street Mall, such as McDonald's, Kentucky Fried Chicken, Jo-Jo's, and Jimmy's. If you are walking the Paddington Circle area around noon-time, one of our favorite Italian restaurants in this area for lunch is **Albertos** (235 Given Terrace, Tel. 369-7511). For good dining in the ambiance of a beautiful old Queensland restaurant, try the **Roseville Restaurant** (56 Chester Street, Newstead, Tel. 358-1377).

Brisbane is one of the best organized cities in providing information to tourists. One of your first stops in Brisbane should be to the **Queensland Government Travel Centre** at 196 Adelaide Street (Tel. 226-5337). This office has a wealth of travel information on the city as well as the State of Queensland. You can book tours and hotels through this office. It also has a small information booth at the airport near the arrival area.

Tourism Brisbane, the city tourist and convention office, is located in the City Hall Building at King George Square (Tel. 221-8411). It also provides maps and brochures on the city. In the middle of Queen Street Mall you will find a tourist information kiosk which has maps and brochures and personnel to answer questions.

Look for several useful publications provided by these tourist information offices both in the city and at the airport: *Beautiful Brisbane!*, *Discover Brisbane*, *Hello Brisbane*, *This Week in Brisbane*, and *Dining Out in Brisbane*.

Brisbane has a great deal to offer visitors in addition to shopping. Within the city you will find several historical and cultural sites worth visiting for their architectural interest: **The City Hall, Parliament House, The Treasury Building, Albert Street Uniting Church, St. John's Cathedral, The Observatory,** and **The State Library of Queensland.**

The **Queensland Cultural Centre**, located along the bank of the Brisbane River and directly across from the Victoria Bridge on Melbourne Street, is especially worth visiting. This is one of Australia's finest cultural centers. Consisting of a Performing Arts Complex, Queensland Art Gallery, Queensland Museum, and State Library, you can easily spend a day exploring this attractive complex. Guided tours are available and take nearly three hours to complete. Look for special art exhibits and special performing arts groups.

You may want to cruise the Brisbane River. The **Kookaburra Queen**, a paddlewheeler, cruises the river daily from Petrie Bight Marina on Howard Street. Call 52-3797 for information on current departure times and costs.

Outside the city center you will find several interesting places to visit:

> • **Lone Pine Koala Sanctuary:** This is one of Australia's most popular attractions and its largest sanctuary for koalas, kangaroos, wallabies, emus, wombats, platypus, and birds. Located on Jesmond Road, Fig Tree Pocket (378-1366), 8 kilometers west of City Hall, it is open seven days a week from 9:30am to 5pm. You can reach this sanctuary by taking a tour coach, taxi, or the ferry from North

Quay at 2pm each day (Tel. 378-1366).

• **Mount Coot-tha Botanic Gardens and Planetarium:** Located five kilometers west of the city at the foot of Mt. Coot-tha, this is a good place to get a panoramic view of the city as well as the D'Aguilar Mountains. The botanic gardens also include a planetarium.

• **New Farm Park:** Located on Brunswick Street in New Farm, this park has nearly 12,000 rose bushes that bloom from September to November, jacaranda avenues that bloom in October and November, and poinciana trees that bloom in November and December.

• **Chinatown:** Located five minutes north of the city center in the suburb of Fortitude Valley, this is a good place for sampling Oriental foods, watching cultural performances, and shopping.

• **Australian Woolshed:** Located at 148 Samford Road in Ferny Hills (Tel. 351-5366 for reservations), this is a good place to see a program of trained rams, sheep shearing, spinning, and sheepdog demonstrations. You can purchase wool products at their award-winning craft shop.

• **Sunshine Coast:** Located two hours north of Brisbane and centered in the town of Noosa Heads, this is a major seaside resort with fine beaches and hotels.

• **Gold Coast:** Located two hours south of Brisbane and centered in and around Surfers Paradise, this is Australia's most popular and commercialized resort area. A booming area of resort communities, high-rise hotels, condominiums, restaurants, entertainment spots, seven golf courses, Dreamworld, and shopping. If you like Miami, Fort Lauderdale, Waikiki, or Costa del Sol and prefer to relax along beautiful beaches with thousands of others, you'll like the Gold Coast.

Whatever you do, don't just pass through Brisbane on your way to the beach resorts or to other cities in Australia. Brisbane offers some wonderful shopping opportunities for unique local and Australian products. Spend at least three or four days here to enjoy its shopping and related activities. If you spend some time exploring its downtown area, suburbs, and craft towns you will be richly rewarded with some of the best shopping in Australia!

Chapter Six

SYDNEY

If you like big cities, delightful weather, lovely harbors, diverse sights, and friendly people, you may fall in love with Sydney. Here's Australia's largest city with a metropolitan population of 3.5 million. Spread over a 50 kilometer area, metropolitan Sydney is where one can live the good life beside beautiful beaches that seem to stretch forever along the emerald South Pacific Ocean. Indeed, many Australian's believe Sydney may well be the best place to live in the world!

In physical appearance Sydney is to Australia what Seattle and San Francisco is to the United States. Sydney's lifestyle, however, resembles that of Los Angeles and Southern California. It's one of the world's most pleasant, cosmopolitan, and liveable cities. Unlike many other big cities, energetic Sydney feels good to be in. It invites you to come to enjoy its many pleasures, and just play, play, and play. And all you need is a little time -- and lots of money, money, money!

Visit Sydney and you will certainly go away with a wonderful collection of Australian memories based on touring the harbor, visiting the museums and historical sites, enjoying its many beaches, prowling its pubs and ethnic restaurants, meeting its friendly people, and shopping its many arcades and neighborhoods.   Sydney is traveling and shopping a big city at its best. It's a wonderful place to spend a week to indulge your shopping, traveling, gastronomic, and hedonistic fancies.

GETTING TO KNOW YOU

Above all, Sydney is a shopper's paradise.   It offers a full range of both imported and Australian-made products presented in a wide variety of exciting shopping settings.

You'll find the latest in Australian and European designer fashion in Australia's most exclusive suburb -- **Double Bay**.   This is Australia's version of Hollywood's "Rodeo Drive", disdained by many Australians for its obstensible elitist and snobbish character.   It's where car and people-watching is as much fun as shopping for quality goods.

Or visit the beautiful and majestic **Queen Victoria Building** to leisurely browse through over 200 shops offering everything from the latest designer fashion to Australiana as well as enjoy its many restaurants and food stalls.   Nearby stands the smaller but ever elegant **Strand Arcade**, still offering some of the best selections of Australian designer-fashion and uniquely designed jewelry in all of Australia.

And don't forget to spend some time in the arts and crafts shops of the quaint, historical, and picturesque area called **The Rocks**. Here you can stroll the streets, browse the shops, climb the stairs, and dine the restaurants -- all accompanied by majestic views of the Sydney Harbour Bridge, Opera House, and Circular Quay.

If your tastes include trendy arts, crafts, and clothing, or you have an eye for good quality antiques and fine arts, you will discover many interesting shops lining the streets and lanes of **Paddington** (Oxford Street), **Woollahra** (Queen Street), and **Mosman** (Military Road).

For those wishing to combine shopping with a social experience, there's the new **Marketplace at Harbourside** (Darling Harbour) as well as **factory outlets** (especially Sully Hills area) and numerous antique and weekend **markets** such as Paddington Market (Oxford Street in Paddington), Paddy's Market (Ross Street in Glebe), Balmain Market (Arling Street and Curtis Road in Belmain), and numerous **auctions** taking place throughout the metropolitan area (see the Saturday edition of the *Sydney Morning Herald* for a listing of upcoming auctions for the week).

Whatever your shopping choices, you will be delighted with the many and varied shopping opportunities offered in

Sydney. Only Melbourne can offer a comparable shopping environment and experiences.

Like so much of Australia, you should come to Sydney to experience its delights rather than expect to discover its bargains. Similar to other large metropolitan areas in the world, Sydney can be a very expensive city, comparable, for example, to New York City. Food and accommodations are expensive, with most deluxe hotels costing more than A$200 a day. Shopping can also be expensive, especially for clothes. But **bargains** can be found at sales and in factory outlet shops. If you come from a country with high import duties on luxury goods, such as New Zealand, Sydney's duty-free shops do offer bargains.

The best buy in Sydney is the local transportation. Taxis, buses, and car rentals are still reasonable compared to other cities in the world. Our recommendation is to spend your money on local transportation to browse shops for truly unique items you cannot find in other Australian cities nor back home. Truly unique items in Sydney are arts and crafts, antiques, jewelry, and Australian-designed fashion clothes. You will find many European imported goods, but you are likely to find the same products with better selections and prices in major cities back home.

Sydney is an especially vibrant, friendly, and cosmopolitan city. The streets are busy with workers and shoppers hurrying from one area to another. Believed by many parochial Australians to have the most beautiful harbor in the world, Sydney's delightful harbor is pretty and pleasant, but by no means a match to the majestic harbors of Hong Kong, Rio, and Acapulco -- or even San Francisco. There's plenty to do in Sydney, be it shopping, touring the harbor, visiting the beaches, taking day trips to the outlying areas, visiting the many museums and historical sites, dining in restaurants with beautiful views of the city and harbor, taking in theatrical performances, or visiting its many pubs and entertainment spots.

Sydney is a cosmopolitan and cultured city that is very easy to get to know and a wonderful place to visit -- and live. The transportation system is excellent, and the weather often cooperates to make this city one of the prime shopping and travel destinations in all of Australia as well as in the Southern Hemisphere. Sydney is the good life, with a booming economy, a delightful natural setting, an attractive skyline, pleasant streets and shopping arcades, and a competitive-spirited chauvinism that delights in putting down supposedly straight-laced Melbourne in comparison to friendly Sydney. Sydney is what many Australians and visitors aspire to -- having the best of everything and living the good life. This is a city where

SYDNEY

1. The Rocks
2. Strand Arcade
3. Queen Victoria Building
4. Market Place at Harbourside
5. Double Bay
6. Woolahra & Queen Street
7. Paddington & Oxford Street
8. Sydney Opera House
9. Museum
10. Regent Hotel
11. Inter-Continental Hotel
12. Hilton Hotel
13. Sheraton-Wentworth Hotel

one should work a little, shop some, and play a lot. Spend a week here and you will want to come back to living the good life, Sydney-style!

THE STREETS OF SYDNEY

The city of Sydney is centered in the protected harbor of Port Jackson. Viewed best from the North Shore or the southwest pylon of the Sydney Harbour Bridge, it's a striking downtown area. From the central business district -- marked by the Sydney Harbour Bridge, The Rocks, Opera House, and Circular Quay to the north, and punctuated by narrow streets darkened by glittering high-rise commercial buildings and elegant shopping arcades to the south -- Sydney's skyline flattens out into numerous residential suburbs sprawling north, south, east, and west. The beaches and upscale residential communities are located to the northeast (Balmoral, Manly, and Palm Beach) and east (Double Bay, Watson Bay, and Bondi). Nondescript, working-class suburbs sprawl to the west for nearly 40 kilometers.

Most of Sydney's quality shopping is confined to the city center, eastern suburbs, and north shore. These are also the areas for visiting Sydney's major historical sites, museums, and beaches and for enjoying harbor tours, restaurants, and entertainment, or just walking around the loveliest areas of this great city.

GETTING ORIENTED

The best way to get oriented to this city is to acquire a good map of the area. Unfortunately, most maps only cover the central business district; they leave out much of the eastern and northern sections of the metropolitan area. We suggest getting a copy of *Inside Sydney* (A$5.95). This 184-page guide includes several useful maps, plus it covers the major shopping areas in the city. Useful guidebooks for those interested in factory outlets and second-hand stores are *The Bargain Shoppers' Guide to Sydney* (A$4.95) and *Secondhand Sydney* (A$4.95). Ropion, Hunt, and Mowe's unique *The Secret Map of Sydney* (A$9.95) is also useful, although by no means as detailed and helpful as their similar map on Singapore. Most bookstores carry these resources as well as numerous maps on Sydney and outlying areas.

You may wish to visit three useful offices for information on the city. The **New South Wales Government Information Centre** (55 Hunter Street, City, Tel. 221-3622) sells an excellent collection of maps and books on

Australia. The nearby **Travel Centre of New South Wales** (corner of Pitt and Spring streets, City, Tel. 231-4444) has one of the best collections of free brochures on tours, attractions, accommodations, and transportation. This Centre will also assist you in booking hotels, tours, and transportation. The **Sydney Convention and Visitor's Bureau** (100 Market Street, Tel. 235-2424) provides similar information on attractions, shopping, restaurants, and tours provided by their members. This organization also operates the **Sydney Information Centre**, a kiosk in Martin's Place (between Castlereagh and Elizabeth streets) providing brochures and advice upon request. These information centers, as well as your hotel and some shops, have free copies of the latest editions of the following useful guides to Sydney's sightseeing tours, shopping, restaurants, and entertainment:

- *This Week in Sydney*
- *Sydney's Attractions*
- *Sydney's Top Ten*
- *Hello Sydney*
- *Sydney Where*
- *Welcome Visitor*

For free telephone information on Sydney, call 669-5111. This tourist information service operates 7 days a week from 8am to 6pm.

While Sydney is Australia's largest city and metropolitan area, it's a relatively easy city to get around. The downtown area -- **The City** -- is small and very compact. It's easy to walk to most shopping arcades and department stores within 10 minutes. The main shopping area in The City is bounded by **Pitt and George streets**, which run North and South, and by **Hunter and Bathurst streets**, which run East and West. Walking these streets, you find the major shopping arcades and department stores in Sydney, such as the Strand Arcade, Mid City Centre, MLC Centre, Imperial Arcade, Royal Arcade, Queen Victoria Building, and the David Jones and Grace Brothers department stores.

Just to the north of the city and immediately northwest of Circular Quay -- Sydney's Harbor Terminal -- is **The Rocks**. The main shopping area here is found along Argyle, Playfair, and George streets. This is another compact walking area which offers a large variety of shops, pubs, restaurants, historical sites, and gorgeous views of the harbor, bridge, and Opera House.

To the west of the city are the popular shopping areas of Double Bay, Woollahra, and Paddington. The exclusive shopping suburb of **Double Bay** is a 10 to 15-minute taxi ride from The City that also passes by Paddington and Woollahra. Another relatively small and compact shopping area great for walking, Double Bay is bounded by three main shopping streets -- Knox, Cross, and Bay.

Woollahra and Paddington are just a few minutes from Double Bay. These two shopping areas are linked together at the intersection of Queen Street (in Woollahra) and Oxford Street (in Paddington). The major shops -- mainly art and antique -- in **Woollahra** are found along Queen Street and in a few streets and lanes to the north, just off Queen Street near the intersection with Oxford Street. You can easily walk this section of Queen Street within 5 to 10 minutes, spending perhaps an hour browsing through the more interesting looking arts and crafts shops.

The **Paddington** area is less compact and more inconvenient for walking. Beginning at the Queen Street intersection, the Paddington shopping area stretches nearly three kilometers west, along Oxford Street past Victoria Barracks to Taylor Square. While most shops are found on the north side of Oxford Street, be sure to also explore the small streets and lanes to the north of Oxford Street, especially near the eastern section of Paddington. You will find many shops along such streets and lanes as Jersey Road, Taylor Street, Elizabeth Street, and William Street. Larger shops, such as Hogath Galleries on Walker Lane, are tucked away on such streets. You will need to spend some time walking these areas.

Harbourside at Darling Harbour is Sydney's newest entry into the latest in trendy harborfront shopping areas. Located southwest of The City, this area is within easy walking distance from the downtown area via Market and King streets. A new monorail system services this area from Market, Pitt, Liverpool, and Harbour streets.

Neutral Bay and Mosman on the North Shore and **Manly** to the northeast are within short driving distances from The City. Manly is a popular beach with an interesting Saturday beachfront market and a pedestrian shopping mall. You can reach Manly by taking a hovercraft (from Circular Quay), bus, taxi, or drive yourself there via the Sydney Harbour Bridge, Military Road (Neutral Bay and Mosman), Spit Road, and Sydney Road.

The **Neutral Bay and Mosman** shopping areas are located along Military Road, with the majority of shops concentrated near the Military Road intersection with Spit Road in Mosman. The best way to get to this area is by bus, taxi, or drive yourself. You may wish to rent a car for the day to visit this shopping area as well as Manly and several beach towns and the Hawkesbury region to the north, or head for the Blue Mountains to the west.

Other shopping areas include **Chinatown** to the immediate south of The City and east of the Marketplace at Harbourside (at Darlinghurst Harbour); **Birkenhead Point** (in Drummoyne) six kilometers west of the city; and several suburban communities with local shopping arcades. While these areas offer some unique shopping opportunities, you may wish to include them only if time permits. Although they are regularly serviced by bus, rail, and taxi, most of these areas are not convenient for visitors.

SHOPPING SERVICES

While you can easily shop Sydney on your own by using this book as well as following the tourist literature, maps, and guidebooks you acquire upon arrival in Sydney, you should also consider joining specialized shopping tours. Two types of tours are available for those who have limited time to shop or prefer the guidance of a professional who knows the ins and outs of shopping in Sydney.

The first type of shopping tour specializes on **shopping in discount factories**. These are half or full-day tours which pick you up at your hotel and take you to factory outlets offering discounts of up to 30 to 50 percent on selected merchandise. The tours primarily center on the factory outlets in the **Surry Hill region**. At present two such tour companies operate this type of tour: **Bargain Buyer's Tours** (21 Elegans Avenue, St. Ives, Tel. 449-7221 or 449-1776) and **Fashion Frolic** (53 Wattle, Haberfield, Tel. 798-7655). Most of these tours cost less than A$30 and include lunch.

The second type of shopping tour specializes on upscale shopping in Sydney's exclusive boutiques, especially for fashion clothes in the Double Bay area. At present **Dimardi** (17 Shellbank Avenue, Cremorne, Tel. 823-3951) operates such a tour. Their three-hour tour costs A$75 and includes a chauffer-driven limousine, special greetings by shopkeepers, and overall deluxe treatment. Dimardi also offers personalized shopping services for people who do not have time to join the tour. For A$50 Dimardi also will do your shopping for you.

WHAT TO BUY

Sydney has everything. All you need is money, walking shoes, and enthusiasm for shopping. If you want the latest in imported fashion or electronic gadgetry, Sydney has it. But be prepared to pay premium prices. Imported goods are not a good buy except for such nationals as New

Zealanders and Japanese who must pay even higher prices in their countries.

In Sydney we seek the **unique** -- designs and products we cannot find elsewhere in Australia nor abroad. And Sydney has plenty of these designs and products to keep you busy shopping for several days!

Opals

You'll find hundreds of shops throughout Sydney offering beautiful opals at duty-free prices. One of the largest concentrations of such shops is found along upper **Pitt Street** near Circular Quay. These are "Duty-Free Shops" which primarily advertise opals, but they also sell the usual duty-free fare of liquor, cameras, candies, perfumes, designer fashion goods, jewelry, and watches as well as typical Australiana, such as Aboriginal arts and crafts, stuffed koalas and kangeroos, fur coats, and sheepskin jackets. The shops offer both unset and set opals at prices ranging from $10 to $20,000. Other shops selling opals are found in and around all of the major shopping arcades in the downtown section and The Rocks. Many shops selling Australiana also sell opal jewelry.

To get the best buys, you will need to shop around to learn about opals and compare quality and prices. A number of factors determine value and hence cost:

- **Know whether you are buying a solid opal, a doublet, or a triplet.** The most expensive would be a solid opal, free of any apparent cracks or flaws, with overall complete play of color. The best solid opals display the full color spectrum including red and violet/purple.

- **The stone should be free of cracks and flaws.** Opals are a porous stone and have a greater tendency to break than other stones of similar hardness--5 1/2 to 7 on MOH's scale. They are more likely to break if there is an evident flaw line or occlusion.

- **Prices vary considerably based on the extent and overall completeness of color.** The actual colors and number of colors also determine value. The highest value has all colors of the spectrum, especially red and purple which are rare.

- **The cheapest opals are the triplets and doublets.** A triplet consists of three thin layers of opal glued together to look like a solid opal. Triplets are usually white or or have very little color; they may have small flaw lines visible to the naked eye. Doublets consist of two thin layers of opal glued together. Inspect opals carefully so you don't pay solid opal prices for douplets and triplets!

The opal business in Sydney is extremely competitive, so be sure to ask questions about the quality of stones as well as differences in prices. Make sure the quoted prices include the standard 30 tax-free discount you should receive as an overseas visitor. Many of the shops will provide you with free transportation to their shop upon request. Refer to page 46 for an expanded discussion about Australian opals.

Some of the largest and most reputable opal dealers in Sydney include:

- **Opal Spectrum:** 37 Pitt Street, Tel. 251-2833. Retail operation of the well known Van Brugge family opal mining company. Claims to have the largest opal, souvenir, and duty-free showroom in the Southern Hemisphere. Has an additional shop at the Cavill Mall in Surfers Paradise, Queensland.

- **Opal Skymine:** Australia Square Tower, Level 6, George Street and Bond Street. Has a model opal mine on the premises which you can tour and learn more about the opal production process.

- **Percy Marks:** The Regent Hotel, 199 George Street, Tel. 27-1322; 65 Castlereagh Street, Tel. 233-1355; Hotel Inter-Continental, 117 Macquarie Street, Tel. 251-3481; and shops in Melbourne and Hayman Island Resort. The oldest jeweler in New South Wales with excellent quality opals.

- **Flame Opals:** 119 George Street, Tel. 27-3446.

- **Allison's:** 15 Park Street, between George and Pitt streets.

- **Bentine Gems:** Corner of Bridge and Pitt streets, Tel. 27-8997.

- **Gemtec Australia:** 50 Park Street, 1st Floor, Tel. 264-2992; and Sydney Hilton Hotel, Lobby Level, 259 Pitt Street, Tel. 267-3883. Also has shops in Melbourne, Perth, Cairns, and Surfers Paradise.

- **Le Classique Duty Free:** 33 Bligh Street, Tel. 223-1455.

- **Darrell James:** 69-73 Pitt Street, Tel. 27-8084. Also has branch shops in Melbourne, Brisbane, Cairns, and Surfers Paradise.

Jewelry

You will find numerous jewelry shops throughout Sydney offering exquisite gems and jewelry. While most of these shops also offer opals, they sell a larger spectrum of jewelry than shops specializing in duty-free goods or Australiana. You will find, for example, Argyle diamonds from Western Australia as well as imported precious and semi-precious stones (amethyst, carnelian, agates, rubies, sapphires) set in a variety of designs. Many of the best jewelers are located in and around the major hotels (The Regent, Intercontinental, Sheraton Wentworth), shopping arcades (Strand, Queen Victoria Building, MLC Centre, Mid Town Center), and in Double Bay.

While much of the jewelry is dutied or taxed, as a foreign visitor you may be able to avoid both and find some pieces crafted in unique Australian styles and settings which you cannot find elsewhere in the world. Some of the most well established, reputable, and quality jewelers in Sydney include:

- **Percy Marks:** The Regent Hotel, 199 George Street, Tel. 27-1322; 65 Castlereagh Street, Tel. 233-1355; Hotel Inter-Continental, 117 Macquarie Street, Tel. 251-3481; and shops in Melbourne and Hayman Island Resort. This is the oldest jeweler in New South Wales.

- **Hardy Brothers:** 74 Castlereagh Street, Tel. 232-2811.

- **L. K. Jewellery:** Kennedy House, 9/11

Knox Street, Double Bay, Tel. 327-2639 or 326-1911.

Jewellery Designers: Shop C12, MLC Centre, King and Castlereagh Streets, Tel. 231-1220.

Masterpiece Jewellery: Shop 10, Strand Arcade, 412-414 George Street,Tel. 231-5569.

Peter Schmidt: 44 Castlereagh Street, Tel. 232-3216.

We are particularly impressed with the unique designs and craftsmanship found at **Robert Clerc** (Shop 28, The Strand Arcade, 412-414 George Street, Tel. 233-2694). This is a truly exciting jeweler and jewelry shop that produces one of the world's most unique collections of gold jewelry. An award-winning artist and jeweler, Robert Clerc produces two fabulous gold collections of pendants, earrings, and pins using traditional and stylized Aboriginal and Egyptian designs. He also works with precious and semi-precious stones and continously develops new and innovative designs. His clients range from the average tourist to Australian and international celebrities. Many tourists who discover this shop become loyal buyers for years to come.

Robert Clerc is a "must" jewelry shop of any visit to Sydney, if not all of Australia! You should also have a chance to meet the affable master jeweler, Robert Clerc, working in the shop on his new designs. You may even catch him sweeping the floors wearing his distinctive trademark -- a beret and two different colored shoes. This is truly a quality shop that produces a style and standard of jewelry you rarely find anywhere in the world. Be sure to get a copy of his catalog since you may want to become another one of his loyal direct-mail customers. He will also do custom work to your specifications. Our recommendation: visit this shop soon. Robert Clerc has become so successful that his custom work will take at least seven months to complete given his present backlog of orders.

Tapestries and Rugs

You will find a few specialty shops which produce unique tapestries and rugs using Australian and New Zealand wools. These shops specialize in doing custom designs for customers throughout the world. You can select from current stocks or commission your own tapestry or rug for your favorite room. Be sure to take pictures and room measurements as well as any drawings you wish to incorporate in a tapestry or rug. All of these shops are experienced in shipping goods overseas. Three such shops are found in various locations in Sydney:

- **Kaminski:** Queen Victoria Building, 2nd Floor, Shop 12, George Street, Tel. 261-3039. Also has a shop in Melbourne (Shop 710, Collins Chase, Hyatt on Collins, Tel. 650-6717). Specializes in producing Polish Gobelin tapestries.

- **Robyn Cosgrove Rugs:** 28 Cross Street, Double Bay, Tel. 32-1845, 328-7692. Also has a shop in nearby Chatswood. Specializes in custom-made rugs using New Zealand wools.

- **Australian Rugs & Design:** Metcalfe Arcade, shop 5, 80 George Street, The Rocks, Tel. 27-3481. Specializes in custom-designed wool rugs. Has a good inventory of samples that can be purchased.

Aboriginal, PNG, and Southeast Asian Arts and Crafts

Several shops throughout Sydney specialize in the collection of arts and crafts produced by various Aboriginal tribes as well as imported from Papua New Guinea and several Southeast Asian countries. Some shops only specialize in Aboriginal, PNG, or Southeast Asian arts and crafts whereas others include arts and crafts from all of these groups and areas.

Many shops mix Aboriginal arts and crafts with such Australiana as stuffed koala bears and kangaroos, T-shirts, Akubra hats, and sheepskin products. You can expect to find some Aboriginal arts and crafts, especially bark paintings, didgeridoos, and boomerangs, in most Australiana shops. But don't expect to find good quality Aboriginal arts and crafts in these shops; most are tourist grade.

Some of the best quality shops specializing in Aboriginal arts and crafts are found in the Strand Arcade, Queen Victoria Building, The Rocks, and in Paddington. These shops in particular offer good quality Aboriginal arts and crafts:

- **Hogarth Gallery:** Also goes by the name

Aboriginal Art Centre. Located at 7 Walker Lane, Paddington. Hard to find in this small back lane. Take Shadford and Liverpool streets off of Oxford Street to get to Walker Lane. Tel. 357-6839. Keeps later daytime hours than most shops: 11am to 6pm, Tuesday to Saturday. · Same owners as Argyle Primitive Art Gallery and Crocodile Rocks at The Rocks.

- **Australian Aboriginal Art:** Level 1 (second floor), Argyle Center, 18 Argyle Street, The Rocks, Tel. 27-1380. Same owners as Hogarth Gallery and Crocodile Rocks.

- **Crocodile Rocks:** #127 Clocktower Square, 35 Harrington Street, The Rocks. Newest shop run by the owners of Hogarth Gallery and Argyle Primitive Art Gallery.

- **Aboriginal Artists Gallery:** Civic House, 477 Kent Street (behind Town Hall), Tel. 261-2929; Sydney Opera House, Upper Concourse Level, Bennelong Point, Tel. 27-4344; and corner of Clarence and Market streets, The City, Tel. 923-2366. Has three additional shops in Perth, Darwin, and Alice Springs.

- **Bindi Gallery:** Shop 2/24, Top Level, Queen Victoria Building, Tel. 261-5402 and 261-5403.

- **Coo-ee Australian Emporium:** Shop 63, The Strand Arcade, 412-414 George Street, Tel. 221-5616.

Shops that mix Aboriginal arts and crafts with tribal and primitive arts from Papua New Guinea and some Australiana include:

- **Coo-ee Emporium:** 98 Oxford Street, Paddington, Tel. 332-1544. Includes a great deal of tourist quality Australiana, but also has a design center offering quality fine arts, prints, and fabrics at 202 Oxford Street.

- **The Australian Museum Gift Shop:** The Australian Museum, 6-8 College Street, Tel. 339-8350.

A few shops specialize in arts and crafts from Papua New Guinea and the South Pacific. If you have an interest in such arts and crafts, visit these shops for an overview of what is available in Sydney:

- **New Guinea Primitive Art:** 6th floor, Dymock's Building, 428 George Street, Tel. 232-4737. Hard to find but worth the visit just to see the massive amount of collected artifacts. Also has a smaller shop with nice displays in the Queen Victoria Building: Shop 42, Second Level, 455 George Street, Tel. 264-5134.

- **Ethnographics:** 46 Oxford Street, Paddington, Tel. 331-3737. Also has a small shop in the Marketplace at Harbourside.

- **Duk Duk:** Shop 114, Second Level, The Strand Arcade, 412-414 George Street, Tel. 235-2971.

If your interests also include the wonderful arts and crafts of South and Southeast Asia, especially those from Indonesia, Thailand, Laos, India, and Pakistan, be sure to visit:

- **Gallery Nomad:** 262 Oxford Street, Paddington, Tel. 331-5015. Good quality arts and crafts, including clothes and jewelry from South and Southeast Asia.

- **Private Life:** 762 Military Road, Mosman, Tel. 969-1173. Nice selections and displays appropriate for home decoration. Talk to Alex Milenko.

- **Java Bazaar:** 304 Oxford Street, Paddington, Tel. 33-6739. A large selection of tourist quality arts and crafts from Indonesia.

- **Peter Lane Gallery:** Shop 3, 14 Martin Place, Tel. 235-0136.

Australian Arts and Crafts

Numerous shops offering quality contemporary Australian arts and crafts are found in The Rocks, Paddington,

The Strand Arcade, and Queen Victoria Building. You'll find delightful items produced by some of the best craftsmen from New South Wales as well as from all over Australia. These shops are filled with some of the best arts and crafts in Australia. You will find good buys on glass, leather, textiles, clothing, wood carvings, ceramics, jewelry, and metal work.

In contrast to the five-day work week of many other shops in Australia, most of these shops are open seven days a week. For best quality and selections, we highly recommend the following shops, most of which are located at The Rocks:

- **Australian Craftworks:** 127 George Street, The Rocks, Tel. 27-7156. Excellent selections made by the enthusiastic General Manager, Greene Kennedy, and lovingly displayed by her dedicated staff. Also has a small shop in Cairns.

- **The Craft Centre:** 100 George Street, The Rocks, Tel. 27-9126. Displays for sale a wide range of Australian crafts produced by over 350 members of The Crafts Council of New South Wales. Includes books and directories.

- **The Society of Arts & Crafts of New South Wales Gallery:** Shop 2, Metcalfe Arcade, 80-84 George Street, The Rocks, Tel. 241-1673. A 60 member cooperative with a large selection of attractive handicrafts produced by its members.

- **Royce Galleries:** Metcalfe Arcade, 80-84 George Street, Tel. 241-3668.

- **The Metal Gallery:** Shop 101A, Argyle Arts Centre, The Rocks, Tel. 27-8202. Specializes in unique metal art.

- **The Small Gallery:** Shop 14, Clocktower Square, 35 Harrington Street, The Rocks, Tel. 274-125. A nice selection of contemporary Australian prints and oils as well as Aboriginal prints at reasonable prices. Affiliated with the Original Australian Art Company in the Argyle Centre.

- **The Original Australian Art Company:** Shop 100, First Floor, Argyle Centre, The Rocks. A good selection of Australian prints, oils, and posters along with quality Aboriginal prints. Affiliated with The Small Gallery across the street at Clocktower Square.

- **The Potters' Gallery:** 48-50 Burton Street, Darlinghurst, Tel. 331-3151. Offers stoneware, earthenware, and porcelain pots made by members of The Potters' Society of Australia.

- **The Handmade Shop:** Level 2, Shop 44, Queen Victoria Building, Tel. 261-3374.

- **Ocean Front Gallery:** Manly Beach Plaza, Ground Floor, 4/49 North Steyne, Manly, Tel. 977-8871. Small shop with good quality and selections of ceramics, pottery, and paintings. May be worth the visit to Manly alone.

The weekends are favorite times to browse through crafts markets in and around the Sydney area. Some of the most popular such markets include:

- **Paddington Market:** Centered at the Uniting Church of Australia yard, 380-390 Oxford, Paddington, 8am to 4:30pm on Saturday, Tel. 331-2646.

- **Paddy's Market:** Harold Park Raceway, Ross Street, Glebe. Offers free bus service on the half hour (8am to 2pm) from Circular Quay (in front of the Custom House) and the Railway Square (bus stop at George Street).

- **Manly Arts & Crafts Market:** Held along the beach walkway in Manly. Open Saturday afternoon and all day Sunday and public holidays.

You will also find arts and crafts shops and markets in towns outside Sydney. Areas such as the Blue Mountains, Berrima, Hunter Valley, and Mudgee are noted craft centers. If you wish to visit and shop in these outlying areas, we strongly suggest purchasing a copy of the latest edition of *Craft Outlets and Galleries in New South Wales* published by The Crafts Council of New South Wales. This

useful directory is available for A$7 at The Craft Centre
(100 George Street, The Rocks). The directory includes a
comprehensive listing of member shops in the areas of
Aboriginal arts, tribal and primitive arts, specialist craft
media, general crafts, retail outlets of craft co-operatives,
non-commercial galleries and museums, and community
galleries. The directory may well keep you busy for several weeks shopping for arts and crafts in Sydney and New
South Wales!

Fine Arts, Antiques, and Collectibles

Treasure hunters and lovers of fine arts and antiques
will find numerous shops and centers offering a variety of
Australian, European, and Asian pieces. Indeed, Sydney is
one of Australia's most important centers for fine arts,
antiques and collectibles. Shops along Queen Street in
Woollahra and William Street in Paddington bulge with
fine Australian, European, and Asian antiques. Art galleries are found throughout the metropolitan area. Several
antique centers and markets offer a wide variety of fine
arts, antiques, and bric-a-brac to satify most connoiseurs of
such selective shopping.

A good way to get oriented to the art and antique scene
in and around Sydney is to pick up copies of various
publications reviewing as well as advertising the latest
collections of arts and antiques:

- *Antiques in New South Wales*: An 80+ page
  free newspaper/magazine available in many
  arts and antique shops. Filled with articles
  and ads.

- *Trade: Art & Antiques*: Catalog published
  by the Boronia Art Gallery in Mosman. Advertises the latest collections of fine arts and
  antiques primarily available through this gallery.

- *Antiques Australia*: Magazine available at
  newstands.

- *Australian Antique Collector*: Magazine available at newstands.

- *Australian Antique Trader*: Magazine available at newstands.

- *W.H.A.T.*: Magazine available at newstands.

- *Vive la vie*: Magazine available at many newstands.

- *Carter's Price Guide to Antiques in Australia*: Book available at bookstores (A$50).

Sydney's antique business is organized into antique fairs, shops, markets, and auction rooms. Many antique shops -- especially stalls in antique centers or emporiums -- offer "collectibles" (old wares and bric-a-brac) of all sorts, from antique jewelry to brass lanterns, and in all price ranges. The best places to shop for such collectibles are the following four centers:

- **Woollahra Galleries Antiques:** 160 Oxford Street, Tel. 327-8840.

- **Sydney Antique Market:** South Dowling Street, East Sydney.

- **Chelsea House:** 160 Parramatta Road, Camperdown.

- **Old Art Antique Market:** 20 City Road, Broadway.

If you are interested in antique auctions -- including the sale of antique cars -- be sure to look at the auction section in the Saturday edition of *The Sydney Morning Star* or contact the Sotheby's office at 13 Gurner Street, Paddington (Tel. 332-3500) to learn about their monthly specialty fine arts and antiques auctions.

Antique shops offering excellent quality furniture and home decorative items are particularly concentrated along Queen Street and Jersey Road in Woollahra, just northeast of Oxford Street in Paddington. This is the area for serious and sophisticated antique dealers who nicely display their goods for discerning buyers. Several quality shops specialize in 18th and 19th century French and English furniture such as **Andre & Cecile Fink** (French and Town Country furniture, 102 Queen Street, Tel. 32-3684; also has a shop at 374 New South Head Road, Double Bay, Tel. 32-2344), **Martyn Cook** (English Regency furniture, 104 Queen Street, Tel. 328-1801), **Gaslight Antiques** (106 Queen Street, Tel. 32-2423), **Wentworth Antiques** (English and French furniture, 36 Jersey Road, Tel. 326-1395), and **Peter Cole Antiques** (19th century English and Australian furniture, 55 Queen Street, Tel. 328-6083). Other shops in the Queen Street area offer fine collections of Oriental arts, antiques, and furniture. Especially worth visiting are **Lynette Cunnington** (92 Queen Street, Tel. 326-2222) and **Earnest Elphinstone** (78 Queen Street, Tel. 328-6641). For an excellent collection of antique Japanese furniture, especially chests, be sure to visit **Tansu-Ya** (90 Queen Street, Tel. 32-4954 or 76-5588). Several other shops in this area offer interesting collections of fine and decorative arts for interior design. Some of the nicest collections of decorative arts are found at **Copeland & De Soos** (66 Queen Street, Tel. 32-5288) and **Brian Moore** (44 Queen Street, Tel. 32-0521 or 327-3310).

Other shops in Sydney specializing in arts and antiques are dispersed throughout the metropolitan area.

You will find several other antique shops within a 15 minute walk of Queen Street. Go to the corner of Queen and Oxford streets and proceed west along Oxford Street going toward The City. You will find the largest concentration of small antique shops offering all types of interesting collectibles -- rare and affordable antique jewelry, silverware, glassware, porcelain, old books, furniture, and antique memorabilia -- in **Woollahra Galleries** at 160 Oxford Street (Tel. 327-8840). Directly opposite Centennial Park, this is one of Sydney's best antique market-emporiums housing 50 antique shops. Be sure to look for **William Street**, a narrow one-way street just off of Oxford Street, where you will find a few additional antique shops, such as **Glenleigh Antiques** (73-75 William Street, Paddington, Tel. 331-1549) for 19th century English and French furniture as well as **Raymond & Victoria Tregaskis** (43 William Street, Paddington, Tel. 331-2427) and **David Ho** (39 William Street, Paddington, Tel. 331-7258), specializing in fine Oriental ceramics, furniture, and works of art. You will also find a few antique shops along Hargrave (**House of Desks**, 120 Hargrave Street, Tel. 32-3663), Glenmore (**The Country Trade**, 2 Glenmore Road, Tel. 33-7809), and Paddington (**Joan Bowers Antiques**, 2 Paddington Street, Tel. 360-1500) streets.

You will find many art and antique shops outside the Woollahra and Paddington areas, but few areas are as concentrated as these two. The next largest center for arts and antiques would be the **Neutral Bay-Mosman area** on the North Shore -- a 15-minute drive from The City and The Rocks areas via the Sydney Harbour Bridge. Head for Military Road, which stretches several kilometers from Neutral Bay to Mosman. You'll find several art, antique, and collectible shops in the area, especially near the intersection of Military and Spit roads. In Mosman look for the **Boronia Art Gallery** (768 Military Road, Tel. 969-

7766), **Normans of Mosman** (627 Military Road, Tel. 969-7766), **Appley Hoare Antiques** (527 Military Road, Tel. 969-3292), **Mosman L. M. Antiques** (646 Military Road, Tel. 969-5294), as well as several stalls in the **Portobello Antique Arcade** (742 Military Road, Tel. 969-4559). You'll also find shops along Ourimbah Road (**The Camden Passage**, Tel. 969-4404) and Major Street (**The Japanese House Gallery**, Tel. 960-3661) in Mosman.

Other art, antique, and collectible shops are found throughout the metropolitan area and in small towns of New South Wales in less concentrated areas than Woollahra, Paddington, and Mosman. In The City you will find one or two shops in the Queen Victoria Building on George St. (**Antiques & Collectibles**, Shop 51, top level, Tel. 261-2861) and **Bundi Fine Antiques**, Shop 41, Second Gallery Level, Tel. 261-2210); and Martin Place (**Antique Porcelain Gallery**, 14 Martin Place, Tel. 231-6619; and **Peter Lane Gallery**, 14 Martin Place, Tel. 235-0136); The Strand Arcade (**Margo Richards**, Shop 76, First Level Gallery, Tel. 232-3870); Hotel Inter-Continental Arcade (**Olde Treasure Fine Arts Gallery**, Tel. 251-3551); Royal Arcade (**Bortignons Antiques**, Hilton Hotel, #612 Royal Arcade, George Street, Tel. 267-6818). Several shops are found in the suburban areas of Double Bay (Bay and Cross streets), Rose Bay (Dover Road), Surry Hills (Riley and South Dowling roads), Camperdown (Parramatta Road), Newtown (King Street), Glebe (Glebe Point and St. Johns Road), Huntsville (Ormonde Parade), Balmain (Darling and Beattie streets and Balmain Road), Haberfield (Dalhousie Street), Drummoyne (Lyons Road), Beescroft (Wongala Crs.), Hornsby (Pacific Highway, St. Leonard, and Gordon), Newcastle (King and Wood streets), Avoca Beach (Avoca Drive), Hamilton (Beaumont Street), Morisset (Dora Street), Windsor (George Street), Kurrajong (Old Bells Road), and the Blue Mountains (Great Western Highway, Lawson; Station Street and Railway Parade, Wentworth).

Art galleries offering fine Australian, European, and North American oils, prints, and water colors are also found throughout the metropolitan area. One of the most extensive collections of Australian fine art -- including special gallery paintings with nautical themes and African artifacts -- is **Boronia Art Gallery** in Mosman (2nd floor, 768 Military Road, Tel. 969-2100). This is a good place for the serious art collector. Be sure to get a copy of their trade catalog/magazine -- *Trade: Art & Antiques* which is available at the gallery or in newstands and bookstores. This 100-page catalog/magazine includes photos of over 300 prints and paintings available through Boronia Art

Gallery and other galleries with prices ranging from A$27 to over A$120,000. It's a good publication to introduce you to the booming Australian fine art market as well as an excellent source to refer to for direct mail ordering once you return home. Boronia and other art galleries are very experienced in shipping art abroad since many of these galleries have a large international corporate and individual clientele that they respond to regularly.

You will find the largest number of fine art galleries concentrated in the Paddington, Woollahra, Darlinghurst, Double Bay, and The city areas. In Paddington and Woollahra look for **Galerie Anne Gregory** (40 Garner Street, Paddington, Tel. 360-2285), **The Bloomfield Galleries** (118 Sutherland Street, Paddington, Tel. 326-2122), **Christopher Day** (Corner of Paddington and Elizabeth streets, Tel. 326-1952), **Windsor Art Gallery** (1186 Windsor, Tel. 328-6013), **The Print Gallery** (73 Jersey Street, Woollahra, Tel. 328-7772), **Wagner Art Gallery** (39 Gurner, Tel. 357-6069), and **Anthony Field Gallery** (38 Gurner, Tel. 331-7378).

In Darlinghurst visit **Beth Mayne's Studio Shop** (corner of Palmer and Burton streets, Tel. 357-6264. In Double Bay, try **Holland Fine Art** (46 Cross Street, Tel. 327-2605) and **Four Winds Gallery** (specializes in American Indian arts, Shop 12, Bay Village, 28-34 Cross Street, Tel. 328-7951). In The City visit **The Blaxland Gallery** (6th floor Grace Brothers, corner of Pitt and Market streets, Tel. 238-9390), and **David Jones Art Gallery** (Elizabeth Street, Tel. 266-5544).

On the North Shore, in addition to Boronia Art Gallery in Mosman, look for **Phillips Antique Prints** (372 Pacific Highway, Crows Nest, Tel. 436-4038), and **The Rainsford Gallery** (328 Sydney Road, Balgowlah, Tel. 94-4141).

Depending on the time of the year you visit Sydney, you may be able to attend one or two annual art and antique fairs. For example, the annual Sydney Antiques Fair, with nearly 150 exhibitors, was held in May 1987 and in July 1988. Ask shopkeepers about upcoming fairs and special exhibits as well as review the publications we suggested on page 108. If you drive through some of the small towns in New South Wales, especially around the Blue Mountain area, you may find all kinds of treasures that have accummulated in the attics and backyards of local residents. Indeed, looking for art, antiques, and collectibles in Sydney and its environs may well become one of the most memorable experiences of your Australian shopping adventure!

Fashion and Sportswear

Sydney is one of Australia's two major centers for fashion and sportswear production and distribution. All of Australia's major designers are represented in Sydney's department stores and boutiques. Several Sydney-based fashion designers operate their own boutiques in and around The Strand Arcade and Double Bay area. You will also find, especially in the Sully Hill area, some factory outlets -- but by no means as plentiful as in Melbourne -- offering designer labels at substantial savings. Exclusive couture shops, high fashion and up-market boutiques, and medium-range clothing stores are all well represented in Sydney. Imported clothes are also widely available in shops throughout Sydney, but especially in the exclusive boutiques of Double Bay and the shopping arcades in The City. Shopping for such designer clothes and sportswear may become one of the major shopping highlights during your stay in Sydney.

If you wander through the women's and men's sections of such major department stores as David Jones and Grace Brothers, you will find fashion and sportswear under the labels of such major Australian designers as Ken Done, Maria Finlay, Jill Fitzsimon, Carlo Zampatti, and Weiss.

If you are interested in some unique fashion and sportswear designs produced by innovative Sydney designers, be sure to visit the shops on the second and third floors of The Strand Arcade. Here you will find **Jenny Kee** (Suite 102, Second Floor, Tel. 231-3027 or 235-2391) and her unique stylized Aboriginal designs in colorful sweaters and sportswear. Also stop by **Lizzie Collins** (Tel. 231-1359) for fashion clothes using beautiful raw silk. Lizzie Collins also has branches in the Queen Victoria Building, Centrepoint, Double Bay, Mid City Arcade, MLC Plaza in Sydney, and The Shop of Shops in Melbourne.

The Queen Victoria Building also houses several boutiques of leading Australian designers. Indeed, you will find 56 ladies' fashion and 24 men's fashion shops here. We especiallly like the **Liz Davenport** shop with its exciting color coordinated wardrobe design concept and its new Sunburnt Country, Corroboree, Snowy River, and Spinnakers collections. Liz Davenport shops are also found in Perth, Melbourne, and Adelaide; and **Lorraine St. Clair** (Shop 6, Ground Floor, Tel. 267-5695) for nicely styled and quality conservative women's clothes.

Centrepoint is another major fashion center in The City. Connected to David Jones and Grace Brothers department stores, this center has 58 women's and 5 men's fashion shops offering clothes, footwear, and accessories which cater to both mid-range and up-market clientele. Many of these shops are branches of shops found in the Queen Victoria Building, The Strand Arcade, and other shopping centers throughout the city. This center houses Cuggi, Just Jeans, Posh, Sportsgirl, Bee Fashions, Designer Savings, Lizzie Collins, Joshua, Laura Ashley, Weiss 'Pringle Shop', and Papoucci.

The Rocks also has several unique fashion and sportswear shops you may be interested in browsing through. For a fun and fashionable collection of women's leather hats and accessories, stop by **Dorothy Furhagen** ("The Rocks Hatters", 47 Argyle Street, Tel. 27-4916). **The Village Leather Boutique** (27A Playfair Street, Tel. 27-1238; also has a shop in Melbourne) has nice Australian-designed and crafted leather goods. For colorful Australian women's fashion and sportswear, visit **Artwear** (77 1/2 George Street, Tel. 27-3668). Men may be interested in the distinctive Australian leatherwear designs at **Morrisons** (105 George Street, Tel. 27-1596).

The **Double Bay** area houses the most exclusive fashion and sportswear shops in Sydney, including an up-market David Jones Department Store. Bay, Cross, and Knox streets are lined with fashionable boutiques offering clothes from $10 to $10,000. For the finest in uniquely designed evening and sportswear, visit **Susan Hannaford** (7 Knox Street, Cosmopolitan Centre, Tel. 32-9607). The rich and famous shop here -- and for good reason. Expensive, but Susan Hannaford's "new wave" and VIP designs and clothes are fabulous. As you look through the samples, remember you will be buying handcrafted, one-of-a-kind pieces that are simply stunning. Considering the quality and workmanship, prices are not unreasonable. This is the type of shop that would feel at home on Rodeo Drive in Hollywood, California. The shop boasts among its clients American film celebrities Farrah Fawcett and Linda Evans.

Femme of Double Bay (Shop 2, Cross Court, 22-26 Cross Street, Tel. 327-7133) also offers a nice selection of dinner and evening dresses. We also like **Simode** (Shop 5, The Georges Centre, Cross Street, Tel. 32-9086) which mainly carries Prue Acton's unique one and two-piece dresses with distinctive applique work. **Mark Foy's** (Cross Street) also has an exclusive shop here offering French and Italian labeled evening wear, sportswear, dresses, and make up. **Antonella** (Shop 2, Cosmopolitan Centre, Knox Street) is also a nice boutique offering many different lines of Australian and imported women's clothes. **Jill Fitzsimon** (Shop 2, Cosmopolitan Centre, Knox Street), **Carla Zampatti** (24 Bay Street, Tel. 326-2248), **Weiss**

'Pringle Shop' (43 Knox Street, Tel. 328-1035), and **Papoucci** (Shop 20, Cosmopolitan Centre, Knox Street, 327-4167) have branch shops here in Double Bay. For nice leather, hat, and scarf accessories visit **D'Aliccia** (Shop 1, Cosmopolitan Centre, Knox Street, Tel. 327-5765).

A few other shops to look for are **Adrienne & The Misses Bonney** (The Regent Hotel, 199 George Street, The City, Tel. 27-2062; and 28 Cross Street, Double Bay, Tel. 32-1723) for elegant and very expensive woolen nightwear, lingerie, and children's clothing, toys, and gifts. Browse through this shop and you will quickly discover the elegant tastes and quality preferences of the rich and famous as well as pick up a copy of their direct-mail catalog.

You will also find several branches of **Designer Savings** promoting the Rodney Clark label in women's designer clothing in the Centrepoint, Darling Harbour, MLC Centre, Wynyard, Mosman, and Neutral Bay shopping areas as well as branches in the cities of Melbourne, Adelaide, Brisbane, and Perth. Ostensibly advertised at "affordable prices", the Rodney Clark label is popular among women seeking middle-range quality and prices in clothing.

Posh (R35, MLC Centre, Tel. 233-1261) sells trendy up-market women's fashionwear created by such leading Australian designers as Prue Acton, George Gross, Peter Weiss, Covers, and Robin Garland. **Rosie Niu** (274 Oxford Street, Paddington, Tel. 331-5844) offers classical clothes and accessories by Marilyn Sainty and Hinke Zieck. **John Lane** (41 Oxford Street, Paddington, Tel. 327-6198) specializes in sportswear, casual suits, shirts, and accessories under the Australian John Lane label as well as such important labels as Etienne Aigner, Cerruti, and Sergio Tacchina. **Maria Finley** (30-36 Bay Street, Double Bay, Tel. 328-7001) is well noted for selling such high fashion imported labels as Fink, Yarell, Bogner, Kanya, Dino Valiano, and Louis Ferandi. **Reads of Woollahra** (130 Queen Street, Woollahra, Tel. 328-1036) is a popular source for high quality designer labels (Tea Rose and Marcus Tush) in women's clothing, shoes, and accessories. **Rhonda Parry** (Shop 8, 19-27 Cross Terrace, Double Bay) offers men's and women's fashionwear under her own designs as well as those from leading European and Japanese designers. **White Ivy** (322 New South Head Road, Double Bay, Tel. 326-1830) provides up-market sleepwear, babywear, and handcrafted gift items.

Factory Outlet Clothing and Accessories

While Melbourne is the center of buying clothing and accessories at **factory outlets**, Sydney has its own factory outlets offering discontinued, end-of-line stock, seconds, samples, and overruns of name-brand men's, women's, and children's clothes, shoes, and accessories at savings from 30 to 70 percent. Some of these shops, such as **Successful Redress** (Gallery Level, Mid City Centre, The City, Tel. 221-7395), also include re-cycled (used) clothes, such as $6,000 wedding dresses for $2,000, whereas others only sell re-cycled clothes. Most of these outlets are scattered throughout the metropolitan area, but many are concentrated in and around the **Surry Hills, Parramatta, Chatsworth, Redfern**, and **Campertown** areas. Factory shops such as **LM Factory Shops** (88 Parramatta Road, Tel. 516-1155 and 218 Church Street, Tel. 891-1552) offer good savings on women's and childrens' sleepwear and outerwear; **Shirt Warehouse** (79 Campbell Street, Surry Hills, Tel. 212-2106) carries well-known brands of casual, business, and designer shirts; and **Clothesline** (713 Darling Street, Rozelle, Tel. 818-1444) offers name brand shirts, dresses, blouses, sportswear, and knits at substantial savings, with most being firsts and samples.

Factory outlet shopping in Sydney is best done by the well informed who know where to go, what to buy, and how to shop. Some factory outlets are open by appointment only whereas others are open to the general public during regular business hours. Our recommendation is to purchase a copy of *Bargain Shopper's Guide to Sydney* (A$5.95) which is available at most bookstores and newsstands or can be ordered directly from the publisher: Universal Magazines, Private Bag 154, North Ryde, NSW 2113, Australia. In addition to sending the equivalent of Australian $5.95, be sure to add sufficient postage for mailing a two pound package by international surface or air mail (check with your local post office).

The most convenient way to shop these outlets is to join a local shopping tour. Try **Bargain Buyer's Tours** (21 Elegans Avenue, St. Ives, NSW, Tel. 479-7221 or 449-1776) or **Fashion Frolic** (53 Wattle, Haberfield, NSW, Tel. 798-7655). These groups charge less than A$30 per person, including lunch, for at least a half-day tour to the major factory outlets -- one of the best travel bargains in Australia.

Australiana, Souvenirs, and Gifts

Sydney's shops are big on offering a large range of

Australiana, souvenirs, and gifts to visitors. The quality ranges from tourist junk to some very fine quality arts, crafts, and jewelry classified as Australiana. Every major shopping area will have one or more shops specializing in knickknacks they term "Australiana".

One of the best places in all of Australia to purchase good quality Australiana is **The Rocks** area of Sydney. Several shops here offer good quality and selections of Australiana. **The Didjeridu Shop** (Shop 16, Argyle Centre, 18 Argyle St., Tel. 251-2294), for example, has an excellent selection of boomerangs, clothes, musical instruments, and books on Australia. Next door is the **Platypus Gallery** (Shop 15, Argyle Centre, 18 Argyle Road, Tel. 241-1590) with many unique handicrafts, such as puzzles, wind chimes, wood carved pieces, stuffed animals, puppets, scarves, coasters, placemats, and Aboriginal bark paintings. In the nearby Metcalfe Arcade you will find the **Lambswool Trader** (80/84 George Street, Tel. 27-9174) offering quality leather and sheepskin goods and related souvenirs. **Beenelong Boomerangs** (29-31 Playfair Street, Tel. 24-1121 or 909-1988) has a unique collection of boomerangs designed by Australia's leading boomerang specialist, Paul Bryden.

Other shopping areas are filled with Australiana and souvenir shops. In the Queen Victoria Building, for example, look for **The Best of Australiana, The Australian, Nik Nak, Koala Bear Shop,** and **Victoria Souvenirs.** In The Strand Arcade, browse through **Strand Souvenirs and Opals, Coo-ee,** and **Martinvale.** In Centrepoint look for **Centrepoint Souvenirs, Oasis Aussie Wares, Sydney Tower Souvenirs,** and **The Wool Shop.** For imported gifts, stop at Centrepoint's **Georg Jensen** for top quality tableware and **Christopher James** for excellent quality leather briefcases, purses, and related leather goods. The **Marketplace** at Harbourside is another major area with numerous small shops and pushcarts catering to tourists with all types and qualities of Australiana, souvenirs, and gifts.

Leathergoods and Furs

You will find several shops selling leather goods as well as a few specializing in furs in Sydney. **Bernhard Hammerman Furs** (119 King Street, Sydney, Tel. 233-5399 and also in David Jones Department Store, Elizabeth Street) offers a large selection of nicely styled quality furs as well as fur and leather coats. As part of their sales campaign, they will pick you up and whisk you off to their store in a chauffered Rolls Royce, greet you with champagne, and show you a video presentation on the crafting of furs.

If you are looking for some "*citified outback clothes*", you're in luck in Sydney. A local branch of the popular **Morrisons** (105 George Street, The Rocks, Tel. 27-1576) store sells good quality and fashionable leather clothes for men. Look for oilskins, moleskins, leather coats, bush hats, sports jackets, and sheepskin coats at Morrisons. The local branch of **R. M. Williams** (71 Castlereagh Street, Tel. 233-1347) sells similar ranges of leather clothes, especially Driza-Bone oilskin rain coats and riding jackets, moleskin pants, kangaroo-hide belts, and Akubra hats -- everything you ever needed to look like Crocodile Dundee or the Man from Snowy River or attend those hoe-downs and bush dances you have been waiting for!

Duty-Free Goods

Sydney has the largest concentration of duty-free shops in the country. They are especially popular with Japanese and New Zealand tourists who feel they are getting a bargain on everything from opals to liquor.

The majority of duty-free shops are found in and around the Pitt Street area in downtown Sydney. Many of the shops are local branches of chain stores found in other cities. Some of the largest duty-free shops include **Downtown own Duty Free** (Queen Victoria Building, Shop 50, Second Floor, 429-481 George Street; 20 Hunter Street, 84 Pitt Street); **Orbit Duty Free** (74 Pitt Street; 276 Pitt Street); **Bridge Street Duty Free** (13-15 Bridge Street); **City Duty Free** (62 and 249 Pitt Street; and 416 George Street); **Martin Plaza Duty Free** (4-10 Martin Place); **Le Classique Duty Free Shops** (33 Blight Street, Tel. 223-1455); and **Angus and Coote Duty Free** (496 George Street, Hilton Hotel, Tel. 267-1363).

Books

You'll find books everywhere in Sydney, from large chain stores to small used and antique book stores. Some of the largest book stores include **Grahame's Books** (34 Hunter Street, Mid City Centre, 197 Pitt Street), **Angus & Robertson** (Imperial Arcade, 168 Pitt Street, Tel. 235-1188), **Abbey's Bookshop** (131 York Street, Tel. 264-3111), **Dymock's** (424 George Street, Tel. 233-4111), and **Ariel Books** (42 Oxford Street, Paddington, Tel. 332-4581).

WHERE TO SHOP

Sydney offers a wide variety of settings for doing your Australian shopping. This energetic city is always on the move with new and controversial office and shopping complexes either being planned or under construction. From The Rocks along the harbor to the new Harbourside development in Darling Harbour, Sydney's commercial development is increasingly moving to the southern part of the city and into the suburbs.

The best shopping in terms of quality and convenience will be found in the shopping arcades, neighborhood shops, and markets of The Rocks (Argyle Centre, Clocktower Square, Metcalfe Arcade, and George, Argyle, and Playfair streets); The City, or central business district (The Strand Arcade, Queen Victoria Building, Centrepoint, MLC Centre, Mid City, Royal Arcade, Imperial Arcade, Martin Place, and George, Pitt, and King streets); Darling Harbour (Marketplace at Harbourside); Double Bay (Knox, Cross, and Bay streets); Woollahra (Queen Street); Paddington (Oxford and William streets); and the North Shore (Neutral Bay and Mosman). Such seaside communities as Manly and Bondi also offer some unique shopping opportunities.

We have not included several additional suburban areas which also offer shopping opportunities, because these areas primarily function as shopping centers for local residents. Most of these areas have few unique items to offer visitors. Sydney's bustling Chinatown, for example, is not included because it offers nothing uniquely Australian to visitors. Go there for some good Oriental restaurants. We also have not included Pier 1 and Birkenhead Point because these areas are presently in decline. Pier 1, adjacent to The Rocks and just beneath the Sydney Harbour Bridge, was Sydney's attempt to create a local version of the San Francisco Wharf. For all intents and purposes, Pier 1 is a failure. Birkenhead Point, just a few kilometers west of Darling Harbour, has declined substantially; competition from the new Marketplace at Harbourside will further accelerate the decline of this once popular harborside shopping area.

The Rocks

The Rocks, nestled just south of the Sydney Harbour Bridge and west of the Sydney Opera House and Circular Quay, is Sydney's most historical area and one of Australia's most successful urban renewal projects. This harborside village and hilly commercial area is where the first settlers -- an unwitting gang of nearly 1000 prisoners -- landed in 1788. It's where much of Sydney's colorful commercial, maritime, and bawdy history developed. It's where over 100 citizens died of the bubonic plague in 1890; where high levels of crime, prostitution, and disease as well as occasional fires characterized what was a slum area until the 1930s when the Sydney Harbour Bridge sliced through the area for ostensible "urban renewal" purposes. But neither fires nor the bridge project could renew this area in the direction of the positive urban renewal that took place in the 1970s. Completely transformed in recent years to become one of Sydney's beautiful and charming tourist attractions and shopping destinations, The Rocks is a "must" stop for anyone visiting Sydney.

The Rocks is one of the most charming, quaint, and colorful shopping areas in all of Australia. Stroll down its cobblestone streets, climb the stairs connecting shops and streets, take a leisurely walk along the charming harbor that bounds this area, duck into a popular pub or two, or dine in one of its fine restaurants and you will be in for a most delightful day of sightseeing and shopping at The Rocks.

Although The Rocks has a reputation among locals for being a "touristy area", it has not succumbed to becoming a tacky tourist trap. The Rocks is one of our favorite shopping areas in all of Australia. We especially like the ambiance of this area. But most important of all, we find in this area numerous quality shops offering some of Australia's finest arts and crafts. Because of the arts and crafts shops, much of The Rocks is open seven days a week. If you are like us, you will want to visit this area more than once during your stay in Sydney. At night the area is alive with people enjoying the harbor views and dining at the many fine local restaurants.

Major shopping at The Rocks is centered in and around George, Argyle, and Playfair streets as well as in three shopping centers: Argyle Centre, Clocktower Square, and Metcalfe Arcade. **George Street** in The Rocks begins just north of the Regent Hotel. This street is filled with shops, pubs, and restaurants. It is lined with horse drawn carts and carriages to take you around The Rocks and surrounding areas. You'll find a **Morrisons** (105 George Street) men's leatherwear shop here as well as two of Australia's finest arts and crafts shops -- **Australian Craftswork** (127 George Street) and **The Craft Centre** (100 George Street). For anyone interested in Australian arts and crafts these are two "must" shops in Sydney. The quality of arts and crafts in these two shops is simply superb. Also, stop by **Artwear** (77 1/2 George Street) for some unique and colorfully designed womenswear.

Along adjacent **Argyle Street** you will find a few shops, such as madhatters **Dorothy Furhagen** (47 Argyle Street) for fashionable hats and accessories, the newly completed Clocktower Square, and the older, historical Argyle Centre.

Two art shops in **Clocktower Centre** are worth visiting: **The Small Gallery** (Shop 14) for a nice selection of reasonably priced Australian and Aboriginal paintings and prints and for excellent service. **Crocodile Rocks** (Shop 127) offers outstanding and pricy Aboriginal art. Both shops have branch shops offering similar quality art directly across the street at the Argyle Centre (**The Original Australian Art Company** and **Australian Aboriginal Art**).

The **Argyle Centre** has over 50 shops selling everything from koalas to candles. Browse through the three stories of shops and you will certainly find something you will treasure. At ground level you will find shops offering quality Australiana, such as **The Didjeridu Shop** and **Platypus Gallery**. For leather, try **Argyle Leather** and **Aussie Ewe and Lamb**. On level one you'll find such diverse and quality arts shops as the **The Original Australian Art Company**, **The Medal Gallery**, and **Australian Aboriginal Art**. If you love candles, go to Level Two to browse through **The Candle Factory**. And don't forget the Argyle Terraces Level with the **Village Leather Boutique** and **Cowboy From Down Under**, for American Indian jewelry.

Along adjacent **Playfair Street** you'll find such distinctive shops as **Beenalong Boomerangs** (29-31 Playfair Street), **The Village Leather Boutique** (27A Playfair Street) as well as an American Indian shop among the more than 12 shops lining this street. Just down the street, off George Street, is the Metcalfe Arcade found in the historical Metcalfe Stores building. Several shops on the First Level sell unique furniture, arts, crafts, and Australiana. **Australian Rugs and Designs** (Shop 5) will custom-make any rug or tapestry design you desire. Stop by to see the samples and unique work being done in Australian and New Zealand wools. Nearby is a delightful arts and crafts shop operated by volunteers: **The Society of Arts and Crafts of New South Wales Gallery** (Shop 2). **Royce Galleries** and the **Lambswool Trader** are well stocked with arts, crafts, and Australian items.

While visiting The Rocks, you may wish to dine at one of the harborside restaurants. The historical Campbells Storehouse has several good restaurants with nice views of the harbor. Sydney's best Chinese restaurant, Imperial

Peking, is found in this complex along with the popular Phantom of the Opera. The restaurant with the best view of the harbor is the new Rocks branch of the famous Doyles Seafood Restaurant located just across from Campbells Storehouse. Be sure to make reservations since most of these popular restaurants are heavily booked for both lunch and dinner.

For a fun evening of food and Australiana entertainment, try the Jolly Swagman Show at the Argyle Tavern (18 Argyle Street, Tel. 27-7782). If you like history, you'll want to stop at the Visitors Centre, Cadmen Cottage, Geological Mining Museum, and Garrison Church--all within short walking distance of each other. For one of the best views of Sydney Harbor and the Opera House and a review of the history of bridge building, climb the stairs and walk out to the southeast pylon of the Sydney Harbour Bridge, where you will climb 200 stairs to get a beautiful view of this area. Take your camera for some wonderful shots of the harbor.

The Strand Arcade (City)

Here is one of Sydney's most elegant historical shopping areas located in the heart of the city's commercial district between Pitt Street Mall and George Street. First built in 1892, this beautiful four-story Victorian building houses over 50 shops, many of which are Sydney's finest boutiques and jewelry stores, offering goods and services galore. This is where you can purchase the latest in Australian fashion; design your own jewelry; get your shoes repaired and clothes altered; buy gifts and accessories; order wedding invitations and a wedding dress; get a tooth filled; or buy freshly roasted coffee and a bouquet of flowers! This is also where many of the rich and famous like to shop -- where such international celebrities as David Bowie, Lauren Bacall, Tina Turner, Sophia Loren, and Cher are known to stop when in Sydney. It is one of the most pleasant and friendly shopping areas in all of Australia to visit -- one you may return to several times during your visit. Best of all, its many shops offer some of the best quality shopping you will find anywhere. Next to Double Bay, this is Sydney's most up-market shopping area. It is a shopper's and browser's paradise.

If you are looking for the latest in Australian fashion, you'll find most major designers represented in the many boutiques on Ground Level and Level One. Especially look for Jenny Kee's **Flamingo Park, Lizzie Collins,** and **Von Troska.** Young people looking for trendy clothes head for **Black Vanity** and **Love and Hatred.** Fashion conscious men visit **Tony Barlow Menswear** as well as indulge themselves at **The Body Shop**.

If you are looking for unique pieces of jewelry, you've come to the right place. **Robert Clerc** (Shop 28, Ground Floor) is doing some of the most creative and innovation gold designs (Aboriginal and Egyptian) we have found anywhere in the world. Look for his pins, pendants, and earrings, and perhaps talk to him about his current work or any custom designs you may have in mind. Many visitors to Australia regularly return to Robert Clerc on subsequent visits. You'll also find a few watch makers and other quality jewelers in The Strand Arcade, such as **Masterpiece Jewellery** (Shop 10, Ground Floor).

If your interests include Aboriginal and tribal arts and crafts, you may want to browse through **Coo-ee Australian Emporium** (Shop 63) and **Duk Duk** (Shop 114). For unique gifts, visit **Martinvale** on the Lower Level. If you are in need of a bakery, a cup of cappuccino, flowers, gifts, or a shoe repair, you will find the right shop here to take care of your needs.

Queen Victoria Building (City)

Located directly across from the Hilton Hotel and Royal Arcade, bounded by George, Market, York, and Druitt streets, and linked to the Town Hall, Railway Station, and Grace Brothers Department Store, the Queen Victoria Building (QVB) houses one of Australia's largest, most elegant, and colorful up-market shopping centers. Similar in character to The Strand Arcade, but on a much grander scale, this is a gorgeous building with a sandstone and domed exterior resembling a Byzantine Palace. Noted for its spacious interior with elegant arches, intricate and colorful tiled floors, and beautiful stained glass, the Queen Victoria Building is an outstanding example of Victorian architecture.

First constructed in 1898 and lovingly preserved, converted, and modernized for the convenience of shoppers, browsers, and diners alike, the Queen Victoria Building is jammed with nearly 200 shops, cafes, and restaurants. It's a place where you can easily spend half a day strolling the four long levels connected by stairs, escalators, and elevators; browsing through nice boutiques; selecting a perfect gift; stopping for a cup of cappuccino or having a full course lunch or dinner; or watching the unique Royal Clock on the top floor (Victoria Walk) on the hour present six famous events from British history, including the beheading of King Charles I!

The Queen Victoria Building is filled with boutiques,

jewelry, gift, souvenir, art, antique, beauty, kids, and service shops as well as numerous take-away eateries and restaurants. For womenswear, you will find such shops as **Liz Davenport, Cherry Lane, Papoucci, Lorraine St. Clair, Country Road, Monsoon, Joshua, Esprit, Just Jeans, Lizzie Collins,** and **Liz Newman's Designer Knits.** For menswear, look for **Najee, Joe Bananas, Canterbury, Numac Leather, Leatherall Boutique, Grand Leather, Roger David,** and **Oasis for Men.** On the Victoria Walk Level these shops have nice selections of Aboriginal and tribal arts: **Bindi Gallery, Aboriginal Arts,** and **New Guinea Primitive Arts** (also has a main shop on the 6th floor of the Dymock Building, 428 George Street). Several jewelry shops specialize in opals: **Opal Beauty, Maurice Schneider Duty Free,** and **Skippy Opals.** For gifts and Australiana, check out **Nik Nak, The Australian Connoisseur, Koala Bear Shop, Victoria Souvenirs,** and **The Best of Australiana.** One of Australia's finest tapestry shops is found on the Victoria Walk Level: **Kaminski Gallery.** Duty-free shoppers will find **Downtown Duty Free** also located on the Victoria Walk Level.

One of the highlights of visiting the Queen Victoria Building is watching the unique Royal Clock on the hour, from 10am to 9pm, present its historical tales. Crowds normally gather on the hour and delight in this presentation. Also, you will find numerous cafes, restaurants, and take-away food stalls serving everything from health foods and fresh juices to pasta and seafood. Several good take-away food stalls -- table nearby -- are found on the bottom floor near the entrance to the underground passageway connecting the Queen Victoria Building with the Grace Brothers Department Store.

City Shopping Arcades

The downtown commercial area, bounded by Bridge, George, Castlereagh, and Market streets and intersected by Pitt and Kings streets as well as Martin Place, houses several large and small shopping arcades and department stores in addition to the elegant Strand Arcade and the Queen Victoria Building. The names and locations of these arcades can be confusing since one shopping complex tends to feed into another and thus all of them appear to merge into one large shopping complex along Pitt and George streets. These are the shops and shopping arcades in and around what is better known as **Martin Place,** a plaza centered around major banks, insurance companies, and airline offices, and where lunch time crowds gather for musical entertainment. This is a vibrant area offering numerous shopping opportunities. The shops in this area will vary considerably in quality.

The largest shopping arcade in this area is **Centrepoint**. This shopping arcade is bounded by Market and Castlereagh streets as well as Pitt Street Mall and the Imperial Arcade. Located at the base of the famous Sydney Tower, the tallest structure in the Southern Hemisphere, and connected to David Jones and Grace Brothers department stores, Centrepoint is a three-level shopping complex with over 100 shops selling everything from the latest in women's fashion to magic tricks. The first floor (Pitt Level) is filled with small eateries as well as a few clothing, shoe, and jewelry stores, such as **Just Jeans, Angus and Coote**, and **Kimberley Jewellers**. The second floor (Castlereagh Level) has a larger concentration of clothes, jewelry, and leather shops with such well known names as **Sportsgirl, Lizzie Collins, Joshua, Designer Savings, Jorgen Jensen**, and **Jeans West**. This floor also connects to Grace Brothers Department Store and the Imperial Arcade. The third floor (Gallery Level) has the largest concentration of up-market shops in Centrepoint. Here you will find **Mark Foy's, The Silver Crystal Shop, Levy Furs, Papoucci, Georg Jensen, Signature**, and **Bugatti**. Many of the shops, such as **Oroton** and **Christopher James** which sell leather items, primarily stock imported goods. This level also connects to David Jones and Grace Brothers department stores and is where you enter the elevator to ride to the top of the Tower or to the Tower Restaurant for a panoramic view of the Sydney metropolitan area.

The adjacent **Imperial Arcade** is a small shopping center containing a few small shops selling clothes, furs, shoes, art, and jewelry. While you may find some good shopping here, the best quality shopping is still on the third floor (Gallery Level) of the Centrepoint shopping arcade.

The nearby **MLC Centre** is a modern trendy shopping center. A railway station connects to the bottom floor. Here you will find nearly 80 shops selling fashion, footwear, menswear, jewelry, gifts, and computers. **Designer Savings, Sportsgirl**, and **Posh** have branch stores in this shopping arcade.

The nearby **Mid City Centre** is a four-level shopping center with over 100 shops selling the usual combination of clothing, jewelry, footwear, gifts, homewares, and food.

Marketplace at Harbourside (Darling Harbour)

This is Sydney's and Australia's most ambitious urban

redevelopment project. It is an attempt to create an integrated cultural, entertainment, commercial, and shopping complex on the city's historical Darling Harbour located southwest of the city center and adjacent to Chinatown. Developed around a much larger concept of waterfront shopping than the failed Pier 1 and the declining Birkenhead Point, Marketplace at Harbourside is nearly identical in appearance and structure to Baltimore, Maryland's (U.S.) harbourside development -- but on a much grander scale. Nestled in Darling Harbour and surrounded by the Sydney Aquarium, Darling Walk amusement center, Exhibition Centre, Chinese Garden, Pump House Tavern and Boutique Brewery, the Sydney Seaport, the huge Powerhouse Museum, the Convention Centre, Tumbalong Park, and luxury hotels, Marketplace has quickly become one of the most popular shopping areas in Sydney for local residents.

The popularity of Marketplace is probably due more to the ambiance of its architecture and harborside setting than to any special shopping opportunities found here. Marketplace is clearly a social event for local residents; shopping is its side show. Young people, especially families, love to come here to enjoy the atmosphere of people, restaurants, shopping, sightseeing, and the water views. If you have been to similar developments in the United States (Baltimore and Norfolk), you know what to expect. This is a nice place to go for a relaxing day of strolling, browsing, eating, and sightseeing. Marketplace is filled with small shops and pushcarts selling gift items, souvenirs, Australiana, and clothes. Many are small branches of larger stores in The City. However, Marketplace's greatest strength is its large number of restaurants, food stalls, and surrounding sites for family entertainment. We like this area but not because of its shopping. Shopping opportunities are much better elsewhere in Sydney. Our recommendation: go here for the full range of tourist attractions and do some shopping at the same time. It's a pleasant change from some of the indoor shopping malls found in downtown Sydney. It's easy to get to this area by walking west from the city center along Market Street. Taxis, buses, and a monorail system service this area.

Double Bay

Double Bay, a wealthy suburb located eight kilometers east of the city center, is Sydney's most exclusive shopping area. It's a shopping village in the midst of being transformed into an international shopping center. It's the place where Australia's rich and famous find their social identity along Knox, Bay, and Cross streets as well as the latest fashions from London, Paris, and Rome. It's where you will see the largest concentration of Rolls Royces, Mercedes, Jaguars, BMWs, and Porches competing for parking spaces or just cruising the streets to see and be seen. It's the area toward which the not so rich and famous Australians enjoy expressing their deep-seated class and egalitarian attitudes. They joke by calling this area "Double Pay" rather than "Double Bay" because of its pricy nature. They take pleasure in noting that after 200 years of egalitarian history, there are still snobbish and pretentious people in Australia -- and many can be found in Double Bay.

For all this local nonsense aimed at bringing the people and places of Double Bay down a social notch or two, Double Bay remains one of the best places to shop in all of Australia. It has a nice ambiance, more in line with a Carmel, California than with its more frequent comparison to Rodeo Drive in Hollywood, California. Ongoing redevelopment efforts will further transform Double Bay into one of Australia's most attractive shopping areas.

Despite what you may hear about the "expensive" nature of shopping in Double Bay, the prices are not that different from other quality shopping areas. The major difference is that this area offers a large concentration of high quality products and custom services you cannot find elsewhere in Sydney. After all, that's exactly why people with good tastes and an eye toward quality like to do their shopping in Double Bay. Many of Australia's super rich and famous by-pass this area altogether as they jet off to London, Paris, and Rome to do what they consider to be "real quality" shopping.

And despite what locals may tell you, we do not find this area to be at all snobbish or pretentious. Indeed, the opposite is more apparent. You can easily spend half a day shopping here. You'll want to browse through the numerous shops and stop for a cup of coffee or tea or have lunch. Start with the shops at the east end of the Cosmopolitan Centre on Knox Street, near New South Head Road, and work your way along both sides of this street as well as along the adjacent Cross and Bay streets. This is the heart of the Double Bay shopping area. You'll find dozens of small boutiques selling the latest in Australian designed and imported fashion clothes, shoes, and accessories. Such shops as **Susan Hannaford** (7 Knox Street, Cosmopolitan Centre) designs gorgeous women's clothes for those who have the desire and money to accent their wardrobes with clothes fit for international movie stars and exclusive shops along Hollywood's Rodeo Drive. **Femme of Double Bay** (Shop 2, Cross Court, 22-

26 Cross Street) creates beautiful dinner and evening dresses. If you like Prue Acton's designs, stop at **Simode** (Shop 5, The Georges Centre, Cross Street) for a nice selection of her women's clothes. Major Australian designers, such as **Jill Fitzsimon** (Shop 2, The Cosmopolitan Centre, Knox Street) and **Carla Zampatti** (24 Bay Street), also have their own boutiques in Double Bay. For good selections of imported clothes, visit **Mark Foy's** (Cross Street), **Antonella** (Shop 3, Cosmopolitan Centre, Knox Street), and **Papoucci** (Shop 20, Cosmopolitan Centre, Knox Street). **David Jones** (The Georges Centre, Cross Street) also has a small department store catering to the up-market tastes of the Double Bay clientele.

If your interests include custom-made wool rugs, be sure to stop at **Robyn Cosgrove Rugs** (28 Cross Street, Bay Village). For jewelry, see **L. K. Jewellry** (Kennedy House, 9/11 Knox Street). For country French fabrics for home furnishings and dresses, see the nice selections at **Les Olioades** (29 Cross Street). A tasteful shop selling nice quality North American Indian jewelry, paintings, and rugs is **Four Winds Gallery** (Shop 12, Bay Village, 28-34 Cross Steet). A unique, interesting, and fun shop selling imported chests, bowls, flatware, dishes, candles, pots, tables, and chairs is **Made Where** (6 Cross Street).

Woollahra and Queen Street

The suburb of Woollahra is also located east of the city center, adjacent to Paddington and near Double Bay. If you love antique furniture, Woollahra is the place to go. This is Sydney's major up-market antique center. Shops along Queen Street in Woollahra sell a large variety of excellent quality and expensive 18th and 19th century European and Australian antique furniture and home decorative pieces. A few shops specialize in Asian furniture and collectibles. Additional antique shops are found along Jersey Road in Woollahra.

It's best to start your antique shopping adventure in the 100 block of Queen Street and work your way South until you come to Jersey Road and Oxford Street in Paddington. You can easily spend two hours browsing through the many shops along Queen Street and Jersey Road. Look for such shops as **Gaslight Antiques** (106 Queen Street), **Andre & Cecile Fink** (102 Queen Street), **Peter Cole Antiques** (55 Queen Street), **Lynette Cunningham** (92 Queen Road), **Tansu-Ya** (90 Queen Street), **Ernest Elphinstone** (78 Queen Street), **Copeland & De Soos** (66 Queen Street), **Brian Moore** (44 Queen Street), **Wentworth Antiques** (36 Jersey Road), and **Galleries Primif**

(174 Jersey Street). Once you reach Oxford Road, you begin entering another major shopping area, the historical Paddington.

Paddington and Oxford Street

Paddington is one of Sydney's best known historical and cultural areas. Stretching several blocks north from Oxford Street between Queen Street in the east to Glenmore Road in the west. The shops and homes in this area have retained their traditional 19th century architecture which you may or may not find attractive. This area is noted for its mix of antique, clothing, secondhand, Australiana, and arts and crafts shops. The area especially comes alive on weekends when the famous Paddington Market on Oxford Street draws large crowds of weekend shoppers who browse along Oxford and the adjacent streets of Paddington and Woollahra.

Contrary to local recommendations on the area as a "must" shopping stop, we find Paddington overrated and somewhat run down. It's a very mixed area where we were disappointed in finding so few good quality shops, especially after shopping in Double Bay and Woollahra. The area looks and feels like it is in transition, having seen better days. The walk along Oxford Street is long, and quality shops are few and far between. You will find a few shops along such side streets as William, Walker, Hargrave, and Glenmore.

Nonetheless, if you persist in walking the length of Oxford Road and exploring adjacent streets, you will discover a few excellent shops that will make the trip to Paddington well worth while. But be forewarned that you will have to walk some long distances. For example, one of Australia's best international arts and crafts shops -- **Gallery Nomad** at 262 Oxford Street -- offers a good selection of South and Southeast Asian arts, crafts, jewelry, and clothing. **Ethnographics** (46 Oxford Street) has a large selection of recently acquired tribal woodcarvings from Papua New Guinea. **Coo-ee Emporium** (98 Oxford Street) offers mixed quality Aboriginal arts and Australiana for tourists. If you persist in taking Shadford and Liverpool streets off of Oxford Street until you come to Walker Lane -- which is even hard to find on a map -- you will discover one of Sydney's finest Aboriginal and fine arts galleries, **Hogarth Gallery** (7 Walker Lane, open 11am to 6pm, Tuesday through Saturday).

Paddington also houses several art and antique shops. **Woollahra Galleries** (160 Oxford Street) is one of Sydney's more popular antique centers with over 50 antique shops. Along William Street you will find a few small but good quality Asian antique shops such as **Raymond Victoria Tregaskis** (43 William Street) and **David Ho** (39 William Street). If you explore Hargrave, Glenmore, Paddington, Sutherland, and Garner streets, you will come to such art and antique shops as **House of Desks** (120 Hargrave Street), **The Country Trader** (2 Glenmore Road), **Joan Bowers Antiques** (2 Paddington Street), **Galerie Anne Gregory** (40 Garner Street), **The Bloomfield Galleries** (118 Sutherland Street), and **Christopher Day** (corner of Paddington and Elizabeth streets). If you are in Sydney on a weekend and your shopping interests include arts, crafts, clothing, and secondhand markets, be sure to stop by **Paddington Market** (Uniting Church yard, 380-390 Oxford Road) to browse through the many stalls selling a wide variety of arts, crafts, clothes, and jewelry. The market opens at 8am on both Saturday and Sunday. It is this market that breathes a great deal of life into the shops lining the streets of Paddington and Woollahra.

The North Shore--Neutral Bay and Mosman

Few tourists ever venture north across the Sydney Harbour Bridge to explore additional shopping opportunities. A major shopping area you should consider, time permitting, is the North Shore area between Neutral Bay and Mosman along Military Road. Numerous art, antique, home decorative, clothing, and jewelry stores as well as ethnic restaurants line both sides of this road. The majority of shops are concentrated at the east end of Military Road near the intersection of Spit Road in Mosman. Here you will find the **Portobello Antique Arcade** (742 Military Road) with over 20 antique stalls selling jewelry, furniture, glass, ceramics, and a host of bric-a-brac. For a good selection of top quality Australian paintings, stop at **Boronia Art Gallery** (2nd floor, 768 Military Road). A small antique, art, and gift shop specializing in country themes is **Country House of Mosman** (Shop 3, 713 Military Road on the corner of Gouldsburg Street). For a nice selection of Asian home decorative items, be sure to visit **Private Life** (762 Military Road). You'll also find a branch of **Designer Savings** here as well as several trendy fashion and footwear shops. The best thing to do is to spend an hour or two just browsing up and down both sides of Military Road.

Manly

Manly, a popular seaside town, is approximately 10

minutes north of Mosman by car. If you are already in Neutral Bay and Mosman, you may want to go a little further on to Manly. Shopping opportunities here are limited to the typical tourist kitsch found at beachside resorts -- T-shirts, souvenirs, and beachwear. However, if you are looking for unique arts and crafts, we highly recommend one shop in Manly -- **Ocean Front Gallery** (Manly Beach Plaza, Ground Floor, 4/49 North Steyne) -- for its fine collection of quality ceramics, pottery, and paintings. Manly also has a popular beach front arts and crafts market -- **The Manly Arts and Crafts Market** -- Saturday afternoon and all day Sunday.

Department Stores

If you are in the market for an upscale department store selling every conceivable Australian and imported item, you're in luck. Sydney's two major department stores -- **David Jones** and **Grace Brothers** -- are located in the heart of the city, along George, Market, Castlereagh, and Elizabeth streets. Both are connected to Centrepoint by walkways; Grace Brothers is also connected to the Queen Victoria Building by an underground walkway at the corner of George and King streets.

Grace Brothers is bounded by George and Market streets as well as the Strand Arcade and the Pitt Street Mall. This massive store sells everything from ladies fashion to housewares.

David Jones, Sydney's version of Harrod's, has two stores, both connected to Centrepoint at Market Street. Beautifully appointed, their two stores are Sydney's premier stores for clothes, jewelry, and home furnishings. Don't miss the popular food centers at both Grace Brothers and David Jones.

Weekend Markets

You will find several weekend markets in the Sydney metropolitan area selling everything from fresh fruits, vegetables, flowers, and junk to quality arts and crafts. Most of these markets are open from 8am to 5pm Saturday and Sunday. The three most interesting weekend markets are Paddington Market, Paddy's Market, and Manly Arts and Crafts Market.

Paddington Market, located at the Uniting Church of Australia yard at 380-390 Oxford Street, is one of Australia's largest outdoor arts and crafts markets. Depending on the weekend, you may find up to 200 vendor stalls selling clothes, jewelry, pottery, paintings, toys, handbags, records, cassettes, candles, and plants. On a beautiful day this can be a fun place to browse for arts and crafts, people watch, and explore the shops in the Paddington and Woollahra areas. Saturday morning is the best time to visit Paddington Market.

Paddy's Market is a popular weekend flea market. Relocated in 1988 from its Haymarket location to the Harold Park Raceway on Ross Street in Glebe, Paddy's Market offers a mixture of fresh produce and an assortment of arts, crafts, and bric-a-brac. Paddy's Market offers free bus service on the half hour (8am to 2pm) from Circular Quay (in front of the Custom House) and the Railway Square (bus stop at George Street).

The **Manly Arts and Crafts Market** is a fun weekend market held along the pleasant beach walkway in Manly, just north of Mosman on the North Shore via Military and Spit roads. This market is open Saturday afternoon and all day Sunday as well as public holidays. You may want to rent a car on a Sunday to visit this market for an hour or two and then proceed further north to explore some of Sydney's beautiful beaches. Alternatively, you may wish to visit the shops along Military Road in Mosman on a Saturday morning and then proceed to Manly and nearby beach towns in the afternoon.

Hotel Shopping Arcades

Hotel shopping arcades in Sydney tend to be small by most standards. None are as well developed and elegant, for instance, as the Hyatt on Collins or Collins Place, in Melbourne. Most deluxe hotels will have a few shops selling jewelry, fashion clothes, and souvenirs.

The four largest hotel shopping arcades are found at the Sheraton Wentworth, Regent of Sydney, Inter-continental, and Hilton International -- all located in the center of the city within easy walking distance of most shopping centers, department shorts, and shops. The **Sheraton Wentworth** (61-101 Phillip Street, Tel. 230-0700) has the best of the hotel shopping Arcades. Consisting of two levels with 10 shops, the shops here sell excellent quality jewelry, clothes, Australiana, and souvenirs.

The **Regent of Sydney** (199 George Street, Tel. 238-0000) has a small shopping arcade. Two of Sydney's best shops are located in this arcade: **Percy Marks** for exquisitely designed jewelry and opals, and **Adrienne & The Misses Bonney** for elegant woolen nightwear, lingerie, and children's clothing, toys, and gifts.

The **Inter-continental** (177 Macquarie Street, Tel. 230-0200), Sydney's most attractive hotel and rated by many travelers as Australia's best, also has a small shopping arcade with some nice shops offering clothes, jewelry, and gift items.

The **Hilton International** (259 Pitt Street, Tel. 266-0610), located directly across the street from the Queen Victoria Building, is attached to the Royal Arcade. Here you will find several shops selling clothing, jewelry, antiques, foods, and Alaskan furs. If you enjoy antiques, stop at **Bortignons Antique** (#612 Royal Arcade) to browse through their nice selections.

ENJOYING YOUR STAY

Sydney is a five-star city with hotels and restaurants galore and with prices to match those of some of the most expensive cities in the world. Compared to many other cities you may visit, do not expect to get top quality for your dollar in Sydney's hotels. They are overpriced due to the general shortage of rooms and the high cost of labor. Sydney's **best hotels** are the the Inter-continental, Regent of Sydney, Sheraton-Wentworth, and the Hilton International which also house Sydney's major hotel shopping arcades. Expect to pay A$200 and up for a double at these hotels. All of these hotels are centrally located in downtown Sydney. Medium-priced hotels are the Old Sydney Inn, The Russell, Hyde Park Plaza, The York, Wynyard Travelodge, and Gazebo Ramada. Budget-priced hotels -- under A$80 a day -- include the Canberra Oriental, Gresham, Sydney Tourist Hotel, and the Texas Tavern.

Some of the best restaurants in Sydney include the Imperial Peking Harbourside Restaurant (Tel. 27-7073), Shanghai Village (65 Dixon Street), Fortuna Court (Tel. 438-4604), and Bangkok (Tel. 33-4804) for Oriental food; La Cafe Nouveau (Tel. 33-3377), Kables (Tel. 238-0000), Bayswater Brasserie (Tle. 357-2749), Pegrum's (Tel. 357-4776), Kinsela's (Tel. 331-3100), Chanterelle (Tel. 660-6050), and Manor House (Tel. 810-4914) for Continental and French cuisine; Beppi's (Tel. 357-4558), Darcy's (Tel. 32-4512), Mario's (Tel. 331-4945), and Arriverderci (Tel. 356-6809) for Italian dishes; Balkan II (Tel. 331-7670) and Claude's (Tel. 331-2325) for steaks; and Doyle's on the Beach (Tel. 337-2007), Doyle's on the Wharf (Tel. 337-1572), Waterfront Restaurant (Tel. 27-3666), and Sails (Tel. 920-5998) for seafood. You will find numerous ethnic restaurants (Greek, Lebanese, Indian) as well as most international fast food chains. For some of the best and least expensive food, try the take-away food stalls that are found throughout the city. Some of the best are found at the Lower Level of the Queen Victoria Building.

Sydney has a great deal to offer visitors from seeing historical sites to attending lively shows. You can literally spend two weeks just trying to cover all the major tourist sites.

One of the best approaches to seeing the highlights of Sydney is to purchase a **"Sydney Explorer" bus pass.** This pass enables you to see all the major sites in Sydney at your own leisurely pace. Expect to spend a full day using this pass. The big red Sydney Explorer buses make 20 stops along an 18 kilometer route around Sydney. The buses operate from 9:30am to 5pm every day. You can get off at any of the well-marked stops to visit major sites in Sydney and get on again whenever you are ready to continue on to another stop. The buses stop at the Sydney Harbour, Sydney Opera House, Royal Botanic Gardens, Parliament House, Mrs. Macquarie's Chair, Art Gallery of New South Wales, Kings Cross, Macleay Street, Elizabeth Bay House, Potts Point, The Australian Museum, Central Railway, Powerhouse Museum/Chinatown, Darling Harbour, Queen Victoria Building, Wynyard, The Historic Rocks, Village Green, Pier One, and The Rocks Visitors Center.

Within Sydney, the most popular sites tend to be concentrated in and around The City. Sydney's two major symbols -- the **Sydney Opera House** and the **Sydney Harbour Bridge** -- are located at the northern end of The City at Bennelong Point, Circular Quay, and The Rocks. The Sydney Opera House is well worth a tour, although you may be disappointed with the interior of this building given its majestic exterior overlooking the harbor. The "Evening at the Opera House", a packaged tour which includes dinner at the the Bennelong Restaurant, a guided tour of the Sydney Opera House, and a show, is worth doing during your stay in Sydney. Be sure to make reservations well ahead of your planned visit to Sydney since this popular package tends to be sold out in advance. In the U.S. and Canada, call 1-800-336-9797; in Japan and Europe, book through Qantas if you are using this airline; in New Zealand, call (09) 799650; and in Australia, call (02) 250-7197 and (02) 250-7447, or write to The Tourism Marketing Section, Sydney Opera House, GPO Box 4274, Sydney 2001. If you arrive early enough, you can shop for Aboriginal arts and crafts at the lovely **Aboriginal Artists Gallery** on the Upper Concourse Level of the Sydney Opera House.

Nearby the Sydney Opera House, **The Rocks** is well worth visiting for its historical significance in addition to its excellent shops and restaurants. Stop at the **Visitors Centre** at 100 George Street to get a walking map of the area as well as view a movie and review the history of the area. Near the Centre you can visit **Cadmans Cottage, Geological and Mining Museum**, and **Garrison Church** as well as get a beautiful view of Circular Quay, the Sydney Opera House, the Sydney Harbour Bridge, and the harbor.

While in The Rocks, walk up to the southeast pylon of the **Sydney Harbour Bridge**. The 200 steps will take you through an interesting museum depicting the building of the bridge and offer you one of the best panoramic views of the harbor, including the Sydney Opera House and Circular Quay.

You will also want to take a **harbor tour**. Go directly to Circular Quay, next to The Rocks, where you can purchase a ticket for one of several harbor cruises that departs every hour. The most popular cruises are the 1 1/4 to full day tours operated by Captain Cook Cruises. Two hours on the harbor is probably sufficient to see all the major sights.

For the most panoramic view of Sydney, 304.8 meters above Sydney, you should visit the **Sydney Tower** at Centrepoint Shopping Centre on Castlereagh and Pitt streets. The tower is reputed to be the tallest structure in the Southern Hemisphere. Open 7 days and nights a week, you will get spectacular views of Sydney from either the oberservation level or from the Tower Restaurant. Make restaurant reservations (Tel. 223-3722) for lunch or dinner at the Tower Restaurant Reception desk on the Gallery Level where you also enter the elevator to take you to the top.

If you enjoy good museums, Sydney has three you should visit. The **Australian Museum** (6 College Street) is an excellent natural history museum. It has very good displays of Aboriginal and Pacific Island cultures and arts. The Museum Shop is also worth visiting for shoppin purposes. The **Power House Museum** located behind Marketplace at Harbourside, is part of the Museum of Applied Arts and Sciences with displays of technological change in Australia (the first locomotives, monoplanes, and cars manufactured in Australia). The **Art Gallery of New South Wales**, behind the State Library on Art Gallery Road, The Domain, has permanent collections of Australian and European art as well as special international art exhibits.

Other popular sites to visit during your stay in Sydney include:

- Royal Botanic Gardens
- Taronga Park Zoo

- Government House
- Customs House
- The Domain
- Fort Denison
- St. James Church
- Sydney Observatory
- Sydney Town Hall
- Vaucluse House

For evening entertainment, you have numerous choices from excellent theater and opera at the Sydney Opera House and several other theaters in the city to pub crawling, dining, and sleezy shows found in the Kings Cross area (at the intersection of Kings Cross Road and Victoria Street). For an evening of dining to light and farcical Australian entertainment, the Jolly Swagman Show at the Argle Travern (18 Argyle Street) is a good choice (Tel. 27-7782 for reservations).

If time permits, you may want to take day or overnight trips to several places outside Sydney. If you enjoy beaches and water sports, head for the famous **Bondi** beach, 25 kilometers to the southeast of the city. **Manly, 25** kilometers northeast of the city, is another beach resort with fine hotels, restaurants, and a pedestrian shopping mall.

Other popular areas to visit outside Sydney include:

- Old Sydney Town
- Hawkesbury River
- Blue Mountains
- Hunter Valley vineyards
- Koala Park
- Royal National Park
- Snowy Mountains
- Canberra, the national capital

You can rent a car to drive to all of these places or take a guided tour with one of many tour companies operating from Sydney. For more information on these and other sites, as well as to book tours, contact the tourist information desks at the **Travel Centre of New South Wales** (corner of Pitt and Spring streets, Tel. 231-4444), the **Sydney Convention and Visitor's Bureau** (100 Market Street, Tel. 235-2424), or the **Sydney Information Centre**, a kiosk at Martin's Place (intersection of Castlereagh and Elizabeth streets).

Chapter Seven

MELBOURNE

Melbourne is Australia's best attempt to capture the old world elegance, charm, and culture of Europe. Frequently compared to Boston, Philadelphia, and Edinburgh but regularly contrasted with Sydney, Melbourne is a city of tree-lined boulevards, beautiful parks and gardens, Victorian architecture, fashionable shops, charming street cars, and fine ethnic restaurants. One of Australia's truly unique cities, Melbourne is a melting pot of European ethnic and cultural groups as well as a center of political and financial influence in direct competition with the bolder and brasher Sydney.

Best of all, Melbourne is a shopper's paradise for fashion, arts, antiques, and crafts. You've come to the right city if you want to do some serious, yet fun, shopping in some of Australia's best shopping streets, arcades, department stores, neighborhoods, markets, and craft centers. You should leave this city with a very different view of the "real Australia", a view partially shaped by Melbourne's many shopping discoveries.

GETTING TO KNOW YOU

Melbourne has a certain character, class, and charm largely absent in other Australian cities. Indeed, if Sydney is Australia's Los Angeles, then Melbourne is its London. Compared to its fast-paced arch rival, Sydney, Melbourne is more laid-back and sedate. Whereas Sydney is bold, brash, and innovative, Melbourne is more reserved, traditional, and conservative. Above all, Melbourne projects a refined and cultured image that challenges the more popular stereotype of a male dominated Australia disproportionately populated by crude, vulgar, uncultured, beer-drinking, beach-bumming, Crocodile Dundee cowboys.

Many people fall in love with this city of over 3 million people. It may not have Sydney's fabulous weather nor the symbolism of the uniquely designed Opera House perched on a visually appealing harbor, but it has a compelling style that puts this city in a class of its own. If you take a tram, stroll its wide tree-lined boulevards and parks, attend a play or opera, visit its many museums and buildings, dine its ethnic restaurants, and shop in its fashionable department stores and shops, you will quickly learn why so many Australians love to call Melbourne their home.

If you liked shopping in Sydney, you may enjoy it even more in Melbourne. This is Australia's fashion capital, where the country's leading designers and factories turn out the latest in fashion clothes and accessories. It's the city that boasts the country's largest (Myer) and most elegant (Georges) department stores and the finest collection of designer boutiques (Shop of Shops and Toorak Road). It's where you can spend thousands of dollars on haute couture (Toorak Village) or save up to 70 percent on brand names by shopping in Australia's largest concentration of factory outlets (metro area). It's where you will find Australia's best collection of Asian art and antique shops (Chapel and High streets), its finest arts and craft shop (Crafts Shop in the Meat Market Craft Centre), and its largest and most fascinating open-air market (Queen Victoria Market).

Spend four days shopping in Melbourne and you'll be thoroughly exhausted but forever pleased with your shopping experience. Spend two weeks shopping in Melbourne and you will learn a great deal about Australia's many highly talented designers, artists, and craftspeople. You will have a unique and fascinating travel adventure known to few people who visit Australia.

This is not a city of large shopping arcades or trendy centers such as Sydney's Queen Victoria Building, Strand Arcade, Centrepoint, or Marketplace. In Melbourne the

best shopping is found in the small shops that line the main streets (Toorak, Chapel, High) of suburban Toorak, Armadale, South Yarra, Prahran, and Malvern; in the central commercial district along Collins and Bourke streets; and in the numerous shops and small arcades that feed into or face the Bourke Street Pedestrian Mall. Stroll along these streets and arcades and you will quickly discover Melbourne's -- and Australia's -- many shopping delights.

Walk through the elegant department stores and shopping arcades on Collins and Bourke streets, take a tram to the upmarket suburbs of Toorak and Armadale, and visit the numerous shops that front on the main streets (Toorak, Chapel, High) and in shopping centers (Toorak Village and The Jam Factory) and you will experience some of the best quality shopping found anywhere in Australia.

THE STREETS OF MELBOURNE

Melbourne is a large sprawling metropolis with a high-rise central business district situated next to the charming Yarra River and with suburbs stretching in all directions. In addition to the central business district, you will find major shopping opportunities south and east of the central business district in the upmarket suburbs of Toorak, Armadale, South Yarra, Prahran, Richmond, Brighton, and St. Kilda.

Melbourne is a relatively easy and pleasant city to get around in. The central business district is laid out in a grid plan with major shops and shopping arcades located along Bourke and Collins streets and within easy walking distance of each other. You'll want to put on a good pair of walking shoes to spend a day just walking up and down these streets to explore the many department stores, shopping arcades, and shops that define this area as one of Australia's major shopping areas.

Several of Melbourne's suburbs, especially Toorak and Armadale, are "must" stops for serious shoppers. Located a few kilometers to the southeast of the central business district, they are best reached by tram, bus, or taxi. The most pleasant and inexpensive way to get to these suburbs is to take the tram (Nos. 6 or 9) from Swanston Street, between Bourke and Collins streets, in the central business district. The $.75 tram ride takes only 10 minutes and puts you in the heart of these up-market suburbs. Once there, you can easily spend another day walking the streets to discover numerous shops and shopping arcades along Toorak Road and Chapel and High streets. Since these are long streets, be sure to wear a good pair of walking shoes

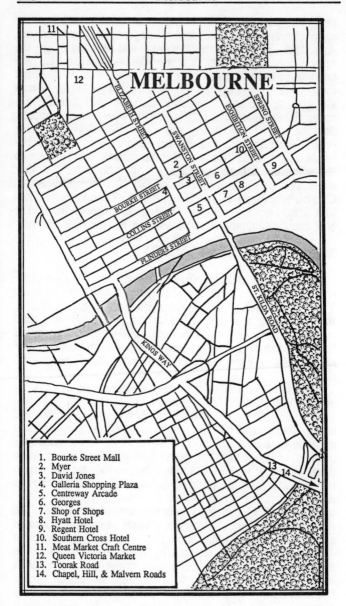

1. Bourke Street Mall
2. Myer
3. David Jones
4. Galleria Shopping Plaza
5. Centreway Arcade
6. Georges
7. Shop of Shops
8. Hyatt Hotel
9. Regent Hotel
10. Southern Cross Hotel
11. Meat Market Craft Centre
12. Queen Victoria Market
13. Toorak Road
14. Chapel, Hill, & Malvern Roads

for a full day of walking.

One other major shopping area is located just to the north of the central business district at the corner of Queen and Victoria streets (Queen Victoria Market) and the corner of Blackwood and Courtney streets (Meat Market Craft Centre). While within 30-minute walking distance from the central business district, we recommend taking a tram from Elizabeth Street or a taxi to reach these areas.

Melbourne's wide streets, tree-lined boulevards, green parks, Yarra River, Victorian architecture, and trams make it an inviting city for most visitors. Melbourne boasts some attractive architecture -- more than any other Australian city -- but contrary to what others may write, this city is not an architectural showpiece. We find Melbourne suffering from large doses of the same dullness and lack of architectural ingenuity so commonly found throughout Australia. It's a quaint, but by no means beautiful, city with character.

GETTING ORIENTED

You will find plenty of resources to help orient you to Melbourne. Most tourist literature provides a general map of the central business district -- the area with the most shops. But this is not necessarily the best area for quality shopping. You will find plenty of bookstores in and around Bourke Street which stock maps of the city. Similar to the maps found in the tourist literature, most of these maps cover the central business district and a few outlying suburbs. Unfortunately, all of these maps cut off the eastern section of Melbourne's two most important shopping suburbs -- Toorak Road (Toorak Village area) and High Street (Armadale). To get detailed coverage of these areas, one must purchase a copy of a thick street atlas used by taxi drivers and local residents -- an expensive and cumbersome publication. Hopefully, Melbourne's tourism specialists will improve on this poor mapping situation in the near future so serious shoppers will have better guidance in reaching these key suburban shopping areas.

You will find a few guidebooks to Melbourne in the local bookstore. However, we found none to be useful for shopping purposes. Most guides cover the usual history, sightseeing attractions, hotels, restaurants, and entertainment you will find in much of the free literature provided by local businesses and available through the **Melbourne Tourism Authority** (50 Collins Street, Tel. 652-2288) and the **Victorian Tourism Commission** (230 Collins Street, Tel. 602-9444).

There is one exception, a useful shopping directory not found in most bookstores. If you are interested in shopping in Melbourne's factory outlets, be sure to get a copy of Pamm Durkin's latest edition of the popular and indispensable *Pamm's Guide to Discount Melbourne*. This book identifies more than 400 of Melbourne's factory outlets by name, address, telephone number, hours of operation and products as well as includes summaries of the best buys in each outlet and money saving coupons. While not presently available in major bookstores, you will find this book in local 7-Eleven stores and in many factory outlet shops. You can also order the book directly from the publisher (send US$11.95 postpaid) or write, fax, or call for information on how to get the book:

> PAMM'S SHOPPING TOURS
> P.O. Box 4900
> Melbourne, Victoria 3001
> Australia
> Tel. (03) 592-6911
> Fax (03) 696-1984

Another useful, but less focused, publication outlines discount buying in Melbourne: *Bargain Shoppers' Guide to Melbourne*. Widely available in major bookstores, this publication is most appropriate for local residents who want to know where to get the best bargains on local household goods, furniture, second hand items, beauty care, pets, gardening supplies, office furniture, as well as items of interest to tourists, such as clothes, Australiana, and crafts. You may find both books useful, but *Pamm's Guide to Discount Melbourne* is our first choice for factory outlet shopping.

Be sure to pick up free tourist literature at the airport, your hotel, and the Victorian Tourist Commission information office at 230 Collins Streets (Tel. 602-9444). You'll find such useful booklets as *Hello Melbourne*, *Discover Melbourne*, *Melbourne Your Gateway*, *Melbourne: The Taxi Drivers Guide*, and *This Week in Melbourne* which include maps, ads, and information on what to do and where to go in Melbourne. A glossy magazine published by the Melbourne Tourist Authority -- *Melburnian* --provides useful information on all aspects of visiting Melbourne, from up-coming events to shopping. You will find numerous brochures on tours, shops, and restaurants at the Victorian Tourist Commission information office.

SHOPPING SERVICES

Equipped with a good map, this book, walking shoes, and dogged persistence, you can eaily do most shopping in and around Melbourne on your own. Hop on a tram and you're on your way to a new shopping area which may be even more rewarding than the last one. But you also may want to consider one of several specialized shopping services that offer group and individualized tours to the major shops and factory outlets in the metropolitan Melbourne area.

The premier shopping service in Melbourne is **Pamm's Shopping Tours** (P.O. Box 38, Brighton North 3186, Tel. 591-6911 or 592-6555). Pamm Durkin, the author of the best selling *Pamm's Guide to Discount Melbourne*, offers an excellent shopping tour which includes visiting six or seven of Melbourne's best factory outlet stores offering clothes, footwear, leather, household goods, toys, and crafts. The items you shop for on Pamm's tours are good quality, name brand samples, seconds, and discontinued stock at savings from 30 to 70 percent. Tours can be arranged during the weekday, weeknight, or on Saturdays. However, it's best to join the weekday tour simply because you will have a chance to visit more factory outlets which are open during the day; many are closed at night. The tour costs only A$27 dollars, which includes all transportation, hotel pick-up, and lunch at Caesars, a very nice Italian-European restaurant in the suburb of Fitzroy. We highly recommend this tour for anyone visiting Melbourne with the yearn for factory outlet shopping. It's inexpensive, well organized, and fun. Not only will you visit key factory outlets you could not easily do on your own, the price of this tour also includes lunch. Participants in past tours have been delighted with the tour service and their factory outlet purchases. In other words, you get top value for your dollar.

Other groups operate different types of shopping tours. **Friends in Town** (576 St. Kilda Road, Tel. 51-8877), for example, provides a personalized shopping service for those interested in shopping in Melbourne's up-market boutiques. **Jackie's Tours** (430 Rathdowne Street, Carlton, Tel. 347-5655) and **Rosalind's Shopping Tours** (Suite 1-4, 401 St. Kilda Road, Tel. 267-1355) focus on factory outlet shopping. **Down Under Shopping Tours** (235 Richardson Street, Middle Park, Tel. 690-4773) and **Shopping Tours Unlimited Australia** (11 Merton Street, Caulfield 3161, Tel. 527-4284) specialize in different types of shopping -- from antiques to furs. You also may find other newly formed shopping groups offering similar ser-

vices.   Check the Yellow Pages of the local telephone
directory as well as the information kiosks at the Victorian
Tourism Commission for brochures on these and other
shopping tours.

WHAT TO BUY

Melbourne is a shopper's paradise for all types of
products.   Shops, shopping arcades, and factory outlets
bulge with the latest Australian-produced and imported
goods.   Your choices range from high fashion and trendy
clothes to fine Aboriginal arts and crafts to great selections
of handcrafted items from all over Australia and the world.
This is a cosmopolitan city which clearly displays its
worldliness in its many city and suburban shops.

Fashion Clothes and Accessories

Melbourne is Australia's fashion center. Here, you find
Australia's leading men's and women's clothes designers as
well as struggling young designers intent on breaking into
the highly competitive and glamorous world of Australian
fashion.   The exciting world of fashion in Melbourne is
very much a cottage industry of creative artists-designers.
Such noted designers and companies as John Cavill, Perri
Cutten, Lou Wiseman, Adele Palmer, Angela Padula,
Anthea Crawford, Teena Varigos, Shelley A. Neill, David
Medwin, Design on Collins, Squire Sport, Dare'e, Feitel,
Stunning, and Bell, Book, and Candle are based in Melbourne. Many of their seasonal designs and collections set
the pace for high fashion and trendy clothes in hundreds of
boutiques and department stores throughout Australia. You
can visit their boutiques in downtown and suburban Melbourne.   While many of the fabrics are imported from
Europe, the finished garments are designed, cut, and as-
sembled in the many workshops of South Yarra where
several top designers also have their own boutiques.
The single best place to shop for top quality Australian
fashion clothes -- classic, trendy, chic, and expensive -- is
The Shop of Shops at 171 Collins Street in the central
business district. Formerly the ultra-exclusive but failed
Figgins Diorama, now The Shop of Shops is where many
of Melbourne's fashion conscious shoppers go.   This
shopping center is filled with exclusive boutiques of major
Australian designers. **Lou Wiseman**, for example, stocks
the latest Lou Wiseman designed clothes for women as
well as the Sydney-based Simona fashion line. **Stunning**
offers simply stunning evening gowns and cocktail dresses
that are one of the most dynamic additions to today's

Australian fashion scene. Sydney-based **Lizzie Collins, Carla Zampatti**, and **Sandra Layt** have branch boutiques here as well as the famous Canberra-based **Shephards**, which also has boutiques in the United States. For beautiful and exclusive knitwear (suits and dresses) designed to project a soft feminine image, be sure to stop at **Angela Padula**, Australia's award-winning designer and favorite of many visitors to Australia. **Bell, Book, and Candle** boutique, which also has a shop at 2 Avoca Street in South Yarra, offers very unique, trendy designs in sportswear and evening dresses. You can even find a **Diane Freis** shop here with its colorful flowing dresses from famous Hong Kong-based designer Diane Freis. For some of the finest in menswear, visit **L'homme**; its main shop is located at 87 Toorak Road, South Yarra.

While The Shop of Shops is Melbourne's designer fashion center, **Toorak Road** in suburban South Yarra and Toorak is Melbourne's fashion street. Here you will find numerous up-market boutiques lining both sides of the road from Punt Road -- look for the 7-Eleven store on the corner -- to Toorak Village. Proceeding west to east along Toorak Road at the intersection of Punt Road, we especially like the quality and selections at **Style, MN Boutique, Migi, Mazzaire, Staggers, Trent Nathan, Trevor West, Fayaz, L'homme, Umano, Rodeo Drive, Jo Bond, Sportempo, Ipanema Boutique**, and **Prue Acton**. Further east at Toorak Village, **Marino and Scott** and **Henry Bucks** offer excellent quality men's clothes. For something different in clothes, especially wedding apparel with 1950s and art themes, stop at the **Gallery of Wearable Art** (315 Toorak Road). If you want a truly unique outfit, using the finest fabrics and individual designs for women, visit the fine couture **Jot** at 475 Toorak Road (Toorak Village) and **Victoria of Balencia** on the corner of Toorak Road and Canterbury.

While the shops on **Chapel Hill** and **High Street** in the suburbs of Prahran and Armadale primarily offer arts, antiques, and ethnic foods, you will find a few nice fashion stores in this area. For example, in Armadale you will find **Top Drawer** at 1039 High Street, for Anne Lewin designer lingerie, and **Centro Fashions**, for a nice selection of conservative-styled German dresses. **The Jam Factory** on Chapel Street in Prahran has a trendy branch of **Georges Department Store**, which carries Weiss and Weiss 'Pringle' labels, as well as branches of **R. M. Williams** and **Morrisons of Australia** for menswear, a **Cuggi** for knitwear, and a few other trendy boutiques. Further north, where Chapel Street becomes Church Street, you will come to the suburb of **Richmond**. This area, especially along Bridge Street, has stores and factory outlets housing many of Australia's young designers. Other suburban areas with shops offering fashion clothes are located along **Lygon Street** (Carlton), **Burke Road** (Camberwell), and **Puckle Street** (Moonee Ponds).

Other fashion and clothes shops are found in the two major department stores on Bourke Street Pedestrian Mall - **David Jones** and **Myer**. David Jones actually has two stores, one across the street from the other. The **David Jones** store next to **Myer** only carries womenswear whereas the other branch across the street specializes in menswear. The **Myer** department store, Bourke Street Building, has women's clothes and accessories on Levels B, G, 1, 2, and 3 and men's wear and accessories on Level 4. You will also find children's clothes and accessories on Level 5. Both the **David Jones** and **Myer** department stores carry fashion clothes created by Australia's leading designers. For high fashion clothes, be sure to visit the exclusive Australian designer boutique on Level 2 of Myer Department Store, Bourke Street Building. The exclusive **Georges** department store at 162 Collins carries some of the finest imported women's clothes and accessories in all of Australia.

You will also discover other menswear and womenswear shops in and around the shopping arcades along Bourke, Collins, and Swanston streets as well as in the shopping arcades at the Hyatt Hotel (Collins Street) and Southern Cross Hotel (Exhibition Street). The **Galleria Shopping Plaza**, for example, at the corner of Bourke and Elizabeth streets, has a **Carla Zampatti** boutique as well as **Jennie** for womenswear and accessories; a **R. M. Williams** for men's leatherwear; and two **Chester's** stores, one for menswear and another for womenswear. Many shops in and around Bourke Street Pedestrian Mall and surrounding shopping arcades, such as those in The Welk, Centrepoint, and the Royal Arcade, carry medium-range, average quality clothes. You will find such chain stores as **Just Jeans** and **Sportsgirl** in this area.

Over on **Collins Street**, across the street from The Shop of Shops, look for the exclusive **Teena Varigos** boutique at 182 Collins Street (also has another store at 67 Toorak Road) with its interesting dressy and evening clothes as well as **Perla Caviglia**, at both 186 Collins Street and 45 Collins Street (Shop 5, Collins Place), for nice blouses and dresses. Further west on Collins Street, near Swanston and Elizabeth streets, you will find local branches of **Designer Savings, House of Merivale,** and **Rodney Clark** offering sportswear and trendy clothes. Next to The Shop of Shops look for **Laura Ashley** and **Bruno Magli** for fine quality imported clothes and shoes. Further east on Collins Street is the **Hyatt on Collins,** Melbourne's most exclusive shopping arcade attached to the Hyatt Hotel. Here, you will find several men's and women's apparel shops selling excellent quality clothes and accessories: **Ipanema, John J. Moore, Mark Muir, Miss Louise, Dorith Unger, Raphael, Triomphe, Adele Chapeaux,** and **Cuggi.** At the Southern Cross Hotel shopping Arcade you will find two nice shops primarily selling imported women's clothes and accessories: **Raphael** and **La Donna.**

Factory outlets offering designer label clothes and accessories are scattered throughout the Melbourne metropolitan area. For example, you can buy samples and seconds of such well-known designer labels as Adele Palmer, Prue Acton, Athea Crawford, and Purri Cutton for nearly half price at the outlets on **Bridge Road** in Richmond. Look for the colorful knitwear of Ken Done at the **Rob Paynter** outlet on Errol Street (near the Meat Market Craft Centre and Queen Victoria Market in North Melbourne). And buy some fabulous trendy and dressy clothes by some of Melbourne's innovative young designers at **Cottage Blossum** on 2 Chapel Street (St. Kilda East). Here, one-of-a-kind $300 samples go for $79! Numerous factory outlets in the Moorabbin and Cheltenham areas stock samples and seconds of good quality Australian designed clothes. The book, *Pamm's Guide to Discount Melbourne,* identifies more than 400 factory outlets, and "Pamm's Tours" also visits several of the best outlets.

Furs and Leather

Melbourne also is Australia's center for elegant furs. Run by several famous Jewish-Greek furrier families who have been in the trade for decades, Melbourne's fur shops offer selections of nicely tailored mink, fox, and opossum coats and jackets. While most of the pelts are imported from Russia, China, Canada, and the United States and then cut and tailored in Melbourne, a few of the furs, such as fox and opossum, come from Australia and New Zealand.

You may find Melbourne's fur selections limited in comparison to what you may find back home. Nonetheless, you may get lucky and find some unique furs and styles not available elsewhere. Indeed, some of the styling here is better than what we find in Hong Kong and Korea. Prices, however, vary; they may or may not be to your advantage.

Most furriers are located in downtown shopping arcades. Several of these also carry leather coats, jackets, and accessories. **Feitel Furs,** one of Melbourne's most stylish furriers, is located on the First Level of **The Shop of Shops** at 171 Collins Street. **James Loustas** is found on the Ground Level (Shop 19) of **Collins Place** at 45 Collins Street. **S. R. McClean** has a small shop at 48 Royal Arcade, just off the Bourke Street Mall and Swanston Street. Also try **Ermina** in the Centreway Arcade (259-263 Collins Street) for furs and leather.

For leather goods, stop at **Eugenes** (148 Swanston Street) and **Morrisons of Australia** (462 Chapel Street, South Yarra). **Leather Cargo** (251 Lonsdale Street) offers high fashion leather jackets, trousers, and shirts. **Eugene of Collins Street** (143 Collins Street) sells furs, leather, and sheepskin goods as well as imported men's shoes, handbags, and accessories. **Siricco House of Leather** (250 Elizabeth Street, 92 Bourke Street, 178 Collins Street, The Jam Factory at 500 Chapel Street in South Yarra, and 189 Toorak Road in South Yarra) for a wide range of Australian and imported leather garments and accessories.

Jewelry

Melbourne has several jewelry stores offering the usual selection of jewelry with special emphasis on set and unset Australian opals. You will find a few jewelers offering fine craft, contemporary, and antique jewelry. **Makers Mark,** for example, at 85 Collins Street, produces some of Australia's most unique silver and gold jewelry with elegant arts and crafts themes. Look for their special displays at the front of their store. Other fine craft jewelry is found at the award-winning **Crafts Shop** at the Meat Market Craft Centre on the corner of Courtney and Blackwood streets in North Melbourne.

For top quality jewelry, **Percy Marks** in the exclusive Georges department store at 162 Collins Street has excellent quality opal jewelry, Argyle diamonds, and other precious stones in beautifully crafted settings. **Hardy Brothers** (338 Collins Street) has top quality jewelry, porcelain, and glassware as well as antique jewelry and silverware. Also, look at the selections and custom jewelry work being done at **MJS** (5th floor, 343 Little Collins Street) and **Andrew Cody** (3rd floor, Manchester Unity Building, corner of Collins and Swanston streets). You will also find local branches of **Proud** and **Edment** jewelers.

A nice shop selling antique jewelry, porcelain, silverware, and related items, such as uniquely handcrafted candlesticks, is **Schlager** at 308 Little Collins Street (corner of Royal Arcade). You should find some very nice new and antique pieces at the beautiful shop of this well-established Melbourne jeweler.

Opals

Many people claim the opal shops in Melbourne are the best in all of Australia for both quality and price. You'll have to judge these claims for yourself. But one fact we know to be true is that you will find numerous shops throughout Melbourne selling opals. Most of the stores specializing in opals are found along Bourke and Exhibition streets, in and around the Southern Cross Hotel. **Lightening Ridge Opal Mine** at 75 Bourke Street, for example, provides demonstrations of opal cutting as well as presents an interesting video on the Australian opal mining process. They have a large selection of unset opals stones which they routinely discount at 50 percent (less the 30 percent sales tax for duty-free purchases and 20 percent commission normally requested by Japanese tour leaders!). Just around the corner on Exhibition Street you will find three of Melbourne's -- and Australia's -- largest opal dealers: **Darrell James** (110 Exhibition), **Altman & Cherny** (120 Exhibition Street), and **Gemtec Opals** (7th floor, 124 Exhibition Street).

Other shops selling opals are found in Melbourne's major hotel shopping arcades: **Regent Jewellers** and **Paragon Jewellers** (Collins Place, Regent Hotel, 35 Collins Street), **Hilton Jewellers** (Melbourne Hilton Hotel, Wellington Parade, East Melbourne), **Master Jewellers** (Collins Chase-Hyatt Hotel, 123 Collins Street), **Melbourne Opal Centre** (Lower Plaza, Southern Cross Hotel, 131 Exhibition Street), **J. R. Johnson** (Lobby, Southern Cross Hotel, 131 Exhibition Street). Additional shops are found along Melbourne's major shopping streets: **Andrew Cody** (3rd floor, 220 Collins Street, Manchester Unity Building), **Opal Cave** (Concourse, Flinders Street Station), **The Opal Den** (17 Howey Place), **Benjamins Jewellry World** (360 Little Collins Street), and **Oplex Opals** (290 Russell Street).

For excellent quality settings, you won't go wrong with the fine opal selections at **Percy Marks** (Georges department store, 162 Collins Street).

Australiana, Gifts, and Souvenirs

Australiana shops abound in the downtown department stores and shopping arcades as well as in the suburban shopping districts. Three shops in particular have good selections of quality souvenirs and curios: **Thingummy-**

bob at 171 Collins Street (The Shop of Shops) and at 58
Ross Street (Toorak Village); **Australiana General Store**
at 1227 High Street, Armadale, and at Collins Place, Re-
gent Hotel; and **Antipodes** at 22 Toorak Road, South
Yarra. Other shops to look for are **Australian Made**
(Swanston Street, Concourse, Flinders Street Station);
Jimmy Smith's Rug and Souvenir Shop (73-75 Victoria
Street); **Australian Spectrum** (126 Franklin Street);
Australian Made Gifts and Souvenirs (Flinders Street
Station); and **The Australian Aspect** (256 Yarra Street,
Warrandyte).

Aboriginal and Tribal Artifacts

Melbourne has a few shops specializing in Aboriginal
and tribal arts and crafts. However, don't expect to find
large selections, top quality, and good prices here. Serious
collectors should go to Alice Springs, Darwin, Cairns, and
Sydney to do their buying.

One of the best shops in Melbourne for Aboriginal arts
and crafts in terms of selections and prices -- 20-40 percent less than most comparable shops in Sydney and Melbourne -- is the Uniting Church's **Aboriginal Handcrafts**
(9th floor, Century Building, 125-133 Swanston Street),
which sells direct from its Aboriginal settlement in central
Australia. You'll find excellent prices here on didgeridoos,
bark paintings, clap sticks, and cassette tapes.

The two **Yarrandoo** shops at Collins Place (45 Collins
Street) and Southern Cross Hotel (131 Exhibition Street)
carry several Aboriginal artifacts along with some good
selections of tribal arts and crafts form Papua New Guinea
as well as tourist-quality Australiana. The Exhibition
Street shop has a larger selection of Papua New Guinea
artifacts than the Collins Street shop.

Both the **Aboriginal Artist Gallery** at 12 Liverpool
Street and the **Tribal Art Gallery** at 103 Finders street
have collections of Aboriginal arts, crafts, books, and
music.

Several Australiana shops, such as **Jimmy Smith's** (73-
75 Victoria Street), also carry some Aboriginal and tribal
arts and crafts.

Australian and Imported Arts and Crafts

Melbourne has a well deserved reputation for producing
excellent quality arts and crafts. These arts and crafts
range from trendy jewelry to fine ceramics. You will find
them in numerous arts and crafts shops in the downtown
and suburban areas as well as in several craft towns out-

side Melbourne.

For one of the best selections of arts and crafts produced in the state of Victoria, be sure to visit the **Meat Market Craft Centre**. This is one of Australia's most unique and innovative centers for promoting the development and appreciation of quality arts and crafts. In addition to offering a series of workshops and exhibits representing over 650 craftspeople throughout Australia (2/3 from the State of Victoria), the Centre houses what is considered by many Australians to be the best arts and crafts store in Australia -- the award-winning **Crafts Shop**. The Crafts Shop sells only the best of Australian pottery, ceramics, leather, basket work, knitwear, craft jewelry, and wood work. Items are nicely displayed, personnel are extremely informative and helpful, and the prices are excellent -- the same items selling for 20-30 percent less than in other shops we visited. The Meat Market Craft Centre also maintains another smaller shop at the airport.

Nearby the Meat Market Craft Centre is the **Queen Victoria Antique Arts and Crafts Centre** at 120 Franklin Street. Claiming to be the largest antique art and craft center in the southern hemisphere, this is a somewhat disappointing area with an assortment of varying quality arts and crafts. The quality here is reported to have declined considerably in the past few years.

You will also find a few arts and crafts shops around the **Queen Victoria Market** at Queen and Victoria Streets. The **Victoria Market Craft Shop** at 83 Victoria Street has a nice selection of country crafts from the states of Victoria and South Australia. You'll also find a leather and sheepskin shop just a few doors from this shop.

Several arts and crafts shops in and around Melbourne also offer good quality Australian arts and crafts. **Australian Trends** (48-50 Bourke Street), for example, has a very nice selection of textile paintings, ceramics, pewter, wood pieces, glasswork, and Aboriginal crafts produced by some of Australia's leading artists and craftsmen. Since they remain open each night until 7pm, this is a convenient place to do your craft shopping. **Craft Link** at 37 Hardware Street offers silks, ceramics, glass, knitwear, textiles, and wood creations crafted by members of The Arts and Craft Society of Victoria.

Look for arts and crafts shops in hotel shopping arcades. **Cache**, for example, at the Hyatt on Collins shopping arcade (Collins Street), has a very nice selection of Australian arts and crafts.

For uniquely crafted metal tableware, be sure to visit **Sheil Abbey** in The Shop of Shops, 171 Collins Street. Don Sheil is producing limited editions of some of the loveliest trays, bowls, and dinnerware we have seen anywhere. Using a special aluminum-based alloy metal he terms "Sheil Silver", his designs are outstanding contributions to the Australian craft industry. He also will do special commissioned pieces. Other shops selling the Don Sheil creations are found in The Jam Factory on Chapel Street in South Yarra, at 21 Carpenter Street in Brighton, Murphy Street in South Yarra, and on High Street in Armadale.

If you are in the market for some unique designs and excellent quality gold and silver crafted jewelry, don't miss **Makers Mark** at 85 Collins Street. They do some of the nicest craft jewelry work we have seen anywhere in Australia. Look for their special exhibits at the front section of their shop.

Further west on Collins Street in the Centreway Arcade at 259-263 Collins Street is a small shop, **Gazelle**, specializing in locally-made as well as imported silver jewelry. We like many of the selections here.

A few shops along Chapel and High Streets offer good selections of Australian and imported arts and crafts. We especially like **Ishka Handcraft** at 409A Chapel Street (Prahran). This shop imports jewelry, pottery, textiles, clothing, and leather goods from over 50 countries. They are particularly strong on Asian arts and crafts. The staff is extremely knowledgeable and enthusiastic about their excellent selections and work. Better yet, they bend over backwards to assist you -- the best service we received anywhere in Australia. Since this shop does no advertising -- just word-of-mouth -- few outsiders know about it. Ishka Handcraft also has four other shops in the Melbourne metropolitan area: 146 High Street (Kew), 541 Riversdale Road (Camberwell), 82 Church Street (Brighton), and 257 Coventry Street (South Melbourne).

Gallery Handmade, a small shop at 467 High Street, has a good selection of quality Australian and Asian arts and crafts. It's one of the few arts and crafts shops found along this High Street which is primarily dominated by antique shops.

If you visit **The Jam Factory** at 500 Chapel Street, you will find a few arts and crafts shops. Nothing of any exceptional distinction here.

And don't forget the weekend craft markets in and around Melbourne. The **St. Kilda Sunday Art Bank**, at Upper Esplanade, St. Kilda, on Sunday from 9am to 6pm, consists of 190 craft stalls selling handcrafted leather, jewelry, pottery, glass, toys, cottage crafts, and woodcrafts. It's also popular for its ethnic foods and pleasant seaside ambiance. The St. Kilda weekend market is located only 5 kilometers south of Melbourne and can be reached by a No. 15 or 16 tram. **Camberwell Market**, Union Street, Camberwell, is open Sunday mornings from 6am to 1:30pm. The **Dingley Village Craft Market** (Marcus Road, Dingley) is located 25 kilometers from Melbourne. It is open the first Sunday of every month from 9am to 2pm.

Several small towns outside Melbourne have craft shops worth visiting. Most are within one or two hours driving distance from the city and make wonderful day trips to discover many unique Victorian arts and crafts. **Mornington Peninsula**, located 50 kilometers south of the city via Nepean Highway, for example, is a center for craft galleries and workshops. Here you will find several shops selling paintings, pottery, ceramics, textiles, leather work, wood work, gold and silver jewelry, and glass. Look for **Portsea Galleries** (3745 Nepean Highway, Sorrento), **The First Settlement Gallery** (141 Ocean Beach Road), **The Grath Gallery** (2843 Nepean Highway, Sorrento), **Manna Gum Pottery Cottage** (Arthurs Seat Road), **Pine Ridge Pottery** (Purves Road), **Post Office Gallery** (Mornington-Flinders Road, Red Hill), **Potters Croft** (141 Red Hill Road, Red Hill), **The Giddy Bullfrog Gallery** (38 Ocean View Avenue, Red Hill), **Periwinkle Potters** (65 Byrnes Road, Shoreham Village), and **Budgery Gunyah Craft Gallery** (3179 Nepean Highway, Sorrento).

Several other arts and crafts centers outside Melbourne are found to the north, east, and west of the city. The **Crafts Council of Victoria** (7 Blackwood Street, North Melbourne, Victoria 3051, Tel. 329-0611), in addition to publishing a directory of arts and crafts shops in Melbourne and its surrounding suburbs, publishes a useful guide to these out-of-town centers, complete with maps, names and addresses, and itineraries for 15 separate trips that will take you to 30 art galleries and 293 craft shops. Indeed, you could easily spend three weeks shopping for arts and crafts outside Melbourne by following these self-directed tours:

- **Day Trips From Melbourne:** 8 galleries and 16 craft shops
- **Princes Highway East:** 2 galleries and 19 craft shops
- **South Gippsland Highway:** 1 gallery and 8 craft shops
- **Hume Highway:** 1 gallery and 20 craft shops
- **Ovens Highway:** 20 craft shops
- **Goulburn Valley/Maroondah Highway:** 1

gallery and 18 craft shops
- **Murray Valley Highway:** 2 galleries and 44 craft shops
- **McIvor Highway:** 1 gallery and 14 craft shops
- **Calder Highway:** 2 galleries and 20 craft shops
- **Western Highway/Wimmera Highway:** 3 galleries and 36 craft shops
- **Midland Highway:** 6 galleries and 22 craft shops
- **Princes Highway West:** 2 galleries and 16 craft shops
- **Geelong/Bellarine Peninsula:** 1 gallery and 11 craft shops
- **Great Ocean Road:** 2 galleries and 10 craft shops
- **Henty Highway/Wimmera Highway:** 2 galleries and 19 craft shops

Fine Arts, Antiques, and Home Decorative Items

Melbourne has a good reputation for offering excellent quality Australian, European, and Asian arts, antiques, and home decorative items. If you are a serious art and antique shopper, be sure to pick up copies of two useful guides to Melbourne's art and antique scene: *The Antique Shops of Melbourne's High Street and Malvern Rd. Area* and *Antiques & Arts in Victoria*. Both are available free from shops along High Street and Malvern Road. The first publication provides a detailed map and summaries of 85 art and antique shops in the Prahran, Armadale, and Malvern areas. The second publication includes informative articles on Australian arts and antiques as well as advertisements from major art and antique dealers in Victoria, arranged by community.

Fortunately for shoppers, Melbourne's art, antique, and home decorative shops are primarily concentrated along Toorak Road, Chapel Street, High Street, and Malvern Road in the suburbs of Toorak, South Yarra, Prahran, Armadale, and Malvern as well as in a few downtown shopping centers and hotel shopping arcades and in small communities outside the metropolitan area.

Numerous shops carry a full line of investment quality traditional and contemporary Australian oils, watercolors, etchings, lithographs, and screen prints. For traditional Australian oils painted by some of Australia's leading artists, visit **Art Gallery** at 43 Bourke Street. If you are looking for antique prints and maps, be sure to stop at

Ebes Douwma Antique Prints and Maps Gallery at 51 Bourke Street. Their collection of 15,000 prints include antique and rare original prints from the 14th to the 19th centuries. You'll find Australian maps and prints, including birds, mammals, and Japanese wood block prints.

Several art galleries outside the central business district offer excellent selections. **Tom Silver Fine Art** at 1146 High Street, Armadale, specializes in pre-1940 art, including the Colonial period and from the Heidelberg School to the post-Impressionists. The **Graphic Illusion Gallery** at 69 Davis Avenue in South Yarra specializes in fine art and craftwork by leading contemporary Australian artists, including jewelry, ceramic sculpture, paintings, drawings, and prints. **Kew Gallery** at 26 Cotham Road, Kew, includes paintings by a large number of leading Australian artists including Colin August, Ian Hansen, David Boyd, and Dorothy Sutton. **The World of Art** at 39-41 Blessington Street, St. Kilda, has permanent and changing exhibitions of paintings and sculptures by such leading Australian artists as Bill Colemen, Robert Dickerson, Norman Robins, Leon Pappas, and Lotte Scharf. Also look for **Olinda Art Gallery** (Main Road, Olinda), **Brian V. Numan Studio Gallery** (109 Main Street, Selby), and **Artist Proof Galleries** (108 Punt Road, Windsor).

You will find several fine art galleries concentrated in the 200 block of Toorak Road. Look for **Andrew Ivanyi Galleries** (262 Toorak Road), **Gould Galleries** (270 Toorak Road), and **Blue Boy Fine Art Gallery** (276 Toorak Road). These galleries carry excellent quality art, including investment quality, by such leading Australian artists as Streeton, Bennett, Wheeler, and Boissevain.

The Gallery Shop (National Gallery of Victoria, 180 St. Kilda Road) offers a full range of art books, exhibition catalogues, hand-painted silk scarves, and replica jewelry from some of the world's leading collections. You'll want to stop at this shop as part of your visit to the National Gallery of Victoria.

For contemporary prints with Australian themes, visit **Billach** art gallery on the ground floor of The Shop of Shops, 171 Collins Street. Shops selling European and Australian antiques and collectibles are found throughout the Melbourne metropolitan area and in nearby small towns. However, the major antique shops are concentrated three to five kilometers southeast of the central business district along High Street in the suburbs of Prahran and Armadale and along Malvern Street in the suburb of Malvern. Several additional antique shops are found on Chapel Street near the intersection of Toorak Road in the suburb of South Yarra and along Burwood, Auburn, and

Burke Roads in the nearby suburbs of Hawthorn and South Camberwell.

The best approach to shopping for antiques in East Prahran and Armadale is to pick up a free copy of *The Antique Shops of Melbourne's High Street & Malvern Rd. Area*. This booklet is an indispensable guide to 85 of Melbourne's shops offering a vast array of arts and antiques. We suggest that you start at the corner of Williams Road and High Street in Prahran and walk east for three blocks until you come to Glenferrie Road. Nearly 60 art and antique shops line both sides of this section of High Street. Turn left at Glenferrie Road, go one block, and turn right at Malvern Road. Another 25 art and antique shops line this section of Malvern Road. And if you proceed west on Malvern Road, between Orrong and Williams Roads, you will come to another five art and antique shops lining both sides of this section of Malvern Road.

The High Street collection of art and antique shops has something for everyone. A shop such as **Edward Clark Antiques** (387 High Street) has a nice collection of French antique furniture and collectibles. **Phoenix Antiques** (458 High Street) includes antique furniture and collectibles from the Georgian to Art Deco periods, with special emphasis on Australiana. If you are in the market for fine and rare books, **Peter Arnold** (463 High Street) and **Kenneth Hince** (485 High Street), noted antiquarians, should be on your shopping list. **Andrew Farmer Antiques** (781 High Street), **Graham Geddes Antiques and Antiquities** (861, 873, and 914 High Street), **Antique Decor** (899 High Street), **Acorn Antiques** (885-9 High Street), and **Copper Kettle Antiques** (960 High Street) are worth browsing through. The **Melbourne Antique Centre** at 941 High Street has over 30 antique shops and stalls under one roof selling a wide range of antique and decorator items. **Kings Arcade** at 976 High Street also has a few small antique shops.

One block away, along Malvern Road, you will find **Marquis Antiques** (1379 Malvern Road) for Georgian and Victorian furniture; **Patrick Davey Antiques** (1377 Malvern Road) for Australian Colonial furniture; **Fiske Antique Galleries** (1421 Malvern Road) for late 18th and early 19th century English oak and mahogany furniture; and **Malvern Village Antiques** (1509 Malvern Road), a collector's treasure house, with 19 stalls selling furniture, clocks, barometers, jewelry, silverplate, and prints.

Other European and Australian antique shops can be found in the city, nearby suburbs, and small towns in Victoria. In the city, you may want to visit the **Queen Victoria Antique Arts and Craft Centre** (120 Franklin

Street) with its many stalls offering antique furniture, jewelry, china, glassware, cutlery, collectibles, and bric-a-brac. **Bruce Ratherford** in The Shop of Shops (171 Collins Street) carries antique silver and jewelry. **Badger Antiques** in the Block Arcade (Elizabeth Street) deals in 20th century jewelry and decorative arts.

You will also find a few antique shops along Chapel Street, Queens Avenue, and Auburn, Burwood, and Burke roads in South Yarra, Hawthorne, and Camberwell South -- suburbs just to the east and south of High and Malvern streets in Prahran, Armadale, and Malvern. Along Chapel Road near the intersection with Toorak Road in South Yarra you will find a few good antique shops: **Yarrabank Antiques** at 588 Chapel Hill and **Lisl Steiner** at 594 Chapel Street. The **Chapel Street Bazaar** has an assortment of varying quality antiques, collectibles, old wares, and vintage clothing. In the nearby suburbs of Hawthorne and Camberwell South, look for **Oscar Prouse Antiques** (corner of Glenferrie and Burwood streets, Hawthorn) for antique desks, bookcases, chairs, paintings, silver, porcelain, and jewelry; **Dove Antiques** (103 Burwood Road, Hawthorn) for late 17th to early 19th century furniture; **Clockwise** (65 Burwood Road) for antique clocks; **Carvill's Baltic Original Furniture** (641 Burwood Road, Hawthorn) for dressers, tables, bookcases, and desks; **Old'N Days** (569 Burwood Road, Hawthorn) for baltic pine furniture -- dressers, tables, desks, bookcases, and corner cupboards; **Stephen Haughton Antiques** (32 Queens Avenue, Hawthorne) for leather desk inlays; **Giltwood Antiques** (394 Burke Road, Camberwell) for one of the world's largest collections of antique mirrors; **Westbury Antiques** (499 Burke Road, Hawthorn South) for Georgian town and country furniture and decorative items; **Renaissance Antiques** (1013 Burke Road, Hawthorn) for furniture, lamps, and bric-a-brac; **L. J. Cook & Company** (404 Burke Road, South Camberwell and 439-449 Burke Road, Glen Iris) for Georgian and Regency antiques as well as Victorian antique furniture and silver.

We are especially impressed with the small number of high quality shops offering Asian arts and antiques. Most are concentrated along High and Chapel Streets. Japanese arts and antiques have been very popular in Melbourne during the past few years. One of the best shops for lovely Japanese interior items -- antiques, chests, ceramics, and furniture -- is **Kazari Japanese Interiors** at 531-533 Chapel Street (South Yarra). This shop is somewhat confusing because it is located in the rear of another shop selling Japanese household items. Just walk through the front door and proceed to the rear. **Acquisitions** at 550-

552 High Street carries a good collection of Japanese furniture along with Chinese, Australian, and English antiques. This shop, too, is somewhat confusing because it is divided into two separate shops adjacent to one another. Just go in and browse until you find what you like.

Two of Melbourne's outstanding Asian art and antique shops are located on High Street in East Prahran and Armadale. **Soo Tze Orientique** at 531A High Street (East Prahran) has a beautiful collection of Burmese, Thai, Tibetan, and Nepalese arts, antiques, and home decorative items, with special emphasis on furniture and textiles. Further east on High Street you will come to **East West Art** (665 High Street). This is a pleasant shop with beautiful Oriental collectables. East West Art specializes in Oriental art and antiques, with an emphasis on Southeast Asian ceramics. Further east on High Street at the **Kings Arcade** in Armadale you will find one of Australia's few shops specializing in Indian fine arts: **Chowringhee**, 974 High Street. Chowringhee also stocks books and arranges tours to India.

In the central business district you will find **The Jade Gallery** (Upper Plaza, Southern Cross Centre) offering a nice range of Oriental jade, jewelry, lacquer furniture, bronzes, porcelains, lacquers, and ivories.

Other Asian art and antique shops to look for are **Arts of Asia** (1383 Malvern Road, Malvern) which specializes in Korean chests, Chinese screens, Thai and Korean celadons, and Korean and Thai folk art; **Asian Antiques** (519 Camberwell Road, Camberwell), which specializes in Oriental furniture and decorative objects from Korea, Japan, and China; and **Tri-Kalum Gallery Craft** (Olinda Village) that has a mixture of arts, antiques, and crafts from Asia, including cloisonne, Rosewood carvings, Thai bronze sculpture, jewelry, rugs, amulets, porcelain, jade carvings, lacquerware, and clothes.

Duty-Free Shops

Like Sydney, Brisbane, and Adelaide, Melbourne has similar duty free shops offering the same types of duty-free goods -- liquor, electronics, perfumes, clothes, opals, jewelry, leather goods, and sporting equipment. Since we are not duty-free shoppers and we have yet to find any real bargains in these stores, we have nothing in particular to recommend. Again, if you are from New Zealand, Japan, India, or any other country that puts high import duties on such items, these stores offer good bargains in comparison to prices back home.

All of the duty-free shops are located in the central

business district along Swanston, Collins, and Queen Streets. **City International Duty Free Shop** is located at 185 Swanston Street. **Downtown Duty Free** is on 128 Exhibition Street. **Orbit Duty Free** has a branch shop at 261 Elizabeth Street. **International Duty Free** is found at 189 Collins Street. **Queen Street Duty Free** is at 43 Queen Street. **West End Duty Free**, specializing in spinning wheels, weaving looms, fleeces, and accessories, is located at 53 Queen Street. **Tasman Discounts** (215 Little Collins Street), run by an ex-Kiwi, primarily caters to visitors from New Zealand.

WHERE TO SHOP

The shopping scene in Melbourne can be best divided into city, suburban, and small town areas as well as into distinct styles of shopping -- hotel shopping arcades, department stores, factory outlets, and markets. Each area and style of shopping tends to specialize in particular types of products.

The City

The city shopping area is located in the central business district. Here you will find Melbourne's only pedestrian mall, shopping arcades, major department stores, small shops and restaurants, and Chinatown. The area is bordered by Spring, Flinders, King, and Latrobe Streets and bisected by two major shopping streets -- Bourke and Collins. Despite efforts to transform this into Melbourne's central shopping area, it remains a mixed area. You will find Australia's finest department store (**Georges**) and several high quality fashion shops (**The Shop of Shops**) here -- especially in the 100 block of Collins Street -- as well as it's largest department store (**Myer**). But this area also has some relatively nondescript stores in and around the Bourke Street Pedestrian Mall in such shopping arcades as The Walk, Centrepoint Mall, and the Royal Arcade.

One of the best ways to shop the city area is to start at the top of **Bourke Street**, beginning at the intersection with Spring Street, directly opposite the Parliament House. To the north of Bourke Street is Little Bourke Street which houses Melbourne's colorful Chinatown, between Exhibition and Swanston streets. To the South of Bourke Street is Little Collins, which has few shops, and Collins Street, which is one of Melbourne's major upmarket shopping areas.

As you proceed west along Bourke Street from Spring Street, you will come to such shops as **Australian Trends**

(48-50 Bourke Street) which has a very nice selection of quality Australian arts and crafts, and **Art Gallery** (43 Bourke Street) for fine quality Australian oil paintings. If you are interested in opals, stop at the shop with the white Cockatoo in the window -- **Lightning Ridge Opal Mines** at 75 Bourke Street. Along with offering a large selection of unset opals, they will give you an opal cutting and polishing demonstration as well as present a video on the opal mining process in Australia. If you turn left at the corner of Exhibition Street, you will come to three of Melbourne's major opal dealers: **Darrell James** (110 Exhibition Street), **Altman & Cherny** (120 Exhibition Street), and **Gemtec Opal** (7th floor, 124 Exhibition Street). Directly across the street is the Southern Cross Hotel Shopping Arcade with several small shops selling opals. Also in and around this arcade are a few fashion stores (**Raphael** and La Donna), a nice Asian arts and antiques shop (**The Jade Gallery**), and a well noted shop for Aboriginal and tribal arts, **Yarrandoo.**

If you go north on Exhibition Street a few yards, turn left, and proceed along Bourke Street for two blocks until you reach Swanston Street, you will see several shops on both sides of the street as well as three small shopping arcades on the north side of the street near the G. J. Coles department store. The stores as well as the three shopping arcades -- **Mid-City Cinema and Arcade, Village Centre,** and **Midtown Plaza** -- are relatively nondescript.

The major shopping section along Bourke street is found along the **Bourke Street Pedestrian Mall,** a crowded pedestrian mall between Swanston and Elizabeth streets. A tram traverses the center of the mall. **Myer** and **David Jones** department stores and three shopping arcades -- **Centrepoint Mall, The Walk,** and **The Royal Arcade --** feed into the mall. You will encounter several representatives of jewelry shops in the mall handing out literature on their shops as well as sidewalk vendors from Myer Department Store selling discounted items.

Both Myer and David Jones department stores dominate the mall. **David Jones Department Store** occupies two buildings across from one another on the mall. The first building is on the south side of the mall, next to Centrepoint Mall. This branch specializes in menswear. The second branch is directly across the mall next to Myers; it specializes in women's wear and accessories. Another small David Jones store is behind this store off of Little Bourke Street. The **Myer Department Store** on the Mall is the largest in all of Australia. It's the most popular department store for local residents. A monsterous complex, it extends to two blocks, stretching from the Bourke

Street Mall to Little Bourke and Lonsdale Streets and connected by overhead walkways.

We have little to recommend in the **three shopping arcades** that feed into the Bourke Street Mall. You may be able to shop all three arcades within 25 minutes. **Centrepoint Mall** has several nondescript shops selling clothing, shoes, and jewelry -- none of particular note. **The Walk** has an assortment of jewelry, shoes, clothes, leather, gift, and boutique shops of varying quality. Next door is a branch of **Just Jeans** for men's and women's clothes. The **Royal Arcade** extends from Bourke Street Pedestrian Mall to both Elizabeth and Little Collins streets. This arcade has the usual assortment of small clothing, jewelry, leather, and fur stores. You will find a small fur shop here, **S. R. McClean**, which carries some nicely tailored furs using New Zealand opossum and Australian fox. At the end of the Royal Arcade on Little Collins Street is one of Melbourne's nicest antique jewelry stores -- **Schlager**. A well established and reputable firm, Schlager carries a fine selection of old and new jewelry, porcelain, and paintings. You will find several unique pieces here.

If you exit the Royal Arcade on Elizabeth Street, directly across the street on the corner of Bourke and Elizabeth streets you will see the **Galleria Shopping Plaza**. This upscale shopping plaza has a branch of **Carla Zampatti** for ladies fashion clothes, **Oroton** for imported leather goods, and **R. M. Williams** for men's Australian leather. You also will find two **Chester's** stores, one for womenswear and the other for menswear, shoe stores, jewelers, boutiques, and restaurants.

The remainder of Elizabeth and Bourke streets have several book shops, restaurants, and gift shops. If you continue south on Elizabeth Street, between Collins Street and Flinders Lane, you will come to the state travel service offices for South Australia and Western Australia. These are good offices to visits for information and reservations should your travel plans include stops in Adelaide and Perth. At this point we recommend turning east on Collins Street to explore the shops along Collins Street between Elizabeth and Swanston streets.

The 200 block of **Collins Street**, between Elizabeth and Swanston streets, is a mixture of office buildings, shopping arcades, shops, and state travel offices. You will find the state travel service offices for Victoria, Tasmania, Canberra, and Queensland clustered along this block. **Centreway Arcade** (259-263 Collins) houses a few worthwhile shops, such as **Gazelle** for unique Australian and imported silver jewelry and gift items and **Ermina** for furs. You will also find a Melbourne branch of **Downtown Duty Free** on the

lower level of Centreway Arcade. A few doors east of
Centreway is the trendy **House of Merivale** (243 Collins
Street) offering fashionable men's and women's clothes.

Directly across the street from Centreway Arcade is
another small shopping arcade, the **Australia Centre**
which also houses the Hotel Australia. You will find a
few shops selling clothings, shoes, handbags, luggage,
leather, and food in this center. A few doors east on
Collins Street look for branches of **Designers Savings** and
Rodney Clark for fashionable women's clothes.

Once you reach Swanston Street, you can either turn left
on Swanston Street or proceed further east on Collins
Street. **Swanston Street** is a major transportation artery
for taking trams to the southern suburbs of South Yarra,
Toorak, Prahran, Armadale, and St. Kilda. You will also
find several gift, jewelry, shoes, and clothing shops along
both sides of this street but primarily on the west side.
We particularly recommend **Aboriginal Handcrafts** at
125-133 Swanston Street. A small shop located on the 9th
floor of the Century Building, it offers some of the best
prices on its limited selections of Aboriginal bark paintings, didjeridoos, clap sticks, music, and books we have
found in either Sydney or Melbourne.

Returning to Collins Street, turn left and go east into
the 100 block. This area, from the 100 block of Collins
Street to Spring Street, is one of Melbourne's classiest and
most upmarket shopping areas. On the north side of the
street, for example, you will find Australia's most exclusive
department store -- **Georges**. This store is filled with top
quality merchandise from all over the world, especially
clothing, accessories, home furnishings, jewelry, porcelain,
glassware, and china. As you enter Georges you will
immediately see on your right a branch of the famous
Percy Marks, one of Australia's best jewelers offering fine
opals, Argyle diamonds, and jewelry in lovely settings.
Nearby you will find the exclusive boutiques **Teena Varigos** (182 Collins Street) and **Perla Caviglia** (186 Collins
Street) for uniquely designed fashion clothes.

Directly across the street from Georges department store
is the fashionable **The Shop of Shops** (171 Collins Street).
The first two floors of this exclusive shopping center are
filled primarily with boutiques of Australia's leading designers. You will find **John Cavill, Shepherds, Lou
Wiseman, Carla Zampatti, Sandra Layt, Stunning,
Lhomme, Prue Acton, Lizzie Collins, Angela Padula,
Bell Book and Candle,** and **Feitel Furs** here. The international designer **Diane Freis**, with her colorful dresses,
also has a shop here. On the ground floor you will also
find a very nice Australiana shop, **Thingummybob**, and

Sheil Abbey, a shop offering beautifully crafted aluminum-alloyed silver tableware by Don Sheil. The top floor (second level) has a few shops selling less expensive and more youthful and trendy clothes. Many of these shops also have workshops and boutiques in the suburbs of Richmond, South Yarra, and Toorak.

Next door to The Shop of Shops you will find the fashionable **Laura Ashley** for imported clothes, **Bruno Magli** for imported shoes, and **La Maison** for lovely glassware. Just a few doors west is **City Square Plaza** which is all but dead. No need to stop here since it has little or nothing to offer shoppers.

If you proceed to the next block on Collins Street, going east, you will come to Melbourne's finest hotel shopping arcade -- **Hyatt on Collins** -- attached to the Hyatt Hotel on the corner of Collins and Exhibition streets. A somewhat confusing shopping arcade to find if you enter through the hotel lobby (supposed to be located on the 6th and 7th levels!), this two-level shopping arcade is best entered directly from Collins Street. Here you will find many exclusive shops catering to the tastes of international tourists and upmarket shoppers. On the First Level you will find **Ipanema** for women's clothes, **John J. Moore** for men's clothes, **Louis Vuitton** for handbags and luggage, **Miss Louise** for women's shoes and accessories, **Piaget** for fine crafted watches, **Master Jewellers** for jewelry, **Dorith Unger** for women's nightwear, **Raphael** for women's clothes, and **Tinsel Trading** for costume jewelry and accessories. On the Second Level look for **Triomphe** for women's clothes, **Adele Chapeaux** for bridal clothes and evening wear, **Kaminski Gallery** for lovely tapestries, **Koala Beaut** for gifts, **Cache** for arts and crafts, **Cuggi Tricot** for knitwear, and **Billich Gallery** for paintings and lithographs.

Just a few doors east of the Hyatt on Collins shopping arcade is **Makers Mark** (85 Collins Street), one of Melbourne's and Australia's finest craft shops offering uniquely designed and exquisitely crafted jewelry and accessories in silver and gold. If you are looking for something special, Makers Mark will design jewelry to your specifications.

The next block on Collins, between Exhibition and Spring streets, is **Collins Place,** a shopping arcade attached to the Regent Hotel. Here you will find a few specialty shops such as **Yarrandoo** for Aboriginal and tribal arts and crafts, **Henry Bucks** for menswear, **Regent Jewellers** for opals, and **James Loustas** for nicely tailored furs.

You will find a few other shops scattered throughout the downtown section. However, the Myer and David Jones department stores on Bourke Street Pedestrian Mall, Georges department store, and the shops and shopping arcades from the 100 block of Collins Street to Spring Street offer the best of the city shopping. The rest of the city area is mixed for shopping. You will discover an occasional shop or two in the downtown area that offers special items for international travelers interested in unique quality products. But most such shops will be found in exclusive suburban shopping areas which have a reputation for upmarket shopping.

The Suburbs

Suburban shopping areas tend to specialize by products with similar shops congregating in the same areas. Therefore, your suburban shopping strategy should focus on particular products of interest to you. If, for example, you are interested in **arts and antiques**, then you will want to go to High and Malvern streets in East Prahran, Armadale, and Malvern. If you are interested in **fashion clothes**, then head for Toorak Road and Bridge Road in South Yarra, Toorak, and Richmond. If you are just out for the day exploring suburban shopping opportunities, we suggest concentrating on **Toorak Road** in South Yarra and Toorak, **Chapel Street** in Prahran, and **High Street** in Armadale. All three of these streets are connected to one another within a two to three kilometer radius.

Toorak Road

One of the best ways to shop these suburban areas is to take a No. 8 tram on Swanston Street in downtown Melbourne to Toorak Road. This four kilometer ride costs $.75 and is a pleasant way to see part of the city. It's best to get off near Punt Street, within one minute after the tram enters onto Toorak Road. You shouldn't have difficulty finding this stop -- you will see a 7-Eleven store on the corner of Punt Street and Toorak Road.

Begin your shopping adventure at this corner and proceed east along Toorak Road until you come to Toorak Village at the corner of Canterbury Road. It's a long, long walk from Punt Street to Canterbury Road. You may want to take a tram part of the way, skipping sections of Toorak Road, that offer few good shopping opportunities. We will point out those sections as we take you down Toorak Road.

Beginning at the intersection of Punt Road and Toorak Road, walk east along Toorak Road until you come to Darling Street. This section of Toorak Road has several of Melbourne's leading boutiques, Australiana stores, and menswear shops. Look for **Style** (17 Toorak Road) for lovely wedding, evening, and cocktail dresses; **MN Boutique** (19 Toorak Road) for sequin evening dresses and beaded sweaters; **Antipodes** (22 Toorak Road) for a nice selection of Australiana and sweaters; **Migi** (31 Toorak) for evening wear and dressy dresses; **Staggers** for trendy menswear and womenswear; **Trent Nathan** (68 Toorak Road) for conservative cut womenswear; **Trevor West** (79 Toorak Road) for a nice selection of menswear; **Fayaz** (80 Toorak Road) for very nice cocktail dresses and formal wear; and **L'homme** (87 Toorak Road) for menswear. If you find yourself in this section of Toorak Road around lunch time, you might try **Maxim's**, a good French restaurant at 60 Toorak Road.

In the 100 block of Toorak Road you will come to the **South Yarra Arcade** (101-105 Toorak Road) which has a nice menswear shop, **Umano**, several specialty shops, and an outdoor restaurant. Across the street is **Rodeo Drive** (118 Toorah), a trendy shop offering Anne Klein womenswear and shoes. If you are interested in flowers, stop at **Kevin O'Neill** (199 Toorak Road) for some truly exotic flowers and wonderful floral arrangements. **Jo Bond** (125 Toorak Road) offers dressy suits and dresses. **Sportempo** (137 Toorak Road) has some very nice imported sportswear, knits, and sweaters; their sale prices are very good.

At this point you will be near Darling Street. You will find very few shops from here until you reach the 200 block of Toorak Road. Rather than walk the long distance, you may want to take a No. 8 tram to the next shopping section along Toorak Road.

At the 200 block of Toorak Road, you will see three art galleries with paintings of major Australian artists: **Andrew Ivanyi Galleries** (262 Toorak Road), **Gould Galleries** (270 Toorak Road), and **Blue Boy Fine Art Gallery** (276 Toorak Road). At the corner of Cunningham and Toorak Roads is **Keith Miles and Associates Interior Designers** with a nice selection of Oriental interior decorating items.

The 300 block of Toorak Road has a few shops worth visiting. Here you will find two Oriental rug shops, **Kamel Persian Rug Gallery** (300 Toorak Road) and **John Gaidzkar** (309 Toorak Road); a **Prue Acton** boutique (307 Toorak Road); and a unique clothing store with dresses, wedding gowns, and shoes with a decided 1950s theme at the **Gallery of Wearable Art** (315 Toorak Road).

There is very little shopping between the Gallery of Wearable Art and Toorak Village, a 20-minute walk. On a beautiful day this can be a lovely walk. However, you may want to take another No. 8 tram to the 400 block of Toorak Road at Tintern Avenue. Here you will find **Andy** (433 Toorak Road), a men's tailor that works with beautiful wools. **Trac Centre** and **Tok H Shopping Centre** have several eateries as well as a few gift and clothing shops of average quality. **Jot** at 475 Toorak Road is in a class of its own; this is one of Melbourne's finest coutures offering fabulous imported fabrics and unique designs for the truly discerning shopper who seeks the very best in women's clothes. Just a few doors down from Jot are **Village Way** and **Place**, small Toorak Village shopping centers with clothing, shoe, jewelry, art and antique (**Toorak Antique and Art Gallery**), hardware, and food shops. **Marino & Scott** (505 Toorak Road) offers exclusive menswear and tailoring. **Henry Bucks** (476 Toorak Road) is also a nice men's shop. **Victoria of Balencia**, just around the corner on Canterbury Road, is another exclusive couture which is part of this Toorak Village area.

You complete your Toorak Road shopping adventure once you reach the intersection of Toorak and Canterbury Roads. At this point you can take another No. 8 tram going west toward the city, but get off near the intersection of Toorak Road and Chapel Street, a 10-minute ride that may have taken you 40 minutes to walk. Alternatively, you can return to the tram stop on Swanston Street in The City and take a No. 6 tram which will put you directly on Chapel Street.

Chapel and High Streets

As soon as you get to Chapel Street, walk south until you come to the intersection of Chapel and High streets. This is another major suburban shopping area -- **South Yarra and Prahran** -- which is filled with a large variety of varying quality shops offering antiques, clothes, trendy jewelry, and home decorative items, along with several inexpensive ethnic restaurants. This, too, is a long street to walk, but the shopping here is continuous from Toorak Road to High Street. Starting near the intersection of Toorak Road and High Street, you will find two antique shops close to one another: **Yarrabank Antiques** (588 Chapel Street) and **Lisl Steiner** (594 Chapel Street). If you are in the market for Japanese antiques and interior decorative items, be sure to stop at **Kazari Japanese Interiors** (531-533 Chapel Street) for fine selections and quality items. You will have to enter through the front door of **Made in Japan Imports** to get to Kazari Japanese Interiors.

Across the street on your right is **The Jam Factory, a** trendy shopping arcade with a branch of **Georges** department store and several small boutiques, gift, household, and arts and crafts shops along with a Safeway grocery store. The Georges department store carries more trendy and boutique-type clothes, such as Weiss and Weiss 'Pringle' label clothes, than their more exclusive store on Collins Street. You will also find a branch of the popular Australian menswear store, **R. M. Williams,** at The Jam Factory.

The remainder of Chapel Street is a mixture of trendy boutiques, clothing stores, arts and crafts shops, and home decorative stores. You will find **Morrisons of Australia,** a "citified" Australian outback clothing store, **Presents** for interior decorative items, and **Cuggi** for knitwear. A branch of **Shepherds** at 459 Chapel Street offers distinctive and colorful womenswear. **Christopher Chronis Designs** (448 Chapel Street) offers trendy menswear. **The Antique Garden** (438 Chapel Street) specializes in antiques for fireplaces and home exteriors. The nearby **Chapel Plaza** has a few boutiques and art and leather shops.

One of our very favorite shops in all of Melbourne is **Ishka** at 409A Chapel Street. This is one of Australia's best shops for buying good quality imports -- especially artifacts, textiles, clothes, and jewelry -- from all over the world. We especially like the selections from South and Southeast Asia. The service is exceptional and the prices are reasonable. This Chapel Street shop is one of five Ishka stores in the Melbourne metropolitan area. If you can't find what you need at this branch, the personal will check their other branches for you.

From here until you reach High Street, you will pass several ethnic restaurants and a few clothing stores and antique shops. **The Chapel Hill Bazaar** at 217 Chapel Street is an antique emporium with a few stalls selling secondhand clothes, furniture, and collectibles. It looks more like an organized garage sale than a serious antique business. **G. D. McPhee Antiques** at 202 Chapel Street carries similar secondhand items.

High and Malvern Streets

If you turn left at the intersection of Chapel Street and High Street, you will enter into another major shopping area. **High Street,** in the upmarket suburbs of East Prahran and Armadale, and **Malvern Road,** in the suburb of Malvern, are two of Melbourne's most famous antique streets. Alternatively, you can take a No. 6 tram to High Street or a No. 72 tram from Malvern Road along Swanston Street and St. Kilda Road. Here, you will find over 80 shops selling everything from European, Australian, and Asian antiques to secondhand junk. Be sure to pick up the latest copy of *The Antique Shops of Melbourne's High Street & Malvern Rd. Area* for detailed information on 86 shops along these two streets. This useful publication is available free from most shops along High Street and Malvern Road.

It's a very long walk from Chapel Street to Glenferrie Road via High Street. You may wish to skip the first section of High Street altogether since few shops in the Chapel Street and William Road area offer quality goods; most shops in this rather run-down area sell household items, office furniture, and auto parts. It's best to start shopping this street just before Williams Road. Take a tram or taxi to the first major quality antique shop along High Street, **Edward Clark Antique** (385 High Street) which specializes in French furniture and collectibles. Starting here, keep walking east along High Street until you reach Glenferrie Road. You'll find over 50 shops offering a large variety of antiques and collectibles as well as a few clothing, arts, and crafts shops.

Some of our favorite High Street shops include **Gallery Handmade** (467 High Street) for arts and crafts; **Soo Tze Antique** (531A High Street) for Korean, Chinese, Burmese, Thai, Laotian, Tibetan, and Indian antiques and home decorative items; **Centro Fashions** (714 High Street) for German dresses; **Graham Geddes Antiques and Antiquities** (861, 873, and 914 High Street) for a large variety of indoor and outdoor items; **Melbourne Antique Centre** (941 High Street) with 40 antique shops; **Copper Kettle Antiques** (960 High Street for Victorian and Edwardian antiques; and **Evan Mackley Fine Art** (954 High Street) for Australian investment paintings.

One of the most concentrated shopping areas along High Street is between Kooyong and Glenferrie roads. This is a more diverse section of antique, home decorative, rug, clothing, and jewelry shops. A few of our favorites include **East-West Art Gallery** (1019 High Street) for fine Oriental arts and antiques; **Carla Zampatti** (1104 High Street), and **John Cavill** (1108 High Street) for top quality designer clothing for women; **Park Lane Antiques Centre** (1170 High Street) for furniture and silver collectibles offered by 20 different dealers; **Monte Cristo** (1199 High Street) and **Exotica Gallery** (1703 High Street) for very nice quality antiques, and **The Australiana General Store** (1227 High Street) for one of the best collections of Australiana in Melbourne. At this point, the intersection of Glenferrie Road and High Street, you have reached the end of the High Street shopping area.

If you walk one block to the north on Glenferrie Road, you will reach the Malvern Road shopping area. This area primarily has art and antique shops similar to the High Street shops. Going east along Malvern Road, look for such shops as **Scandinavian Country Furniture** (1292 Malvern Road), **The Cobweb** (1361 Malvern Road), **Tooronga Hall Antiques** (1365 Malvern Road), **Arts of Asia** (1383 Malvern Road), **Lighthouse Antiques** (1425 Malvern Road), and **Malvern Village Antiques** (1509 Malvern Road). You will also find a few shops three blocks directly west on Malvern Road, between Orrong Road and Williams Road.

Other Suburbs

Nearby these major suburban shopping areas are several other suburbs offering unique shopping opportunities. Bridge Street in **Richmond**, one kilometer north of the Chapel Street and Toorak Road intersection, has several retail outlets of Australia's top designers as well as factory outlet shops of Melbourne's garment manufacturers selling seconds and discontinued stock. For haute couture, visit Lygon Street in **Carlton**, Burke Road in **Camberwell**, and Puckle Street in **Monee Ponds**. Burwood, Auburn, Burke, Camberwell, and Canterbury roads in the suburbs of **Hawthorne, Camberwell,** and **Canterbury** are noted streets for fine antiques and collectibles. You'll also find art galleries in the southern seashore suburbs of **St. Kilda** and **Brighton**.

Hotel Shopping Arcades

Three of Melbourne's major hotels have shopping arcades worth visiting. Located near one another in the downtown commercial section, they are three of Melbourne's major shopping areas for clothes, jewelry, arts, and crafts.

Hyatt on Collins, at the corner of Collins and Russell streets, is Melbourne's most upmarket hotel shopping arcade. Centrally located just one block from such fine stores and shops as Georges department store, The Shop of Shops, and Makers Mark, Hyatt on Collins consists of two levels of 17 specialty shops attached to the Hyatt Hotel. This is one of Melbourne's most pleasant and well-appointed shopping arcades. While many of its shops offer imported items, such as watches, clothes, shoes, handbags, and luggage, others primarily sell Australian-made clothes, arts, crafts, and gift items. Shops with a distinctive Australian flavor include **Koala Beaut** for gift items, **Cache** for arts and crafts, **Cuggi Tricot** for knitwear, **Billich Gallery** for paintings and lithographs, **Kaminski Gallery** for tapestries, and **Dorith Unger** for women's nightwear.

Collins Place, located one block east of the Hyatt on Collins, is attached to the Regent Hotel. While not as upmarket an area as the Hyatt on Collins, Collins Place does have a few shops worth considering. If you are interested in Aboriginal and tribal arts as well as Australiana, visit the popular **Yarrandoo**. For nice furs, especially those using Australian red fox, stop at **James Loustas**. **Regent Jewellers** offers opals, and **Henry Bucks** has a nice selection of menswear.

Southern Cross Hotel Arcade, just one block north of the Hyatt on Collins and Collins Place hotel shopping arcades on Exhibition Street (between Little Collins and Bourke streets), has several jewelry, clothing, arts, and crafts shops. Here, you will find several opal and jewelry shops catering to Japanese tourists with advertised 30, 40, and 50 percent discounts. Keep in mind when buying opals that a 30 to 50 percent discount should be the normal retail price -- not a truly discounted or bargain price. The reasons for this are twofold: (1) you automatically get a 30 percent discount, because as a foreign tourist you are exempt from the hefty 30 percent Australian sales tax; and (2) many shops give another 20 percent discount, because they take off a 20 percent mark-up they already put into their price as a "*Japanese tour guide commission*". Such commissions are standard practice in many Australian opal shops. Guides bring groups of Japanese tourists to these shops and receive a 20 percent commission on the total amount spent by the group as an "incentive" to bring tourists to these shops. Other shops worth visiting in the Southern Cross Hotel Arcade are **The Jade Gallery** for Oriental arts, crafts, jewelry, and ivory, especially their nice collection of Japanese Netsukes; **Yarrandoo** for Aboriginal and tribal arts and Australiana; **Shoppers Paradise** for gifts and souvenirs; and **Raphael** for nice imported women's clothes.

Department Stores

Melbourne has three major department stores each found in the central business district within a few minutes walking distance of each other. The most elegant department store in all of Australia is **Georges** at 162 Collins Street, directly across the street from The Shop of Shops. This six-level department store consists of two buildings: the main department store on Collins Street and a Hostess Store on Little Collins Street, directly behind the main store. This place shouts "class". This is where Melbourne's rich and famous shop. Owned by the David Jones department store chain, Georges is filled with top quality clothes, accessories, jewelry, and household goods, many of which are imported from abroad. The fine **Percy Marks** jeweler, with its exquisite opal and Argyle diamond jewelry, is located on the Ground Level immediately to your right as you enter the front door of Georges' Collins Street entrance.

Myers Department Store is located on the Bourke Street Pedestrian Mall next to and directly across the street from the two David Jones Department Stores. This is the favorite department store of local residents because of its size, service, and prices. It's the largest department store in all of Australia consisting of eight levels and two huge buildings (Bourke Street Building and Lonsdale Street Building) spanning two blocks which are joined by bridges and a subway. You can easily spend a day shopping the numerous departments of this mammoth place as well as get lost several times as you become overwhelmed attempting to find different departments and products! As soon as you enter the store from Bourke Street, look for the Information Desk which will give you a map of the store as well as answer any of your questions. You'll quickly discover one of the great strengths of this department store -- Myer's service. It's a big, big store, but the personnel are extremely service-oriented. Some of the major highlights of this store are the designer clothes center on the Second Level of the Bourke Street Building where you can see garments produced by several of Australia's top designers; and Australiana, souvenirs, Settlers & Company's leather goods, and huge deli on the Ground Level of the Lonsdale Street Building. There are few department stores in the world that can match the sheer size and variety offered by this department store.

David Jones Department Store consists of two stores on the Bourke Street Pedestrian Mall. The first store is located next to the Myer Department Store and primarily offers good quality womenswear. The second building is located directly across the mall from the first building and Myer Department Store and is located between Centrepoint Mall and The Walk shopping arcade. This store primarily sells menswear and has a very nice food and deli center on its Lower Level. While not as large as the Myer Department Store, these two David Jones Department Stores offer excellent quality products -- not as exclusive as Georges but better overall quality than Myer.

Factory Outlets

Melbourne is Australia's factory outlet center, reflecting the fact that the garment industry is centered in and around Melbourne. The combination of leading clothing designers and manufacturers producing millions of garments each year in Melbourne has given rise to numerous factory outlet shops that sell direct to the public at savings ranging from 30 to 70 percent on seconds, irregulars, and discontinued stock. This is a considerable savings given the general high costs of Australian clothes.

As we noted earlier in our discussions of shopping services and fashion clothes and accessories on pages 142-146, several groups sponsor shopping tours to Melbourne's major factory outlets. In addition, you should purchase a copy of the latest edition of Pamm Durkin's *Bargain Shoppers' Guide to Melbourne* which outlines the where and what of nearly every factory outlet -- over 400 -- in the Melbourne metropolitan area. We also highly recommend "Pamm's Shopping Tours" (P.O. Box 4900, Melbourne, Victoria 3001, Tel. 592-6911) for a guided tour to visit these outlets.

Markets

Melbourne's markets are also reputed to be the biggest and best in the country. You'll have to see for yourself. The markets here are a colorful mix of ethnic groups, craft products, food, and entertainment. You can easily spend a few days shopping the many markets in and around Melbourne.

Melbourne's largest and most colorful market is the **Queen Victoria Market** at the corner of Victoria and Elizabeth streets. This market is also reputed to be the largest in Australia and the Southern Hemisphere. Consisting of several covered buildings (labeled as sheds A-F) with open air stalls, vendors here sell everything from fresh fruits and vegetables to clothes and handicrafts. This is a very colorful and festive market to explore, reminiscent of many ethnic and Third World markets found in Europe and Asia. You can buy imported clothes, leather, jewelry, and crafts at one-third to one-half the price you might pay in department stores and shops downtown. You will find inexpensive sweaters, clothes, shoes, toys, textiles, real and fake leather goods, and luggage imported from several Asian countries. While the market is open every day except Monday (Tuesday to Thursday, 6am to 2pm; Friday, 6am to 6pm, Saturday, 6am to 1pm), the best day to go is Sunday (9am to 4pm) when selections are better and crowds are the largest. While visiting this market, be sure to explore some of the nearby shops, such as **It's Australian,** for additional handcrafted items.

The **Meat Market Craft Centre,** located near the Queen Victoria Market at 42 Courtney Street), is one of Australia's finest craft centers. Housed in the historic Meat Market building, with cobblestoned floors and high arched timber ceilings, the Meat Market Craft Centre is a place where you can observe exhibits and craftsmen at work as well as attend workshops. Its award-winning **Crafts Shop** has some of the nicest selections of arts and crafts in all of Australia. This shop alone is worth the visit to the Centre.

The **St. Kilda Sunday Art Bank** market is another popular market for those interested in handcrafted leather, jewelry, pottery, glass, toys, cottage crafts, photography, paintings, woodcrafts, and Australiana. Located along the Upper Esplanade in the southern seaside suburb of St. Kilda -- just 5 kilometers from the city -- this market is open every Sunday from 9am to 6pm. Here you will find numerous stalls selling good quality handmade items. This area is also famous for its food and cake shops as well as stores along nearby Acland, Therry, and Fitzroy streets. Shops here remain open on the weekends in anticipation of lively crowds descending on St. Kilda on Saturday and Sunday. St. Kilda is a good place to shop on Sunday -- especially since most shops in the city are closed.

Other markets in the Melbourne metropolitan area include:

- **Camberwell Market:** arts and crafts market located in the car park opposite Target, Union Street, Camberwell; open Sunday 6am to 1pm.

- **Dandenong Market:** A produce and consumer goods market located at corner of Cleeland and Clow streets. Has a special 'Trash and Treasure' auction every Tuesday Open Tuesday, Friday, and Saturday morning.

- **Dingley Village Craft Market:** A fine crafts market open the first Sunday of every month, 9am to 2pm. Located on Marcus Road, Dingley, 25 kilometers from Melbourne.

- **Melbourne Westend Market:** Offers 600 undercover stalls and foodhalls in a multicultural atmosphere. Open Saturday and Sunday, 8:30am to 5:30pm. Located at 47 McIntyre Road, Sunshine.

- **Moonee Ponds Market:** A colorful food market offering meats, fish, poultry, vegetables, and fruits. Open Thursday, 8am to 6pm; Friday, 8am to 9pm, and Saturday, 8am to 1pm. Located on Homer Street, Moonee Ponds.

- **Pipeworks Market & Leisure Complex:** Large entertainment and leisure complex with over 600 variety stalls. Open Saturday and Sunday, 9am to 5pm. Located at 400 Mahoneys Road, Campbellfield.

- **Prahran Market:** A popular market offering a wide variety of products. Open Tuesday and Thursday 7:30am to 5pm; Friday, 6am to 6pm; and Saturday, 6am to 12:30pm. Located at 177 Commercial Road, Prahran -- near Chapel Street.

- **Preston Market:** Offers fruits vegetables, leather goods, footwear, and jewelry. Open Thurdays, 8am to 6pm; Friday, 8am to 9pm; and Saturday, 8am to 1pm. Located at 30A Centreway, Preston (next to the Preston Railway Station).

- **The Village Market:** A weekend market with over 650 undercover stalls, restaurants, and amusements. Open Saturday and Sunday from 8:30am to 5pm. Located at 8 Leakes Road, Laverton.

Craft Towns

As we noted earlier in our discussion of Australian and imported arts and crafts on pages 149-153, greater Melbourne and the State of Victoria abound with small craft towns featuring fine art galleries and craft shops. Again, you can easily spend three weeks visiting the various towns and shops tucked away along the seaside and in the valleys and hills. These are the areas where some of Victoria's master craftspeople live and work.

If you want to visit some of the best craft towns outside Melbourne, we strongly recommend contacting the **Crafts Council of Victoria** (7 Blackwood Street, North Melbourne, Victoria 3051, Tel. 329-0611) for a copy of their directory to the arts and crafts shops of Melbourne and Victoria. The directory outlines 15 separate trips you can take to visit 30 art galleries and 293 craft shops outside Melbourne. If you have the time, these can be wonderful trips in and of themselves as you immerse yourself in the arts and crafts of Victoria, meet some of Australia's leading craftspeople, and make some memorable, quality purchases. We suggest renting a car to drive to these areas.

ENJOYING YOUR STAY

Melbourne abounds with many things to see and do in addition to shopping. It has excellent hotels, fine ethnic restaurants, attractive historical sites, first-class museums, cultural events, and numerous sports activities and sporting events to keep you busy for several days during your stay.

Hotels in Melbourne range from the deluxe to budget. Similar to Sydney, deluxe and first-class hotels are very expensive. Expect to pay around A$150-200 a night for a double at one of Melbourne's deluxe hotels. Five of Melbourne's best hotels are centrally located in and around one of Melbourne's finest shopping areas, Collins Street: **Hyatt On Collins** (123 Collins Street), **Regent Melbourne** (25 Collins Street), **The Windsor** (103 Spring Street), **Menzies at Rialto** (495 Collins Street), and **Southern Cross Hotel** (131 Exhibition Street). While a few minutes outside the central business district, the **Hilton International Melbourne** (192 Wellington Parade) is also an excellent hotel. The Regent Melbourne has the nicest view of the city from the 35th floor restaurant and bar. The Regent Melbourne, Hyatt On Collins, and Southern Cross Hotel have Melbourne's three best hotel shopping arcades. The historical Windsor is a classy hotel lovingly restored to its old world elegance. From these hotels you can easily walk to the major downtown shops, shopping arcades, and department stores as well as catch trams to the northern and southeastern suburban shopping areas.

Melbourne is reputed to have the best **restaurants** in all of Australia. You'll have to judge for yourself. Like many Australian restaurants we find, the reputed best are often good to excellent and always very expensive. We have yet to find a truly outstanding restaurant in Australia, and we tried our best to do so here in Melbourne.

Given its ethnic diversity with strong European roots and Asian immigration, Melbourne has numerous ethnic restaurants, pubs, and take-away eateries ranging from expensive to inexpensive. For French/Italian dining, we found **Florentino** (78-82 Bourke Street) to be a good restaurant. **Vasili's** (265 Johnston Street, Abbotsford) is our favorite Greek restaurant. If you seek excellent Oriental food, just walk through Chinatown on Little Bourke Street and you will find several good Chinese and Southeast Asian restaurants: **Express of China** (120-122 Little Bourke Street), **Coconut Hut** (43 Little Bourke street), and **Fortuna Village** (235 Little Bourke Street). **Stephanie's** (405 Tooronga Road, Hawthorne East), **Mietta's** (7 Alfred Place), **Grand Dining Room at the Windsor** (115 Spring Street), **Two Faces** (149 Toorak Road, South Yarra), and **The Willows** (462 St. Kilda Road) are considered by many discerning diners and critics to be some of Melbourne's best restaurants. However, you may also discover the many less expensive take-away eateries offer some of the best food in Melbourne.

Melbourne is famous for its architecture, parks, arts, museums, and shopping events. It's a great walking and tram-riding city. While shopping you may also want to visit some of Melbourne's major landmarks:

- **Victorian Arts Centre:** Melbourne's attempt to provide its own alternative to Sydney's Opera House. Located on St. Kilda Road adjacent to the Yarra River and the downtown commercial area (walk south on Swanston Street which becomes St. Kilda Road as soon as you cross the bridge), this huge complex is topped by an uninspiring Spire (Melbourne's "Eiffel Tower") and houses a concert hall, theater, and playhouse. Take a one-hour guided tour (A$2.75) of this building to see it thoroughly. However, you may want to call ahead as many of the scheduled tours are fully booked by large groups, and personnel are unwilling to add additional tours to accommodate waiting tourists -- a very disappointing public service!

- **The National Gallery:** Located next to the Victorian Arts Centre, it houses Australia's largest collection of paintings by traditional masters (Rembrandt) and noted Australian artists, including Aborigines.

- **Melbourne Town Hall:** Located on the corner of Collins and Swanston Street. The beautiful Council Chambers and function rooms are worth visiting.

- **Parliament House:** Located at the east end of Bourke Street and across from the Windsor Hotel. Beautiful Victorian building built in 1856.

- **Royal Botanic Gardens:** Located between Alexandria Avenue and Domain Road in South Yarra. Considered by many observers to be one of the best botanic gardens in the world with over 12,000 species of plants.

Two of Melbourne's **ethnic groups** also have their own museums. If you are interested in the Australian Jewish community, consider visiting **The Jewish Museum of Australia** (corner of Toorak Road and Arnold Street; open Wednesday and Thursday, 10am to 4pm) and the **Jewish Holocaust Centre** (13 Selwyen Street, Elsternwich; open Monday to Thursday, 10am to 2pm). The Chinese also have their own museum depicting the colorful history of the Chinese in Australia: **Museum of Chinese Australian History** (22 Cohen Place; open Monday, Wednesday, Thursday, and Friday, 10am to 5pm, and Saturday and Sunday from 12 noon to 5pm).

Sports in Melbourne play a very important role in defining the character of this city. This is a sports-minded city and a center for several national and international sporting events. It boasts superb golf courses, horse racing (Melbourne Cup), soccer, football, cricket, tennis (Australian Open), motor races, sailing, and hot-air ballooning. If you love **sports and sporting events,** be sure to pick up information on upcoming sports events at the Victorian Tourism Commission office (230 Collins Street). You may also want to visit Melbourne's popular **Australian Gallery of Sport** (Melbourne Cricket Ground, Jolimont; open Wednesday to Sunday, 10am to 4pm) to get an excellent overview of the sporting traditions in Australia as well as the **Victorian Racing Museum** (Caufield Racecourse Station Street, Caufield; open Tuesday and Thursday, 10am to 4pm).

Several tour companies offer a variety of tours to further enjoy the city and surrounding countryside. You can choose city tours, walking tours, cruises on the river and bay, helicopter and hot air balloon flights, vintage railway tours, vineyard and Australiana tours, and adventure tours into Australia's outback. You may want to see the Penguins at the highly touristed Phillip Island Penguin Reserve south of Melbourne; head into the hills and valleys for a day of wine tasting in Victoria's many vineyards; or just lie on the beach in St. Kilda, Elwood, or Mornington

Peninsula. It's all here in Melbourne. All you need is lots of time, money, and information on where to go and what to see. Again, be sure to pick up information at the Victorian Tourism Commission office. Their *Melburnian* magazine guide lists most of these and other tours, activities, and sites to visit during your stay in Melbourne.

Chapter Eight

ADELAIDE

Adelaide, Australia's fourth largest city with a population of 1 million, is a charming community of beautiful architecture, green parklands, and a festive atmosphere. It's a surprising city for visitors who primarily think of Australia as being made up of Sydney, Melbourne, and the beaches of Queensland.

We're unabashed fans of Adelaide. We like its leisurely pace, openness, and convenience. It's a big city, but with a small town feel to it best captured by walking its many downtown and suburban streets. It's a surprising city for shopping, touring, and enjoying the ambiance of a friendly and inviting South Australia. It has the look of a frontier city but with all the amenities of a modern metropolis. It's Denver without Denver's elevation, snow-capped mountains, and lingering pollution. Wide streets and squares laid out on an inviting grid scheme make this one of the easiest cities to navigate in all of Australia.

Come to Adelaide and you will discover one of Australia's best kept secrets for shopping and traveling, all done on the edge of the Outback. Come here before you venture further north into the interior Outback, the Nor-

thern Territory of Alice Springs and Darwin. For Adelaide
makes a wonderful transition from the more cosmopolitan
metropolises of Melbourne and Sydney.

GETTING TO KNOW YOU

Once considered to be Australia's most conservative
city, today Adelaide is a city of great diversity and energy.
Host to the annual Australian Grand Prix and the biennial
Adelaide Arts Festival, world famous for its opals and
wines, renowned for its arts and crafts, noted for its gambling casino and vibrant central business district, and
considered the gateway to the Outback and the center for
Australia's movie industry, Adelaide has placed itself in
league with Australia's other cosmopolitan cities. It's a
city with a great deal of character. Best of all, it offers
some excellent shopping opportunities.

Stroll down Rundle Mall in downtown Adelaide or head
for the upmarket suburbs of Hyde Park (King William and
Unley roads), Glenside (Burnside Village at Greenhill and
Portrush roads), and North Adelaide (Melbourne Street),
and you will quickly discover a unique city which has
much to offer shoppers. You will find excellent arts and
crafts shops, chic boutiques, department stores, and opal
and jewelry stores. While not on the same scale as Sydney and Melbourne, shopping in Adelaide does hold its
own in comparison to Brisbane and other cities in
Australia. Better yet, shopping in Adelaide is easily
managed because of its smaller population size and convenient street system. You can easily shop this city in two
days and then head for even more shopping in the many
charming arts and crafts towns in the surrounding hills
(Aldgate and Hahndorf) and valleys (Barossa).

THE STREETS OF ADELAIDE

Adelaide is Australia's best planned city. **Downtown
Adelaide** is laid out as a grid system, surrounded by green
parklands, and situated along the charming Torrens River.
This whole area is bounded by North, South, East, and
West Terrace roads.

Downtown Adelaide is best approached on foot. As
you will quickly discover, this is a walking city for shoppers. The main shopping area is concentrated along **Rundle Mall**, a pedestrian mall between King William and
Pultney streets, similar in appearance to the pedestrian
malls in Brisbane and Darwin. Within this highly congested three block commercial area are hundreds of shops
and three department stores crammed into 16 different

shopping arcades, centers, and plazas that feed into Rundle Mall. Here you can spend hours -- day and night -- walking from one shopping arcade to another as you untangle Adelaide's many clothing, arts and crafts, jewelry, and sporting goods shops as well as dine at its many restaurants and fast-food establishments. At the eastern end of Rundle Mall, beginning at East Terrace, the road is used annually by the Australian Grand Prix as part of its downtown trackway.

Just one block off Rundle Mall to the north along North Terrace are major hotels and Adelaide's famous gambling casino. Other surrounding streets define the central business district of commercial and government offices. King William Street, for example, is where you will find the post office and the city's major banks and insurance offices.

Outside the downtown area are a few suburban areas worth including in your shopping plans. You can easily get to these areas within 10 minutes by bus or taxi. **North Adelaide** was Adelaide's major upmarket shopping area until recently. Centered along **Melbourne Street,** just a five minute taxi ride from the downtown area, the shops here offer a nice mix of clothes, accessories, arts, and crafts. You can easily spend two to three hours browsing through the many boutiques and curio shops that line both sides of this pleasant street.

Other popular suburban areas for shopping include **Burnside Village** (Greenhill Road), a small upmarket shopping center in Glenside to the southeast of the city center, and **Hyde Park** (King William and Unley roads), a major upmarket shopping area filled with boutiques. The Hyde Park area requires a major walking effort especially given the length of King William Road.

Outside Adelaide you will find several small towns with shops selling some of South Australia'a best arts and crafts. While you can join bus tours of these areas, it may be more convenient to rent a car and drive yourself. You will pass through some lovely countryside of rolling hills and colorful vineyards. **Hahndorf,** 40 kilometers southeast of Adelaide, is a popular craft town with tourists. Shops here offer everything from the latest tourist kitsch to good quality arts and crafts. Nearby is the quaint and less touristed town of **Aldgate** with a few nice arts and crafts shops. To the north of Adelaide is the popular **Barossa Valley,** best known for its vineyards, but an excellent center for quality arts and crafts. Here you can visit galleries and shops throughout the valley but especially in the small towns of Bethany, Tanunda, Nuriootpa, and Angaston.

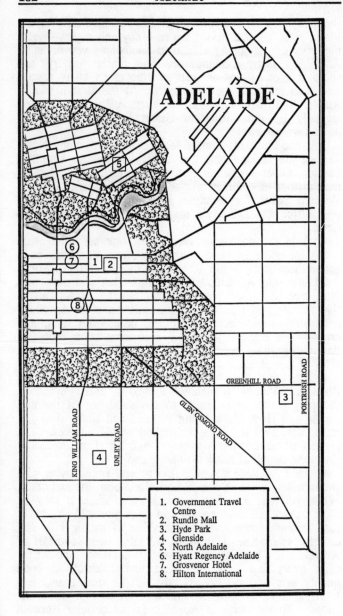

ADELAIDE

1. Government Travel
   Centre
2. Rundle Mall
3. Hyde Park
4. Glenside
5. North Adelaide
6. Hyatt Regency Adelaide
7. Grosvenor Hotel
8. Hilton International

GREENHILL ROAD

GLEN OSMOND ROAD

PORTRUSH ROAD

KING WILLIAM ROAD

UNLEY ROAD

GETTING ORIENTED

Given the size and planned nature of Adelaide, it is very easy to get oriented to this city. It's best to start your Adelaide shopping adventure at Rundle Mall in the downtown area. From here you can visit the major shopping centers and gather information on the city and surrounding area. One of your first stops should be the **S.A. Government Travel Centre** (Tel. 212-1644) at 18 King William Street, near the corner of Rundle Mall. This office has maps and tourist literature and can answer your questions and help you book tours. Be sure to pick up maps as well as current copies of *Your Guide to Adelaide*, *The Week in Adelaide*, *The Adelaide Tourist Guide*, *Adelaide Your Gateway*, *What's On In Adelaide and South Australia*, and *Adelaide For the Visitor*. Your hotel also should have copies of these and other helpful publications.

A good way to get oriented to the city is to purchase an unlimited day travel pass (adults A$10, pensioners A$9, children A$5, family of four A$25) on the **Adelaide Explorer.** This bus-tram stops at Adelaide's major attractions, such as the HMS Buffalo restaurant and Museum, Adelaide Casino, Old Parliament House, Marineland, Festival Centre, Botanic Gardens, and Adelaide Zoo.

You should be able to shop Adelaide and the surrounding areas on your own. We recommend renting a car and driving to the suburban areas as well as Hahndorf, Aldgate, and the Barossa Valley. Several rental car firms are located in downtown Adelaide. It's best to reserve a car the day before since many of the firms have few cars available, and those that are seem to be gone by 9am. Alternatively, you can book day and overnight tours through several tour companies or through the S.A. Government Travel Centre.

Should you wish assistance with your shopping, contact **A Little Shopping** (Tel. 274-1101) or **Dial A Shopper** (Tel. 223-6749). These are personalized shopping services that will take you through Adelaide's many boutiques and antique shops.

WHAT TO BUY

Adelaide's major shopping strengths are handcrafted items, clothes, and opals and jewelry. Outside Adelaide crafts and wine predominate as major shopping attractions. At the same time, you will find art, antique, leather, Australiana, gift, and duty-free shops to round out your shopping adventure.

Arts, Crafts, and Wine

The city, towns, and hills are alive with some of Australia's finest arts and crafts as well as some of the best shopping for handcrafted items in all of Australia. Indeed, many of the arts and crafts found in the shops of Brisbane, Sydney, and Melbourne come from artists and craftspeople who live and work in South Australia. Adelaide is the city that hosts the popular biennial Adelaide Arts Festival which attracts hundreds of craftspeople from all over Australia.

You will find numerous shops in the shopping arcades along Rundle Mall offering good quality arts and crafts. One of the nicest shops in all of Australia is **Quality 5 Crafts** (Shop #47) in the City Cross Arcade. This award-winning shop carries some truly unique and high quality arts and crafts primarily (90%) from South Australia. We also like **L'Unique** on the First Level of the Gallerie Shopping Centre and The Renaissance Arcade (Shop 6) for beautiful South Australian handcrafted pottery and related arts and crafts. **International Handicrafts** (22-23 Renaissance Arcade), operated by volunteers with the nonprofit Community Aid Abroad Project and also known as a CAA Trading Limited shop, offers a unique collection of handcrafted items from all over the world.

Adelaide also has its own state promotional craft center which is operated by the South Australian Craft Authority. Known as **The Jam Factory** (169 Payneham Road, St. Peters, Tel. 42-5661), it is similar in concept to The Meat Market Craft Centre in Melbourne. The Jam Factory has a gallery as well as offers training workshops in four major craft areas: knitted textiles, ceramics, glass, and leather. It also has a retail craft shop which sells handcrafted items to the public.

A few good quality arts and crafts shops are also found in the suburbs. We especially like the beautiful patchwork designs created at **The Patch Box** (106 King William Road) in Glenside. If you are interested in handcrafted clothes and knitwear, you will love this shop.

Some of the most interesting shopping for arts and crafts is found outside Adelaide in Aldgate, Hahndorf, and the Barossa Valley. If you rent a car, you can cover all three areas in a single day. However, it will be a long and rushed day, especially once you get into the Barossa Valley where you may be tempted to go wine tasting while doing arts and crafts shopping. The little town of **Aldgate**, located southeast of Adelaide just off the Princes Highway (before approaching Hahndorf, 2 kilometers beyond Stirling, and on Mount Baker Road), has one large art and craft shop -- **Aldgate Crafts** -- with excellent selections of pottery, textiles, clothes, basketry, hats, and stained glass. Affiliated with Quality 5 Shop in Adelaide, this shop alone is worth the trip to Aldgate. Another nice shop is **Aldgate Cottage** which is located next door to Aldgate Crafts. This shop tends to specialize in country crafts -- dried flowers, wood plaques, cuttings, and figures which would go well with Early American decors. Across the street in the Aldgate Valley Shopping Centre (226 Mount Baker Road) you will find two nice shops: **Aldgate Village Workshop**, which offers a very nice selection of hand-crafted pottery, pots, stained glass items, and clothes produced by craftsmen living in the hills of South Australia; and **Tootsies Village Clothing and Gallery** for unique costume clothing.

The nearby town of **Hahndorf**, located 33 kilometers southeast of Adelaide and 8 kilometers from Aldgate, is Australia's oldest German town. In recent years it has become an arts and crafts mecca for tourists. Disdained by many locals for its commercial atmosphere and heavy emphasis on tourist kitsch, it does have a few quality shops worth visiting. It's true, on a busy weekend as many as 30 tourist buses will descend on this small town and disgorge its camera-toting tourists as they proceed to overwhelm many of the small shops. Try to visit this town during a weekday so you may miss much of this activity.

Hahndorf's one main street is lined for 1 kilometer with restaurants, arts and crafts shops, trash and treasure stores, and antique bric-a-brac shops offering a wide range of handcrafted items. You can buy arts, crafts, antiques, opals, Australiana, skins and hides, and clothes in Hahndorf's many shops. You will find, for example, a branch shop of **L'Unique** here which offers good quality arts and crafts. We especially like a small shop called **Bamfulong Fine Crafts** (34 Main Street) for its uniquely designed hill crafts (clothes, pots, etc.) and **The Wool Factory** (54 Main Street) for handspun and hand knitted wool garments. However, most of the shops here tend to offer an overbundance of Australiana, gifts, and souvenirs. You will have to visit many shops before you will find unique and good quality items.

The **Barossa Valley** is another excellent source for arts and crafts. A one hour drive north of Adelaide, the Barossa Valley is most famous for its vineyards, wineries, and small craft towns. The best place to shop for quality arts and crafts is a small shop in Bethany -- **Bethany Art & Craft Gallery**. Located two kilometers from the town of Tanunda, this shop offers an excellent collection of handcrafted pottery, textiles, and woodcarved items. You will find, for example, exquisitely handcrafted blue and gold pottery by Marian Cole and unique scarves of wool challis by The Marble Art Studio. This shop makes an excellent first stop in the Valley, because it also functions as an information center on other nearby shops, restaurants, hotels, wineries, and the history of the Valley. Here you can pick up literature on the valley, especially the helpful "Land for All Seasons Visitors Guide to the Barossa Region" and the "Explorer" map of the Valley.

In Tanunda, the largest town in the Barossa Valley, look for several art and craft shops lining the main street: **Balloons** for nice pots, pottery, planters, and wicker items; **Joy Day Woodburns** for unique wood burnings and paintings; **The Raven's Parlor** and **Pioneer Antiques** for antique furniture and bric-a-brac; **The Fancy Bazaar** for country crafts and gifts; and the **Barossa Museum Shop** for similar quality handcrafted items as found in its sister shop, the Bethany Art & Craft Gallery.

North of Tanunda is the Barossa Valley's commercial center, **Nuriootpa**, which has little shopping of interest to visitors. If you turn right in Nuriootpa onto Angaston Road, you will go directly into the small town of **Angaston** which has a few shops worth visiting. You will find four antique, bric-a-brac, and craft shops on the main street: **Cavendish Antiques, Angaston Cottage Industries, Angaston Antiques,** and **Angaston Galleria.** Angaston Galleria, located in an old church, has an unusual collection of Australian arts and crafts also with many items from Mexico and Taiwan! The prices at this shop for local pottery are some of the best we have found anywhere in Australia. You also may want to visit the popular **Angas Park Dried Fruit** company, which is located a few blocks west of these shops at the corner of Murray and North streets. This company has a retail shop (Angas Park Promotions Centre) offering a very good selection of assorted dried fruits, many of which are exported to the United States.

On your return trip to Adelaide, you may want to take the road directly south of Angaston which goes through Eden Valley and Springton. In Springton you will find one major shop, the **Springton Gallery** (Miller Street, open 11am to 5pm), which offers a large assortment of excellent quality arts and crafts. And, of course, don't forget to stop at the many wineries that dot the Valley. Many of these wineries offer tours and have retail shops where you can taste wines and purchase some of Australia's best wines directly from the manufacturers.

Clothes and Fashionwear

Similar to other cities in Australia, Adelaide has its own budding group of fashion designers who produce some very attractive and trendy garments. Local designers, such as Walter Kristensen, Bowie's, Harry Who, George Gross, Naffines, and Skins and Things, produce some of Australia's most attractive and fashionable clothes for women. While by no means as large and well known a group as the designers in Melbourne and Sydney, nonetheless, they do offer unique designs which attract the eyes of many visitors to Adelaide.

You will find numerous clothing stores and boutiques in the various arcades of Rundle Mall. However, the best concentration of good quality boutiques and clothing stores is found in the suburbs of Hyde Park, Burnside, and North Adelaide.

Indeed, King William and Unley roads in Hyde Park have quickly become the fashion centers for all of South Australia. This is to Adelaide what Toorak Road is to Melbourne and Double Bay is to Sydney. Here you can easily spend a full day walking these two long streets to visit the numerous boutiques and shops along the way.

Along King William Road, for example, you will find such shops as **DiHill** and **Chrisdi** (116), two local de-signer-label shops producing unique evening wear, casual outfits, knitwear, and nicely designed silk garments; **Front-Cover** with its all Australian designed clothes from Rae Ganim, Lisa Barron, Cliche, Lisa Ho, Shiman, Teena Vargos, and Jill Fitzsimon; **Bowie's** (165A), a local desig-ner producing very attractive womenswear in both casual (Town & Country label) and upmarket (Bowie label) col-lections; **Lorenzini** (165B) for menswear; **Toffs Fashion House** for a good selection of designer label clothes from such Australian designers as Harry Who, George Gross, Covers, Susie Gallagher, Jill Fitzsimon, Perry Cutten, Peter Metcheve, Lisa Ho, and Trent Nathan and New Zealand leather designer Brigid Brock; **Liz Davenport** (173) for fashionable womenswear; **Pellissimo** (150A) for attractive leatherwear; and **Kerley's** (185), at the corner of King William Road and Mitchel Street/Park Street for fine qua-lity menswear (David Freiz, Trent Nathan, and Don Vag-nato labels).

Unley Road is a 10 minute walk from the intersection of King William Road and Mitchel Street/Park Street. Newly transformed into a street of upmarket boutiques, the major shopping center is the new **Metro**, on the corner of Park Street and Unley Road. This is Adelaide's designer fashion center, similar in concept to Melbourne's The Shop of Shops. Here you will find boutiques of **Sportscraft, Maggie T, Palmer & Palmer, Midas Shoe, Najee, Brian Rochford, Cherry Lane, Canterbury, Sportsgirl, Perri Cutten, Adele Palmer, Cue Design,** and **New Image Fashion.** Directly across the street in a row of old shops are several nice boutiques and clothing stores: **Carla Zampatti, Panache Boutique, Punch Menswear,** and **Country Road.** Further north along Unley Road at Oxford Corner (corner of Oxford Terrace) is a **Sportsgirl** and **Kristensen's Boutique** (includes the designer labels of Walter Kristensen and Teena Varigos). Nearby is a branch of **Just Jeans** and **Robert Miels Menswear** (154 Unley Road), a nice men's shop with good prices.

Burnside Village and Village Shopping Centre in Glenside (corner of Greenhill and Portrush roads) also have a few nice clothing stores and boutiques. The **Demasius Department Store** stocks several designer labels, and locals like to shop here because of prices and selections. You will also find two of Adelaide's major designers offering attractive clothing for women: **Walter Kristensen** and **Bowie's.** Also look for **Francesca Boutique** and **Sportsgirl Design.**

North Adelaide, especially along Melbourne Street, used to be Adelaide's most upmarket fashion center. However, this has all changed in the last few years with the continuing development of the Rundle Mall area as well as the dynamic growth of King William Road and Unley Road as the fashion center for Adelaide. As a result, several boutiques along Melbourne Street have relocated to these other areas, and Melbourne Street is beginning to look a little worn and tired. Nonetheless, you will still find some of Adelaides best boutiques along Melbourne Street. Look for **Vinnie Tessile** (168) for nice sleepwear; **Country Road** (116-120) for a good selection of sportswear; **Alta Moda** (104) for attractive menswear; **Francesca Boutique** (84) for nice womenswear; and **Witchcraft Boutique** (78), **Chatterbox Boutique** (74A), and **New Image Fashion** (60) for locally designed clothes.

In downtown Adelaide the **Gallerie Shopping Centre** has the largest collection of upmarket boutiques and clothing stores. Here you will find two of Adelaide's leading designer boutiques -- **Walter Kristensen** and **Bowie's.** Also look for **Laura Ashley, Posh, Carla Zampatti, Breaking Rules,** and **R. M. Williams. City Cross Arcade** also has some very nice boutiques, clothing, and accessory shops: **Shepherds, Country Road, Body Shop, South Girl, Joshua Shoes, Canterbury Clothes,** and **Cue.** For nice menswear and womenswear, look for **Fletcher Jones** on Main Street, next door to Johns Decor. A small shop in Twin Plaza (38), **Royal Designs**, does beautiful made-to-order womenswear -- cocktail dresses, evening wear, suits, and dresses.

If you are interested in furs, two shops in downtown Adelaide can help you: **Fashion Furs** (Shop 202, Rundle Street) and **Hodders & Hunter** (Shop 15, Adelaide Arcade). And Adelaide also has its own branch of **Morrisons** (Rundle Street) for Australian menswear.

Opals and Jewelry

Adelaide and South Australia are also the centers for Australia's opal industry. One of Australia's largest opal mining areas, for example, is found in Coober Pedy (960 kilometers northwest of Adelaide) as well as in Andamooka. Opals mined in these areas find their way into numerous shops in Adelaide.

Some of the better known opal and jewelry stores include: **Adelaide Gem Trading Company** (26 Currie Street, Tel. 212-3600); **Opal Field Gems** (29 King William Street, Tel. 212-5300); **Olympic Opal Jewellers** (5 Rundle Mall, Tel. 211-7440); **The Opal Mine** (30 Gawler Place, Tel. 223-4023); **Gemstone Corporation of Australia** (48 Gawler Place, Tel. 272-6444); **Jackson Jem and Opal Centre** (Lobby, Adelaide Hilton International, Victoria Square, Tel. 212-2939); **Precious Gems of Australia** (7 Hindley Street, Tel. 212-3493); and **Twin Plaza Gems** (Shop 1, Twin Plaza Arcade, Twin Street, Tel. 223-4828). Duty-free shops as well as some souvenir shops also carry opals and jewelry.

Australiana, Gifts, and Souvenirs

You will find the usual assortment of Australiana, gifts, and souvenirs -- stuffed fur animals, leather goods, mugs, spoons, pottery, kangaroo and lambskin rugs, jumpers, tea towels, boomerangs, postcards, and T-shirts and sweatshirts -- in many of Adelaide's downtown and suburban shops. The Rundle Mall area has the largest concentration of such shops. Look for **Lawrence** (111 Rundle Mall), **Bank Street Souvenirs** (Shop 12A Bank Street), **City Souvenir Centre** (Shop 43A, City Cross Arcade), **Festival City Souvenirs** (36A King William Street), **Aussie Gifts** (173 Rundle Street), and **Grande Leather Goods & Australiana** (Shop 14, Renaissance Centre, Rundle Mall).

Arts and Antiques

Several shops in and around Adelaide offer arts and

antiques from Australia and abroad. Look for **Bernadette's Gallery** (90 Carrington Street) for over 150 artworks and changing exhibits. The **South Australia Museum Shop** (North Terrace) -- has a good selection of Aboriginal and modern Australian arts and crafts as well as Egyptian replicas, jewelry, toys, books, posters, and postcards. **Adella Gallery** (28 Currie Street) also sells Aboriginal art. **Pedestal Gallery** (Gays Arcade, Rundle Mall) offers original paintings by Australian artists. In North Adelaide you will find two art and antique shops along Melbourne Road: **Elder Fine Art Galleries** (106) and **Ruth Irving Antiques** (79).

We found one very interesting shop selling Asian arts and antiques in the midst of Adelaide's suburban fashion center, Glenside: **Zen Oriental Design** (148 Unley Road). This shop offers some of the best selections of Asian arts and antiques in all of Australia, especially Japanese chests, Chinese panels, Thai Buddhas and lacquerware, and textiles. It also has a unique collection of tribal arts and crafts from Papua New Guinea and Africa, many of which are collector's items of museum quality.

WHERE TO SHOP

If you want to fully shop Adelaide, your shopping adventure should take you to six shopping areas: downtown (Rundle Mall and adjacent streets), suburbs (Hyde Park, Glenside, North Adelaide), and small craft towns (Aldgate, Hahndorf, Barossa Valley) each within one hour of Adelaide. You will also find some shops, such as **The Jam Factory**, in other suburbs and craft towns.

Downtown Shopping Arcades

Downtown Adelaide is the city shopping center. **Rundle Mall**, stretching from Pulteney Street to King William Street, is one of Australia's largest and most compact pedestrian malls, similar to the ones found in Brisbane and Darwin. This is where you will find Adelaide's major shopping arcades, department stores, and shops. It's where most visitors to Adelaide begin their shopping, where Adelaide's young people congregate, and where the annual Grand Prix races draw crowds at the Rundle Street section of the race track. The nearby streets house Adelaide's major banks, hotels, restaurants, and the Adelaide Casino.

The **Rundle Mall** area consists of 16 separate shopping arcades that feed into Rundle Mall, adjacent streets, and each other:

- Southern Cross Arcade
- City Cross Arcade
- De Costa Arcade
- Regent Arcade
- Adelaide Arcade
- Gays Arcade
- Renaissance Centre
- Twin Plaza Arcade
- Renaissance Arcade
- John Martins Plaza
- The Gallerie Shopping Centre
- Rundle Arcade
- Millers Arcade
- Station Arcade

Most of these arcades are small to medium size, housing 10 to 50 shops. The most upscale shopping arcade is **The Gallerie Shopping Centre** which houses several of Adelaide's best boutiques, clothing stores, and jewelers. The **Renaissance Arcade, John Martin Plaza**, and **City Cross Arcade** are also relatively upscale. You will also find three major department stores in this area: **Myer, David Jones**, and **John Martin's**.

Some of our favorite shops in the Rundle Mall area include **L'Unique** and **International Handicrafts** in the Renaissance Arcade for excellent selections of both Australian and international handcrafted items; **Hunters** in the John Martin Plaza for unique seamless sweaters and gift items; **Royal Designs** in Twin Plaza for made-to-order fashion clothes and dresses; **Quality 5 Crafts** in City Cross Arcade for one of Australia's finest collections of arts and crafts; **The Cue Shop** in City Cross Arcade for nice women's clothes; and **Michael's** and **Nicholas Pike** in Gallerie Shopping Centre for jewelry. You will find some familiar shops -- mainly boutiques and clothing stores -- in downtown Adelaide that you also found in most other major Australian cities: **Morrisons, R. M. Williams, Alta Moda, Laura Ashley, Posh**, and **Carla Zampatti**.

Hyde Park

Adelaide's three major shopping suburbs are within 10 minutes driving distance from the downtown area. **Hyde Park**, located 3 kilometers directly south of Rundle Mall, is Adelaide's second major shopping area. Here you can easily spend the day walking up and down two major parallel streets -- King William Road and Unley Road -- that are lined with Adelaide's finest boutiques and clothing stores. This is definitely the most upscale shopping area in

Adelaide, similar in concept and style to Double Bay in
Sydney as well as Toorak Road and The Shop of Shops in
Melbourne.   It's best to start shopping this area at the
northern end of King William Road at **The Patch Box**
(102 King William Road) and continue walking south until
you reach the intersection with Park and Mitchel streets.
Turn left onto Park Street and walk approximately 1 kilometer until you reach Unley Road.   Take another left and
walk north along Unley Road for approximately two kilometers.   You will initially see the **Metro**, Adelaide's new
fashion center with its numerous designer label boutiques,
on the corner of Park Street and Unley Road.   Similar to
King William Road, you will find shops along both sides
of Unley Road.

Some of our favorite shops along **King William Road**
include **The Patch Box** (102) with its beautiful hand
produced patch work clothes and hand knit sweaters;
DiHill and **Chrisdi** (116) for some lovely evening wear,
sportswear, and sweaters locally designed and produced;
Front-Cover (155-165) for its nice collection of Australian
designer clothes representing Rae Ganim, Lisa Barron,
Cliche, Lisa Ho, Shiman, Tenna Vargos, and Jill Fitzsimo-
n; **Bowie's** (165A) for uniquely designed causal and formal
wear by one of Adelaide's top designers; **Pellissimo** (150)
for leatherwear; **Toffs Fashion House** (169-171) for major
designer label clothes and accessories by Harry Who,
George Gross, Covers, Susie Gallagher, Jill Fitzsimon,
Perry Cutten, Peter Metchev, Lisa Ho, and Trent Nathan;
Circe (173) for nice sleepwear and lingerie; and **Kerley's**
(185) for menswear with such famous Australian labels as
David Freiz, Trent Nathan, and Don Vagnato.   A good
coffee shop in this area is **Jekyll's of Hyde Park.**

While the shops along King William Road primarily sell
upmarket clothes, many shops along **Unley Road** offer arts
and antiques along with top name brand clothes.   At the
new **Metro** fashion center, look for such famous designer
shops as **Sportscraft, Maggie T, Palmer & Palmer,
Brian Rochford, Cherry Lane, Canterbury, Sportsgirl,
Perri Cutten, Adele Palmer,** and **Cue Design.**   Across
the street you will find boutiques such as **Carla Zampatti**
(211) and **Panache Boutique** (221), an antique shop (**Bar-
oque Antique**), and **Country Road**, a popular sportswear
shop.   As you proceed further north on Unley Road from
the Metro area, you will find few shops until you reach the
corner of Oxford Terrace.   It's a long walk to this next
shopping area.   When you come to Oxford Terrace you
will see a building on your right named **Oxford Corner.**
This building houses a **Sportsgirl** and a **Kristensen's
Boutique.**   Across the street on Unley Road is a **Just**

Jeans and a nice men's shop, **Robert Miels Menswear** (154). Next comes one of Australia's best Asian art and antique shops -- **Zen Oriental Design** (148). This shop has a fine collection of top quality Japanese furniture, Chinese screens, Thai Buddhas and lacquerware, Sumba textiles, and primitive arts from Africa and Papua New Guinea. Indeed, compared to anywhere else in Australia or Papua New Guinea, we discovered some of the finest quality artifacts from Papua New Guinea in this shop.

Glenside

Glenside is another upscale shopping area you may wish to visit if time permits. Located 3 kilometers southeast of Rundle Mall, Glenside's major shopping area is the **Burnside Village Shopping Centre/Atrium Mall.** Located at the corner of Greenhill and Portrush roads, across the street from the Glenside municipal office, this is small but upcoming shopping area frequented by many of Adelaide's upmarket shoppers. You will find a small but nice department store here, **Demasius**, which carries many designer label clothes. **Walter Kristensen**, the noted Adelaide designer, and **Sportsgirl Design** have trendy boutiques in the Burnside Village Shopping Centre section. The newly completed **Atrium Mall**, which is adjacent to the Burnside center, has 24 shops. Here, you will find a branch boutique of another noted Adelaide designer, **Bowie's.**

North Adelaide

North Adelaide used to be the major upmarket suburban shopping area. Centered on **Melbourne Street,** just a five minute drive from Rundle Mall, this area still has some very nice shops and restaurants although it has the appearance of an area in decline. It's best to start shopping this area just west of the intersection of Jerningham and Melbourne streets, which is directly across the street from **The Old Lion Hotel.** The first place to visit is **Vinnie Tessile** (168) with its nice selection of sleepware. As you proceed east along Melbourne Street, you will come to such shops as **Olympic Opal Jewellers** (142) which does good handcrafted jewelry work; **Country Road** (116-120) for Australian designed sportswear; **Elder Fine Art Galleries** (106); **Francesca Boutique** (84) for nice womenswear; **Ruth Irving Antiques** (79); **Witchcraft Boutique** (78); **Chatterbox Boutiuqe** (74A); and **New Image Fashion** (60). You will also find some good restaurants along this street, such as Picasso's Reaturant (73) and Zapata's Mexican Restaurant (42).

Craft Towns

You will find numerous small towns with craft shops in South Australia. However, you may want to concentrate your shopping on two major areas within a day's drive of Adelaide. The first area, **Aldgate** and **Hahndorf**, is located approximately 40 kilometers southeast of Adelaide just off Route 1. The small town of **Aldgate** has very few shops. However, **Aldgate Crafts** on Mount Baker Road is well worth the visit to Aldgate. Owned by the Studio 5 Group, an award winning group of craft shops, Aldgate Crafts offers some of the best quality hill crafts -- pottery, basketry, stained glass, fabrics, oil lamps -- you will find in South Australia. Also look for **Aldgate Cottage** next door for country crafts and the **Aldgate Village Workshop** (226 Mount Baker Road), another good quality arts and crafts shop offering some unique pottery collections.

Hahndorf, located just 5 kilometers from Aldgate, is the oldest German town in Australia. In recent years it has become a major tourist attraction because of its many arts and crafts shops. Both sides of the street are lined with arts and crafts shops and German restaurants. While the town is somewhat overrun by tourists and disliked by many South Australians for its touristy atmosphere and trinket quality shopping, you can still find some good quality shopping in this town. We especially like **L'Unique** (Market Place Shopping Centre), a branch shop of two similar shops found in the Renaissance Arcade and Gallerie Shopping Centre in downtown Adelaide, with its fine collection of South Australian arts and crafts; **Bamfurlong Fine Crafts** (34 Main Street) with many good quality handcrafted items produced by Hahndorf craftspeople; and **The Wool Factory** (54 Main Street) for handspun and hand knitted garments and gift items.

The **Barossa Valley** is another good place to go shopping for South Australian arts and crafts. Located a little more than one hour from Adelaide by way of Route 1 and Main North Road, the Barossa Valley is dotted with numerous wineries and small craft towns. While you may wish to spend two or three days relaxing, tasting wine, and shopping in this lovely valley, you can easily drive to and from the Valley in one day. We recommend that you first stop at one of the best shops in all of the Barossa Valley, **Bethany Art & Craft Gallery**, which is located just before you reach the town of Bethany. You will find excellent quality arts and crafts here as well as maps and literature on restaurants, hotels, and activities within the

Barossa Valley. The owner is very helpful, and you will be treated to nonalcoholic wine while you shop. Next, go to the nearby town of Tanunda where you will find several arts, crafts, and antique shops along the main street. The **Barossa Museum Shop**, operated by the owners of the Bethany Art & Craft Gallery, has an excellent shop worth visiting along with the interesting museum. Also look for **The Raven's Parlor** and **Pioneer Antiques** for antique furniture and bric-a-brac; **Joy Day Woodburns** in the Kavel Arcade for woodburnings and paintings; and **Balloons** in the Kavel Arcade for nice pottery, wicker items, and gifts. In the midst of this main shopping street is one of the Barossa Valley's best restaurants--**Zinfandel Restaurant**. A small, homey, and extremely popular restaurant, it serves some of best German food, including excellent desserts, in Australia -- and all at reasonable prices.

Further north of Tanunda is the Valley's commercial center, Nuriootpa. You may decide to skip this town altogether as you head directly east along Angaston Road for the town of **Angaston**. This town has a few interesting arts, crafts, and antique shops. **Angaston Galleria**, an old church converted to a craft shop, has a large but eclectic collection of arts and crafts from all over Australia as well as from Mexico and Taiwan. The prices here are very good, especially on pottery. **Cavendish Antiques** and **Angaston Antiques** both carry small antiques and bric-a-brac for antique treasure hunters. Also, be sure to stop at the **Angas Park Dried Fruit** company, which has a retail shop at the corner of Murray and North streets. This shop has a good selection of freshly packed dried fruits.

You may want to leave Angaston via North Street to the south toward Keyeton or Eden Valley. This road will eventually take you into the small town of Springton which is home to the **Springton Gallery** (Miller Street). This shop has a large selection of arts and crafts, from pottery to Japanese kimonos.

ENJOYING YOUR STAY

Adelaide has several good hotels and restaurants. The best hotel is the new **Hyatt Regency Adelaide** on North Terrace, next to the new Adelaide Convention Centre and Adelaide Casino and directly across the street from the popular **Grosvenor Hotel** (125 North Terrace). Both of these hotels are conveniently located just one block from Rundle Mall. After the Hyatt Regency, the **Hilton International Adelaide** (233 Victoria Square) competes as Adelaide's best hotel. Other good hotels include the **Ade-**

laide **Parkroyal** (226 South Terrace), **Earl of Zetland** (44 Flinders Street), **Gateway** 147 (North Terrace), **Hotel Adelaide** (62 Brougham Place, North Adelaide), **Old Adelaide Inn** (O'Connell and Gover streets, North Adelaide), and **Richmond** (128 Rundle Mall). If you plan to arrive in Adelaide without reservations, you may want to visit one of the South Australian tourist offices in other major cities where you can pick up a copy of a useful guide to accommodations in Adelaide, the suburbs, resorts, and towns: *Adelaide South Australia Accommodations*. This guide lists the names, addresses, and telephone numbers as well as price ranges for accommodations. You can also book accommodations through these offices prior to arriving in Adelaide.

You will find numerous restaurants throughout Adelaide offering everything from German specialties to Oriental dishes and seafood. Some of Adelaide's best restaurants include: **Henry Ayers House** (Tel. 224-0666); **The Grange** (Tel. 217-0711); **Chelsea** (Tel. 217-7552); **Bangkok** (Tel. 223-5406) for Thai food; **Jarmer's Restaurant** (Tel. 332-2080) in Kensington Park; **Magic Flute** (267-3172) in North Melbourne; **Ellinis** (Tel. 212-6793) for Greek food; Further outside Adelaide are **Pataluma** (Tel. 339-3422) in Bridgewater; **Duthy's** (Tel. 272-0465) at 19 Duthy Street in Malvern; **Pheasant Farm** (Tel. 62-1286) on Samuel Road (Nuriootpa); and **Zinfandel** (Tel. 63-2822) at 58 Murray Street in Tanunda.

Adelaide and South Australia have a great deal to offer visitors who have a few days to enjoy the many and varied pleasures of this city and state. In addition to shopping, the area offers a number of attractions to make any holiday a memorable experience. Within Adelaide, the major tourist sites include:

- **Adelaide Casino:** located on North Terrace next to the luxury Hyatt Regency Hotel, the Adelaide Convention Centre and the restored railway station, this is Adelaide's premier gaming center.

- **Adelaide Festival Centre:** Located on the banks of the Torrens River, this is the city's performing arts complex. Tours are available, but you may want to attend one of the many regularly scheduled theatrical or musical performances.

- **Art Gallery of South Australia:** Houses a substantial collection of Australian, English, and European paintings.

- **Ayers House:** Located on North Terrace, this old mansion serves as the headquarters for the state branch of the National Trust.

- **Botanic Garden:** Located on North Terrace, this 40 acre (16 hectares) area displays Australian and exotic plants.

- **HMS Buffalo:** Located at Adelphi Terrace in the suburb of Glenelg. A full scale model of the Buffalo, the ship that brought the first colonist to Glenelg in 1836. Contains a good maritime museum and restaurant.

- **Light's Vision:** Located on the corner of Pennington Terrace and Montefiore Road, North Adelaide, this hill provides you with a panoramic view of the city, Adelaide Hills, Torrens River, and parklands.

- **Old Parliament House:** Located on North Terrace, this is Australia's only museum devoted to political history.

- **St. Peter's Cathedral:** Located at Pennington Terrace, North Adelaide, this is one of Adelaide's most famous historic and architectural landmarks. Noted for its beautiful towers and spires and pealing bells.

- **South Australian Museum:** Located on North Terrace, this museum houses the world's best collection of Aboriginal artifacts as well as excellent displays on Melanesia and the Pacific Islands.

- **Zoological Gardens:** Located on Frome Road, the zoo is particularly noted for its fine collection of Australian birds as well as its ability to breed rare animals. Includes a special Children's Zoo.

In addition to visiting the Barossa Valley, Hahndorf, and Aldgate **outside Adelaide**, you will find several other interesting towns and hill areas worth visiting for their historical sites, museums, wineries, and recreational opportunities: Belair, Birdwood, Blackwood, Bridgewater, Clarendon, Cudlee Creek, Glen Osmond, Gumerache, Hersbrook, Lobethal, Mount Baker, Mount Lofty, Norton Summit, One Tree Hill, Springfield, and Windy Point. Further outside the metropolitan area -- requiring more than one day to visit -- are such popular destinations as Coober Pedy for opal mining; the Eyre Peninsula for its coastal resorts; Flinders Ranges for its spectacular mountain scenery and bushwalking; Kangaroo Island for its wildlife and beaches; the Murray River for its cruises; and Mt. Gambier for its lakes.

Adelaide also offers over 32 kilometers of lovely **beaches** and seaside resorts within a 30 minute drive from the city. The beaches have excellent facilities for swimming and boating. If you enjoy fishing from jetties, go to the popular fishing beaches at Brighton, Glenelg, Henley Beach, Grange, Semaphore, and Largs Bay.

The **Barossa Valley**, as noted earlier in our discussion of craft towns, is a popular destination for both its wineries and craft shops. Located less than two hours drive north of Adelaide, the Barossa Valley begins around the town of Grawler. Many visitors to Adelaide plan to stay two or three days in this area enjoying the wineries, quaint towns, interesting historical sites, excellent restaurants and bakeries, friendly accommodations, and varied recreational opportunities. Indeed, you will find 50 wineries open to the public for tours, wine tasting, and retail sales. Settled by German Lutherans in the early 1800s, the Valley has retained much of its old world charm and hospitality. There's plenty to see and do, from touring the many wineries to taking hot air balloon rides to sampling the many marvelous old bakeries and restaurants in the towns. You will find many small country hotels, motels, traditional farms houses, and camping sites for accommodations. The **South Australia Government Travel Centre** at 18 King William Street (Tel. 212-1644) in Adelaide as well as the **Barossa Information Centre** at 66 Murray Street (Tel. 62-1866) in Nuriootpa can assist you with your plans to visit the Valley.

Another popular area for famous South Australian vineyards and wineries is the **Clare Valley**, located in the hills of the northern Mt. Lofty Ranges. The historic town of Clare is the center for visiting this area.

Known as the "Festival City", Adelaide is a great place to visit during the biennial crafts festival that draws hundreds of craftspeople from all over Australia. This festival is held during the month of March in even-numbered years. The Australian Grand Prix is held every October. Small towns, such as Hahndorf, Tanunda, Willunga, and McLaren Vale, also have festivals.

Chapter Nine

ALICE SPRINGS

Alice Springs is a relatively isolated frontier town of 25,000 people that is noted for hosting 200,000 visitors a year. Located in the heart of Australia's famous Outback, Alice Springs is the second largest town in the Northern Territory. The largest city, Darwin, is situated 1,500 kilometers directly north via the Stuart Highway.

Also known as The Red Centre, for its deep orange and red colored soil, this is the area of Ayers Rock and The Olgas -- two of the world's most unique and impressive rock formations. It's also an area of Aborigines, festivals, camels, a casino, pedestrian shopping mall, shopping arcades, boutiques, and unusual festivals.

Once a shabby town of rugged individualists, Alice Springs still retains its Outback frontier character while it also functions as a major tourist destination for those who want to sample the sights of the unique Outback. While by no means a shopper's paradise, it can claim to be a shopper's oasis. For it offers some surprising buying opportunities for those who are particularly interested in Outback art and the local Aboriginal cultures.

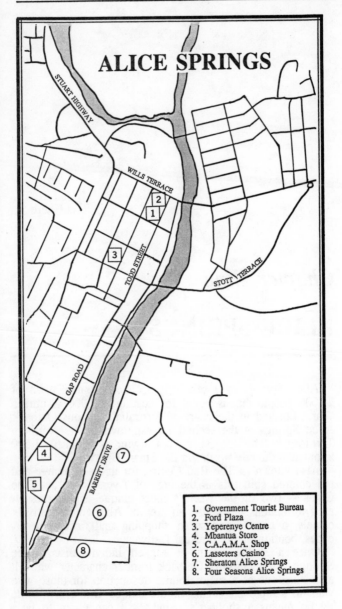

ALICE SPRINGS

1. Government Tourist Bureau
2. Ford Plaza
3. Yeperenye Centre
4. Mbantua Store
5. C.A.A.M.A. Shop
6. Lasseters Casino
7. Sheraton Alice Springs
8. Four Seasons Alice Springs

GETTING TO KNOW YOU

If you arrive in Alice Springs from any of Australia's major cities, you will experience a very sudden and striking transformation in Australia's physical, social, and cultural landscapes. First of all, Alice Springs is a small town with some big-city ideas about attracting tourists with unique festivals, a casino, hotels, tour companies, recreational opportunities, and a shopping mall. Arrive at the airport and you quickly discover what a small town this is as you walk through a small terminal to pick up your bags from a loading cart next to the bus and taxi stand. Attend its famous Camel Cup races or Henley-On-Todd Regatta bottomless boat races on the dry bed of the Todd River, and you sense that some things are very different here in the Outback!

Secondly, Alice Springs is surrounded by an arid, harsh, and barren landscape exhibiting dramatic contrasts -- temperature extremes, beautiful floral, unique fauna, unusual rock formations, and spectacular hues and colors. The landscape itself generates a sense of timelessness, an ethereal quality captured in many Aboriginal paintings. At night you can look up at the sky and see fabulous constellations, especially the Milky Way and Southern Cross.

Third, this area impresses you with its flies, wind, dust, and sand. The Outback flies are everywhere. You can't escape them except for fleeing into a fly-free air-conditioned vehicle or building. Depending on the time of year you visit, the flies can be either a mild annoyance -- the winter months -- or a major irritation -- the rest of the year. The wind is often strong, blowing tons of dust and sand in all directions -- but not removing the flies from your body! On a hot day, the mixture of flies, wind, dust, and sand confirms the fact that Alice Springs and its surrounding countryside is indeed a harsh area for rugged individualists.

Fourth, Alice Springs quickly introduces you to the Aborigines and their culture as well as their socioeconomic problems. Walk along the Todd Street Mall and you will see several groups of seemingly poor, dirty Aborigines sitting around socializing with each other or drinking. Socially and economically dislocated, many of these Aborigines live on the outskirts of town or sleep in the dry bed of the Todd River next to trees and logs. And still others are visiting town from settlements to sell their paintings and carvings to local shops, galleries, and middlemen as well as to purchase additional art supplies, food, drink, clothing, and household provisions. The sight of these Aborigines in Alice Springs' major shopping areas may at first startle you with their primitive looks, charcoal skins, deep features, unkept appearance, odor, social distance, and loud and aggressive manners amongst themselves. Nonetheless, they are a very shy people with outsiders and tend to keep to themselves; they will not bother you. Remember, you should not take photographs of them since they may take offense at such an invasion of their privacy.

THE STREETS OF ALICE SPRINGS

Thanks for small towns after shopping in Australia's big cities! Alice Springs is very easy to get around on foot and by taxi. The city is somewhat spread out over a 12 kilometer area. Upon arriving in Alice Springs, you should pick up a map and tourist literature which are available at the airport and hotels as well as through the **Northern Territory Government Tourist Bureau.** The Bureau is conveniently located on the Ground Floor of the Ford Plaza at Todd Mall and is very helpful in providing literature, answering questions, and booking hotels and tours.

Alice Springs has one main shopping street, Todd Mall-Todd Street-Gap Road. Like many other streets in Australia, this one changes its name three different times. The street stretches for more than 7 kilometers and is where all the major shops and shopping centers are located. Being a very long street and not conveniently located within easy walking distance from such major hotels as Lasseters Casino and the Sheraton Hotel, you may need to take a hotel bus or taxi into the center of town at the Todd Mall to begin your shopping adventure. After shopping along the Todd Mall and a few adjacent streets, you may wish to take a taxi for a three kilometer ride until Todd Street becomes Gap Road and resume shopping at a few shops along Gap Road between Strehlow and Kempe streets.

WHAT TO BUY

Alice Springs has full service shopping centers and shops selling the latest in fashionwear, accessories, gift items, and Australiana. However, Alice Springs' major shopping strength is **Aboriginal arts.** Next to Darwin in the north, this town functions as the most important center for marketing arts and crafts produced by numerous Aboriginal groups in the Northern Territories.

Compared to similar quality items found in Sydney and Melbourne, Aboriginal art prices in Alice Springs are very good. A similar acrylic or bark painting to one selling for

$1,000 in Sydney or Melbourne may sell for $350 in Alice Springs. The prices are less here, because you buy with only one or two middlemen between you and the artists; in Sydney and Melbourne you may be buying items that have already passed through the hands and mark-ups of three or four middlemen. However, a Tiwi bark basket that sells for $50 on Melville Island off the coast of Darwin, may cost $80 in Darwin, $100 in Alice Springs, and $200 in Sydney, because it first passes through middlemen who collect such items on Melville Island before marketing them in Darwin, Alice Springs, and Sydney. Bark paintings that primarily originate in the Darwin area will be cheaper there than in Alice Springs, but cheaper in Alice Springs than in Adelaide, Melbourne, Sydney, or Brisbane.

Several shops in downtown Alice Springs sell a good variety of Aboriginal arts and crafts from the western desert. The best buys in this area are the unique **acrylic dot paintings** which used to be done only in sand and then destroyed. Lacking trees for wood and bark -- found more abundantly further north near Darwin -- the local Aboriginal art traditions were committed to sand and rocks until the twentieth century. First developed by Geoff Bardon, an art and craft teacher at the nearby Papunya School, today there are over 100 Aboriginal artists using the acrylic and canvas mediums to paint colorful dreamtime themes and stories. Associated with the Papunya Tula art school, this is one of Australia's most important contemporary art movements, and it's centered here in Alice Springs. Consequently, you will find the best prices on these paintings in the shops of Alice Springs; prices are higher in Darwin, Adelaide, Melbourne, and Sydney. If you appreciate this art style, you can spend a great deal of time going from one shop to another to learn more about this school of art as well as discover just the right painting with the right colors, designs, and dream time story.

Another good buy in Alice Springs are the beautiful handmade **batik cloth designs** which we have not seen outside Alice Springs. Marketed under the name Utopia Batik, this textile work is being done on Aboriginal settlements near Alice Springs and marketed through two branches of the **C.A.A.M.A. Shop** (on Gap Road and in the Yeperenye Centre on Hartley Street).

Several shops also sell **woodcarvings** of small animals using a traditional Aboriginal wood burning process; **bark paintings** from the Darwin area; **carved poles** and **bark baskets** from the Tiwi tribe of Melville Island; didjeridoos, clap sticks, boomerangs, and music.

We are especially impressed with five shops offering good quality Aboriginal arts and crafts. The ordering scheme reflects our preferences:

- **Central Australian Artifacts:** Located on the ground floor of the Ford Plaza, Todd Mall. Has an excellent selection of acrylic paintings which it commissions from local Aboriginal artists. Offers some of the best quality bark paintings, didjeridoos, wood burnt animals, and Tiwi woodcarvings and bark baskets we have found anywhere in Australia. Experienced in shipping items abroad. Also opening a new gallery that will only sell top quality Aboriginal acrylic paintings.

- **C.A.A.M.A. Shop:** Has two shops -- located at the Yeperenye Centre on Hartley Street and near the corner of Kempe Street on Gap Road (continuation of Todd Street). Offers excellent selections of acrylic paintings, woodcarvings, and the unique Utopia Batik. The Gap Road shop is the main shop.

- **Mbantua Store:** Located at 55 Gap Road approximately four kilometers from the Todd Mall via Todd Street. This is one of the most interesting general stores you will find in Australia; it also functions as an art gallery selling acrylic and bark paintings, woodcarvings, and didjeridoos. Offers some of the best prices anywhere in Australia. This is due in part to the fact that the shop buys direct from the Aborigines, extending them lines of credit to purchase food, clothes, and household goods from the general store side of this shop. This guarantees the owners a steady supply of arts and artifacts at good prices which they, in turn, pass on to their customers. This is an interesting shop for just observing the trading and credit activity taking place between the managers and Aboriginal artists and families who frequent the shop.

- **Centre for Aboriginal Arts:** Located at 86-88 Todd Street, just a three minute walk from the Todd Mall. This is one of five branch shops of the Aboriginal Artists Australia Ltd. which is also found in Sydney, Darwin, and Perth under the name Aboriginal Artists

Gallery. Offers acrylic paintings, weavings, woodcarvings, weapons, didgeridoos, prints, fabrics, jewelry, books, records, and cassettes.

- **Papunya Tula Artists:** Located at 78 Todd Street. Only sells acrylic paintings done by the Papunya Tula school of artists. Also has a limited selection of woodcarvings and didjeridoos.

WHERE TO SHOP

Knowing where to shop in Alice Springs is very simple: go to the shops and shopping centers in and around Todd Mall, the town's only pedestrian mall, as well as Todd Street/Gap Road. All the shops and shopping centers are conveniently located within walking distance of each other except for two shops on Gap Road which are best reached by taxi from the Todd Mall/Todd Street area.

Alice Springs has two major shopping centers: Ford Plaza on Todd Mall and Yeperenye Centre on Hartley Street, which is located one block north of Todd Mall. **Ford Plaza** will probably be your first shopping stop in Alice Springs, because it also houses the **Northern Territory Government Tourist Bureau** which dispenses a great deal of useful tourist information on Alice Springs and all of the Northern Territory, including Darwin. The Ground Floor of this small but nice air-conditioned shopping mall has a mixture of local retail and tourist shops. You will find, for example, an Australiana shop, **Centre Souvenirs**, which has a good collection of postcards, booklets, boomerangs, T-shirts, stuffed animals, and other gift items to help remember your trip to Alice Springs.

One of our favorite Aboriginal arts shops, **Central Australian Artifacts**, is also located in the Ford Plaza. It offers very good quality acrylic and bark paintings, woodcarvings, didjeridoos, and Tiwi bark baskets and carvings at decent prices. The service here is also excellent. The personnel are knowledgeable, helpful, patient, and enthusiastic in explaining their collections and arranging for shipping abroad. You will also find a few boutiques, menswear, book, shoe, music, and car rental shops on the first floor along with a supermarket and fast food eateries that primarily cater to the shopping needs of local residents.

Be sure to go to the First Floor (second level) of the Ford Plaza where you will be pleasantly surprised to find the nicest natural history and fine art museum in Alice Springs. Called the **Spencer & Gillen Museum and**

Gallery, it is well worth the A$2.00 admission fee for adults (Children under 15 enter free). The museum has a small, but excellent collection of central Australian Aboriginal art as well as some art from Indonesia, Papua New Guinea, and other parts of Southeast Asia and Oceania. It also has a small shop selling books and cards.

Todd Mall has a few small arcades and several shops feeding into the Mall. Here you will find the Alice Spring branch of **Morrisons Australia** outback clothing store; the **Gem Cave** for opals; the **Art Mart** for pottery, ceramics, souvenirs, paintings, and art supplies; **Outback Arts & Souvenirs** for Aboriginal acrylic and bark paintings, Australian oil paintings, woodcarvings, baskets, pottery, and souvenirs; and **Outcrop Gallery**, on the corner of Gregory Terrace and Todd Street, for Aboriginal art and souvenirs.

Along Todd Street you will find several other shops which may interest you. The **Centre for Aboriginal Artists** at 86-88 Todd Street has a good selection of acrylic Aboriginal dot paintings and woodcarvings. **Arunta Art Gallery** on Todd Street is primarily a book and art supply shop, but it also has a small gallery of paintings. Next door at 78 Todd Street is the **Papunya Tula Artists** gallery with its modest collection of acrylic paintings.

One block north of Todd Mall and Todd Street is Alice Springs' second major shopping street -- Hartley Street. Here you will find the newest shopping center in Alice Springs, the **Yeperenye Centre** (opposite the Post Office). This is a very small shopping center catering primarily to local residents with a few shops selling clothing, cards, magazines, jewelry, records, and prescription drugs. You will also find a fruit and vegetable market and some restaurants here along with a Woolworths supermarket. The most interesting shopping centers on the **C.A.A.M.A. Shop**, which offers a good collection of Acrylic paintings, woodcarvings, and the unique Utopia Batik.

Further south on Todd Street and Gap Road -- approximately four kilometers from Todd Mall and between Strehlow and Kempe streets on Gap Road -- are two good shops selling Aboriginal arts. The **Mbantua Store** (55 Gap Road), a small general store catering primarily to Aboriginals and tourists, has a small but very reasonably priced collection of acrylic and bark paintings, wood carvings, and didjeridoos. This shop is well worth the visit just to observe the trading activity between the managers and the Aboriginals and to compare prices and quality of Aboriginal arts with those found elsewhere in Alice Springs. Further south on the lefthand side of Gap Road, a 5 to 10 minute walk from the Mbantua Store, is the main workshop and retail store of the **C.A.A.M.A. Shop**. You will find some very nice acrylic paintings, woodcarvings, and Utopia Batik here.

That's it for shopping in this town. You can do it all in half a day. And there's no need to hunt for a great variety of product lines nor look for hotel shopping arcades, department stores, suburban shopping centers, and towns outside Alice Springs. Most of your time may be taken in comparing products and asking questions to learn more about the unique Aboriginal arts found in the town's many shops. For shopping in Alice Springs is primarily shopping for Aboriginal arts and souvenirs along one long street that changes it name from Todd Mall to Todd Street to Gap Road. It's the simplest shopping adventure you will encounter in Australia, but it also yields some of the nicest products at relatively reasonable prices for all of Australia. The only thing left is to enjoy the rest of Alice Springs and the Outback, which is, after all, what most people come here to do anyway.

ENJOYING YOUR STAY

Alice Springs is a popular destination for those interested in visiting the popular Ayers Rock, one of the world's largest monoliths located 450 kilometers southwest of Alice Springs, and enjoying adventure tours to the Outback. Many visitors stay in Alice Springs and visit Ayers Rock on a one or two-day tour; others proceed directly to the village of Yulara where they will spend a night or two at one of the resort hotels. And others sign up for several four-wheel drive tours. In any case, you will pass through Alice Springs. The question is what to do while in Alice Springs.

If you decide to stay in Alice Springs for a few days, you will find several things to do in addition to shopping. You will find several good hotels and motels located near the town. Some of the best hotels include **Lasseters Casino** on Barrett Drive. This is a nice casino-hotel complex which offers good service and plenty of entertainment opportunities. The **Sheraton Alice Springs**, located just down the road from Lasseters Casino on Barrett Drive, is a relatively new hotel complex with its own 18-hole golf course. The **Four Seasons Alice Springs** near the corner of Stephens Road and Barrett Drive is also relatively new. The **Oasis Motel** at 10 Gap Road offers good value for your dollar.

For your dining pleasure, try **The Bradshaw Room** in the Sheraton Alice Springs Hotel (52-8000); **The Other Place** at Todd Tavern on the corner of Todd and Wills streets; **Overlander Steakhouse** at 72 Hartley Street (Tel.

52-2159); **Chopsticks Chinese Restaurant** in the Ermond Arcade (Tel. 52-3873); and **Mister Pickwick's** at 20 Undoolya Road (Tel. 52-9400). A popular Outback-style restaurant complete with nightly entertainment, try the **Outback Winery** on Petrick Road (Tel. 21-5771). Another popular bar and restaurant with local entertainment -- yarns and bush songs -- is at the **Chateau Hornsby** (Tel. 53-1011).

While in Alice Springs, you can visit several local **historical sites.** Pick up a copy of *Alice Springs Walkabout* at the Northern Territory Government Tourist Bureau in the Ford Plaza. This guide includes a map showing you where and what to see on foot within the city: Flynn Memorial Church, Adelaide House, The Residency, Stuart Town Gaol, Anzac Hill, John Ross Memorial Park, Coles Wall Mural, Panorama Guth, Stuart Memorial, and the Royal Flying Doctor Service.

Alice Springs has several **museums** you may wish to visit. One of our favorites is the Spencer & Gillen Museum and Gallery (First Floor of Ford Plaza), a fine art and natural history museum. Also look for the Adelaide House Museum (Todd Mall), Central Australian Aviation Museum (Memorial Avenue), Frontier Camel Farm (Ross Highway), Old Timers Folk Museum (south of Stuart Highway), Panorama "Guth" (65 Hartley Street), Royal Flying Doctor Base (Stuart Terrace), Stuart Auto Museum (Ross Highway), and The Residency (Parsons Street).

If you are especially interested in the Aboriginal tribes and cultures, be sure to pick up a copy of *Come Share Our Culture: A Guide to Northern Territory Aboriginal Tours, Arts and Crafts* from the Tourist Bureau in Ford Plaza. The helpful guide outlines 19 different tours, festivals, and galleries relating to Aboriginal arts, crafts, and cultures throughout the Northern Territory. Seven of these are within 450 kilometers of Alice Springs: Ipolera Tour, Aboriginal Artists' Gallery, Dreamtime Tour, Uluru-Maruku Arts and Crafts, Liru Walk, Edible Desert Tour, and the Yuendumu Festival.

Alice Springs, the Macdonnell Ranges, gorges, historical landmarks, and local flora and fauna are interesting to see from the air. If you can get up early in the morning, consider taking a **hot air balloon ride** over the area. **Aussie Balloons** (Tel. 52-4369 or write to P.O. Box 2055, Alice Springs) offers half-hour and one-hour balloon flights over Alice Springs and the Macdonnell Range. You will be picked up at your hotel early in the morning, assist with inflating the balloon, take a peaceful ride, watch the sun rise over the Macdonnell Ranges, and finish with a traditional chicken and champagne brunch. This same company can arrange special balloon tours and also operates a helicopter touring service. Veteran pilot Ken Watts operates these services. You can arrange such tours by contacting Aussie Balloons directly or through your travel agent or the Northern Territory Government Tourist Bureau. Two other companies also offer similar balloon tours, and the prices are the same. Aussie Balloons has the most colorful balloon which is great for picture taking!

You will most likely want to visit **Ayers Rock** and **The Olgas**, the two most popular tourist attractions outside Alice Springs. Ayers Rock is located 450 kilometers southeast of Alice Springs. The Olgas are only 25 kilometers from Ayers Rock. We recommend that you take a scheduled tour to this area rather than drive yourself. It's a long boring drive with little help along the way should you have car trouble. One of the best tour companies is **CATA-/AAT King's Tours** which is located at 74 Todd Street (Tel. 52-5266). You can also fly to the area from Alice Springs. We took the CATA/AAT King's Tour by bus and were favorably impressed with the trip. The bus was comfortable and passengers were able to enjoy the outback scenery during the morning drive to Ayers Rock. Two films relating to Australia were shown on the bus during the return trip. A stop was made for dinner -- included in the price of the tour -- and a later short coffee stop along the highway gave us a view of the southern skies we will never forget. Out on the desert, away from city lights, the Milky Way was a thrilling attraction for those of us who had never seen it before.

Many visitors to Ayers Rock plan to stay overnight at the resort village, Yulara. You will find two major hotels here: **Sheraton Hotel** (Tel. 52-8000) and the **Four Seasons Ayers Rock** (56-2100). The **Ayers Rock Lodge** (Tel. 56-2170) provides budget accommodations, and **Ayers Rock Campground** (Tel. 56-2055) is for campers.

If you only go to Ayers Rock for the day, you will have little time to see the whole area, especially The Olgas. We recommend staying overnight so you can enjoy this interesting area at a more leisurely pace. Ayers Rock itself is a fascinating monolith, 9 kilometers in circumference and 348 meters high. Many visitors choose to climb the Rock, a rather ambitious endeavor considering its steep and exhausting incline. It looks easier than it is and will take you at least two hours to complete. The Rock is a great photo opportunity, especially for its changing colors during the day. The nearby Olgas consist of several smaller but picturesque rocks with huge cliffs and gorges. Both Ayers Rock and The Olgas are sacred areas of the Aborigines who still live in this area.

If time permits, you may want to take some other tours to various Outback locations. Most of these are adventure tours. Again, we recommend CATA/AAT King's Tours, a very reputable firm which offers a wide variety of tours: Palm Valley, Chambers Pillar, Rainbow Valley, Western Macdonnell Ranges, Eastern Macdonnell Rangers, Aboriginal Dreamtime, Standley Chasm, Simpsons Gap, Glen Helen, Historic Arltunga, Kings Canyon, Sunset Camel Safari and B.B.Q. Other firms offer similar tours as well as 7 and 14 day camel tours into the Rainbow Valley, Finke River, and Macdonnell Ranges areas. Brochures on these and other tours are available at the Northern Territory Government Tourist Bureau in Ford Plaza in Alice Springs. The Bureau will also book reservations for you at no cost to you or the tour operators. If you need information on these tours before arriving in Alice Springs, write to: The Northern Territory Government Tourist Bureau, 51 Todd Mall, Alice Springs N.T. 5750 or Tel. (02)52-1299.

Like many other cities and towns in Australia, Alice Springs also has its own unique festivals. The two most popular ones are the annual **Camel Cup Carnival** (April), or camel races, and the madcap **Henley-on-Todd Regatta** (October), a hilarious bottomless boat race that takes place on the dry river bed of the Todd River. Alice Springs also hosts an annual rodeo (August), food and wine festival (October), Beerfest (October), Bangtail Muster (May), and a Taps, Tubs, and Tiles Desert Race (June).

Chapter Ten

DARWIN

Darwin, one of Australia's fastest growing cities of over 75,000, is a surprising city for travelers and shoppers. Situated at the Top End of Australia and the Northern Territory, it is relatively isolated from the rest of the country. Accessible primarily by air, Darwin's closest state capital is Adelaide, a 3,620 kilometer trek south along the hot and boring Stuart Highway.

While more and more tourists are discovering this delightful city and its wonderful hinterland, Darwin still remains off the beaten tourist path. It's a city tourists are likely to visit only after stopping first in Sydney, Melbourne, Brisbane, and Adelaide. It is a popular city for backpackers and budget travelers who arrive here from Thailand, Malaysia, Singapore, and Indonesia on their way to other parts of Australia.

Best of all, Darwin, its suburbs, and the Tiwi islands of Bathurst and Melville offer some of Australia's most unique shopping. Here, you will find some very lovely Aborigine arts, Australian crafts, and uniquely designed jewelry largely unavailable elsewhere in Australia.

GETTING TO KNOW YOU

Darwin is an interesting **city of contrasts, commitment, and cultures.** Begun with Australia's gold rush in 1871, the city survived 60 Japanese bombings during World War II and three devastating cyclones, the most recent being Cyclone Tracy in 1974. Completely rebuilt since the 1970s, today Darwin is a pleasant mix of modern architecture in the midst of Top End residential relics from the pre-1974 cyclone period.

It's a city long ago discovered by Asian immigrants, Greeks, Italians, sailors, fishermen, investors, and budget travelers, and more recently by Asian gamblers, resort-goers, curious fans of *Crocodile Dundee*, and Australians themselves. It's a city that is about to be discovered by more and more tourists who enjoy urban comforts while participating on the edge of the rugged and ever fascinating Outback of Aborigines, natural beauty, and incomparable flora and fauna. Spend a week here and you will feel you have just begun to discover the "real Australia" so many others miss by only confining their visit to the East Coast, Sydney, and Melbourne.

Darwin is Australia's **gateway city to Asia** and an important expression of the Australian character. More than any other Australian city, Darwin is more oriented to its Asian neighbors than to cities in the southeast. International flights from Singapore, Brunei, Jakarta, and Bali, for example, regularly fly in and out of Darwin. Many local residents still find it cheaper to travel and shop in the bargain cities of Singapore and Bangkok or lie on the beaches of Southern Thailand, Eastern Malaysia, and Bali than to head for Australia's more expensive Sydney, Melbourne, and the East Coast. Darwin's multiracial population and ethnic restaurants and markets reflect the fact that this city has become a popular home for Australia's resident Chinese, Vietnamese, Malays, Thai, and Indonesians.

Here's the city of *Crocodile Dundee*, where hard-driving, beer-drinking, Outback cowboys come in from the never-never land of the Northern Territory. Sometimes wild, but often wacky, Darwin is very much a part of the Australian character that is so often communicated abroad. This is where stereotypes of Australia, however true or false, tend to arise and take on a life of their own.

Darwin is also a center for some of Australia's most interesting **Aboriginal tribes** as well as a central marketing and distribution point for **Aboriginal art.** On the one hand, you will find Aboriginal artists from Arnhem Land (east of Darwin, near Kakadu National Park) producing bark paintings in "Dreamtime" themes. On the other hand, you encounter the Tiwi peoples of Bathurst and Melville Islands who produce bark baskets, carved poles, and textiles in colorful abstract designs completely devoid of "Dreamtime" themes. At the same time, and to the dismay of many local residents and visitors, you may meet Aborigines on the streets in downtown Darwin. Some sleep on the streets while others, especially female hookers dressed in fancy clothes and accessories, prowl the streets for sailors and other potential customers.

This is also a **resort city** for tourists who have discovered Darwin's irresistible combination of great weather, fine hotels and restaurants, a colorful Outback, wild and wonderful Kakadu National Park, outstanding boating and sportfishing opportunities, picturesque islands, beautiful beaches and sunsets, dramatic lightning, a fine museum, a fun casino, colorful markets, and some of Australia's most interesting shopping. It's all set here in the bright and bustling town of Darwin where there's plenty to see and do in splendid isolation from the rest of Australia, and Asia.

Darwin also has the feel of tropical Southeast Asia. Famous for its frequent lightning and its two season climate (hot and wet), Darwin's hot and humid weather, palm trees, beaches, and sunny and balmy days remind one of similar places in Indonesia, Singapore, and Malaysia. No need to pack your winter clothes for Darwin. The pleasant sunny, but occasionally wet, climate calls for causal summer clothes, an umbrella, hat, and suntan lotion.

THE STREETS OF DARWIN

Being a relatively small city, Darwin is easy to get around by foot, bus, or car. Taxi stands are plentiful, but taxis seem to be few and far between. Since the city and suburbs are spread over a 25 kilometer area, expect to do a great deal of walking as well as traveling by car or bus between major shopping areas.

Shopping is largely confined to four areas in the city and suburbs: Downtown Darwin, Mindil Beach, Parap Shopping Centre, and Casuarina Shopping Square. Each area can be easily covered on foot, but distances between areas require some form of transportation. Downtown Darwin and Mindil Beach are the major shopping areas for visitors; Parap and Casuarina shopping centers cater primarily to local residents.

Downtown Darwin is the hub of shopping in the Northern Territory. Laid out as a grid system, it is easily accessible on foot from the major hotels on the Esplanade. The center for shopping is the Smith Street Mall, **a**

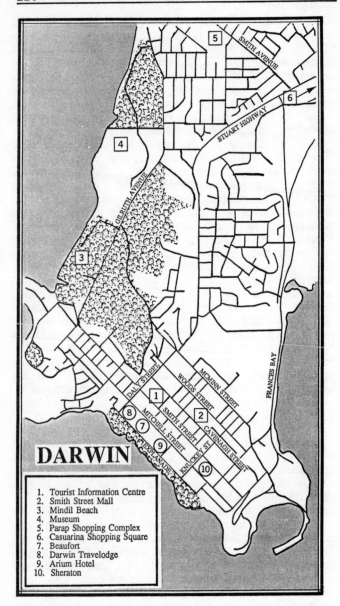

DARWIN

1. Tourist Information Centre
2. Smith Street Mall
3. Mindil Beach
4. Museum
5. Parap Shopping Complex
6. Casuarina Shopping Square
7. Beaufort
8. Darwin Travelodge
9. Arium Hotel
10. Sheraton

pedestrian mall crammed with shopping arcades and bordered by Knuckey and Bennett streets. The adjacent Knuckey, Mitchell, Smith, and Cavenagh streets also have some shops of interest to visitors.

Mindil Beach, located approximately 5 kilometers from Smith Street Mall -- just off the Stuart Highway and next to the Diamond Beach Casino -- is an outdoor food and craft market only open on Thursday evenings. Here you will find numerous Asian food stalls and arts and crafts vendors selling their products while local residents dine on the beach -- complete with their own tables, chairs, candles, and wine -- as they watch the sun produce another gorgeous Darwin sunset.

Parap Shopping Complex is located another 5 kilometers beyond Mindil Beach -- just off Stuart Highway or approximately 10 kilometers from Smith Street Mall -- in the suburb of Parap which is next to the upmarket suburb of Fannie Bay. Here you will find a few small arts, crafts, and clothing stores, but this place really comes alive on Saturdays when the Parap Weekend Market is held here.

The **Casuarina Shopping Square** is located approximately 17 kilometers northeast of Parap Shopping Centre via Stuart Highway, Bagot Road, and Trower Road. This is Darwin's newest and largest shopping mall and one which primarily caters to the upscale local market.

Outside the Darwin metropolitan area is the **Outback** which has little to offer shoppers. One major exception are the islands of the Aborigine Tiwi peoples -- **Melville and Bathurst Islands**. Located 30 minutes by air, just off the northwest coast of Darwin, Melville Island offers some unique shopping opportunities for Tiwi art, clothes, and pottery while one also learns about the local history, culture, flora, and fauna. Here, you can buy direct from the Tiwi at savings of 50 percent over what you will pay for comparable items in the shops of Darwin.

WHAT TO BUY

Darwin's major shopping strengths are in the areas of Aboriginal arts, Australian arts and crafts, jewelry, and locally produced sportswear. Prices for Aboriginal art in Darwin appear to be lower than in other cities because Darwin is located near the production sources and thus prices reflect the involvement of fewer middlemen in the marketing process.

Aboriginal Arts and Crafts

The shops in Darwin offer Aboriginal arts from four different groups in the Northern Territory:

- **Central Australia:** Acrylic Papunya paintings, woodcarvings, and Utopia Batik from artists and settlements near Alice Springs, more than 1,000 kilometers south of Darwin.

- **Arnhem Land:** Bark paintings with "Dreamtime" themes, clap sticks, and totemic objects from tribes east of Darwin in the area of Kakadu National Park.

- **Bathurst and Melville Islands:** Bark baskets, carved Pukamani burial poles, woodcarved animals, silk screen materials, and pottery using distinctive Tiwi patterns that are both colorful and abstract. Since the Tiwi have no "Dreamtime", their designs are less mysterious and thus need little interpretation.

- **New South Wales:** Weapons and utilitarian items, such as boomerangs, clubs, and small shields.

Shopping for Aboriginal arts, artifacts, and textiles is centered in downtown Darwin as well as on Bathurst Island. It's best to start in and around Smith Street Mall. Here you will find several shops selling Aboriginal items. Our favorite is **Raintree Gallery** at 29 Knuckey Street (Tel. 81-2732). This shop offers excellent quality Aboriginal arts and crafts, including bird carvings, Tiwi sculptures, Central desert sand paintings, bark paintings, carvings, didjeridoos, weapons, weavings, pandanus baskets, pottery, and silk screen printed fabrics as well as T-shirts and books. The prices here are the best we have found for any retail shop in Australia, and the service, including packing and shipping, is excellent.

Other good shops offering Aboriginal items include **Aboriginal Artist's Gallery** (local branch of Aboriginal Artists Australia) at 153 Mitchell Street, nearly 2 kilometers from Smith Street Mall, for excellent quality paintings, carvings, and clothes; **Day Night Chemist** at 46 Smith Street Mall for selections similar to those found at the Aboriginal Artist's Gallery since this drugstore functions as their downtown gift shop; and **Arnhem Land**

Yolngu Jarmu, a very small shop located in Anthony Plaza at Smith Mall, offering spears, bark paintings, and didjeridoos.

The other major shopping area for Aboriginal arts is on the Tiwi island of Bathurst. This is one of the most interesting Aboriginal shopping adventures in Australia. If you take the wonderful half-day or full-day tour of this island organized by Tiwi Tours (Tel. 81-6611), you will have an opportunity to shop at the **Tiwi Prima Arts Centre** (variously called "The Keeping Place" and "The Sistine Chapel") in the main settlement town of **Nguiu**. This shop-warehouse has a large collection of colorful bark baskets and carved Pukamani (burial) poles and animal figures. You can purchase the items here at half the price you would pay in Darwin and one-fourth the price you might pay in Sydney. The center takes credit cards, and Tiwi Tours will transport your purchases back to Darwin free of charge. This is the same place dealers from Darwin and other cities come to make their purchases, and they pay the same prices you will pay. In fact, you can easily pay for your tour to this island from the savings on your purchases at the Tiwi Prima Arts Centre!

You will also find three workshops in Nguiu producing uniquely designed womenswear (Bima Wear), menswear (Tiwi Design), and pottery (Tiwi Pottery). The colors, designs, and overall quality of these products may or may not appeal to you, but they are unique.

Australian and Imported Arts and Crafts

Darwin has its own local artists and craftsmen who are producing unique arts and crafts. For fine art, visit the following galleries: **Studio Art Gallery** in the Star Village shopping arcade at 32 Smith Street Mall; and **"Framed" -- The Showcase Gallery** at the corner by Stuart Highway and Geranium Street in Stuart Park (3 minutes by car from the major city hotels). Both of these galleries sell paintings as well as pottery from some leading local and Australian artists.

For good quality Australian arts and crafts, we recommend three shops at **Parap Shopping Complex** in the suburb of Parap: **Potters Place** (2 Parap Village, Tel. 81-7071), one of Darwin's finest craft shops, carries a large range of handcrafted pottery, lamps, and lampshades made in the Darwin area as well as unique fish skin items crafted in Western Australia; **Weavers Workshop** (2 Parap Place) offers pottery, wicker baskets, rugs, and woven items; and **Mango Pottery** (35 Gregory Street, just behind the Weavers Workshop) is a small pottery shop which makes pottery on the premises. Craft lovers will also enjoy the **Parap Village Market** which is held in this shopping area every Saturday from 8am to 2pm. The market offers everything from Asian foods and fresh produce to jewelry and secondhand books.

The Thursday night market at **Mindil Beach** also is a popular area for purchasing local arts and crafts from vendor stalls. Amongst all the Asian food vendors, hot dog stands, and ice cream trucks, you will find several local craftsmen selling pottery, leather goods, jewelry, and candle holders as well as clothes, stuffed animals, and books.

The **Crafts Council of the Northern Territory** has an exhibition gallery at Conacher Street, Bullocky Point, in the suburb of Fannie Bay (Tel. 81-6615).

The **Shady Lady** in the West Lane Carpark Shopping Arcade on Smith Street Mall offers some very unique ceramics along with Akubra hats.

We discovered one nice shop offering good selections of imported arts and crafts from Indonesia, India, and Japan. **Blazez** is located in the Star Village shopping arcade at 32 Smith Street Mall. Next to the Asian Connection shop in Cairns, this is one of the best shops in Australia for Indonesian carvings and ikat textiles.

Jewelry

You will find a few shops selling Australian opals, similar to those you would find in other major cities. Look for **The Black Opal**, Shop 3, Harry Chan Arcade, 60 Smith Street, for opals and jewelry as well as **The Jewellers Workshop** for opals and pearls. A few Australiana and souvenir shops, such as **Casuarina Opal and Souvenirs** in the Casuarina Shopping Square (247 Trower Road), sell opals.

One of our favorite jewelry shops in all of Australia is **The Opal House** at M24 Paspalis Centrepoint. This is a very fine shop which is producing some of the most unique jewelry designs we have seen anywhere in the country. The name of this shop is deceptive since it suggests they primarily deal in opals. While it does sell opals and opal jewelry, the Opal House is primarily noted for its unique handcrafted sterling silver and gold. The owners, Paul and Jeannette Lewis, have created an exquisite Australian Collection consisting of over 100 pendants, necklaces, earrings, bracelets, rings, tie pins, brooches, and cuff links depicting the unique animals, birds, and legends of Australia. This shop also carries a few other unique collections, such as Walkabout Clay Crafts made in Alice

Springs and beautiful stained glass and silver jewelry by Pat Cheney of Scotland.

Other jewelry can be found in shopping centers and the markets. If you visit **Sasuarina Shopping Square**, you will find a few jewelers such as **Hourglass Jewellers, Georges Jewellers, Hallmark Jewellers,** and **Prouds.** Look for craft jewelry at the Thursday night market along **Mindil Beach** and the Saturday morning **Parap Village Market.**

Clothes, Fashionwear, and Accessories

Given Darwin's warm and humid climate, you can expect to find a great deal of light weight cotton clothing in numerous shops throughout the city and suburbs. You will find a few shops with clothes from local designers, such as **Riji Dij** and **Shandy** on Knuckey Street and **Kasandras** in the Parap Shopping Complex. Riji Dij and Shandy have nice sportswear using northern Australian desert and Aboriginal designs. Kasandras stocks a good selection of colorful tropical clothes by the popular local designer Andrea Lee.

Smith Street Mall has several shops offering the latest in fashion design. In the Paspalis Centrepoint shopping center, look for **Sheva** for nice evening and sportswear under the Adele Palmer label and **Lotus Batiks** for Orientique label batik blouses, skirts, and dresses from Sydney. **Shady Lady** at Westlane Carpark Arcade (Smith Street Mall) has a unique collection Akubra hats along with handcrafted pottery.

The **Casuarina Shopping Square** has several clothing stores, many of which are branch stores of the same stores found in Sydney, Brisbane, Melbourne, and Adelaide: **Just Jeans, Jeanworks, Cherry Lane,** and **Sportsgirl.** Other nice clothing stores include **Sussan, Suzanne Crae, Temptations, Trent Lee's,** and **Accessories Plus.**

In a few shops you will see one line of women's clothing under the label of **Bima Wear.** These clothes are made by the Aboriginal Tiwi women on Bathurst Island. If you visit the island, you will most likely stop at the Bima Wear factory and shop in the main settlement town of Nguiu. There you can see the cotton silk screen process and the cutting and sewing of garments. The shop sells women's dresses, blouses, bags, and T-shirts using unique Tiwi motifs. While we are impressed with the entrepreneurial efforts of Bima Wear, the colors and quality of the garments may not appeal to you. Few of the garments have a "finished look" to them. The nearby **Tiwi Design** workshop, operated by Tiwi men, produces menswear, tablecloths, tea towels, shirts, and T-shirts.

Again, you may have problems with the colors and quality. Nonetheless, these are two interesting workshops to visit to see the silk screen process and production methods.

Australiana, Gifts, and Souvenirs

You will find several gift and souvenir shops throughout Darwin offering a wide variety of Australiana, T-shirts, Aboriginal artifacts, stuffed animals, leather goods, and memorabilia. Most of these shops, however, tend to concentrate in the downtown area around Smith Street Mall. Look for **N.T. Aussie Shop** in the Anthony Plaza (Smith Street Mall) for a wide range of gifts, souvenirs, and Aboriginal artifacts; **Crocodile Souvenirs** in The Mall on Smith Street as well as in the Casuarina Shopping Square; **Downtown Duty Free** at 19 Queen Street Mall (Qantas Corner at Bennett Street); **Studio Arts** at 20 Knuckey Street; **Darwin Gift Shop** at 50 Smith Street; **Siesta Souvenirs** at 21 Smith Street Mall; and **Day Night Chemist** at 46 Smith Street Mall. Several hotels, such as the Sheraton Darwin and Travelodge, also have small gift and souvenir shops as well as a shop next to the Food Bazaar and Darwin Transit Centre (Ansett Trailways) on Mitchell Street near the corner of Peel Street.

Casuarina Shopping Square also has a few gift and souvenir shops: **Casuarina Opal and Souvenirs, Granny's Gifts, Casuarina T-Shirts, The Gift Shop, Shamrock Card & Gift**, and **Crocodile Souvenirs**.

A popular gift and souvenir shop just outside Darwin is the **Buffalo Shed**, located at the 10 kilometer point on Stuart Highway. You can't miss this place with its giant pink buffalo waiting for you along the roadside. Here you will find a large selection of kangaroo, sheep, and cow hides as well as leather and felt hats among its many other souvenirs.

WHERE TO SHOP

The most interesting shopping is centered in and around the Smith Street Mall in downtown Darwin, the suburban shopping centers of Parap Village and Casuarina Shopping Square, the markets at Mindil Beach and Parap Village Market, and the settlement town of Nguiu on the Tiwi island of Bathurst. Hotel shopping for the most part involves small gift and souvenir shops that primarily service their own hotel guests.

While you can easily cover each of these shopping areas on foot, it is best to take a bus or car between the shopping areas because of the long distances involved in going from one area to another. If you don't rent your own car, you may find the bus more convenient since taxis tend to be very irregular. In the case of Bathurst Island, you must take an authorized tour (Tiwi Tours, Tel. 81-6611) since this island is not open to the general public. You will travel to Bathurst Island by a DC3 (Air North), by mini bus on both Bathurst and Melville Islands, and by a short boat trip between the two islands. This is a well-organized and thoroughly enjoyable tour for anyone interested in the Tiwi culture or artifacts.

Downtown Darwin

The center of shopping in Darwin is the Smith Street Mall, a pedestrian mall similar to Adelaide's and Brisbane's pedestrian malls but smaller in scale. Bordered by Knuckey and Bennett streets, the mall consists of 12 small shopping arcades crammed with over 250 specialty shops. You can easily spend half a day exploring the arcade and sampling the international foods offered by several restaurants and take-away eateries.

Some of our favorite shops in and around the Smith Street Mall include **The Opal House** (M24 Paspalis Centrepoint) for exquisitely designed sterling silver and gold jewelry in a fabulous Australian Collection -- one of Australia's most unique jewelers; **Blazez** in the Star Village for a nice collection of Indonesian arts and crafts; **Studio Art Gallery** in the Star Village for fine art and pottery; **Shady Lady** in the West Lane Carpark for nice Akubra hats and unique ceramics; and the **N.T. Aussie Shop** for a large selection of gifts and souvenirs.

Just off of Smith Street Mall are a few nice shops along Knuckey Street. **Raintree Gallery** at 29 Knuckey Street is one of our "must see" shops. It has an excellent selection of Aboriginal arts and artifacts and at the best prices we found anywhere in Australia. **Riji Dij** at 11 Knuckey Street has very nice sportswear (Territoriana label) in North Australian desert and Aboriginal designs along with a selection of gift and souvenir items.

If you are interested in Aboriginal arts and artifacts, be sure to also visit the **Aboriginal Artist's Gallery** at 153 Mitchell Street. Located by itself nearly two kilometers northwest of the Smith Street Mall, this shop is part of fine Aboriginal Artists Australia group of shops; it also operates a gift shop from the **Day Night Chemist** at 46 Smith Street Mall.

Suburbs

Numerous suburban shops are located throughout the greater Darwin area: Hibiscus Shopping Town, Malak Shopping Square, Nightcliff Shopping Complex, Northlakes Shopping Centre, Palmerston Shopping Centre, Rapid Creek Shopping Centre, and Winnellie Shopping Centre. However, two suburban shopping areas are of particular interest to visitors: Parap Shopping Complex and Casuarino Shopping Square.

Parap Shopping Complex in the suburb of Parap has four interesting shops: **Potters Place** for one of the best selections of Australian arts and crafts; **Weavers Workshop** for hand woven items as well as pottery and wicker baskets; **Mango Pottery** (behind Weavers Workshop at 35 Gregory Street) for handcrafted pottery; and **Kasandras** for colorful sportswear and casual clothes by the local designer Andrea Lee.

Casuarino Shopping Square is a big shopping center with 150 shops selling everything from health food to opals. Located approximately 22 kilometers from Smith Street Mall, this shopping center can be reached by taking a No. 10 bus from downtown. The bus stops at a depot directly across the street from the shopping center. The Casuarino Shopping Square has three major department stores -- Coles, K-Mart, and Woolworths -- as well as numerous restaurants and specialty shops. You will find several boutiques and clothing stores with such familiar names at **Just Jeans, Jeanworks, Sportsgirl**, and **Cherry Lane**. Also look for **Accessories Plus** for unique and colorful womens' sportswear. For jewelry, visit **Prouds, Hourglass Jewellers**, and **Georges Jewellers**. There are also a few gift and souvenirs shops -- **Crocodile Souvenirs, Casuarino Opal and Souvenirs, The Gift Shop**, and **Granny's Gifts** -- as well as a bookstore (**Angus & Robertson**) and offices of Ansett Airline and Australian Airlines in this shopping center.

Markets

Darwin has two markets you may find interesting for shopping purposes. The **Mindil Beach Night Market** is located along Mindil Beach about 10 kilometers northeast of the Smith Street Mall. This is a fun ethnic food and crafts market held every Thursday evening during the dry season (April to November). It's a social event for many local residents who come here to browse through vendor stalls, picnic on the beach, and watch the beautiful sunset slip behind Fannie Bay. Many people sit on the beach or take their own tables, chairs, and lighting as they eat and drink the night away in the tropical ambiance of a beautiful sunset, cool breeze, and a festive atmosphere. Be sure to get here early (by 6pm in the winter) if you want to watch the sunset. The market itself is an interesting mix of ethnic food stalls and arts and crafts vendors selling pottery, clothes, leather goods, jewelry, candle holders, books, and souvenirs. The quality of food and beachside ambiance tends to out-distance shopping for quality arts and crafts.

Parap Village Market is located further north in the suburb of Parap. Every Saturday from 8am to 2pm this becomes a festive arts, crafts, and food market.

Bathurst and Melville Islands

Bathurst and Melville Islands offer an interesting opportunity to learn about the Aborigine Tiwi as well as shop for Tiwi arts, crafts, and clothing. Located 80 kilometers off the northeast coast of Darwin, these two islands are home to the unique and artistic Tiwi peoples who are noted for their colorful abstract designs.

You cannot visit the Tiwi islands on your own since this area is restricted by invitation only. The best approach is to take a half-day or full-day tour of the island operated by Tiwi Tours in Darwin (27 Temira Crescent, Tel. 81-5115 or 81-5118). This is one of the best tours we encountered in all of Australia. You leave Darwin early in the morning via a DC3 plane operated by Air North. After a half-hour flight, the plane lands on Bathurst Island, the smaller but more developed and more heavily populated of the two islands. The tour includes both islands, with visits to the major towns and through the countryside by minibus.

The central focus of the tour is the town of Nguiu on Bathurst Island, a community of 1,200. Begun in 1911 as a Catholic Church Mission, today it is a center for Tiwi development. This is where you will find the Tiwi Design screen printing workshop, Tiwi Pottery, Bima Wear clothing and screen printing workshop, and the Tiwi Pima Art Centre. You can shop at each of these places. If you are interested in purchasing a Pukamani ceremonial burial pole, carved figures, or bark baskets, be sure to stop at the **Tiwi Pima Art Centre**. This warehouse-shop is the central distribution point for locally produced art. You can purchase items at half the price you will pay for comparable items in Darwin. Tiwi Tours will also ship your purchases back to Darwin free of change as well as arrange shipments elsewhere in Australia or abroad. Better still, you can use your credit card here.

The **Bima Wear** clothing and screen printing workshop is operated by Tiwi women who produce Bima Wear label clothes, including dresses, blouses, T-shirts, and bags with unique Tiwi designs. You can tour the workshop to observe the screen printing, cutting, and sewing rooms. Next to the work rooms is a boutique which sells the finished garments and a few books on the Tiwi people and islands. You will find changing rooms here so you can try on the garments. The same garments are also found in a few gift and clothing stores in Darwin. The quality of the prints and garments may be improving.

Near the Bima Wear shop are two additional workshops worth visiting. The **Tiwi Design** screen printing workshop is operated by Tiwi men who produce shirts, tablecloths, tea towels, T-shirts, and bolts of fabric. The designs are different from those of Bima Wear. You will not find high-quality prints, fabrics, and products here. Some of the items may make souvenir or gift items.

Next door to Tiwi Design is **Tiwi Pottery** which produces a glazed pottery with Tiwi designs. Again, don't expect top quality. Most of the pottery looks like seconds.

ENJOYING YOUR STAY

Darwin and the Northern Territory is a fascinating area to visit. While there is much to do in Darwin, from enjoying the beaches, casino, ethnic restaurants, and shops to visiting the Territory's finest museum, the city is an ideal jumping-off point for exploring the Outback and for sportfishing.

Darwin has several excellent hotels as well as budget accommodations. One of the best places to stay is along the Esplanade. Hotels in this area have an excellent view of the Darwin Harbour. The best hotels here include the **Beaufort** (Tel. 82-9911), one of the most interesting architectural adventures in Australia; it has excellent facilities, great views of the Harbour, and is a pleasant 10 minute walk from the Smith Street Mall. Next door to the Beaufort is the older **Darwin TraveLodge** (Tel. 81-5388). The beautiful new **Atrium Hotel** (Tel. 381-6433) is also located on the Esplanade. Closer to the downtown area, but minus the ocean view, are the **Sheraton Darwin** (32 Mitchell Street, Tel. 32-0000) and **Hotel Darwin** (10 Herbert Street, Tel. 82-9211). Further from town at Mindil Beach is the deluxe **Diamond Beach Hotel and Casino** (Tel. 81-7755).

You will find plenty of good restaurants and ethnic food stalls in Darwin. For fun eating and cheap eats, visit the

Food Bazaar next to the Darwin Transit Centre on Mitchell Street near the downtown, small eateries in and around the Smith Street Mall, and the food stalls at the Mindil Beach Night Market. Some of Darwin's best restaurants include the **Beagle** at the Museum of Arts and Sciences, Conacher Street, Fannie Bay (Tel. 81-7791) -- great food and views for both lunch and dinner; **Peppis** (International) at 84 Mitchell Street (Tel. 81-3762); **Lee Dynasty** (Chinese) at 21 Cavenagh Street (Tel. 81-7808); **Riviera** (Italian) at 41 Cavenagh Street, Tel. 81-9322; **Tai Hung Tol** (Chinese) on Parap Road (Tel. 81-6373); **Orient Teppanyaki** (Japanese) in the Boulevarde Motel on Gardens Road (Tel. 811544); **Kim Phung** (Vietnamese) on Wood Street (Tel. 81-7068); and **Genghis Khan** (Mongolian) at 44 East Pt. Road in Fannie Bay (Tel. 81-3883).

One of the real highlights of visiting Darwin is the **Northern Territory Museum of Arts and Sciences** (Bullocky Point, Fannie Bay, Tel. 82-4211), one of Australia's finest museums. The displays on Aborigines, Papua New Guinea, Oceania, and Southeast Asia are outstanding, some of the most informative we have found anywhere, especially on the Tiwi Pukamani ceremonies and the Indonesia ikat textiles. You will also find a good collection of contemporary art in this museum. A small museum shop sells books on Australia, Indonesian textiles, and prints. One of the additional benefits of visiting the museum is to discover one of Darwin's best restaurants on the premises -- the **Beagle**. It's a great place for lunch or dinner, with excellent food and a great view of the ocean.

If you wish to see the major highlights of Darwin, you can take a walking tour of the city or purchase an all day pass to tour the city by open-air bus. The tourist publication "Top of Australia" includes a walking map of historical Darwin which will take you to such places as Government House, Old Post Office, Christ Church Cathedral, Browns Mart, Old Town Hall, and the Westpac Building. A tour bus service called Tour Tub offers a full-day pass ($7.50) which stops on the hour at 23 locations in the Darwin area, including hotels on the Esplanade, the Aboriginal Artists Gallery, Diamond Beach Casino, Museum and Art Gallery, and the Botanical Gardens. You can get on and off this bus at your own leisure. Look for the Tour Tub along Knuckey Street next to the Smith Street Mall as well as at most of the major hotels.

Outside Darwin we highly recommend a tour of **Bathurst and Melville Island** to meet and learn about the Tiwi people. As outlined earlier, Tiwi Tours (Tel. 81-5115 or 81-5118) offers excellent tours to these two islands.

Another company, **Barra Base B.I.** (Tel. 81-1088), offers sportfishing opportunities for barramundi, sailfish, and threadfin salmon at its fishing lodge at Barra Base on Bathurst Island.

One of the most popular destinations outside Darwin is the Kakadu National Park, located in Aboriginal Arnhem Land approximately 150 kilometers east of Darwin. Somewhat over rated, especially if you have visited the Everglades in the United States or the Kalahari in Africa, Kakadu National Park does offer an excellent opportunity to view unique Northern Australian flora, fauna, wetlands, Aboriginal rock art, and picturesque countryside. Several tour companies operate day tours from Darwin to Kakadu National Park by coach or a combination of air and coach. The tours are mainly designed to view the wildlife in Kakadu National Park, but they also include a few other interesting stops along the way. You will see wildlife and termite mounds, take a boat ride on the wetlands (Yellow Waters) to observe crocodiles and birds, observe Aboriginal rock art, view the Arnhem Land escarpment, and tour around the world's largest uranium mine (Ranger Uranium Mine at Jabiru). You can also rent a car or camper to visit this area on your own. Keep in mind that this is a long drive which you may want to break by staying overnight in Kakadu National Park.

Several other areas outside Darwin, such as Katherine Gorge National Park, 350 kilometers south of Darwin, offer sightseeing, adventure touring, and sportfishing opportunities. A sportsman's country, you can golf, go horseback riding, parachute, sail, swim, or water ski. The Northern Territory has several parks you can visit to observe flora and fauna, swim, camp, and hike. Several tour operators offer trips to these areas as well as specialty fishing tours. You can charter boats, take cruises, or join a river safari to enjoy the northern inland waterways as well as the surrounding Timor Sea, Van Diemen Gulf, and Gulf of Carpentaria.

The best approach to identifying activities and tours is to contact the Northern Territory Government Tourist Bureau (81-6611) at 31 Smith Street Mall in downtown Darwin. The Bureau has comprehensive directories of local tours and tour operators as well as literature on what to see and do in Darwin and the Northern Territory. Their *Holiday Planner* lists more than 400 tours available through local tour operators.

Chapter Eleven

CAIRNS

Cairns is a pleasant surprise for those who spend most of their time in the major beach resorts and cities further south or in the Outback to the south and west. A booming city along the mountainous northeastern shore of Queensland, Cairns has become a tourist mecca within the past few years for those who have discovered the many pleasures of this fascinating area. Once a small tropical town, famous among international game fisherman for offering the world's best Black Marlin fishing, today this sleepy town has awakened to become a major tourist center and gateway city to Papua New Guinea, Indonesia, and the Pacific Islands.

Cairns' population of over 75,000 hosts over 1 million domestic and 200,000 international visitors each year. Still a small city with a decided resort atmosphere, Cairns offers an infinite variety of both hectic and relaxing tourist attractions to keep you busy for days, if not weeks. It's a city that appeals to jet-setters and backpackers alike. Better still for us, it offers some of Australia's best shopping opportunities that are largely unknown to outsiders who primarily treat Cairns as a jumping-off point for recreational activities elsewhere in this part of Queensland. You may be pleasantly surprised with what you find in Cairns as you begin viewing this city as more than just another way-station.

GETTING TO KNOW YOU

Cairns has not been well reported to outsiders nor have recent changes been carefully documented for tourists. Preoccupied with the joys of fishing and reef walking, many visitors neglect Cairns altogether. This is unfortunate because they miss some truly wonderful shopping opportunities in downtown Cairns as well as in nearby craft towns. Indeed, if you read much on Australia, you get the feeling that this is the type of town you should, at best, spend two or three hours in on your way fishing or visiting the Great Barrier Reef.

Until recently, Cairns has had a reputation as a center, gate-way, or jumping-off point for other more interesting attractions and activities in this part of the country: chartering a boat for big game fishing, visiting the Great Barrier Reef, exploring the beautiful beaches and Atherton Tablelands outside the city, or flying from here to Papua New Guinea, Indonesia, or the Pacific Islands. As such, Cairns has exhibited little character of its own that would entice visitors to come to the city to spend more than a few hours or to actually book a hotel in the downtown area.

All this is changing, especially in the past two years with the completion of two elegant deluxe hotels -- The Park Royal and Hilton -- and a cruise terminal and shopping center -- the Trinity Wharf. In addition, many new shops are springing up in downtown Cairns near the hotels and wharf. Many of these shops offer some of the most unique shopping in all of Australia. Now you can easily spend a day or two shopping in Cairns and still need more time to enjoy its fine hotels and restaurants.

Cairns has a great deal to offer visitors, moreso than many other more popular tourist destinations in Australia. This is a booming city and area. New resort complexes, such as Port Douglas 40 kilometers north of the city, are being completed and new shops are opening to cater to Cairn's growing international clientele. It has a sophisticated yet easy-going temperament -- one more frequently associated with international beach resorts located in tropical areas not yet overrun by tourists. Its beautiful and varied typography of mountains, rainforests, Atherton Tablelands, rivers, ocean, reefs, and miles and miles of picturesque beaches make this one of Australia's most attractive areas to visit. Its easy to quickly fall in love with this beautiful and relaxing area.

Shopping in and around Cairns is surprising to many visitors who arrive misinformed about the city. Given Cairns' tropical setting, close proximity to Papua New Guinea and Indonesia, and the continuing strong Australian craft tradition, expect to find some good shopping here for tribal artifacts, Australian arts and crafts, and tropical weight clothing and resort wear. And the shopping in Cairns can be exceptional. Within the downtown area, you will find Australia's best Papua New Guinea tribal art (Gallery Primitive) and Indonesia artifact and textile (Asian Connection) shops. You will also discover some very nice art galleries (Waterfall Place and Grafton House Galleries) and craft markets (Rusty's Bazaar and Karunda) both within and outside the city. In addition, numerous shops offer good selections of fashionable tropical weight clothing, sportswear, and swimwear. Outside Cairns, especially in the hill town of Karunda and the Tablelands as well as Port Douglas, you will find several shops offering exquisite arts and crafts unique to this area.

So plan to spend a little time here shopping and enjoying Cairns' varied recreational opportunities. We recommend spending at least three days -- preferably five days -- in Cairns. You will find this area offers two to three good days of shopping. You may also want to visit the many other attractions in and around Cairns. These can easily take another three days -- if not a week or more!

If you plan to visit Papua New Guinea (PNG), Cairns is the best place to stop in transit to your first stop in PNG -- the capital Port Moresby. In Cairns you will want to introduce yourself to what you will see in abundance in PNG -- tribal artifacts. A few shops offer good selections of artifacts from PNG, many of which you may not find in PNG. You will want to see the range of artifacts as well as compare quality and prices. In general, we find the prices for PNG artifacts in Cairns to be two to three times higher than the prices in Port Moresby which, in turn, are three times higher than what you might pay along the Sepik River or 10 times more than what you might pay in remote tribal villages -- if you can make such an adventure! However, the selections and quality may be better in Cairns and thus you will want to buy here rather than in Papua New Guinea.

If you plan to return to Cairns after visiting PNG, do your window shopping on your first visit to Cairns and then do your buying after you have had a chance to see your alternatives in PNG. But if you do not plan to return to Cairns, buy now since you may not find similar quality items in PNG, and certainly not from shops in other

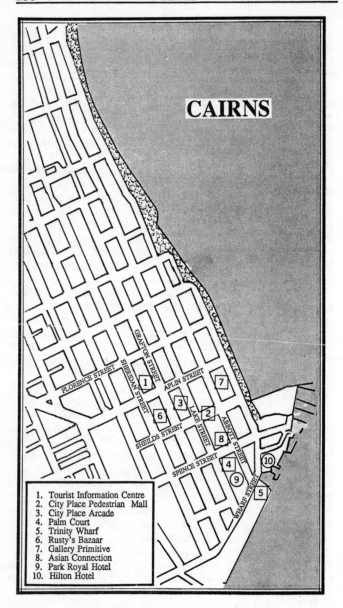

CAIRNS

1. Tourist Information Centre
2. City Place Pedestrian Mall
3. City Place Arcade
4. Palm Court
5. Trinity Wharf
6. Rusty's Bazaar
7. Gallery Primitive
8. Asian Connection
9. Park Royal Hotel
10. Hilton Hotel

Australian cities.

THE STREETS OF CAIRNS AND ITS ENVIRONS

Shopping in and around Cairns primarily centers on three areas: downtown Cairns, the village of Kuranda, and the resort town of Port Douglas. You will find a few craft towns, such as Atherton, Mareeba, Yungburra, and Tolga, in the Tablelands west and south of Cairns.

Cairns is one of the easiest towns to get around in and shop. Similar in size to Darwin, Cairns' downtown area is laid out on a simple grid plan. The major shops, shopping centers, and hotels are concentrated in a four block area which is centered around a pedestrian mall called **City Place**. This area is bordered by The Esplanade, Florence Street, Sheridan Street, and Wharf Street, streets which front on or lead to the waterfront. The major shopping streets are Abbott, Lake, Grafton, Shields, Spence, and Wharf. Within this area you will find the Park Royal Hotel, Hilton Hotel, Pacific Hotel, Trinity Wharf, Park Royal Shopping Village, tourist information center (Cairns Convention and Visitors Bureau), airline offices, restaurants, and banks. Most of the newer shops, as well as the whole downtown shopping area, are moving toward the Trinity Wharf. You can easily walk this whole area within 45 minutes.

The major shopping areas outside Cairns can be reached by car within 45 minutes. The tropical rainforest village of **Kuranda**, a small craft town 27 kilometers northeast of Cairns, can be reached by train or road. The train leaves Cairns everyday at 8:30, 9:00, and 9:30am for the scenic trip to Kuranda. The roundtrip takes approximately 3 hours. By road you can drive to the village within 45 minutes along a winding road that takes you through a tropical rainforest area. Within Kuranda you will find numerous shops and bazaars lining both sides of Kuranda's two main streets. Open primarily between 7am and 1pm on Wednesdays and Saturdays, this is an attractive arts and crafts town offering many unique items for those who enjoy shopping in village bazaars and quaint crafts towns.

Port Douglas, a rapidly developing resort town 65 kilometers north of Cairns, has a few shops worth visiting, especially for Queensland arts and crafts. The town can be easily reached by car within 45 minutes. However, you may want to stop along the way to enjoy the beautiful beaches that stretch for miles along this major highway to the northern end of Queensland. Within Port Douglas the major shopping is confined to Macrossan Street, the main street of the town, as well as to the Sunbird Centre of

Mirage Port Douglas Resort and the newly completed waterfront Marina Mirage shopping complex.

Other shopping areas in the Cairns area include Paradise Shopping Village at **Palm Cove**, a small beachside resort shopping center 20 kilometers north of Cairns, and a few villages in the **Tablelands**. If you plan to drive to Kuranda or Port Douglas, you can easily stop at Palm Cove along the way. The major craft towns in the Atherton Tablelands -- Mareeba, Atherton, Yungaburra, and Tolga-- involve a day trip. You can stop at Kuranda along the way, keeping in mind that it opens and closes early on Wednesdays and Saturdays (7am to 1pm).

To best enjoy the Cairns area, we recommend that you rent a car as soon as you arrive in Cairns. Assuming you arrive by plane, you will find four car rental firms at the airport -- Hertz, Avis, Thrifty, and Budget. If you rent a car here, you can save yourself the taxi fare into Cairns. With a car you will have the freedom to quickly cover all of the major shopping areas in and around Cairns as well as enjoy the beaches, mountains, and rainforests of this delightful area.

WHAT TO BUY

Cairn's major shopping strengths are the areas of ethnic and tribal arts, crafts, leather goods, clothes, resort wear, jewelry, and souvenirs. Unlike most other cities in Australia, the arts and crafts in Cairns come from four major groups and areas: Papua New Guinea, Indonesia, Australia, and Aborigine. You will also find many shops selling the latest in fashionwear, opals, and duty-free items.

Tribal and Ethnic Arts

Two shops in Cairns are responsible for making this one of the best places to shop for tribal and ethnic arts in all of Australia. **Gallery Primitive** at 26 Abbott Street (Tel. 311-641) has what we consider to be the finest collection of primitive art from Papua New Guinea. The is a "must visit" shop for anyone interested in tribal and ethnic arts from PNG. The owner, Ed Boylan, has been in the PNG artifact collection business for more than 15 years. His eye for quality combined with his spirit of adventure takes him to some of the more remote and dangerous areas of PNG where he is able to find unique artifacts not available in other shops in Australia, or even in Papua New Guinea. You will find, for example, some very beautiful masks from the Black Water area in PNG which you seldom find elsewhere. This is the type of shop serious collectors of

PNG artifacts will find interesting. Prices here are not cheap, but they are better than elsewhere in Australia as well as abroad. Best of all, you get unique and good quality items not readily available even in PNG. The shop is also developing a good quality Australian Aboriginal art collection which should appeal to serious collectors. This shop also does the best packing of any shop we encountered in Australia.

Asian Connection, located just one block from Gallery Primitive at 51 Abbott Street (carvings and jewelry) and 39 Shields Street (textiles), has the largest and best collection of Indonesian artifacts and textiles we have found in Australia. The Abbott Street shop also has a good range of tribal artifacts from Papua New Guinea, similar to ones you will find in Port Moresby. The owner, Rick Bennet, regularly travels to Indonesia and Papua New Guinea to replenish his collection. If you plan to visit Indonesia and Papua New Guinea, especially Bali and Port Moresby, this is a good place to get an idea of the types of artifacts you are likely to find there. This shop also carries a few items from India and China.

You will also find a few other tribal and ethnic art shops in and around the Cairns area. In downtown Cairns, look for **Niugini Gallery** with its small collection of PNG pieces and the **Zambezi Gallery** (Shop 10, City Place Arcade, Lake Street) with its international collection of artifacts and jewelry from over 20 different countries. In Kuranda you will find one excellent shop -- **Tropical Pulse** at 1 Therwine Street (Tel. 93-7369) -- offering a unique collection of textiles, woodcarvings, and jewelry from Java and Bali in Indonesia as well as PNG. This shop has one of the best collections of Sumba ikat textiles (from Indonesia) in Australia.

Fine Art

Cairns also has its own artist colony. Several local artists produce excellent quality oils and watercolors that appear in several galleries in Cairns. One of the nicest galleries is the newly opened **Waterfall Place** (Fine Art Australia) in the City Place Arcade at 113-115 Lake Street (Tel. 311-417). This gallery displays the works of many leading artists from all over Australia as well as several local artists: Arthur Boyde, Ray Crooke, Cliften Pugh, John Perceval, Charles Blackman, Heinz Steinmann, Jeffrey Making, Chuck Kehoe, Pam Schultz, Ivy Zappala, and Bill Auld. Other galleries to look for include the **Grafton House Galleries** in the Grafton House at 42 Grafton Street (Tel. 51-1897) and **The Upstairs Gallery** at 13A Shields

Street (Tel. 51-6150).   A few shops in Kuranda, such as
the **Kuranda Gallery** at 26 Coondoo Street (Tel. 93-75-
30), also offer fine arts.   One shop in Paradise Vallage at
Palm Cove -- **The Whole Works Gallery** (Tel. 55-3452) -
specializes in paintings by such noted Queensland artists as
Ray Crooke, Strom Gould, and James Baines.

Australian Arts and Crafts

Artists and craftsmen in the Cairn's area have similar
traditions as artists and craftsmen elsewhere in Australia:
they tend to be a very independent group working from
small houses, studios, and shops in the hills of northeast
Queensland.   They sell their products through several
shops in downtown Cairns as well as in Kuranda, Port
Douglas, and small towns in the Atherton Tablelands. You
will find some exquisite work being done with ceramics,
pottery, jewelry, and wood.

Some excellent arts and crafts shops to look for in
downtown Cairns include the newly opened Cairn's bra-
nch of the fine Sydney craft shop -- **Australian Craft-
works** -- at 3B Earl Court on the Corner of Lake and
Spence streets (Tel. 51-0725); **Orchards** just next door to
Australian Craftwork on Lake Street; **Grafton House
Galleries** at 42 Grafton Street (Tel. 51-1897); **The Pottery
Place** at 59 Sheridan Street (Tel. 51-3985); **Freshwater
Pottery House** at 227 Kamerunga Road, Freshwater (Tel.
55-2837); **Koala Kraft** at 17A Aplin Street; and **Fibres
Etcetera** at 58 Shields Street.   **Rusty's Market** (Grafton
Street) on Saturday from 6am to 1pm is filled with small
stalls selling a large variety of locally produced arts and
crafts similar to those you will find in the markets and
shops of Kuranda.

Twenty kilometers north of Cairns in **Palm Cove** you
will find one excellent arts and crafts shop in the Paradise
Shopping Village on The Esplanade: **The Whole Works
Gallery**.   This shop offers a good range of handcrafted
items -- jewelry, glass, silk, ceramics, and paintings --
from artists and craftsmen throughout northeast
Queensland.

Kuranda has several shops offering good quality arts
and crafts. Some of our favorite shops include the **Kuranda Gallery** at 26 Coondoo Street; **Crackerbox Palace** at 1
Therwine Street; and **Kuranda Inn Crafts**. Also look for
a new upscale shopping center opening in Kuranda which
should house some very nice arts and crafts shops.   The
market area has numerous stalls selling a wide variety of
locally produced arts and crafts. Especially on Wednesdays and Saturdays, when this market area is open from

7am and 1pm, you can easily spend the whole morning browsing through the many arts and crafts shops and market stalls.

Port Douglas also has a few arts and crafts shops worth visiting. We especially like the **Christy Palmerston Gallery** on Macrossan Street. This shop has a very fine collection of some of the best arts and crafts produced in Queensland, especially from the Atherton Tablelands area. You will find ceramics, pottery, jewelry, and unique wood-carvings in this delightful shop. The owners, Raewyn and Paul Oliver, are very helpful and enthusiastic about the local artists and craftsmen. In the newly completed Marina Mirage shopping complex, look for **Australian Art and Artifacts** and **Jennifer Ferrier**.

Other arts and crafts shops are scattered throughout the **Atherton Tablelands** area south of Kuranda. If you visit the towns of Mareeba, Atherton, Yungaburra, and Tolga you will find a few shops and galleries run by local craftsmen.

Aboriginal Art

Shops selling Aboriginal arts and crafts are by no means as numerous in Cairns as you would find in Darwin or Alice Springs. Nonetheless, you will find a few good quality shops offering some Aboriginal arts and crafts. In **downtown Cairns**, look for **Capricorn Galleries** (Tel. 51-0551) and **Yarrandoo** in the Park Royal Shopping Village on Lake Street and **Aboriginial Community Arts & Crafts** at the Trinity Wharf shopping center. **Gallery Primitive** at 26 Abbott Street (Tel. 311-641) is beginning to develop a good quality collection of Aboriginal artifacts. Also look for Aboriginal arts and crafts at **The Upstairs Gallery** at 13A Shields Street (Tel. 51-6150); **Outback Images** in the Central Court Hotel Complex on the corner of Lake and Spence streets (Tel. 31-2167); and **The Big Boomerang** at Rusty's Market (Tel. 51-1827 on Grafton Street.

In **Kuranda** you will find an Aboriginal museum and craft shop on Coondoo Street. Found at the very end of the shopping district, **Jillibinna Aboriginal Crafts and Museum** (Tel. 93-7220) is a museum and co-op offering craft classes. The **Tjapukai Dance Theatre** (Tel. 93-7544) at the corner of Koondoo and Therwine streets, which puts on very interesting Aborigine cultural performances, also has a small shop offering Aboriginal arts and crafts.

At **Port Douglas** you will find one shop selling Aboriginal arts and crafts. **Capricorn Galleries**, which also has a shop in downtown Cairns, is located in the Sunbird Centre at the Mirage Port Douglas Resort (Tel. 993-172). This shop has a nice selection of acrylic desert sand paintings, bark paintings, and Tiwi ceremonial poles.

Jewelry and Opals

You will find several shops in and around Cairns offering jewelry and opals. For uniquely designed silver jewelry, visit **Chibnall of Cairns** at 79 Abbott Street (Tel. 51-5124). This shop has developed two popular collections -- The Aboriginal Collection and the Marine and Rainforest Collection -- using local themes in handcrafted rings, bracelets, pendants, earrings, and charms. **Ridgy's** in the Central Hotel shopping arcade at the corner of Lake and Spence streets has some lovely black and red coral jewelry and opals. Other jewelry shops to look for include **Flair Jewellery** at 50 Lake Street (Tel. 51-2199). The popular **Shiray Gems** at 26 Abbott Street (Tel. 51-2576) has a large selection of investment gems, gold jewelry, and opals. Also look for a jewelry and souvenir shop called **1770** at 43A Sheridan Street (Tel. 51-4776) and the handcrafted jewelry of Jenry Welzman at **The Work Bench** at 77 Esplanade, Trinity Beach (Tel. 55-6473).

While many of the jewelry shops carry opals, other shops primarily specialize in opals: **Gemtec Opals** at 57-59 Abbott Street (Tel. 51-9833); **The Sapphire and Opal Centre** (129 Abbott Street (Tel. 51-6626); **Opal World** in the Hilton International Hotel on Wharf Street (Tel. 31-2466); and **Allisons** at the Parkroyal Hotel on Abbott Street (Tel. 31-1703).

Fashion and Resort Wear

As a major resort area in Queensland, the Cairns area has numerous shops selling the latest in fashion and resort wear, from colorful swimsuits to fashionable evening wear. In downtown Cairns, you will find familiar fashion stores, such as **Brian Rochford** in the Central Hotel shopping arcade (corner of Lake and Spence streets) and **Jeans West, Sportsgirl, Canterbury, Cue & Company,** and **Accessories Plus** in The Boland Centre (corner of Spence and Lake streets). **Judi Guthrie Design** at 74 Sheridan Street (Tel. 52-1132) designs and manufactures her own garments, using only natural fibers, at this shop. Also look for **Lucy Brown's Wardrobe** at 17A Sheridan Street (Tel. 51-0984); **Design 99** at 99 Grafton Street (Tel. 51-6197); **City Girl** in the Westcourt Plaza on Mulgrave Road (Tel. 51-8771); **Sunshine Leather** on Shields Street;

Cairns Resort Store in the Trinity Wharf; and **Aussie Down Under** in the Mellick Centre on the corner of Grafton and Spence streets (Tel. 51-9787). In the Palm Court shopping arcade on Lake Street, just adjacent to the Park Royal Shopping Village, look for **Danzare** for handcrafted and imported shoes and accessories, and **Dishiki** for nice women's sportswear and evening clothes.

Kuranda also has several clothing stores worth visiting. One of the most unique shops is **Cuscus** on Therwine Street (Tel. 937-353). Their handpainted clothing by Fitzpatrick and Raymond makes this one of the most interesting boutiques you will find anywhere in Queensland. Several other shops, such as **Jungle Johns Trade Store** and **Australian Bush Store** offer Outback style clothing for men.

In **Port Douglas** the **Marina Mirage shopping center** has several nice boutiques and clothing stores catering to tourists staying in this upmarket resort community: **Brian Rochford, Canterbury Clothing, Christopher James, Louis Vuitton, Jennifer Ferrier, Nautilus Boutique Marina, Nautical Charm, Sportsgirl, Things Mirage,** and **Umano.**

Australiana, Souvenirs, and Gifts

If you collect souvenirs or are looking for small gift items, especially T-shirts and shells, you've come to the right place. Cairn's abounds with souvenir shops selling everything from good quality arts and crafts to tourist kitsch. If you are interested in shell items, one of the largest and most unusual souvenir shops in Cairns -- as well as Australia -- is **The House of 10,000 Shells** at 32-34 Abbott Street (Tel. 51-3638). This shop is packed with every conceivable item made from shells. For coral and shell souvenirs and jewelry, visit the **Blue Water Coral Factory** at 33-35 Aumuller Street (Tel. 51-5797). For oilskin coats, hats, leather accessories, toys, fabrics, books, and craftworks, stop at **Australiana Aspect** and **Possums Gift Shop** in the Hilton International Hotel Shopping Promenade on Wharf Street (Tel. 31-2040). For T-shirts and Australiana, visit **Aussie Down Under** at the Mellick Centre on the corner of Grafton and Spence streets (Tel. 519-787); **Crocodilliacs** on the Esplanade (Tel. 81-3176); **The Big T-Shirt** at 393 Sheridan Street (Tel. 53-5052; and **Gum-nut Creations** at 62A Shield Street (Tel. 513-052). Other shops include **Cairns Souvenir Shop** in the Cominos Arcade at 88 Lake Street and their outlet at Trinity Wharf, **Tropical Souvenirs.** On Saturday morning **Rusty's Market** on Grafton Street is filled with vendor stalls selling all kinds of souvenir items.

Kuranda and Port Douglas also have several souvenir shops. In **Kuranda** look for vendor stalls in the market as well as shops along Therwine and Coondoo streets. The Marina Mirange at **Port Douglas** has a few souvenir shops, such as **Everything Australian** and **Exclusively Australian**.

Duty-Free Shops

Cairns has a few duty-free shops. Look for **Le Classique** at Palm Court (38-42 Lake Street) and in the Cairns International Airport. **City International Duty Free** is located at 77 Abbott Street. Like duty-free shops elsewhere in Australia, the ones in Cairns carry a similar range of liquor, perfume, Australiana, souvenirs, and gifts.

WHERE TO SHOP

The Cairns area has three major shopping areas you can visit during your stay: downtown Cairns, Kuranda, and Port Douglas. You will also find a few shops in Paradise Shopping Village at Palm Cove and in the crafts towns of the Atherton Tablelands.

Downtown Cairns

Downtown Cairns is the major center for the region. Here you will find a pedestrian mall -- City Place -- surrounded by small shopping arcades, street shops, hotel shopping arcades, Trinity Wharf, and Rusty's Market. This is a pleasant area to stroll along Cairns seven major shopping streets: Abbott, Lake, Grafton, Aplin, Shields, Spence, and Wharf. Most of the best shopping is located near the southern end of Abbott Street toward the Parkroyal Hotel and Trinity Wharf.

It's best to start shopping the downtown area at the **City Place** pedestrian mall, which intersects at Shields and Lake streets, and ends at the Trinity Wharf. Along **Lake Street** you will find several small shopping arcades each with 10 or more shops. One of the city's newest arcades is the **City Place Arcade** at 113-115 Lake Street. Here you will find **Waterfall Place** (Fine Art Australia), one of Cairn's best fine arts galleries; and **Gallery Zambezi** for African art and jewelry. The nearby **Andrejic's Arcade** (55 Lake Street) houses the **Niugini Gallery**, which has a small collection of artifacts from Papua New Guinea. **Lake Street** also has one of Cairn's best arts and crafts shops -- **Australian Craftworks** at 3B Earl Court on the corner of

Lake and Spence streets. Also look for two good jewelry stores -- **Flair Jewellery** (50 Lake) and **Rigby's** -- as well as several clothing stores along this street.

Abbott Street is our favorite shopping street in Cairns. Here you will find two of Australia's finest ethnic and tribal arts shops: **Gallery Primitive** (26 Abbott Street) for Australia's best collection of artifacts from Papua New Guinea; and **Asian Connection** (51 Abbott Street) for Australia's best collection of Indonesian artifacts and textiles as well as several artifacts from Papua New Guinea. Abbott Street also is home for Cairn's largest and most unique souvenir shop -- **The House of 10,000 Shells** at 32-34 Abbott Street. You will also find a few nice jewelry stores, such as **Chibnall of Cairns** (79 Abbott) and **Shiray Gems** (26 Abbott), on this street.

Grafton Street is a mixture of souvenir shops, restaurants, and clothing stores. Here is where you will find **The Craft Shop**, for stockman and riding supplies, **Eastern Emporium**, and the entrance to **Rusty's Bazaar** which has several small shops open during the week as well as during the Saturday morning market at Rusty's Bazaar.

Two of the best places to shop in downtown Cairns are the shopping arcades adjacent to the Parkroyal Hotel on Abbott Street and the Hilton Hotel on Wharf Street. The Parkroyal Hotel has two adjacent shopping arcades -- the **Parkroyal Shopping Village** and the **Palm Court**. The Palm Court is connected to the hotel shopping arcade but actually fronts on Lake Street (38-42 Lake Street). These two shopping arcades are Cairn's most upmarket shopping centers. Here you will find **Capricorn Galleries** with its Aboriginal arts and crafts; **Yarrandoo** for souvenirs, Australiana, and Aboriginal and PNG artifacts; **Le Classique** for duty-free goods; **Danzare** for handcrafted and imported shoes and accessories; **Dishiki** for nice women's clothes.

The **Hilton International Shopping Promenade** has a few nice shops worth visiting. Here you will find the **Opal World** for good quality opal stones and jewelry; **Australiana Aspect** for souvenirs and Australiana; **Tilli** for nice women's clothes; **Brian Rochford** for fashionable swimwear; and **Possums Gift Shop** for Australiana.

Immediately south of the Hilton International Hotel is the **Trinity Wharf**, Cairns' new waterfront pier, restaurant, entertainment, and shopping complex housing 35 specialty shops. This is a mixed area consisting of eateries, travel and tour companies, and clothing, souvenir, art, and nautical shops. Trinity Wharf is especially noted for its nice view of the harbor which is dotted with sailboats, powerboats, and reef touring ships.

Cairns also has a weekend market specializing in arts and crafts. Located on Grafton Street, directly across from the Andrejic's Arcade, **Rusty's Market** is open every Saturday from 6am to 1pm. Numerous vendor stalls are crammed together along the walkway as well as under a covered area adjacent to small shops. Here you can buy a large assortment of handcrafted items, such as arts, crafts, clothes, accessories, jewelry, T-shirts, woodcarvings, paintings, opals, rugs, wicker, shoes, watches, and plants. You can also get a $12 foot massage here! Several of the vendors displaying their wares in this market are also found at the Kuranda Market on Wednesdays and Saturdays. Therefore, if you don't have time to visit Kuranda, Rusty's Market will give you some feel of the atmosphere and products you would most likely find in Kuranda. The shops surrounding Rusty's Market are open 7 days a week. Look for such places as **Rocky's Home of the Black Opal**, **Big Boomerang**, and **Tony's Trinkets and Gems**.

Kuranda

The small town of Kuranda is located 27 kilometers northwest of Cairns. A gateway town to the Atherton Tableland area, Kuranda is in picturesque mountain and rainforest country. You can get there by either train or car. The train departs from the Cairns Railway Station everyday at 8:30, 9:00, and 9:30am for a scenic trip through sugarcane fields and rainforests and up the Barron Gorge. The train leaves Kuranda for Cairns at 12 noon, 2:10pm, and 3:15pm. The drive takes about 1 hour and is a scenic adventure along winding mountainous roads.

The town of Kuranda is famous for its arts and crafts, and especially for the Wednesday and Saturday market days. You will find numerous shops lining Kuranda's two main streets -- Therwine and Coondoo streets. Most of these shops are open 7 days a week and they offer some of the best selections of arts, crafts, and clothes in the Cairns area. However, on Wednesdays and Saturdays the town really bustles as two open-air markets open just for these two days. Over 100 vendors set up tables to sell their products: arts, crafts, clothes, leather goods, T-shirts, Australiana, souvenirs, and gifts. There's a little of something for everyone here. The markets are larger versions of Rusty's Market found in downtown Cairns on Saturdays.

While Kuranda is more crowded, touristy, and festive during the Wednesday and Saturday market days, you may want to visit Kuranda on other days of the week when there are fewer crowds and tour groups descending on the town. Most of the shops remain open during the week, and these other days will give you an opportunity to shop Kuranda at a much more leisurely pace. While the markets are the big drawing card to visiting Kuranda, they are by no means exceptional given their decidedly tourist orientation. The really good shopping in Kuranda is found in a few quality shops that line the two main streets of Kuranda.

Some of our favorite shops in Kuranda are the **Cracker Box Palace** at 1 Therwine Street with its unique objects and home decorative pieces; **Tropical Pulse** at 1 Therwine Street for its handcrafted artifacts from PNG, Indonesia, and Australia, especially their handwoven ikat textiles; **Cuscus** for its unique handpainted clothing; and **Kuranda Gallery** at 26 Coondoo Street for its nice collection of art work and handcrafted items from the area.

Plans are proceeding to further expand Kuranda's shopping area with more new shops and shopping arcades as well as to attract more and more high quality shops. Indeed, Kuranda is quickly becoming a major shopping center in the Cairns area, one which is a "must do" destination on many visitors' travel agendas.

Port Douglas

Port Douglas, located approximately 65 kilometers north of Cairns, is a rapidly developing resort of special appeal to upmarket travelers who enjoy the comforts and convenience of a full service resort complex, complete with a golf course and marina. The shopping here is beginning to expand rapidly with the recent completion of the Marina Mirage, a classy waterfront shopping, restaurant, and entertainment complex.

Port Douglas has three major shopping areas. The downtown area of the original town has one main street -- **Macrossan Street**. Here you will find several restaurants and shops. We especially like **Christy Palmerston Gallery** with its nice selection of handcrafted arts and crafts from northern Queensland. You will find some lovely pottery, jewelry, and woodcarved pieces in this shop.

Less than 1 kilometer from the main street is the **Sunbird Centre** of the Mirage Port Douglas Resort. This is a small shopping complex with a few clothing stores and one nice Aboriginal arts and crafts shop -- **Capricorn Galleries** (Tel. 993-172). This shop is worth visiting. It has a good selection of nicely displayed bark and acrylic paintings, Tiwi ceremonial poles, and woodcarved pieces. You will find another Capricorn Galleries shop in the Parkroyal Shopping Village on Lake Street in downtown Cairns.

The new **Marina Mirage** shopping complex has several upmarket shops catering to the shopping tastes of Port Douglas' resort clientele. For fashion and accessories, look for **Brian Rochford, Canterbury Clothing, Christopher James, Louis Vuitton, Nautilus Boutique Marina, Nautical Charm, Sportsgirl, Things Mirage,** and **Umano.** Specialty stores include **House of Stokes, Imageland,** and **The Opal Cave.** For souvenirs and gifts, look for **Everything Australian** and **Exclusively Australian.**

Palm Cove

Palm Cove is located 20 kilometers north of Cairns. You can easily stop here on your way to either Kuranda or Port Douglas. As you travel north of Cairns, look for a small sign on your right which directs you to the Ramada Reef Resort. This is the Palm Cove area.

Palm Cove is a lovely, quiet beachside resort area where you will also find the Ramada Reef Resort hotel and a few other smaller hotels. It has one small shopping center -- **Paradise Shopping Village** -- with a few shops selling resort wear and arts and crafts. You will find one excellent arts and crafts shop here that alone makes the trip to Palm Cove worthwhile. The **Whole Works Gallery** (Tel. 55-3452) has a unique selection of contemporary Australian arts and crafts, with emphasis on jewelry, glass, silk, ceramics, and paintings. In addition to offering the works of such famous Queensland artists as Ray Crooke, Strom Gould, and James Baines, the shop also includes works of contemporary Aboriginal artists. **Mango** has a nice selection of designer resort wear. **Sandprints Resort Shop** offers clothes, Australiana, and gifts.

Atherton Tablelands

Time permitting, you may want to drive to the Atherton Tablelands area which is located approximately 40 kilometers south of Kuranda. Four roads lead into this area. Lying at an elevation of 760 meters above sea level, the Atherton Tableland has a temperate climate, up to 10 degrees cooler than the tropical coastline. Here you will find several small towns with arts and crafts shops.

The major towns to visit for shopping purposes are Mareeba, Atherton, Tolga, Kairi, and Yungaburra -- all within 100 kilometers of Kuranda. In Tolga, visit **Tolga Woodworks** for uniquely crafted wood bowls, platters vases, knife blocks, plates, and boxes. Several of Tolga Woodworks' pieces are also on display at Christy Palmerston Gallery in Port Douglas. In Kairi look for **De Olde**

Craft Shoppe and **Lee Art Gallery.** In Atherton visit the **Underground Crystal Caves** at 69 Main Street. In Yungaburra look for **Nap's Next** with its extensive range of local handcrafted products -- pottery, timberware, homespun hand knits, paintings, soapstone carvings, and wooden toys.

ENJOYING YOUR STAY

As noted earlier, most people come to Cairns for everything other than shopping. It's only after being in the area for a few days that they begin discovering many of Cairns' shopping delights. And some visitors leave too little time to shop downtown Cairns, Kuranda, Port Douglas, Palm Cove, or the Atherton Tablelands. If you enjoy shopping, we recommend that you include two days in your schedule just for shopping. We also suggest that you rent a car to shop this area on your own. Use tours to do what most other visitors to the Cairns area do -- see the Great Barrier Reef and go sportfishing.

Your choice of **hotels** will largely depend on the purpose of your visit to Cairns. If, for example, you enjoy lying on the beach, then stay somewhere along the beach rather than in downtown Cairns. The city does not have such beaches -- only wharfs and docks for ships and boats. Go instead to the **Ramada Reef Resort** at Palm Cove (20 kilometers north of Cairns) where you can enjoy a fine resort hotel just across the street from a lovely beach. Alternatively, head further north to the **Mirage Port Douglas Resort.** Keep in mind, however, these hotels are not conveniently located in relation to Cairns. Although the hotels have a shuttle bus service, you may choose to rent a car to drive from these hotels to the city.

But if you could care less about sitting on the beach, we highly recommend the two best hotels in Cairns: **ParkRoyal Hotel** on Abbott Street and the **Hilton International Hotel** on Wharf Street. These are excellent hotels conveniently located in pleasant downtown surroundings. We especially like the unique architecture and tropical ambiance of the Parkroyal Hotel. The Hilton International Hotel has a lovely view of the harbor. Both hotels are ideally located in the heart of downtown Cairns near the Trinity Wharf. They are within easy walking distance to all of the major shops, shopping centers, and restaurants. You will find several other hotels in Cairns, ranging from budget to first-class.

If you don't know where to initially stay, take the shuttle bus from the airport to the downtown Cairns. The bus will stop at the **Cairns Convention and Visitors Bureau** at 41 Shields Street (Tel. 51-7366) where you can arrange for different categories of accommodations as well as pick up tourist literature and get answers to any questions you might have about planning your stay in Cairns, including tour reservations. This office has copies of a few tourist newspapers and booklets that summarize all of the major activities and attractions in the Cairns area as well as northeast Queensland: *Coral Coaster*, *Travel & Tourism*, *Tourist Scene*, *Welcome to Cairns*, and *The Cairns Tourist Guide*.

Most visitors come to Cairns to see the **Great Barrier Reef** to do reef walking, snorkeling, scuba diving, or just lying on the sandy beaches to soak up the sun. Indeed, Cairns is one of the major departure points along the East Coast for visiting the reef. Green Island is the major reef watching destination from Cairns. Several tour groups sponsor day cruises to the Great Barrier Reef. One of the most popular such cruises is on the large catamaran **Quicksilver** which departs every morning from Port Douglas. You can arrange for this tour in Cairns through the **Cairns Tour Services** (87 Lake Street, Tel. 51-8311) or through **Quicksilver Connections** in Port Douglas (99-5500). Some tour companies also offer helicopter trips to the Great Barrier Reef.

You will find a great deal of literature in your hotel and at the tourist information center which advertises these and other tours to the Great Barrier Reef. We do not recommend any particular tours since each one is slightly different in terms of cost, itinerary, and group and ship size. Some tours, for example, allow you time to walk on the reef, snorkel, and swim whereas others spend most of the time getting to and from the reef, with little time available for recreational activities. On the other hand, you may not want to spend four hours waiting for everyone else to enjoy the water. Therefore, it's best to look over the literature, compare tours, and decide on which tour best meets your interests and needs.

If you enjoy **sportfishing**, you've come to the right place. Cairns has a well deserved reputation as the world's center for Black Marlin fishing. Sport fishermen come from all over the world to fish in the waters outside Cairns where Black Marlins weighing more than 1000 lbs. (455 kgs.) have been caught. You can charter fully equipped boats in Cairns to take you on a fishing adventure of a lifetime. If you don't catch the big Black Marlin, there are plenty of good-sized sail fish, Spanish mackeral, tuna, dolphins, barracuda, and sharks to keep your fishing interests high.

The Cairns area is also famous for its **rainforests and**

Tablelands. As we noted earlier, Kuranda is one of the gateways to the tropical Atherton Tablelands. This picturesque area includes rainforests, extinct volcanic lakes, waterfalls, gorges, rich farmlands, ancient limestone caves, and rolling plains. You can easily spend a full day or two exploring this area. While you can take a tour to Kuranda as well as into the Tablelands, you can also rent a car and easily drive to this area. We recommend starting in Kuranda and then proceed to Mareeba, the largest town in the Tablelands only 37 kilometers from Kuranda. Proceed from there to Tolga, Kairi, Lake Tinaroo, Atherton, Yungaburra, and Malanda. In addition to seeing interesting sights in the Tablelands, you will also find several small arts and crafts shops in these towns. You can return to Cairns by way of Lake Barrine or Innisfail.

Whatever you do, you will find plenty to do in Cairns. More adventuresome visitors might head further north to the **Cape York area**, the northern most point in Australia. Indeed, you will find regular air service from Cairns to Australia's remote northern areas such as Cooktown, Mt. Isa, Normanton, Karumba, Buretown, Mornington Island, and Doomadgee as well as nostalgic 'Gooney Bird' air tours of Cape York Peninsula (contact DC-3 Queensland at 53-7819). Others might want to try a wilderness safari into the **Daintree River** and **Daintree National Park** areas northwest of Port Douglas (call Australian Wilderness Safari at 981-666) or go whitewater rafting, hot air ballooning, or para-sailing.

If you plan to proceed on to **Papua New Guinea**, Cairns is a good place to relax before encountering a totally different culture and society. In Cairns you can prepare for your new adventure. For Papua New Guinea is different -- wild, colorful, and intriguing. Get a glimpse of this fascinating country by visiting the tribal artifact shops in downtown Cairns (Gallery Primitive, Asian Connection, and Niugini Gallery) as well as the the New Guinea Adventure Centre at 44B Aplin Street (Tel. 51-0622) for information on tours to the Highlands (Ambua Lodge) and the Sepik River (Karawari Lodge). Papua New Guinea is a different world than what you have seen in Australia thus far. You will be entering a country that has quickly moved from the Stone Age into the 20th century, a country where over 700 languages are spoken amongst its hundreds of diverse ethnic and cultural groups. This is a beautiful and fascinating country of former headhunters, remote valleys and villages, raging rivers, steaming jungles, colorful tribes, proud warriors, and incredibly rich and continuously productive artistic traditions. However you travel and wherever you stay in Papua New Guinea, you will have fond memories of your Cairns experience and look forward to returning there again.

PART III

SECRETS OF EXOTIC
PAPUA NEW GUINEA

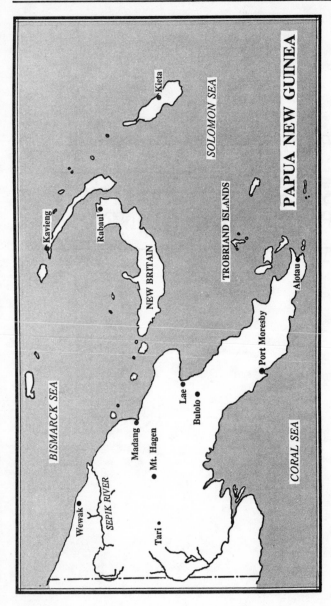

Chapter Twelve

WELCOME TO PAPUA NEW GUINEA

Welcome to one of the world's most intriguing lands and peoples. Located north of Australia, East of Indonesia, and West of the South Pacific islands, Papua New Guinea occupies the eastern half of the world's second largest island. Its population of 3.5 million, divided into nearly 700 different cultural and linguistic groups, is scattered throughout the hills, valleys, and islands of this rugged but extremely beautiful and intriguing country.

Papua New Guinea, popularly referred to as PNG, is a land of great diversity, challenge, and adventure. Long noted as a haven for the world's 3M's -- missionaries, misfits, and mercenaries -- Papua New Guinea is one of today's best kept traveling and shopping secrets. A paradise for those who want to experience a true adventure in travel, it is unlike any other country you have ever visited or are likely to experience in the future. A country in the midst of experiencing rapid changes -- from the primitive Stone Age to the modern 20th century -- within a space of only a few decades, Papua New Guinea is experiencing political, economic, social, and cultural changes unparalleled in the history of mankind.

Visit Papua New Guinea as soon as you can. It's a wonderful and exciting travel experience which will forever change your perceptions of this part of the world. Do it now, because the PNG of today is quickly disappearing with the onslaught of modernization. Better still, PNG is a shopper's paradise for some of the world's most fabulous tribal artifacts and crafts. If you get there soon, you can still witness the emergence of new art and craft developments, meet emerging artists, commission textiles, paintings, and sculptures, and purchase one-of-a-kind works of art that have yet to appear on the local commercial market or be exported abroad. All of this will change in the next 5 to 10 years as the arts and crafts increasingly become commercialized in response to tourists and export markets.

THE BASICS

Location and Geography

Situated just south of the Equator and immediately to the north of the northeastern tip of Australia, Papua New Guinea is a beautiful and rugged country consisting of a large mainland island and several smaller islands. The mainland island is actually the eastern half of the world's second largest island, New Guinea, which is shared with Indonesia's province of West Irian. The island portion of PNG consists of several islands lying off the east coast and facing the South Pacific Islands. The largest and most heavily populated islands are Manus, New Britain, and New Ireland islands to the north and Milne Bay and the North Solomon islands to the east.

PNG is a mountainous country. A high range of mountains, with an average height of 3,000 meters, runs down the spine of the main island, splitting it into northern and southern basins: the Markham, Ramu, and Sepik rivers to the north and the Strickland, Purari, and Fly rivers to the south. While the Sepik and Fly are PNG's largest rivers, the Sepik River is PNG's "Amazon River" and one of its major tourist destinations. The islands fall into three groups of mountainous islands: the Bismark Archipelago to the north consisting of Manus, New Britain, and New Ireland; the Milne Bay Islands to the east consisting of 160 islands and 500 islets and atolls; and the northeastern islands of the Solomons, Buka, and Bougainville.

Climate, Seasons, and When to Go

PNG's climate is definitely equatorial but with major variations due to its high mountain ranges and island settings. This is a warm country with two distinct seasons: wet and dry. However, the extent and intensity of these seasons will vary from one part of the country to another. Port Moresby, for example, tends to be dry all year long. The wet season is most pronounced during the months of November to March. The driest time of year is between May and October. In many areas of the country the wet season primarily brings showers during the evening or for short periods of time during the day rather than continuous torrential downpours normally associated with equatorial and monsoonal climates.

Temperatures can vary greatly depending on altitude. In coastal areas temperatures tend to be relatively stable, ranging from 25C to 30C. However, temperatures in the Highlands can become cold at night. We recommend taking casual clothing for summer as well as a jacket for cool evenings in the Highlands.

The best time to travel to PNG is during the dry season, although anytime during the year can be good depending on where you plan to travel. A few companies operate tours on the Sepik River, into the Highlands, and to the Trobriand Islands year-round. The months of June to September are especially good for most parts of the country. However, it can be very hot and dry in Port Moresby, and the rivers the lakes may be very shallow at this time of year.

What to Pack and Wear

It's best to pack lightly for your trip to PNG. Given the warm and humid climate and the informal social atmosphere of this country, we recommend packing summer weight, casual clothes made of natural fibers. Avoid polyesters or wools since they are not comfortable in such climates. Men can get by with slacks and sport shirts. Women can wear slacks, culottes or skirts, with blouses. Be sure to take a comfortable and sturdy pair of walking shoes that you don't mind getting scuffed, muddy, and wet. If you are going into villages, especially those along the Sepik River and the islands, expect to get your shoes wet and muddy. You should also take another pair of shoes to change to when you complete your village walks, especially if you are on board one of the cruise ships.

If you plan to visit the Highlands, take along a lightweight jacket and sweater. You are likely to experience some cool evenings and mornings in the Highlands.

Leave things of value, especially expensive pieces of jewelry, at home. Thievery and assaults are well and alive in PNG, so don't advertise the fact that you may be carrying a lot of money!

Getting There

Most visitors to Papua New Guinea arrive by air via Cairns, Australia's major gateway city to PNG.   **Air Niugini**, the national carrier of PNG, and **Qantas Airline** operate flights from Cairns to Port Moresby. We suggest both entering and departing PNG by way of Cairns. We especially recommend this routing for shoppers, because Cairns provides a good introduction to the types of artifacts you are likely to find in PNG. You may, for example, discover some lovely PNG items in the shops of Cairns which are not available in PNG. Survey the major shops in Cairns, especially Gallery Primitive and Asian Connection on Abbott Street, before arriving in PNG and then return to Cairns and these shops after you leave PNG.

Qantas also flys to Port Moresby from Brisbane and Sydney and Air Niugini flies from Sydney, Brisbane and Townsville in Australia as well as Hong Kong, Manila, Singapore, Jayapura (Indonesia), and Honiara (Solomon Islands). For information on Air Niugini's flight schedule, contact one of their offices which are listed at the end of this chapter.

Documents

Many visitors to PNG do not need a visa prior to arrival if they are bona fide tourists. Citizens from Australia, New Zealand, Canada, the USA, most Western European countries, and near Pacific neighbors are issued visas upon arrival at Port Moresby's Jackson International Airport. These visas cannot be issued for more than 30 days. If you are going to PNG for business purposes, are a citizen of another country, or plan to stay more than 30 days, apply for a visa through a PNG diplomatic office nearest you or inquire through an Australian Embassy.

Arrival and Departure

Arrival in PNG by air is relatively hassle-free. If you enter Port Moresby from Cairns, Australia, the flight takes less than 2 hours. Jacksons International Airport is relatively small and convenient. Immigration, baggage retrieval, and Customs are all together in one small room. If you are a foreign tourist without a visa, go to the Immigration line on the left, present your passport, and pay US$6 for a visa. Free baggage carts next to the baggage trolley. Retrieve your bags and proceed through Customs. This process should not take more than 30 minutes.

As you come out of the main terminal building, you will find a branch of the PNG Banking Corporation which should be open to exchange your money. The bank is normally open during international arrival times (9am to 2pm, Monday thru Thursday, and 9am to 5pm on Friday). Change as much money as you need to here since the exchange rates at the airport bank are the same as at the banks downtown. Directly across from the bank and to your left as you exit the terminal building is a Tourist Board Information Desk. It may or may not be open. The same tourist information is available in the major hotels and through the Air Niugini office in town.

Arrival experience at other airports in PNG will vary considerably, from landing on a grass airstrip in the Highlands where you unload and carry your own bags to small airports where there is some degree of baggage handling. However, do not expect many airport services -- sometimes the phones don't work!

Be especially cautious with your **departing times and flights**. Always confirm your flight in plenty of time, and get to the airport at least an hour early. Flights are known to leave **before** the stated departure time. This may never happen to you, but it nearly had disasterous consequences for us. Bruce, but not his luggage, missed a critical connecting flight to Kieta because the plane left 15 minutes early. What was most disturbing was this scenario: Bruce arrived at the airport one hour early, checked several times with airport personnel on the departure time to be sure he would not miss this flight, and the flight still left without him! Bruce was left standing with some rather incongruous possessions -- a laptop computer in one hand and a bilum bag filled with five penis gourds in the other hand.

Needless to say, this was not his idea of a good time, although in retrospect it makes for an amusing story since it fits in with three other disasters that we shared on this same day -- the airport car left the hotel without us; our airplane had to make an emergency landing due to a failed jet engine during take-off; and Bruce's taxi from the airport to the hotel ran out of gas! While the airline apologized, put Bruce up overnight in Port Moresby, and retrieved his bags the next day, he had to cancel the remainder of his flight plans. Our advice on good airport departure behavior: expect your plane may leave early, keep a close eye on any locals taking the same flight, and when they suddenly move to the departure gate, you move with them. We subsequently learned that such early departures are a common occurrence. The result of this missed flight for Bruce was to cancel a series of flights to the Solomon

Islands, Fiji, and the United States and to re-route the
remainder of his trip to other locations in PNG and in
Australia. Fortunately he found a friend who invited him
to sail with his group to the Trobriand Islands. He was
flexible enough so that everything worked out in the end.
But few people have such flexibility when traveling on
tight schedules. So, when in PNG, always keep an eye on
your departure gate!

Currency and Credit Cards

The local currency is the **kina**. At present, one kina is
roughly equivalent to US$1.16. In Port Moresby you can
exchange your money at the airport or at banks in the city.
Towns also have banks that will take traveler's checks and
major international currencies. While major hotels and
some shops take traveler's checks and credit cards, those
accepting credit cards primarily take American Express --
not Visa or MasterCard. Some shops will also take personal checks for goods to be shipped later.

Be sure to take enough local currency with you when
you travel outside Port Moresby and major towns. Foreign
currency, travelers checks, and credit cards are not accepted in these areas. When shopping outside the urban areas,
you should take lots of small denomination kina bills with
you since few villagers have change.

Tipping

PNG follows the same simple tipping pattern as
Australia and Melanesia -- no tipping. However, you may
encounter tour situations where local guides attempt to get
tips from the group. Even in these situations, it's perfectly
acceptable to follow the local practice in this part of the
world -- no tip. Americans, Europeans, and Japanese are
most likely targets for such tip requests; Australians and
New Zealanders will lead a revolt!

Security

You need to be very careful in PNG with your valuables and your personal safety. The crime rate is steadily
increasing in PNG to the point where many foreigners
claim PNG is in a state of anarchy. This is somewhat of
an exaggeration, but crime is widespread in PNG, it occurs
in daylight as well as at night, and it is getting worse.
Towns such as Lae and Mount Hagen have been especially
hard hit with major increases in crime over the past year
or two. And many long-time expatriate residents are

extremely concerned about their safety.

The most common crimes are thefts, assaults, and gang rapes. Increased social dislocation accompanied by high unemployment amongst unskilled men residing in urban areas is largely responsible for the deteriorating security situation. Termed the "rascal problem", because of the large number of unemployed men wandering the streets and getting into trouble, this is something you can avoid by being very cautious where you go and what you do. Our advice: It is not safe to walk around urban areas and wander into villages on your own. When you go out, do so during the day and with a friend or in a group. Women should be especially cautious given the high incidence of "pack rapes" in PNG: in 1988 there were 290 victims of 1900 rapes! The most common rape involves five men -- a pack -- raping one woman.

The increased crime situation in PNG makes a strong argument for staying at the best hotels, taking taxis or hiring a car and driver, and joining experienced tour groups. You may pay more for such services, but your personal safety is well worth the extra costs.

Language

PNG is a multi-lingual nation with over 700 languages spoken throughout the country. English is widely spoken in the urban areas and is the official language of government and business. Pidgin English is also widely spoken. When shopping outside the urban areas, use sign language to negotiate prices. Most of the sellers understand English numbers and the concepts of "first price", "second price", and "third price" -- different price and discount levels central to the bargaining process in many villages. When in doubt, use your fingers or show your kina for prices.

Business Hours

Most stores in the urban areas are open for business between the hours of 8am and 5pm, Monday thru Thursday, have extended hours on Fridays, and may open from 9am to 12 noon on Saturdays. Offices are open from 8am to 4pm, and banks stay open from 9am to 2pm, Monday thru Thursday, and from 9am to 5pm on Fridays.

Most villages are open for business whenever visitors arrive. As soon as a tour boat or bus approaches a village, the villagers move into position with their goods and wait for you to approach them in and around the *haus tambaran* or a central open space in the village.

Transportation

PNG is a challenging country of dense jungles, rugged mountains, remote Highland and river villages, small trading towns, and limited transportation and communication. With very limited roads, the only way to get around the country is by plane. Air Niugini regularly flies into 20 major urban centers. Talair flies into over 100 airstrips throughout the country. More remote areas are serviced by the missionary airline -- MAF, the Missionary Aviation Fellowship -- as well as Douglas Airways, Bougair, and Provincial Air Services. Many of the flights will be in prop planes piloted by bush pilots who fly by sight rather than by radar and tower communication. Don't be surprised if you see your pilot looking at a map and staring out the windows to locate a grass airstrip on which to land the plane. This form of transportation may be one of highlights of your visit to PNG!

Several ships and vessels ply the waters and stop in coastal towns around Papua New Guinea. If you have a great deal of time and flexibility and don't mind spartan accommodations, you can easily and inexpensively arrange transportation on these vessels for trips to mainland ports and islands. However, there are drawbacks to this mode of transportation. As we arrived in the Trobriand's, the local passenger freighter was aground in the harbor. When we left a few days later, it was still in the same position where it most likely remained until a storm brought in the next unusually high tide. In this case patience is more than a virtue -- it is a necessity!

Transportation within urban areas is normally by **PMV** (Public Motor Vehicles) or taxis. The PMV's are mini buses in Port Moresby but they may be trucks with wooden benches in other urban areas. These are cheap forms of public transportation where you will have a chance to rub shoulders with local residents. If you ride these vehicles, be sure to watch your wallet since these are also good places to meet the local "rascals"!

Taxis tend to be expensive. In Port Moresby they are available at the airport and major hotels, and they can be called to come to any location. Although they are metered, negotiation is also possible. We learned this the hard way. One driver at the airport, for example, quoted us a flat rate into town. Thinking the amount was high, we asked him to use the meter instead. When we arrived at our hotel, we discovered the amount showing on the meter was twice the "off-meter" rate the driver had initially quoted! The best approach is to ask a local how much you should pay, and negotiate ahead of time.

If you **rent a car,** be sure to remember one important rule of the road. If you get into an accident, flee the scene as quickly as possible! Chances are you may be assaulted by the victim who decides it is "payback" time, regardless of whether or not the accident was your fault. Better still, don't drive in PNG.

Food

PNG is not a gourmet's delight. However, you will find some good restaurants in Port Moresby, and the food is tolerable elsewhere in the country. In Port Moresby, the best restaurant is reputed to be **The Galley Restaurant** (Aviat Street, Konedobu, Tel. 21-2167). Nothing fancy, but the food is good and the prices are reasonable. Other decent restaurants in Port Moresby include the restaurants in the **Travelodge Hotel** as well as the Tropicana Restaurant and **Shanghai Gardens.** In fact, we thought the restaurant upstairs in the Travelodge competed well with the Galley Restaurant; although the price may be a bit higher, the decor is more plush.

When you book tours at the various lodges as well as on ships that tour the Sepik River and Trobriand Islands, all meals are included in the tour price.

Accommodations

We recommend that you stay in the best hotels during your stay in PNG. While these hotels may be more expensive than other accommodations, they have one advantage -- security and safety. Given the prevalence of the "rascal" problem and the high incidence of thefts and robberies, we recommend that you spend a little more money to stay at the best hotels. Be forewarned that neither accommodations nor food are inexpensive in PNG. Whatever level of services you choose, you will feel the price is high relative to what you get. Accept it as an economic fact-of-life in PNG. Port Moresby's three best hotels are the **Port Moresby Travelodge** (P.O. Box 1661, Tel. 21-2266), **Islander Hotel** (P.O. Box 1981, Boroko, Tel. 25-5955), and the **Davara Hotel** (P.O. Box 799, Tel. 21-2100). We highly recommend the Port Moresby Travelodge for its location, service, and amenities.

You will find plenty of accommodations in towns outside Port Moresby. While they may not be the same quality as the best hotels in Port Moresby, accommodations will be clean and comfortable. Tourist publications such as *Travellers Times* and *Insait* have a current listing of the major hotels throughout the country.

Tour groups, such as Melanesian Tourist Service and Trans Niugini Tours, have their own accommodations. Melanesian Tourist Services operates the Madang Resort Hotel as well as lodges in the Highlands. Trans Niugini Tours owns the Karawari Lodge and Ambua Lodge. Both companies also operate cruise ships which have on-board accommodations.

Electricity and Water

Electricity in PNG is 240 volts. If you bring 110 volt appliances with you, be sure to bring a voltage convertor. We do not recommend drinking local tap water. Drink bottled drinks instead.

Health

The major health problem in PNG is malaria. If you plan to travel outside the urban areas, be sure to take adequate anti-malaria medication before, during and after, your stay in PNG. Assuming your tetanus innoculation is up to date, other than malaria, you should not have any health problems in PNG. It is always a good idea to check with your doctor regarding what precautions are recommended at the time you are traveling. Keep in mind however, that most physicians in the developed world are overly conservative when prescribing for travellers to less developed areas.

Convenience

On a scale of 1 to 10, PNG gets a 5 for convenience if you try to travel there on your own. However, if you join a tour, PNG gets an 8 for convenience. Remember, this is still a frontier country in the process of development. While it is not organized to handle a large number of tourists, it does have a few excellent tour operators that offer some of the most convenient tours you will find anywhere in the world. As we outline later, these tours are highly recommended for anyone wishing to visit PNG. They are all inclusive -- transportation, accommodations, meals, and guides. Perhaps most important, the operators are knowledgeable regarding the safety of places to visit.

If you try to do PNG on your own or on the cheap, you will find this country both inconvenient and expensive. Transportation both inside and outside the urban areas is inconvenient, and accommodations are limited. In addition, you will have difficulty communicating with the locals and few tours are organized to be booked upon arrival. Again, your best approach is to book ahead and join an all inclusive tour.

Resources

Many books have been written on PNG, but most are either out of print or difficult to find. Some of the best books on PNG art were published in the 1960s. If you are lucky you may be able to find some of these books in libraries or used book stores.

One of the best sources for introducing yourself to PNG artifacts is the Michael C. Rockefeller collection in the South Wing of the Metropolitan Museum of Art in New York City. This is a truly fine collection of artifacts collected by Michael Rockefeller during the 1960s. You should enjoy seeing this display both before and after visiting PNG. The museum bookshop at the Metropolitan Museum of Art also sells a few books on PNG art: Douglas Newton's *New Guinea Art in the Collection of the Museum of Primitive Art, Crocodile* and *Cassowary: Religious Art of the Upper Sepik River, New Guinea*, and *Massim: Art of the Massim Area, New Guinea*; and Cherry Lowman's *Displays of Power: Art and War Among the Marings of New Guinea*.

You will not find many books available in bookstores and libraries outside PNG. The tourist literature is extremely limited, confined to a few brochures available through Air Niugini and local tour companies (see addresses at the end of this chapter) and small sections in a few guide books.

One of the most comprehensive guidebooks focusing solely on PNG is the Lonely Planet's *Papua New Guinea: A Travel Survival Kit*. Designed primarily for budget travelers who are used to traveling on their own, this book includes some interesting information on PNG history, ethnography, sightseeing, and local hotels and restaurants. At times difficult to read because of language and editing problems and in parts esoteric, the book is useful for its coverage of the whole country. However, it could be a less than helpful book if you followed its every detail. Ironically, the book is designed for do-it-yourself traveling in a country where do-it-yourself traveling is no longer recommended! We still highly recommend this book because it's the only detailed book available on traveling in PNG.

The *South Pacific Handbook*, published by Moon Publications, has a section on PNG. Like the Lonely Planet guidebook, this one is also designed for budget travelers who are used to traveling on their own with a little money but a great deal of time, tolerance, and perseverance.

You will also find a series of booklets on the various provinces in PNG. Published by Robert Brown and Associates in Bathurst, New South Wales, Australia, this *PNG Series* is primarily a set of 18 photo books with some narrative on each province. You may want to purchase copies of *The Sepik*, *The Southern Highlands*, and *The Highlands*. These books are available in a few arts and crafts shops in Port Moresby.

Once you arrive in PNG you will find several books on the history, geography, and ethnography of PNG. The Girl Guide Hand Craft Shops have a limited selection of some of the best books of interest to tourists. However, the University Bookstore on the campus of the University of Papua New Guinea in Waigani has the best selection of such books. Especially recommended for background reading are James Sinclair's *Sepik Pilot* and *Kiap: Australia's Patrol Officers in Papua New Guinea*; Christina Dowell's *In Papua New Guinea*; Buckley and Klugman's *The Australian Presence in the Pacific, Burns Philip 1914-1946*; Margaret Mead's *Growing Up in New Guinea*; Gardner and Heider's *Garden's of War -- Life and Death in the New Guinea Stone Age*. A good coffee table photo book is Kirk and Strathern's *Man as Art: New Guinea* which focuses on the Highland tribes.

Serious shoppers should purchase a copy of *The Artifacts and Crafts of Papua New Guinea* which is available in artifact and handicraft shops as well as at the University Bookstore. This is used as a "catalog" by sellers and dealers in PNG. In fact, some shops may show you "our catalog" which is this booklet published by the Handcraft Industry of Papua New Guinea. It is "everyone's catalog" to use and abuse at will! This fully illustrated booklet is a "must buy" item which will quickly become your buying guide to PNG artifacts. Take it with you wherever you go to compare items with the booklets classification system. You will begin seeing major differences in quality by comparing potential purchases to the color photos in the booklet.

You will not find many maps available on PNG. Most hotels will have basic city maps to assist you in navigating the local streets. The best commercial map available on PNG is published in Australia -- *Map of Papua New Guinea* -- by Universal Business Directories Pty. Ltd. in Macquarie Park, New South Wales. This map includes maps of the country, Port Moresby, and 12 towns. You will find this map in several major bookstores in Sydney and Melbourne and some shops in Port Moresby. Shell Oil of Papua New Guinea also publishes a Tourist Guide *to Papua New Guinea* which includes maps of the country, Port Moresby, the Sepik River, and eight towns.

If you join a cruise sponsored by the Melanesian Tourist Services, you will find a fairly comprehensive library of books on board. Many of these books are now out of print. They also have several videotapes on PNG, but the quality varies and some may not be of interest to the casual traveler. One tape -- the powerful *First Contact* showing the actual arrival and reaction of local tribes to the first Europeans in the Highlands in 1930 -- is "must" viewing for any visitor to PNG.

Costs

Traveling in PNG is not cheap, although it is no more expensive than traveling in many parts of Australia. Major hotels will cost K90 or more a night. Food costs about the same as in Australia, and the best restaurants are very inexpensive compared to Australian restaurants. Transportation, however, is a major cost because you will depend on flying into most towns in small aircraft that can be expensive. In addition, the all-inclusive tours will cost between K100 to K400 per day. As we will see later, shipping can also be a major expense.

Shopping prices vary depending on where and what you are buying. The prices of artifacts increase the closer you get to urban centers where more middlemen are involved in the transactions. A mask purchased for K10 in a village along the Sepik River, for example, may cost K30 in Madang and K50 in Port Moresby. Overall, however, artifacts purchased in the villages and urban shops are still good buys compared to the prices you would pay for the similar items outside PNG. The item purchased for K10 in the village, K30 in Madang, or K50 in Port Moresby, for example, is likely to cost the equivalent of K200 in Australia and K500 in Germany, United Kingdom, and the United States. However, you are likely to find some items in the shops of Port Moresby that you didn't see out in the villages.

GETTING TO KNOW YOU

Many first-time visitors have difficulty relating to Papua New Guinea, because their past experiences have not prepared them well for such a place or warp in time. Indeed, when was the last time you visited a Third World village? It probably wouldn't make much difference because PNG is much more than just another Third World country, and many of its villages and people have a decidedly primitive character about them. Here's a country where people outside the urban areas still practice warrior traditions, walk around scantily clad, paint their bodies in bright colors, and use shells, cassowary feathers, boar tusks, and crocodile teeth for body decoration. It's a country where there is always the smell of smoke. Even in most urban areas, there is always smoke, smoke, smoke from the fires used to keep the jungle at bay only a few miles away. PNG is a country stained red by the spittle of betel nut chewers, a traditional chewing habit with some narcotic affects. But the greater drug problem lies in alcoholism which goes hand in hand with the recent growth in violence.

Above all, PNG is a country of vast contrasts, colors, and contradictions -- one that assaults you visually, challenges your tolerance, and educates you about a little-known but fascinating world occupied by an extremely diverse, physical, and colorful people.

Understanding the New PNG

You must be open-minded about this country if you want to really enjoy it. Unfortunately, you will find many critics of PNG -- from conservative journalists, disgrunted expatriates, failed businessmen, misfits, racists, and ethnocentric Australians -- who view PNG through the eyes of their own culture and society. What they say about this country may at first make sense, but only if you share their narrow and hardened views of peoples different from themselves. For many of these social critics, PNG is a Third World country of inherent ignorance, incompetence, corruption, inefficiency, and lawlessness. If you listen to their redundant complaints for very long, you get the impression that this country is going to hell in a handbasket!

However, these critics fail to put this country into a proper context -- the broader perspective of a newly emerging nation undergoing some difficult nation-building processes. PNG, for example, was under colonial rule until it received independence from Australia in 1975. The interior of the country was not discovered by Europeans until 1930, and many of PNG's peoples still live a near-Stone Age existence. Here is a country that has had to move from the Stone Age to the 20th century in a space of only 50 years! It's an extremely diverse country where family, clan, and tribal loyalties take precedence over identity with a larger culture, society, and nation.

Intensely committed to creating a democratic nation in the midst of incredible diversity -- a commitment unparalleled in the history of most Third World nations -- in PNG you witness the Founding Fathers debating the shape of their nation. They are attempting to create a nation in the midst of perceived security threats from Indonesia, the problems of ethnic and linguistic diversity, the complexities of lingering colonialism, and the competing economic interests of plantations and mining and shipping companies. Added to this are increasing numbers of tourists who come to this country with expectations more appropriate for countries with well developed tourist infrastructures.

PNG is in the midst of profound changes that few outsiders fully appreciate. It's a classic case of a new nation being hurled into the 20th century of urbanization, industrialization, education, technology, and management without a great deal of 19th, 18th, 17th, or even 5th century experience and with an unclear vision of its future. It's a rich country, but its resources have yet to be fully exploited and mobilized. High crime rates, attendant with social dislocation, continue unabated as unemployed tribal villagers migrate to the towns and Port Moresby and become tomorrow's "rascals". The problems will most likely get worse before they get better as this brave new nation proceeds to chart an unclear course through troubled waters. It will create a nation, but it also must go through some difficult growing pains in the process -- not unlike many other nations that were founded on democratic principles and proceeded to penetrate their frontier while experiencing major social changes and periods of lawlessness. Australian critics of PNG, for example, would do well to take a more sobering look at present-day PNG by viewing it through the more appropriate lenses of 19th century Australian history -- one of the least noblest nation-building histories of mankind.

Adjusting to PNG

Therefore, one can be both critical and sympathetic to PNG at the same time. This is perhaps the world's most exotic travel destination, but it poses some problems for travelers: high costs but low value for your travel dollar; inefficiency and occasional rip-offs; and the potential for crime and physical danger for the unwary. It is everything you might imagine in an exotic location, and much more. Please don't go to PNG with Western lenses honed by living and traveling in Australia, Europe, or the United States. This is a unique adventure which may frustrate you at times. But it should not deter you from making PNG one of the most unique, challenging, and rewarding travel experiences of a lifetime. You can meet some of the world's most ferocious-looking tribes in the Highlands, complete with warriors and their burdened wives; cruise through jungle waterways and see exotic flora and fauna; visit friendly villages; enjoy enthusiastic and smiling children; sun yourself on gorgeous beaches; or scuba dive in some of the world's most fabulous waters. But you must first understand PNG before you can fully participate in and learn from its many travel delights.

If you are used to the comforts and conveniences of five star hotels and restaurants, resort accommodations, numerous tour options, excellent roads and railway systems, a well managed tourist infrastructure, and the freedom to explore new places on your own, Papua New Guinea may not be ready for you, or vice versa. Above all else, this is frontier country. It requires a totally different orientation from most other countries you have visited.

Our recommendation: keep your eyes, ears, and mind open to new sights, sounds, and practices without drawing conclusions until the end of your adventure. There is much to absorb and learn in Papua New Guinea. Yes, it has its downside, such as the "rascals" -- the local term for male hooligans, thieves, robbers, and rapists. But there is no reason you should encounter the "rascals" unless you travel alone or fail to take adequate security precautions after having been fully briefed on their existence and advised on what you should and should not do. If, for example, you would not venture into areas controlled by street gangs wielding knives, handguns, or automatic assault rifles in Los Angeles, New York, or Washington, DC, why would you want to do such a foolish thing in an unfamiliar city such as Port Moresby?

Unique Attractions

In PNG you will most likely travel on the edge of steaming jungles, majestic mountains and valleys, roaring rivers and streams, and fascinating peoples drawn from another age and exhibiting unfamiliar cultures. This is the country that intrigued such noted social anthropologists as Bronislaw Malinowski and Margaret Mead, attracted fanatical missionaries, confounded the advancing Japanese during World War II, laid claim to national independence from Australian colonial rule in 1975, and periodically vies with Indonesia for control of its western border -- and perhaps its ultimate destiny. Given difficulties with the typography and the transportation and communication systems as well as exotic nature of this country, you will welcome assistance in getting from one area to another and from one travel and shopping experience to another.

Papua New Guinea is a beautiful but rugged country of small isolated communities primarily accessible by small plane, boat, canoe, and foot. Unless you are simply foolish, you should not travel to remote areas or wander around at night on your own. The people are as fascinating as they may at times appear frightening. The 700 cultural and linguistic groups live relatively isolated from each other. The warrior traditions and payback and compensation systems still persist as tribes and individuals frequently engage in violent confrontations amongst themselves. Coupled with this is a great deal of social change and dislocation -- most evident in towns and cities -- accompanying the movement from Stone Age tribal communities to 20th century urbanization. The result is a clash of cultures, values, and economic expectations and the widespread prevalence of thievery and assaults in the towns and cities of PNG.

Highlands, Lowlands, and Islands

The peoples of PNG are divided into three general groups, each of which provides a different type of travel and shopping adventure for visitors. The **Highland tribal peoples** are primarily found in the hills and valleys of PNG's vast interior. They are especially noted for their colorful ceremonies, body painting, and warring traditions periodically exhibited in "sing-sings" -- unique gatherings where different tribes demonstrate their singing, dancing, artistic, and warrior talents. Only recently (1930s) discovered by the outside world, the Highlanders are the most primitive of the PNG peoples. You may quickly notice that the Highland women do most of the work and are often treated as beasts of burden; the men do little or nothing aside from attempting to perpetuate their warrior role which has been greatly diminished by the government's law and order system. The Highlands have little to offer shoppers other than an occasional penis gourd, kina shell, jewelry, or weapons. Tourists go to the Highlands primarily to see the colorful people and learn about their cultures.

The **lowland tribes** are primarily found along the coastal areas and rivers. The most famous lowland tribes -- and the ones you are most likely to visit -- are found along the Sepik River in northern and central PNG. These people are especially noted for being some of the world's most prolific artists and craftsmen who produce a fabulous array of wood carvings, jewelry, and woven items. Now largely producing for the commercial market rather than for tribal ceremonial markets, these peoples are the objects of travel-

ers who wish to learn about tribal societies while shopping
for arts and crafts at the same time.

The **islanders** are found to the east and northeast of the
mainland in three major island groupings. The Bismarck
Archipelago in the north consists of three major islands:
Manus, New Britain, and New Ireland. New Ireland,
especially along the northern shore, is most famous for its
intricately carved ceremonial figures unlike any others
found in Papua New Guinea or other parts of Melanesia.
The Milne Bay Islands directly east of the mainland consist of 160 islands and over 500 islets and atolls. This is
the smallest and most isolated province in PNG which was
famous during World War II as a major American air and
naval base; It also includes the famous Trobriand Islands,
first popularized by the father of social anthropology,
Bronislaw Malinowski, noted for its unique yam festivals,
sexual practices, and wood carvings. The final islander
grouping are the northern islands of the Solomons, Buka,
and Bougainville -- mineral rich islands which are geographically, ethnically, and culturally more closely related to
the Solomon Islands further to the east than to the PNG
islands to the south and west. Several of these islands,
especially the Trobriands and New Ireland, offer interesting
shopping adventures unlike any found in the highlands and
lowlands of mainland PNG.

Cities and Towns

There also is a fourth PNG you should not overlook --
cities and towns. Because of the uniqueness of tribal
PNG, most tours and travelers advise you to quickly pass
through the cities and towns of PNG and head directly for
the Highlands, Sepik River, or Trobriand Islands. The
capital, Port Moresby, is primarily viewed as a transit stop
on the way to other areas in PNG. It is dismissed as an
ugly, uninviting city best left to shippers, bankers, politi-
cians, and the local rascals. Towns such as Lae, Madang,
and Mt. Hagen are treated as frontier trading towns which,
like Port Moresby, are transit points to the more interesting
interior. We understand the biases of outsiders who seek
the more unusual and exotic places for discovering the
"real PNG" of missionaries and anthropologists.

However, as is often the case, the towns can be as
interesting and fulfilling as many of the more remote areas.
Ironically, the towns are largely untouched by tourists
whereas many villages may have seen too many tourists.
After all, the towns are centers of social change, even
though at first glance they may look unattractive and over
run by thieving rascals who will steal anything that's not

nailed down! But most important of all, these are centers of social change, economic exchange, and commercial development that will tell you more about the future of PNG than a trip into an ostensibly remote village. The so-called "real PNG" will most likely have been visited by a few too many tourists. There you are likely to discover locals who lazily wait in the shade of another haus *tambaran* to sell you another round of recently produced "authentic PNG artifacts" at inflated tourist prices. They may even put on a pathetic version of a Sing-Sing for a paid photo opportunity.

The cities and towns in PNG deserve more than a passing glance in transit to touristed villages. For it's in the cities and towns that you may discover the "real PNG" and the best shopping in the country. Port Moresby, for example, is the most significant shopping center in PNG -- not the Sepik River, Highlands, or Trobriand Islands. In Port Moresby you will find the major warehouse-shops selling the largest variety of PNG artifacts anywhere in the world. You will also find a few jewelry shops offering unique black coral jewelry designs and silk screen fabrics and clothes. You may even discover an emerging group of highly talented artists working in oils, lithographs, textiles, and sculpture -- art not available in shops or galleries yet, but acquired directly from the artists. This is where you will find some of the most exciting shopping available in PNG -- but it takes place in homes, studios, workshops, and a university in an urban area rather than in villages or from a boat along a river. Similiar shopping discoveries are found in such towns as Lae, Madang, and Mt. Hagen.

Four Travel and Shopping Adventures

Taken together, these four distinct areas of PNG constitute four different types of traveling and shopping adventures. If, for example, you are primarily interested in learning about the culture and customs of the various tribes, you may be more interested in traveling to the Highlands than to the Sepik River, Islands, or urban centers. On the other hand, if you are primarily interested in the traditional cultural products of different tribes transformed into readily produced commercial products for dealers and tourists -- their arts and crafts -- then you may be more interested in learning about the peoples of the Sepik River. If your interests also include sailing, scuba diving, beaches, interesting cultures, and arts and crafts, then a trip to the Trobriand Islands may be just the thing for you. And if you are interested in the next stage of artistic development and creativity in PNG -- the adaptation of traditional motifs to modern art forms and commercial mediums -- be sure to spend some time exploring the shops and artist circles in Port Moresby and a few other urban centers. Indeed, and contrary to what others may tell you, Port Moresby and these towns may prove to be some of the most interesting travel and shopping discoveries of your PNG adventure!

Realistic Expectations

A few words of caution before you embark on your PNG shopping adventure. First, *don't try to do PNG -- especially the Highlands and Sepik River -- on your own.* It can be dangerous, less informative, and more expensive in the long-run than joining the many well organized and informative tours, such as those offered by the Melanesian Tourist Services and Trans Niugini Tours.

Second, *don't expect to find exceptional quality artifacts for sale in PNG.* Old collector's pieces are either prohibited from export or they were exported many years ago by collectors, missionaries, and colonial administrators. The best quality PNG artifacts are found in collections in Australia, Germany, England, and the United States. They periodically appear on the art and antique markets in these countries at prices that may astound you. Occasionally you may come across some excellent quality old pieces in art, antique, and home decorative shops in Australia as a result of family collections being sold at auctions or directly to shops. For example, we found some of the best PNG artifacts in four cities in Australia -- Brisbane (Decorators Gallery and Karavan), Sydney (New Guinea Primitive Art), Adelaide (Zen Oriental Design), and Cairns (Gallery Primitive and Asian Connection).

In the meantime, what is left for sale in PNG are mainly tourist quality artifacts produced primarily for the tourist market rather than for their original ceremonial purposes. This is not to say you will not find lovely contemporary pieces in PNG that will make wonderful home decorative items. Indeed, we discovered many unique items along the Sepik River as well as in the Highlands, the Trobriand Islands, and Port Moresby. But they are by no means collector's items nor pieces of exceptional quality. You can best purchase quality pieces in the Australian cities of Cairns and Brisbane; we most recently found quality pieces in Adelaide, Australia and Santa Fe, New Mexico USA! Many serious, addicted, and wealthy collectors, spend time in Germany, London, and New York searching for quality pieces that long ago left with the missionaries, colonial administrators, and travelers of a by-gone era.

THE STREETS OF PNG

Traveling in PNG is unlike traveling in most other countries of the world. Your assumptions about how to get around in the country are challenged by local realities - few roads other than those within towns. Be prepared to travel in PNG by plane or boat. If you fly, be sure to arrive at the airport an hour early, and carefully watch any movement among fellow passengers toward your assigned gate. Flights sometime leave early without announcing the fact to passengers. The locals seem to know when this will happen -- frequently attributed to some form of telepathic communication -- but you may be left behind as your plane takes off into the sunset 20 minutes early!

The Highlands

You will find a few roads in the Highlands and along the coastal areas. The main roads run along the northeastern coast between Lae, Madang, and Bogia and again around Wewak. In the Highlands a road connects Lae, Goroka, Mt. Hagen, Mendi, Tari, and Koroba. There is one main road along the southeastern coast which connects Kupaino, Port Moresby, and Berenao. Roads are also found on the major islands of Bougainville, New Ireland, and New Britain. The rest of the country is largely inaccessible except by plane or boat. Indeed, the fastest and most convenient means of transportation between towns and village communities is by plane. Air Niugini, Talair, and the missionary MAF airlines maintain an extensive network of regularly scheduled flights to all corners of the country. Many of the flights are in small 6 to 18 seat prop engine planes that fly by sight only. The flights alone into many of PNG's remote areas, or into such major tour centers as Tari and Ambunti, can be a thrilling experience in and of itself.

We do not recommend driving on what limited roads exist in the Highlands. The drive between towns can be rigorous and dangerous. Remember, this is frontier country where the traditional warrior, payback, and compensation systems operate alongside the contemporary rascal problem. Assaults, rapes, and robberies have increased markedly along these roads during the past few years. Should you become involved in an accident, for example, you could become the target of a violent payback. If you are ever involved in an accident, the first rule is to flee the scene as soon as possible because the locals have a reputation for dealing out immediate justice on the spot (payback), and justice takes on various forms of violence in this very physical culture. You may be lucky to get out of the situation alive. Head for the nearest police station for protection and stay there! You can deal with the question of compensation later.

The Sepik River

Transportation along the major tourist and shopping attraction in PNG -- the Sepik River -- is by boat. Your choices here are either the new luxurious cruise ships of the Melanesian Tourist Services and Trans Niugini Tours or by more basic, adventuresome dug-out canoes. Considering the distances involved, malarial mosquitos, and the inconveniences of camping along the river, you may want to opt on the side of air-conditioned luxury by booking a tour through either the Melanesian Tourist Services or Trans Niugini Tours.

The Trobriand Islands

If you wish to visit the Trobriand Islands, you can either fly or take a boat. We opted for a tour sponsored by the Melanesian Tourist Services, but unfortunately the tour was cancelled at the last minute because of too few people to justify the trip. We, instead, found a friend with a 50-foot sailboat who invited us to join him in sailing to the islands on our own. This was one of those wonderful serendipitous events that allowed us to shop the Trobriand Islands differently from the average tourist. Once on the Trobriand Islands, we were able to get around by car on the local dirt roads.

Port Moresby

Getting around Port Moresby is at best inconvenient. Its population of nearly 150,000 is spread over a 30 kilometer stretch of road, from Port Moresby Harbour and Walter Bay in the south to Waigani and the University of Papua New Guinea in the North. As indicated in the shopping map on page 283, two major roads run through the expansive area: Ela Beach Road/Hubert Murray Highway, running southwest to northeast from downtown Port Moresby to the airport, and Waigani Drive which runs north of the Hubert Murray Highway. The side streets and neighborhoods are a confusing maze of streets that go in several seemingly unplanned directions.

Transportation in the city is by bus (PMV) or taxi. Again, even though the city is best driven on your own for convenience sake, we do not recommend driving yourself since you could have a serious problem should you get into an accident. The taxis tend to be very expensive and inconvenient to find outside the major hotels. You will need a good map of the city and lots of time and money to get from one section to another. Should you opt to use the local bus system, be sure to hold on to all of your valuables since you could become the subject of a pick pocket, purse snatcher, or a simple mugging.

Towns

Most of the towns in PNG are very small. The downtown areas are normally concentrated at the intersection of two main roads. You can easily walk the downtown section and explore the markets on foot. Taxis and cars and drivers are usually available through your hotel. Even though these towns may be small, you may encounter local rascals. Lae and Mt. Hagen have reputations for having many such rascals. Again, avoid going out alone in these towns even during the day, and especially avoid walking around town at night.

Chapter Thirteen

WHAT TO BUY

Papua New Guinea is one of the world's most fascinating centers for the production of tribal arts and crafts. Here you can travel into villages where you observe craftsmen carving and weaving their latest tourist creations, buy directly from the village stores (*haus tambaran*), or visit dealers in the towns and cities who have already collected artifacts from several tribal groups throughout the country. At the same time, PNG offers some unique contemporary jewelry, textiles, fine art, and sculptures in shops, studios, and schools in Port Moresby and the towns. You will find plenty to buy in PNG. Your only problem may be deciding how to ship everything home!

TRIBAL ARTS AND ARTIFACTS

PNG's major shopping strength is in the area of tribal arts and artifacts. The country is the world's leading producer of tribal arts and crafts. It's one huge emporium of artifacts. Prolific artists and craftsmen produce some of the world's most fascinating arts and crafts. The sheer volume of artistic output is staggering to many visitors.

You may find as many different artifacts being produced as there are tribes and ethnic groups. While the art and artifacts have spiritual and ceremonial meanings, they appeal to many visitors who purchase them for their aesthetic appeal and with an eye toward collecting, reselling, or decorating their home with primitive art and artifacts.

A Unique World of Art and Shopping

When you shop for tribal arts and artifacts in PNG, you enter into an entirely different world of art. It's a mystical world of primitive art produced by societies where art plays an integral role in the daily lives of clans, tribes, and villages. This art will quickly introduce you to the fascinating spirit, clan, ceremonial, and warrior worlds of PNG's numerous tribes. While many Westerners buy this art for its aesthetic qualities, the artifacts have important meanings in the daily lives of PNG tribes. Indeed, the sheer proliferation of this art is indicative of the important role these artifacts continue to play in the spirit, clan, ceremonial, and warrior worlds of PNG.

Many visitors purchase the tribal arts and crafts for home decorative purposes. Many of the colorful and dramatic masks make wonderful accent pieces to contemporary Western homes and offices or complement rooms devoted to the collection of tribal arts and artifacts. Whatever your purpose, you may become intrigued with this art; you may want to better understand this unique society as you begin developing your own collection of masks, weapons, shields, jewelry, basketry, and pottery.

Art Centers

The largest output of tribal arts and crafts is produced along the Sepik River and its tributaries (see map on page 290). Divided into the Upper, Middle, and Lower Sepik River, the Middle Sepik River -- between Angoram and Ambunti -- is the most prolific area for artifacts. Many river tours concentrate on visiting the villages in this area.

Within each village, the men produce the woodcarvings and store them in the men's spirit house, or *haus tambaran*, which also serves as the general store for visiting tourists who wish to purchase the artifacts. The women primarily produce woven products, such as bilum bags, head ornaments, and woven figures (*tumbuans*), as well as pottery. They sell their products either by displaying them on the ground or approach visitors laden with the products around their heads, shoulders, arms, and hands.

Do not expect to find many old tribal arts and artifacts

for sale in Papua New Guinea. Government regulations to preserve the national heritage prohibit the export of any works that are more than 20 years old. Many pieces have been declared National Cultural Property, and it is illegal to remove these from the country. Many villages do have old collector's pieces that are occasionally sold to the national museum or to collectors who pay exhorbitant prices and then smuggle them out of the country. Newer pieces of varying quality -- from very fine craftsmanship to tourist kitsch -- are found in abundance along the Middle Sepik as well as in villages along the Lower and Upper Sepik and along several tributaries flowing into the Sepik. If you are looking for older collector's pieces, you should visit art and antique shops and auctions in Australia, Germany, London, and New York City that specialize in PNG arts and artifacts.

Understanding PNG Arts and Artifacts

If you are unfamiliar with the various arts and crafts offered by these tribes, we strongly recommend that you get a copy of PNG's universal catalog: *The Artifacts and Crafts of Papua New Guinea*. Published by the Handcraft Industry of Papua New Guinea, you may have difficulty finding this publication outside PNG. The booklet is widely available in the art and artifact shops of Port Moresby as well as through various tour companies. Published for the purpose of promoting trade with PNG, this beautifully illustrated catalog is used by most dealers and shops as the key guide to buying and selling. It's classification system and colored photos provide buyers with an excellent overview of the types of arts and artifacts to be found in the villages and shops of PNG.

You can expect to find the following types of arts and artifacts in PNG:

PNG ARTIFACTS

- **Masks:** Wood carved, woven, and turtle shell masks used as *haus tambaran* gable, spirit, ancestral, dance, canoe prow, or souvenir masks. Come in many different shapes, forms, sizes, and colors, depending on the tribe and region. Masks are the most common artifact found in PNG.

- **Tumbuans:** Large woven figures used in ceremonies and dances.

- **Boards:** Ancestral, door, and gable and ceiling boards used as protective spirits and for ceremonies and decoration. Carved story boards are a recent (1960) art form, depicting village scenes, primarily developed for tourists.

- **Prows:** Carved prows and splash boards from canoes depicting crocodile figures (Sepik River) or colorful abstractions (Trobriand Islands).

- **Shields:** Wood carved, painted, and hide shields used by warriors for protection from enemy arrows. Produced in several shapes, sizes, colors, and mediums. Painted figures on shields have spiritual significance.

- **Stools, tables, and headrests:** Artistically carved items with utilitarian functions.

- **Weapons:** Ceremonial axes, clubs, bone daggers, bows and arrows, arrow throwers, swords, and spears used in battle and for hunting and decoration.

- **Hooks:** Cult hooks associated with spirits and ceremonies. Food hooks used to hang food to keep it from vermin.

- **Skull racks:** Racks for placing the severed heads of enemies or relatives. One of the most important symbols of supernatural powers.

- **Musical instruments:** Hand and slit-gong (garamut) drums, flutes, bullroarers, horns, and pottery whistles.

- **Bowls, dishes, mortars:** Most of these are made from wood or coconut shell and come from the Trobriand and Tami islands.

- **Implements, utensils, and tools:** Wood carved and woven items such as fish traps, walking sticks, paddles, adzes, fish hooks, fire sticks, oil pots, fish nets, betel nut sticks, and drills.

- **Jewelry:** A variety of necklaces, headbands, armlets and head dresses made from pig's teeth, dog's teeth, pig's tusk, snake, cassowary feathers, bone, kina (mother-of-pearl) shells, hornbills, and shells.

- **Body ornaments, clothing, and accessories:** Wigs, belts, phallocrypts, tapa cloth, armbands, woven face masks, lime pots, and pipes.

- **Pottery:** Sago storage pots, water jars, cooking pots, and figurines.

- **Basketry and other woven items:** Trays, baskets, bags, purses, bilums, and birds.

- **Carved figures:** Ancestral, spirit, and animal figures. Some of the largest and most dramatic figures are orator's stools and the bird-human carvings (roof finial).

The list tends to go on and on. If you collect any of these objects, you will find an incredible number of such arts and artifacts in several different styles -- representing different regions, tribes, and clans -- to keep you busy shopping for weeks. Your shopping adventure will take you into the shops of cities and towns as well as into the lowland and highland villages on the mainland and the islands.

Shopping in Villages and Shops

If you tour the Highlands, Sepik River, and the islands, you will be able to shop for primitive arts and artifacts in small towns and villages. Given limited time, we recommend that you take a tour along the Sepik River, one which thoroughly covers the Middle Sepik, the most prolific area for arts and artifacts. Here you will be able to purchase artifacts in such villages as Korogo, Kanganaman, Palimbe, Yenchan, Aibon, Wombon, Tambanum, Timbunke, Angoram, and Taway. In each case you will go into the village *haus tambaran* to view a large collection of carved artifacts produced by the men. Most of the items in the *haus tambaran* will be available for purchase. Outside this building you can purchase handcrafted products displayed on the ground, especially woven items and jewelry produced by women.

You will find a few shops selling arts and artifacts in such towns as Madang, Mt. Hagen, Goroko, Lae, and Wewak. In Madang, for example, the two major hotels -- **Madang Resort Hotel** and **Smugglers Inn** -- have haus tambaran set up on the hotel grounds where you can buy a large variety of artifacts from the Sepik River. The **Madang Museum and Cultural Centre** also has a good selection of artifacts at excellent prices. In Lae, the **Melanesian Arts Centre** (8th Street), operated by Robin Leahy, has a good selection of Sepik River arts and artifacts. In many towns the local open-air markets, which primarily sell fresh fruits, vegetables, and meats, also sell a few handcrafted items, such as bilum bags and textiles.

However, the most extensive collections of PNG arts and artifacts are found in two major warehouses-shops in Port Moresby. You should visit these two places before going to the Sepik, Highlands, or islands to see the range of artifacts as well as to compare prices. The largest dealer is **PNG Art** (Spring Garden Road, Hohola, Tel. 25-3976) which is operated by the affable and unflappable Joe Chan. He has a huge warehouse that is packed with artifacts from all over PNG, but especially from the Sepik River. Just two streets from Joe Chan's operation is the second largest warehouse and shop -- **Hanuacraft** (Ahuia Street, Hohola, Tel. 25-1878).

If you have a chance to attend a "sing-sing", you will have an opportunity to buy artifacts during these large gatherings of tribes. Villagers bring artifacts, including some paintings and handicrafts, to these gatherings and offer them for sale to tourists attending these functions. Buying normally takes place before the performances.

Prices, Bargaining, and Discounting

Shopping for arts and artifacts in PNG is not cheap. In general you will find prices to be cheapest at the point of origin -- the villages. Middlemen tend to increase prices from 3 to 5 times each time they become involved in a transaction. For example, an item that can be purchased for K50 (US$60) along the Sepik River will cost K150 to K250 (US$175-300) in a Port Moresby shop. If found in Australia, the same item will cost K450 to K750 (US$530-US$900). If found in London or New York, expect to pay US$1350 to US$3750.

Contrary to what others may say, you can and should seek discounts in PNG. But discounting in PNG is not what you might expect, especially if you are used to bargaining in Asian countries. In PNG cities and towns it is perfectly acceptable to ask for a discount by asking the shopkeeper the following question: *"What kind of discount can you give me?"* The standard discount is 10%, but you may do better -- possibly 20% -- if you buy in volume.

Pricing and discounting in villages is unpredictable. Some villages ask exorbitant prices for the same items that are inexpensive in other villages. While villagers do not bargain in the traditional give-and-take manner commonly found in many other Third World countries, they do discount prices one or two times, depending on how you approach them. You must first understand their pricing system which invoices "First Price", "Second Price", and "Third or Final Price". Each price is determined by the disposition of the seller -- not the buying skills of the buyer. So be friendly and don't upset the seller in the process of reaching an agreeable price!

A common discounting scenario goes something like this. You ask *"What is the price?"* and a villager responds with an amount. You should then ask, *"Do you have a second price?"* In most cases, the villager will drop the first price by 20 to 40 percent in giving you a more reasonable "second price." The second price is usually the last price, but you might ask, *"Do you have a third or final price?"* In a few cases you will find third prices at another 10 to 20 percent discount. You should never accept the first price; most villagers do have a second price -- and maybe a third. This is a typical exchange:

> BUYER: *"How much is this mask?"*
> SELLER: *"50 Kina."*
>
> BUYER: *"Do you have a second price?"*
> SELLER: *"35 Kina."*
>
> BUYER: *"Do you have a third price?"*
> SELLER: *"30 Kina."*

While this scenerio works well along the Sepik, it may not in the Trobriand Islands, which we will examine later.

This discounting scenario takes little time at all since it does not involve haggling or bargaining. Just get the first quote and immediately ask for the second price. Within a few seconds you will have a final price. We've experienced discounts ranging anywhere from 20 to 70 percent. We never pay the first asking price.

CONTEMPORARY JEWELRY

You will find a few shops in PNG offering some unique contemporary jewelry. Look for the award-winning **House**

of Gemini (Ori Lavi Building, Kwila Plaza, Nita Street, Boroko). This is PNG's premier jewelry designer and producer of black coral, silver, and gold jewelry. The black coral is found locally in several reef locations around PNG. At the House of Gemini local craftsmen create unique black coral designs influenced by traditional Papua New Guinean art forms: bird of paradise, drums, adzes, and masks. Using sterling silver and gold with the black coral, the House of Gemini produces a good range of attractive necklaces, earrings, bangles, pendants, and rings. They also offer a line of unique pendants produced with boars tusk and crocodile teeth.

Another excellent jeweler is **Kara Jewellers**, located in the nearby Brian Bell Plaza in Boroko. This jeweler produces similar black coral, silver, and gold jewelry as House of Gemini. Indeed, several jewelers at the House of Gemini were trained by Kara Jewellers, and many of their designs have been borrowed from Kara Jewellers. You will find the workmanship here to be of similar quality as the House of Gemini. The major differences tend to be that the House of Gemini markets itself more aggressively, and Kara Jewellers tends to do more work in gold as well as more made-to-order and custom work than the House of Gemini. Kara Jewellers major strength is in working with gold, although they still do excellent work in black coral and silver. They do a great deal of gold made-to-order work. They will custom design jewelry based on your own designs or copy designs found in the many catalogs available at the store.

In Madang you will find one arts and crafts shop offering some unique jewelry using crocodile teeth. **Palms Boutique**, located on the grounds of the Madang Resort Hotel, has a small but very nicely crafted collection of necklaces, arm bands, bracelets, and earrings made from crocodile teeth. Operated by Bev Blackley, the shop designs its own jewelry.

TEXTILES, CLOTHES, AND FABRICS

Textiles, clothes, and fabrics in Papua New Guinea include everything from traditional tapa cloth to contemporary skill screen fabrics and imported garments.

Tapa cloth, a fibrous material made from the inner bark of trees, is produced in island PNG. Painted with natural ochre and gray pigments in traditional village designs, this cloth is used as clothing, bedding, room dividers, and carpets. A few shops in Port Moresby -- especially PNG Art -- carry some tapa. It is not widely marketed throughout PNG.

Within the past decade, the Textiles Department at the National Arts School, located on the campus of the University of Papua New Guinea in Port Moresby (Waigani), has been instrumental in developing a new and exciting **contemporary textile movement**. Students attending this institution receive extensive training in silk screen design and printing. While the department does do commissioned work, many of its graduates work for local businesses that need textile design and print capabilities. At present these graduates and businesses are just beginning to become major players in a contemporary textile movement which should expand considerably over the next few years.

The pattern of this contemporary textile movement appears to be the same for most graduates from the National Arts School and the businesses: a shop sets up a print table and hires one graduate to develop designs and supervise the printing of fabric and T-shirts. The fabric is either sold by the meter or designed into clothing and marketed through a few shops selling handcrafted items. Most of the shops are found in Port Moresby, although some factory-shops operate in Lae, Rabaul, and Arawa (Bougainville).

The two major producers of textiles are **Hamamas Prints** in Lae (P.O. Box 230, Tel. 42-3645, see Mrs. Gamma) and **Tiara Designs** in Arawa, Bougainville (P.O. Box 1350, Tel. 95-1250, see Rae Smart). Other shops with design and print capabilities include **Crow Designs** in Lae (P.O. Box 4004, Tel. 42-2193, see Pauline Ponifasio), **Haus Laplap** (P.O. Box 330, Rabaul, Tel. 92-1315, see Rohi Mills), **Niugini Arts** in Boroko, Port Moresby (Gavamani Mall, Korobosea, P.O. Box 3080, Tel. 25-3035, see Susan Chang), and the **Craft Hut** in Boroko, Port Moresby (Garden City Plaza, 1st Floor, Tel. 25-5999, see Kim Lowe).

You can purchase fabrics, clothes, and T-shirts directly from these factory-shops as well as through a few additional outlets in Port Moresby. The three shops of the popular **Girl Guides' Hand Craft Shops** (main shop, Tel. 21-7699, located next to the Koki Market and other shops in the Travelodge Hotel and Islander Hotel), for example, sell the Hamamas label fabrics and clothes. **Studio Y** in Boroko, Port Moresby (Y.W.C.A., 3 Mile Hill, P.O. Box 1883, Tel. 25-6522) also sells textiles. While in Port Moresby you may have a chance to visit special textile shows or exhibits which are periodically held at hotels and the National Arts Schools. For further information on these textiles, contact the Textiles Department at the **National Arts School** (Tel. 25-5477, 25-663, 25-5368). This department keeps in close contact with all businesses involved in producing textiles. In addition, the department will do commission work, especially fashion design and home furnishings, such as drapes and upholstery using contemporary PNG designs.

FINE ARTS AND SCULPTURE

Contemporary fine art and sculpture are two of the most exciting shopping discoveries in PNG. In many respects we find this art more interesting than much of the more touristy traditional arts and artifacts found along the Sepik River and in the huge warehouse-shops of Port Moresby. Judge for yourself, but at least introduce yourself to PNG's other world of art.

Since contemporary art and sculpture in PNG is urban-based art, shopping for it primarily takes place in Port Moresby and thus provides a good excuse to extend one's stay in this much-maligned city. If you really get interested in this art, you may need three to four days in Port Moresby just to locate the art, visit with artists, and commission works -- one of the most interesting and rewarding shopping adventures in PNG.

Little known to outsiders, the contemporary art movement in PNG is producing some of the most creative and attractive art found anywhere in the Pacific. It's a relatively new movement which began about 20 years ago and which is destined to take a respected place in international art circles in the coming decade. Our recommendation: shop for this art now before it becomes discovered and prices skyrocket! Had we known about this art before arriving in PNG, we would have prepared better for commissioning some lovely metal sculptures. Our next trip will result in some commissioned works that can be nicely integrated into our homes.

For centuries art in PNG was mainly confined to the mediums of wood, shell, bone, and stone and produced by villagers for ceremonial and religious purposes. However, colonialism introduced Western concepts and mediums of art. Schools and universities, led by expatriate teachers and professors, have been instrumental in encouraging local talent as well as training a new generation in Western art. But unlike many other countries where locals followed the landscape, portrait, and abstract expressionist movements of the West, in PNG contemporary artists have adapted traditional abstract designs to modern oil paintings, prints, and metal sculptures. A commercial market for this art is just beginning to develop, centered around special exhibits and commissioned works for companies, to help sustain a small but growing number of talented artists.

The **National Arts School** plays an important role in the development of contemporary fine arts and sculpture inspired by traditional PNG designs. Within the past few years a group of talented PNG artists have begun to produce some very exciting works in oils, prints, and metal -- new mediums for a growing number of urban-based artists. However, unlike many other countries where one can walk into a gallery or shop to see and buy such works, in PNG the fine art and sculpture movement is centered at the National Arts School and in the studios of individual artists. If you are interested in seeing such works, you will have to visit the gallery at the National Arts School, attend a special show or exhibit, or contact the artists directly.

Contemporary PNG artists tend to come from similar backgrounds and express similar themes in their works. Most have not completed secondary school; many were laborers inspired by the works of other contemporary artists and encouraged by teachers to continue to develop their artistic talents; and most were born in villages but acquired their interests in contemporary art while living and working in urban areas. What is particularly interesting is how these artists have transformed traditional village themes into new designs influenced by their urban experiences. In this sense, their works are uniquely PNG -- not a mere transfer of traditional themes to new mediums nor adapting Western themes to the PNG setting.

PNG's two most famous contemporary artists are now deceased: **Timothy Akis** and **Cecil King Wongi**. Akis, one of the leading artists of the Pacific, for example, created highly stylized and abstract depictions of themes from village and bush life -- cassowaries, lizard, wallabies, hunters, and spirits. His works have been exhibited internationally. You may be able to find a few of his signed prints in Port Moresby. However, most of Akis' works are now in museums or private collections.

Some of PNG's present noted artists include **Kauage**, who works with acrylics on canvas, as well as with wood cuts and textile designs, in depicting urban themes on politics and society. Born near Kundianwa in Simbu Province, Kauage is now a full-time artist who works from his studio in Port Moresby. **Jakupa**, who works form his studio in Goroka and who is in residence at the National Arts School, paints themes from daily village life and legends. Other famous artists include **Martin Morobobuna** and **Joe Nalo**.

The contemporary sculpture movement is centered at the National Arts School where two of PNG's leading sculptors -- **Gickmai Kundun** and **Benny More** -- are in residence.

Gickmai Kundun, currently studying in India, is perhaps PNG's most famous sculptor who has received international acclaim and who produces some of the most attractive metal sculptures we have seen anywhere. Another noted sculptor -- **Ruki Fame** -- also works from Port Moresby. All of the sculptors work in metal and have produced very distinctive designs that you will find on many buildings in Port Moresby and in homes of expatriates. You will find examples of such sculptures in the international departure lounge of the airport in Port Moresby as well as on a few commercial buildings in Boroko.

Similar to artists who work with acrylics on canvas, the metal sculptors have adapted traditional village themes to urban settings. And similar to purchasing paintings, you will not find metal sculptures in galleries or shops in PNG. If your timing is right, you may be able to attend a special exhibit at one of the hotels in Port Moresby where you can purchase this art. For the most part, however, sculptures are sold on a **commission basis**. You must meet with the artists and decide on designs, prices, and delivery arrangements. The best place to go shopping for this type of art is the **National Arts School** (Tel. 25-5477, 25-5663, 25-5368) on the campus of the University of Papua New Guinea. There you can visit the gallery where you can purchase art, meet sculptors in residence, and get information on how and where to contact other artists who work from their own studios. The School also can provide information on upcoming shows and exhibits.

HANDICRAFTS

You will find a few shops in Port Moresby and small towns selling locally produced arts and crafts. Some of these shops combine traditional PNG artifacts, textiles, and other handcrafted items into one big potpourri of arts, crafts, and souvenirs. Given the limited number of tourists to PNG who help support such shops, shopkeepers tend to offer a wide range of items to appeal to many tastes. Expect to find masks, baskets, trays, jewelry, shells, story boards, tapa cloth, T-shirts, post cards, occasions cards, tablecloths, tea-towels, carvings, pottery, books, rugs, and grass skirts in these shops. While most of the handcrafted items come from villages, you will find a few items -- especially textiles and needlework -- produced in the urban areas.

The best places to shop for arts and crafts are in Port Moresby. The three **Girl Guides' Hand Craft Shops** (near Koki Market, Islander Hotel, and Travelodge Hotel) have a good range of handcrafted items, especially baskets,

trays, T-shirts, shells, masks, story boards, tapa cloth, and
books, as well as Hamamas label fabrics and clothes.
Studio Y, the Y.W.C.A. at 3 Mile Hill in Boroko (Tel. 25-
6522), has a nice selection of jewelry, pottery, carvings,
trays, T-shirts, shells, tea-towels, tablecloths, baskets,
Highlands rugs, books, bilums, grass shirts, post cards, and
copper beating. **Niugini Arts** (Tel. 25-3035), located in a
two-story building at the Gavamani Mall in Boroko, includes baskets, carvings, pottery, Sepik Art, bilums, sand-
paintings, tapa cloth, PNG butterlies and insects, musical
instruments, trays, black coral and shell jewelry, storyboards, and walking sticks. Niugini Arts recently acquired
a print table and artist-designer to produce its own fabrics
in traditional PNG designs. **Craft Hut** (Tel. 25-5999), a
small crafts shop at the Garden City Plaza in Boroko, does
excellent quality needlework as well as prints its own line
of T-shirts and fabrics. The duty-free shop in the **Jacksons International Airport** departure lounge offers a
selection of black coral jewelry (bracelets, pendants, necklaces, and earrings) from the House of Gemini and woodcarvings from the Solomon Islands and Trobriand Islands.

In other PNG towns you will find a few small shops
selling handcrafted items. If you are in Madang, visit
Palms Boutique at the Madang Resort Hotel; in Lae, stop
at the **Melansian Arts Centre** (8th Street, Tel. 42-1604)
and the **Morobe Handcrafts Centre** (Tel. 43-1770); in
Yomba, visit the **Haus Tambuna** (Tel. 82-3199); in New
Lorengau, visit the **Manus Handcraft Shop** (Tel. 40-
9136); in Alotau visit the **Milne Bay Women's Co.** (Preston White St., Tel. 61-1074); and in Wewak, stop at
Sepik Handicrafts (The Centre, Tel. 86-2427). These are
shops to visit if your itinerary includes these towns. We
do not recommend scheduling these stops just for the
shopping.

BOOKS

You will find very few shops offering books on PNG
and the Pacific. While most of the craft and souvenir
shops will have a few popular as well as esoteric travel,
ethnographic, and history books for sale, if you are a
serious book buyer your best approach is to go directly to
the **University Bookstore** on the campus of the University
of Papua New Guinea. Here, you will find a good range
of books on all aspects of PNG -- history, geography, ethnography, economy, culture, society, and politics. While
visiting the bookstore, you may want to wander through
the university library which is located just around the
corner from the bookstore. The library has a good collec-

tion of local and regional newspapers just to the left of the front entrance to the library.

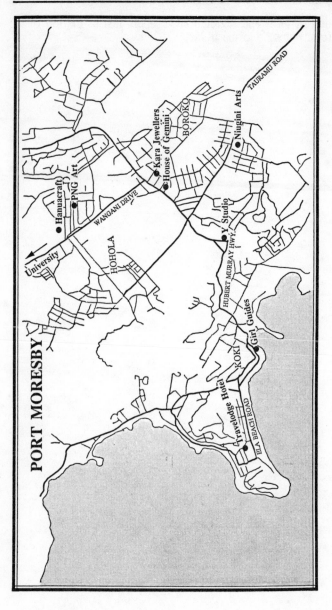

Chapter Fourteen

WHERE TO SHOP

Major shopping in PNG takes place in Port Moresby and several towns, along the Sepik River and its tributaries, and on several islands. Except in the case of Port Moresby and a few towns, we recommend that you take a tour to many of the other areas which provide shopping opportunities. Wherever you go, we do not recommend that you shop on your own given the uncertain security situation in PNG. Go with a friend or a group and keep your valuables close at hand. Although taxis are expensive, they are safer than taking the inexpensive PMVs.

PORT MORESBY AND ITS SUBURBS

Port Moresby is by no means a shopper's paradise. You will find few shops offering the types of goods you would expect to find in most capital cities. While Port Moresby does have its own department stores and shopping plazas, these are very limited in terms of the types of goods of interest to you. Most of stores and plazas cater to the local expatriate community and elites with numerous imported clothes and household goods of limited appeal to visitors. However, in the midst of these stores and shopping plazas you will find a few shops offering some unique items, primarily jewelry, arts, and crafts.

Limited Shopping and Time Considerations

Shopping in Port Moresby is limited to a few hotels, shopping centers, department stores, artifact and handicraft shops, the university, and the airport which are located both within the city and the surrounding suburbs. If you are primarily interested in PNG artifacts and handicrafts, you could shop the whole metropolitan area in one day. However, if you are a more serious shopper who also wishes to include contemporary textiles, paintings, and sculpture in your shopping plans, you may need another day or two to complete your shopping in Port Moresby.

Given the spread-out nature of this city as well as safety considerations, it's best to take taxis or rent a car with driver to cover the whole area.

The Port Moresby area is divided into downtown Port Moresby, which is located on a hilly peninsula southwest of the metropolitan area, and several suburbs to the east and north. The major shopping areas are found in downtown Port Moresby and the suburbs of Koki, Boroko, Hohola, and Waigani.

Downtown Port Moresby

Downtown Port Moresby houses the major banks, airline offices, shipping companies, and the city's best hotel -- the Travelodge. It is not a significant shopping center for visitors. The best shopping in this area is largely limited to the hotel. Here you will find a branch of **Girl Guides' Hand Craft Shop** and a boutique and jewelry shop. You will also find one of Port Moresby's major department stores just around the corner from the hotel on Douglas Street -- **Steamships**. Like most department stores in PNG, this one primarily caters to local residents with a large selection of imported clothes and household goods as well as a grocery and liquor store.

Koki

Approximately 1 kilometer east of downtown Moresby, along Ela Beach Road, is the suburb of **Koki**. This area is famous for its large open-air fruit and vegetable market as well as for one art and craft shop located nearby -- **Girl Guides' Hand Craft Shop**. The main reason to stop in Koki is the Girl Guides' Hand Craft Shop. Being the main shop, this is the largest of the three Girl Guides' shops. Here, you will find a good selection of arts and crafts: artifacts, tapa cloth, storyboards, shells, masks, baskets, trays, jewelry, T-shirts, butterflies, clothes, and fabrics as well as colorful postcards and greeting cards.

Koki is also an area where the "rascals" congregate. Be sure to take precautions here by traveling in a group and safeguarding your valuables.

Three Mile Hill

If you go further east along Hubert Murray Highway for about 1 kilometer, you will come to **Y Studio** on the corner of Hubert Murray Highway and Korobosea Drive at Three Mile Hill. This shop is operated by the Y.W.C.A. Located on the second floor, it has a good selection of arts and crafts: jewelry, pottery, baskets, rugs, carvings, trays, shells, tablecloths, bilums, and grass skirts as well as books, post cards, and greeting cards.

Boroko

Boroko is located approximately 2 kilometers northeast of Koki by way of the Hubert Murray Highway. This is the major shopping area in Port Moresby. It's where most expatriates do their shopping. Here, you will find the major shopping plazas (Garden City Arcade, Kwila Plaza, and Brian Bell Plaza), department stores, restaurants, and commercial buildings. If you are looking for jewelry, you'll find the **House of Gemini** in Kwila Plaza and **Kara Jewellers** in the Brian Bell Plaza. In the nearby Garden City Arcade is the **Craft Hut** with its beautiful needlepoint work and printed T-shirts and materials.

Just south of Boroko, near the intersection of Taurama and Gavamani roads and directly east of the Port Moresby General Hospital and Papuan Medical College in Korobosea, is **Niugini Arts** (Gavamani Mall). This two-story shop has a small but nice selection of PNG artifacts and handicrafts: baskets, Trobriand carvings, pottery, Sepik art, bilums, sand paintings, tapa cloth, PNG butterflies and insects, musical instruments, trays, black coral and shell jewelry, storyboards, walking sticks, and fabrics printed at this shop.

Hohola

From Boroko, the metropolitan area meanders to the north and becomes industrial in character. The next major shopping area is **Hohola**, located less than 1 kilometer north of the Boroko shopping area. In Hohola you will find PNG's two largest artifact emporiums: **PNG Art** (Spring Garden Road) and **Hanuacraft** (Ahuia Street). PNG Art, operated by Joe Chan, has the largest collection of PNG artifacts found anywhere in the world. You have to see this place to believe it. It's a huge warehouse with thousands of artifacts acquired from the Sepik River, Trobriand Islands, and villages throughout PNG. You can easily spend a couple of hours browsing through this place. PNG Art is very reliable -- offers good quality products, operates an efficient service, and ships everything in good condition. Hanuacraft, originally developed with the assistance of U.S. Peace Corps Volunteers, also offers a good selection of PNG artifacts. While the management here is not as efficient as Joe Chan's operation, it does try hard and offers some good selections -- about 30% of the volume offered by PNG Art. Our recommendation: visit both emporiums since they are within 10 minutes walking distance of each other.

Approximately 1.5 kilometers north of Hohola is the University of Papua New Guinea in Waigani. On the way to the university you may want to stop at the **Islander Hotel** which is located at the intersection of Waigani and Wards roads. One of the best hotels in Port Moresby, the Islander Hotel is frequented by the local elites and is often the site for special art shows and exhibits. The hotel has a small shopping arcade which includes a branch of the **Girl Guides' Hand Craft Shop**. Further along Waigani Road are the major government buildings -- Supreme Court, National Library, and National Parliament Building -- foreign missions, golf course, and the **National Museum and Art Centre**. The museum is well worth visiting. It has a good collection of PNG artifacts as well as displays of flora, fauna, and the history of PNG. It also has a small bookstore located on the left, just before entering the museum.

Waigani

The University of Papua New Guinea offers two major shopping opportunities -- the University Bookstore and the National Arts School. The **University Bookstore** is located amongst the main campus buildings. Just enter the campus by following the main entrance sign on the right of Waigani Road. Primarily serving students on campus, the bookstore also has the best collection of books in PNG on the history, peoples, culture, society, economics, and politics of PNG.

Just 400 meters north of the main entrance to the university on Waigani Road is the **National Art School.**

Turn left and follow this road to the end where you will find several buildings -- a gallery, classrooms, workshops, and offices. The gallery also houses the central administrative offices. Here you can view the paintings and sculptures on exhibit as well as purchase many of the works. You may also notice a piece of furniture at one end of the room that has several drawers. This is where prints are kept. In fact, you may find the most interesting pieces stored in this unit. Depending on when you visit the gallery, you may have an excellent range of art from which to purchase. Sometimes, however, the exhibits are on loan and the gallery will look empty. Whatever the case, be sure to ask someone about the current displays and any additional art for sale. You may have to spend some time locating someone to help you purchase the art since the gallery is not set up in a normal commercial manner. If you walk into the gallery and no one is there to help you, just proceed through the door at the opposite end of the gallery and you will enter the administrative office area. People here will be able to answer your questions and find someone to assist you with your purchase.

If you are interested in meeting artists and having commissioned work done -- especially with textiles and sculptures -- ask the personnel in the gallery where you should go. The Textile Department, with its administrative office and design and print workshop, is located within a few meters of the gallery. The sculpture workshop is found a couple of buildings from the Textile Department. Here you may find a few sculptors in residence working on their latest creations and commissioned works. However, we only suggest you do this if you are a serious buyer. These are busy people who are not in the business of entertaining curious tourists who may think this would make an interesting addition to visiting the sights in Port Moresby!

When you leave PNG on an international flight you will find a duty-free shop in the departure lounge of the Jacksons International Airport. This shop offers black coral jewelry from the House of Gemini and woodcarvings from the Soloman and Trobriand islands.

TOWNS AND THE HIGHLANDS

Most towns in PNG are small coastal or interior towns which function as frontier trading and commercial centers for the export of raw materials. Towns such as Rabaul on the island of New Britain and Kieta on the island of Bougainville are pleasant towns with a long and colorful history of colonial and commercial development. Other towns, such as Goroko, Mt. Hagen, and Mendi in the

Highlands are frontier towns for missionaries and traders which developed over the past 50 years with the opening of the Highlands to the outside world.

All of PNG's major towns are regularly serviced by domestic airlines. Many visitors who tour the Highlands and the Sepik River will pass through Mount Hagen and Madang. Both of these towns serve as the headquarters for the two largest tour operators in PNG -- Mount Hagen for Trans Niugini Tours and Madang for the Melanesian Tourist Services. These towns offer a few good shopping opportunities for Highland and Sepik River artifacts. The Highlanders are not noted for producing many products, but you will find a few items of interest -- woven baskets, bilum bags, pottery, and jewelry made with beads, pigs feet, and boar tusks, as well as ceremonial axes. The Sepik River, of course, is a treasure-trove of all types of artifacts and this area is a shopper's paradise.

Downtown Mount Hagen consists of two main parallel streets where you will find several trading stores and a few shops selling artifacts. Many shops post a sign stating *"Thank you for not eating, smoking, drinking, or chewing betelnuts in this shop"*. Red stained streets, sidewalks, and walls of buildings testify to the preoccupation with betelnut chewing which at times makes the downtown area look like a bloodied war zone!

If at all possible, do not go out on your own during the day or night in Mount Hagen. The people environment here is not conducive to a nice friendly stroll through the town. Be especially careful with your valuables, and hold on tightly to all your possessions! This town has a notorious reputation for thieves, and you may see them prowling the downtown shops in broad daylight. It's not unusual to see shopkeepers chasing thieves from their stores, and tourists are fair game for such people. If you stop anywhere and put a camera or bag unattended on a counter, table, chair, or floor, it is most likely to disappear in a wink. Hotels are located within barbed wire compounds. The problem here is that there are too many male Highlanders roaming the streets doing what they normally do in the Highlands -- nothing. You will quickly discover that this is indeed a tough frontier town where law and order continues to disintegrate as more and more male Highlanders come to this town in search of opportunities.

Two shops in downtown Mount Hagen sell artifacts from the Highlands and the Sepik River. The **Cultural Gallery** has a small shop and museum selling books, bilum bags, spears, arrows, drums, mats, and tapa cloth. It is has a very small but interesting exhibit of Highland artifacts. You will see a sign to this shop and museum.

You will have to walk upstairs along a dark and narrow stairwell and hallway to get to this place. To the dismay of some visitors, this shop and museum has no postcards!

Just down the street from the Cultural Gallery and across from the Post Office is **Jara Artifacts**, a popular if rustic coffee shop (serves great quiche!) which also functions as an artifact shop and tour company. The owner, an expatriate who has lived in Mount Hagen for more than 35 years, has a small but growing collection of Highland and Sepik River artifacts on display in her office-shop to the right of the restaurant area. The department or trade stores in the downtown area primarily carry local consumer goods of little interest to visitors.

To the west of the downtown area you will find an open-air market where hundreds of Highlanders gather to buy and sell fresh produce as well as bilum bags and colorful sarongs and dresses. The market is interesting to walk through just for the cultural experience. This is a great photo opportunity, although some individuals may ask you to pay for taking their photo. You may even get a good deal on nicely woven bilum bags which are more colorful than those sold along the Sepik River.

Madang is located on the east coast, southeast of the mouth of the Sepik River, and is the major center for the Melanesian Tourist Services. Their popular Sepik River and Trobriand Island tours originate from Melanesian Tourist Services' headquarters at the Madang Resort Hotel, a lovely tropical compound facing the Bismarck Sea. A relatively quiet and easygoing resort town, Madang offers a few good shopping opportunities for artifacts from the Sepik region as well as from the Trobriand Islands and the Madang area. Two hotels have constructed replicas of *haus tambaran* where you can buy a large assortment of PNG artifacts -- carvings, bilum bags, shell jewelry, pottery, and baskets: **Madang Resort Hotel** and **Smugglers Inn**. The *haus tambaran* at Madang Resort Hotel has the largest selection of artifacts. However, the *haus tambaran* at Smugglers Inn tends to have a nicer selection of masks and carvings and prices seem to be better; the men working here are more willing to discount prices.

You should also visit the **Madang Museum and Cultural Centre** which is just down the street from Smugglers Inn on Modilon Road. This is a small but very nice museum displaying many artifacts from the Madang area. The museum also has a shop selling carvings -- war shields, masks, boards, and figures -- and paintings at very reasonable prices. In fact, this museum and cultural center sells the works of several local artists and craftsmen who bring their carvings and paintings here to be sold on consign-

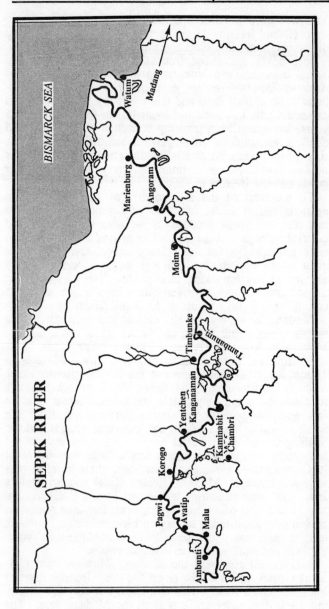

ment. Most of the pieces are signed by the artists and craftsmen, and you may have a chance to meet some of them while shopping in the museum shop. Some of the prices here are much better than in the villages along the Sepik River and 1/4 of what you might pay for similar items in the hotel *haus tambaran*.

If you are interested in jewelry and handicrafts, visit **Palms Boutique** at the Madang Resort Hotel. This shop has a nice selection of carved bowls from the Tami and Trobriand islands, unique hand painted silk scarves, hand painted T-shirts in traditional PNG designs, Highland baskets, and crocodile teeth jewelry. The distinctive necklaces, arm bands, bracelets, and earrings are designed by the owner, Bev Blackley, an expatriate who is one of the most popular tour leaders with the Melanesian Tourist Services. This shop also sells by the jar a delicious local nut called *galip*, which is worth trying; these attractively packaged nuts make nice gifts for friends back home.

You will find artifact and handicraft shops in a few other PNG towns. In Lae, for example, look for **Melanesian Arts Centre** (8th Street, Tel. 42-1604), **Morobe Handcrafts Centre** (Tel. 3-1770), **Hamamas Prints** (Tel. 42-3645), and **Crow Designs** (Tel. 42-2193); in Wewak visit **Sepik Handicrafts** (The Centre, Tel. 86-2427) and the **East Sepik Development Corporation**; in Kainantu visit the **Eastern Highlands Cultural Centre**; in Alotau look for the **Milne Bay Women's Co.** (Preston White St., Tel. 61-1074); in Yomba visit the **Haus Tambuna** (Tel. 82-3199); in New Lorengau look for **Manus Handcraft Shop** (Tel. 40-9136); in Rabaul see **Haus Laplap** (Tel. 92-1315); and in Arawa visit **Tiara Designs** (Tel. 95-1250).

THE SEPIK RIVER

The Sepik River, the country's largest river where nearly 100,000 people live along its banks, is a shopper's paradise for PNG artifacts. The river itself is 1126 kilometers in length and is navigable most of the way. Here you will encounter numerous villages along the river and its tributaries that produce thousands of colorful and dramatic looking artifacts. It's a virtual living museum of different tribes producing numerous styles of carvings, woven items, pottery, body ornaments, and jewelry. Many travelers to the Sepik River who have also traveled the Amazon River in Brazil much prefer the Sepik River for its cultural and shopping experience.

The Sepik River is the major travel destination for many visitors who come to PNG to learn about local cultures, take pictures, visit villages, meet exotic people, watch cultural performances, and purchase artifacts directly from craftsmen. However, getting to the Sepik, visiting the villages, and shopping for artifacts requires some advance planning -- preferably several months to a year before your planned arrival date. This is not a place you should attempt to travel on your own.

Travel Options

You must travel the Sepik by boat, but the type of boat depends on how you wish to approach this river adventure. On the budget end, you can rent or buy a dug-out canoe and hire a guide to take you from one village to another. This, however, is not a particularly safe way to travel, and such a trip can be very uncomfortable given the heat, mosquitos, and village sleeping accommodations. After hearing many tales of rip-offs, thefts, and over-charging, it is questionable if this so-called budget approach to the Sepik is in fact inexpensive!

Two of PNG's major tour operators offer informative tours of the Sepik. The **Melanesian Tourist Service**, headquartered at the Madang Resort Hotel in Madang, operates the luxurious "Melanesian Discoverer". This is the premier cruise ship on the Sepik and it is operated by an experienced firm that pioneered the Sepik River tours. Their cruise ship can accommodate 50 passengers with comfortable air-conditioned cabins, private baths, lounges, a restaurant, bar, closed circuit television, videos, and a library stocked with literature relevant to the peoples of the Sepik River. The ship is equipped with a water jet ferry that takes passengers from the ship into the villages. The "Melanesian Discoverer" offers different itineraries along the Sepik River. For serious shoppers, one of the most interesting tours is a five-day cruise along the Middle and Lower Sepik River. This tour either originates in Madang and travels up the Sepik to the town of Ambunti or originates in Ambunti and travels down the Sepik to its headquarters in Madang.

Trans Niugini Tours, based in Mount Hagen, also offers tours of the Sepik and its tributaries. At present it offers two different approaches to the Sepik. Its Kaminimbit Lodge and Karawari Lodge are situated on the Sepik River and the Karawari River respective; the Karawari River is a tributary of the Sepik River. These lodges shuttle guests into villages along the Sepik and Karawari rivers where one can purchase artifacts. Trans Niugini Tours also offers tours of the Karawari and Sepik rivers on its new "Sepik Spirit" cruise ship. Fully air-conditioned and accommodating 18 passengers with 9 cabins, private baths, a dining room, lounge, bar, and observatory deck, the "Sepik Spirit" leaves Karawari every Friday for a 4-day and 3-night cruise of the middle Sepik, an area between Tambanum and Korogo. It also leaves every Monday for a 4-day and 3-night cruise of the Blackwater area, a tributary of the Sepik River which is visited by very few tourists but yields some of the most fascinating PNG artifacts. These river segments are part of larger 9 or 10-day tours that include a few days in the Highlands as well as some time in Port Moresby. They are nicely balanced itineraries for travelers with limited time.

Traveling and Shopping Rules

When you visit the villages along the Sepik be sure to put on plenty of mosquito repellent. In several villages mosquitos are everywhere; you may leave wondering why more mosquitos did not bite you! Take a good supply of strong mosquito repellent with you before you arrive in PNG.

You may also want to take a good supply of items to entertain the children, who are one of the real delights of traveling on the Sepik River. Inflated balloons seem to be a popular item for the many childen who love to dive in the water to recover them. Other popular items for children -- both boys and girls -- are marbles and whistles. You can buy these items in department stores in Port Moresby or in the trade stores in towns such as Madang and Mount Hagen.

When shopping in the villages, you should follow a few procedures in buying from the villagers:

--- **BUYING PROCEDURES ON THE SEPIK** ---

- Most of the woodcarvings are housed in the *haus tambaran* which is operated by the initiated in the village. This building usually has two levels. The first level is the area underneath the pillars of the building. You will usually find several men sleeping or socializing in this area as well as offering items for sale. At times you may be overwhelmed by the smoke from a low burning fire which is supposed to ward off the hoards of mosquitos that congregate in this area. The second level is inside the building and it may or may not house a large number of artifacts. Each item tends to belong to a particular craftsman who will determine the

final price for an item. In some of the more
commercialized villages, such as Tambanum,
most artifacts are sold from the homes of
individual craftspeople rather than from the
haus tambaram.

- **Spend some time looking in every nook
  and cranny of a *haus tambaran* for quality
  carvings.** Most artifacts are poorly displayed
  in these buildings. Often the best quality
  items are found in the rafters or underneath
  other items. These are truly disorienting
  buildings which should be surveyed two or
  three times to uncover the best quality items.

- **Other items, especially woven items made
  by the women, may be spread on the gro-
  und near the entrance to the village or
  around the outside of the *haus tambaran*.**
  Items for sale in this area are usually handled
  by women. In some cases women will approach to sell you goods hanging from their
  heads, shoulders, arms, and hands -- usually
  bilum bags, jewelry, and body decorations.

- **Avoid taking pictures of sacred objects in
  the *haus tambaran* which you may think
  are for sale.** Not everything you see in the
  haus tambaran is for sale. In many of these
  buildings, for example, you may see an attractive orator's stool that is considered a
  sacred object. When in doubt, ask if you can
  take pictures in the *haus tambaran*.

- **Take plenty of small change with you,
  especially K2, K5, and K10 denominations.**
  Many items you may want to buy will cost
  less than K20. Villagers only accept local
  currency, and they generally do not have
  change.

- **Never accept the first price quoted since
  all prices are negotiable in the villages.**
  While Highlanders tend to have fixed prices
  but will give a little when asked for second
  and third prices, Sepik villagers give much
  larger discounts -- 30, 50, and even 70%!
  When in doubt, ask for a second price and
  expect to receive at least a 30% discount.

Never pay the asking price.

- **Villages differ in terms of the style, quality, and pricing of artifacts as well as in the entrepreneurial skills of its craftspeople and sellers.** Some villages produce only tourist quality artifacts while others continue to create good quality pieces. In many villages artifacts are not well displayed and the men operating the *haus tambaran* are very inert, preferring to sleep or gamble rather than sell their products to visitors. However, in other villages, such as Taway, products are nicely organized and displayed, and the local villagers are excellent entrepreneurs.

- **If you are with a group tour, try to be the first one off the boat so you will have the first pick.** While many of the items available in the villages are tourist quality, you can usually find one or two unique quality items. Remember, the early bird gets the worm on the Sepik River!

- **If you are with a group tour, buy as soon as you see an item.** After a day or two of visiting villages and shopping, group members tend to become very competitive. Everyone knows there are a limited number of quality goods for the number of members in the group. If, for example, you are on tour where 40 tourists descend on a small village at the same time, only a few members of the group will be fortunate enough to buy a limited number of quality goods. Group members tend to buy the best quality items available. If you don't buy immediately, someone else in the group is likely to buy the item from under you. Indeed, he who hesitates on the Sepik River is lost!

- **If you take one of the tour boats on the Sepik and its tributaries, the boat will be able to handle large purchases as well as arrange for shipping.** Don't pass up some lovely large items, such as an Orator's stool, just because you think you might have trouble shipping it home if it is an item you really want. However, know that shipping costs will add to the purchase price. (See the section on shipping for more information.)

- **Be sure to take pictures and inventory all of your purchases before trusting them to a local shipper.** While you will find reliable shippers in PNG, it's best to err on the side of being overly cautious when dealing with local shippers. For example, as we go to press one should not have to pay more than K400 per cubic meter for shipping goods to the east coast of the U.S. If you are charged more, you are being ripped-off which is exactly what happens to many visitors to PNG.

The Journey Through Villages for Artifacts

We approached the Sepik River via Port Moresby, Mt. Hagen, Tari, and Ambunti, and then cruised the Middle and Lower Sepik with our final destination being Madang. Our trip was handled through the Melanesian Tourist Services. We chose this route because we knew we would be buying artifacts along the way, and we wanted to take care of the final disposition of our purchases when the ship docked at the end of the tour in Madang. Had we chosen the alternative routing -- from Madang to Ambunti -- we would have had to leave all of our purchases on board and trusted they would be handled properly when the ship returned to Madang. This proved to be a wise decision since we quickly learned the shipper in Madang was overcharging by approximately 300%, and we would have been in for a shock when the bill arrived at home. The Ambunti to Madang routing enabled us to meet with the shipper, determine we were being ripped-off, pull the shipment from under him, and save a few thousand dollars in the process. See the section on shipping if you expect to make purchases larger than you can pack in your luggage.

We flew from Port Moresby to overnight in Mt. Hagen in order to take the early morning charter to Ambunti. The flight from Mt. Hagen to Ambunti made one stop in transit -- at the Highland village and resort of Tari. Our flight to Ambunti was in a small 18-seater plane. You will see some spectacular mountain and valley scenery during this flight and learn that PNG is still a relatively unexplored country. The landing at Ambunti is interesting if you are not used to landing on small grass airstrips. The plane gets one pass since a mountain wall is situated at the end of the runway!

Ambunti is a relatively nondescript village. The biggest event here is the landing of the plane which the locals turn out to greet with enthusiasm. The tour of the Sepik River begins here -- or it ends here -- depending on whether you have arrived on the boat from the Upper Sepik or Madang or by plane from Mt. Hagen or Tari. The area from Korogo to Angoram is considered the Middle Sepik, the most prolific area for artifacts. The Lower Sepik runs from Angoram to the mouth of the Sepik River on the Bismarck Sea.

The tour of the Middle and Lower Sepik river visits several villages along the way. The Melanesian Discoverer has a launch which takes you into the villages where you can meet the people, see cultural performances staged for your arrival, and purchase artifacts. A typical day involves stopping at three villages and cruising from 1 to 3 hours between villages. Some of the more interesting villages along these sections of the Sepik River include:

VILLAGES ALONG THE SEPIK

- **Korogo Village:** One of the first stops after leaving Ambunti on your way east toward Madang. This village offers a large selection of tourist quality artifacts. Rather overly commercialized due to its popularity with tourists and dealers, the prices here tend to be high. However, expect to get from 10 to 50 percent discounts on any purchase. Korogo is especially popular for the long-nose Mai Masks and Orator's stools. If you are in the market for an Orator's stool, and find one you like, buy it since you are not likely to find many elsewhere along the Sepik River.

- **Kanganaman Village:** You will need to take a 10-minute walk along a mosquito infested foot path to reach the main area of this village. Famous for its historical *haus tambaran* which has collapsed, you can buy artifacts and handicrafts in three areas of the village. The village is noted for its carved hooks. Here you will find many women displaying baskets, jewelry, and carvings on the ground.

- **Palembei and Malingai Villages:** These two villages are within two kilometers of each other and involve a 25-minute walk through mosquito infested jungle paths. The two *haus tambaran* in Malingai have numerous tourist quality artifacts -- masks, drums, tumbuan, lime betelnut stoppers, and Orator's stools. Some of the best buys here are the colorful bilum bags and jewelry sold by the women outside the *haus tambarans*.

- **Yenchen Village:** This village has a famous *haus tambaran* made in part by Sago Palm. Again, you will find more tourist quality masks, tumbaum, and Orator's stools as well as bilum bags and shell necklaces.

- **Chambri Lakes -- Aibon and Wombon Villages:** A long trip by launch along a chanel and through swamp lands is rewarded with visits to two villages that produce different styles and types of artifacts. Aibon Village has a large collection of masks in its *haus tambaran* as well as unique pottery made by women in the village. Wombon Village is also noted for its pottery making and puts on a pottery demonstration for visitors. The distinctive pottery from the Chambri Lakes area is very fragile, so be sure to pack it well when shipping it home.

- **Timbunke Village:** Located along a canal, this village is famous for its missionary presence and the infamous massacre of 99 men and 2 women during World War II by the Japanese in collusion with villagers from Koroga. The *haus tambaran* here has some nice quality carvings at reasonable prices. This is one of the more friendly and interesting villages along the Sepik River. This is one of three villages that can be reached by road via Wewak.

- **Tambanum Village:** This is the famous village where the noted anthropologist Margaret Mead did her initial work in PNG. It is also one of the largest villages along the Sepik River that is famous for production of numerous carvings. Frequently visited by tourists and dealers, it nonetheless continues to produce some nice quality carvings -- masks, hooks, Orator's stools -- and woven items -- animals and gables -- and ceremonial bone daggers. Each house in this village produces its own artifacts, so you will have to spend some time going from one house to another in search of artifacts. The selections here are better than in many other villages along the river. This village is also does face-painting.

- **Angoram Village:** This is the largest and most commercialized village along the Sepik River which is also accessible by road via Wewak. The *haus tambaran* is well organized and has some nice selections not found in other villages on the Sepik River. The women here are very entrepreneurial. You should find some unique items of quality, especially masks, flutes, and jewelry.

- **Taway Village:** This is one of the best organized villages on the Sepik River for shopping. The *haus tambaran* is organized like a supermarket. The men here are some of the most energetic entrepreneurs you will find along the Sepik River -- especially after having visited so many lethargic and inert villages along the way. The quality of artifacts is mixed, but you will find some nice pieces and at good prices. You should enjoy shopping here and meeting the people.

- **Murik Lakes -- Mendam Village:** This village is more Polynesian in appearance than other villages along the Sepik River. And the artifacts for sale here are less primitive and more Polynesian in appearance. This is a village that sells many small items you can pack in your suitcase or carry on a plane: carved bowls, spoons, forks, and walking sticks.

You may visit many other villages along the Sepik River and its tributaries. While all of the villages have something to sell, the villages most frequently visited by the tour groups tend to offer the largest selections. You will probably find better quality artifacts -- less responsive to the tourist market -- and better prices in the more remote villages along the Upper Sepik River and several tributaries off the Sepik River. However, you won't find many artifacts on the Upper Sepik, and the designs and workmanship in this area are much cruder than those found along the Middle and Lower Sepik.

One area few tourists or dealers visit, but which produces some of the most interesting carvings in PNG, is the **Blackwater River area**, a tributary south of both the Sepik and Korosameri rivers at Mindimbit. Villages in this area produce some truly stunning masks. Beginning in 1989 Trans Niugini Tours will open this area to visitors with its new "Sepik Spirit" cruise ship. Our recommendation: get there soon before too many tourists result in commercializing the production of poorer quality artifacts. If you are in Cairns, Australia, you should visit the Gallery Primitive at 26 Abbott Street to see Blackwater River artifacts collected by one of the few dealers who ventures into this area to purchase excellent quality items.

THE TROBRIAND ISLANDS

The Trobriand Islands lie in the Soloman Sea 300 kilometers to the northeast of the PNG mainland. These islands achieved international fame after World War I through the academic works of the German anthropologist Bronislaw Malinowski. His series of books -- *Coral Gardens and Their Magic*, *Argonauts of the South Pacific*, and *Sexual Life of Savages* -- are now classics.

The Trobriands are an excellent destination for those interested in combining shopping with exploring an exotic culture. The peoples on these islands are a unique mixture of Melanesians and Polynesians. They have a unique life style found no where else in the Pacific. They are a fascinating destination for both amateur and professional anthropologists.

Yam cultivation plays a central role in the Trobriand society. Far more than just a staple food, the cultivation of yams is surrounded by ritual and ceremony, with the male members of the society drawing much of their prestige from their relative abilities in growing yams. The role of the yam is at its high point during the July and August harvest period. The harvest festivals are a time of bizarre sexual ritual when entire villages meet to engage in massive promiscuity among both the married and unmarried members! If you visit the Trobriands during this time, expect your shopping and sightseeing to get caught up in some of these ritual events.

The Trobriands are not a major tourist destination. All the better for the few adventurous travelers each year who put it on their itinerary. The islands offer the shopper the chance to purchase directly from the artisans who produce some of the highest quality woodcarvings in the Pacific. These artifacts combine the craftsmanship of the Solomon Islands with the creativity of mainland PNG. The carvings are executed in Kerosene and Quela wood which are available locally on the island. You will also find a few carvings made from Ebony. The wood for these carvings is imported from Woodlark Island.

The Trobriands participate in the Kula Ring. This involves the ritual trading of shell money and various items of body decoration such as necklaces and armlets. The by-product of this trading is that you might be offered some shell money by the occasional villager. We saw some pieces, Rossel Island shell money, of very high quality.

In addition to carvings and jewelry, you might find a stray canoe prow, grass skirts, some intricately detailed pieces of the famous "Yam Houses", or even a dried exotic butterfly.

When shopping and traveling in the Trobriands, keep your eyes open and bring your sense of humor. The locals enjoy having fun with the tourists. Their name for tourists, *dim-dim*, should give you an idea of what is in store for you. Enjoy these wonderful people as much as they enjoy you.

Travel Options

The Trobriands are accessible by plane and ship. How you approach the islands will be dependent on both your budget and the amount of time you have to spend.

Two of PNG's major tour organizations -- Melanesian Tourist Service and Pacific Expeditions -- operate in the Trobriands. Each offers a different approach to the islands. The **Melanesian Tourist Service**, headquartered at the Madang Resort Hotel in Madang, operates the luxurious "Melanesian Discoverer" on a regularly scheduled basis in the Trobriands. It is worth noting that this service is conditional on a minimum number of passengers, and to the chance of a last minute cancellation.

As noted earlier, the new "Discoverer" is the premier cruise ship in PNG. It is operated by an experienced firm that pioneered the Sepik River tours. This new ship can accommodate 50 passengers with comfortable air-conditioned cabins, private baths, lounges, a restaurant, bar, closed circuit television, videos, and a library stocked with literature relative to the peoples of PNG. The ship is equipped with water jet ferries to transfer the passengers to the various villages and islands along its route.

Pacific Expeditions, based in Port Moresby, also offers a tour to the Trobriands. Their 5-day stay attempts to show a different side of the islands. Their accommodations at the Kaibola Beach Resort are "native" -- huts constructed in the local manner and complete with kerosene lanterns and mosquito nets hung over your bed. The Resort does have a mini-bus which can be rented for excursions into the villages in the countryside, and the good shopping.

Kiriwina Lodge is the only facility on the island offering modern accommodations. The rooms are basic, however, with neither air-conditioning nor fans. The main room of the facility is a combination bar and pool hall which serves as home to local characters and expats. The lodge also has a mini-bus available for rent.

In addition to these facilities, most of the villages will be happy to arrange other accommodations. Most are very reasonable in price, if rustic in character. But be careful of the occasional rip-off. To forestall any potential hassles, be sure you know the price and exactly what it is you are getting before committing yourself to such accommodations.

Traveling and Shopping Rules

Shopping in the Trobriands is more difficult than anywhere else in PNG. Because of the lack of tourist traffic, the people primarily deal with wholesale buyers and middlemen from the various shops on the mainland who arrive unexpectedly on the islands. To be an effective shopper, your first mission upon arrival is to "get the word out" that you are looking and ready to buy. It may take several days for your message to sift through the local communication infrastructure. Since there are no telephones or any other form of mass communication on the island, all communication is strictly word-of-mouth.

But to truly shop the Trobriands, your best approach is to hire a car with a good guide and go beat the bushes. To be successful with this approach, there are a few basic rules you should follow:

BEATING THE BUSHES
FOR TROBRIAND TREASURES

- **Rent a vehicle to get out into the villages.** Each village produces unique artifacts, and only with a good guide and a vehicle can you get out to where the interesting artifacts are produced. Be very specific in spelling out your rental car deal, and terms with your guide. Keep track of your mileage, and be sure to write the mileage down if the vehicle is going off to do an "errand". You should also address "overtime charges" if there is a chance you might be out late. Determine exactly who you are to pay. Your best deal will probably be paying for the car and driver separate from the guide.

- **Plan on carrying your purchases off the island with you.** We were unable to locate a reliable shipper. The small planes that serve the island can take your artifacts loose; you can then have them packed correctly with a Port Moresby shipper. If you are using the Melanesian Discoverer, the same advice applies that we give in Chapter 15 in relation to the Sepik River cruise: if you plan to purchase items in the Trobriands and have them picked up by a shipper when the boat returns to Madang, negotiate your deal before you leave Madang.

- **Ask before taking pictures.** Several villages ask a fee for allowing photographs. Our suggestion is not to pay the fee; move on to the next village. To pay the fee only encourages this kind of practice and makes it difficult for others who visit this area.

- **Carry a lot of low denomination currency.** Many items in the Trobriands are small and inexpensive, and few villagers carry change. Unless you have the correct change, you will find yourself walking away with several additional items in lieu of change. Chances are you really don't want or need such items, and you probably overpaid for them.

- **Guard your personal belongings.** A tropical paradise it is, but crime free it isn't. The relaxed, smiling, and overall good nature of the place can easily cause you to let down your guard.

- **Do comparative shopping at one of the major mainland shops prior to visiting the islands.** Since the various carvings are produced in different villages, visiting one of these shops can give you an idea of the variety of items available on the islands. Also, the pricing will give you a perspective as you should be paying something in the neighborhood of 30 to 50 percent for the same items in the islands.

- **Learn to distinguish between different types and qualities of wood used in carvings.** While in one of the mainland shops, pick up a carved piece done in Ebony. Pay close attention to the piece, especially its weight and density. Note the hardness of the wood's surface. This exercise should help you spot any pieces made of Kerosene wood and treated with black kiwi polish that may appear to be made of Ebony wood.

- **Learn the difference between real shell money and plastic immitations.** Once again while in one of these shops, look at some shell money. Carefully note the texture, the weight, and the feel of the pieces of shell that make up the string. When in doubt, remember that stone will not burn, and putting a lighter to the string is the ultimate test. Please make sure that this exercise is okay with your prospective seller, as it can and frequently does burn through the inner string holding the necklace together. This can leave you with a wonderful mess, particularly in a string that was closely graded with stones moving from lighter to darker, or smaller to larger. Perhaps the best rule in this case is when in doubt, don't.

- **Never accept the first price quoted since all prices are negotiable in the villages.** Since villagers expect you to bargain, they set their prices accordingly.

- **Expect your bargaining skills gained on the Sepik River to fail you in the Trobriands.** The concept of "first price" and "second price" does not exist in the Trobriands. The seller will normally quote you a price -- sometimes outlandish, sometimes reasonable -- where upon he or she will expect a counter offer if you are interested. Along the Sepik River, however, bargaining scenarios are very predictable. After getting a first price, you immediately ask for the second price. Within a few seconds you will have a final price. In most cases the final price is 30 to 60 percent of the first price. Knowing we would probably pay 30 or 60 percent of the first price, we wasted little time bargaining along the Sepik River. In the Highlands, we received smaller percentage discounts. But the Trobriands turned out to be very unpredictable.

• **Expect asking prices to have no relationships to the final price in the Trobriands.** We got lazy along the Sepik where we knew that the final price was going to be somewhere between 30 and 60 percent of the initial asking price. In the Trobriands, there is no fixed relationship between the initial price and the final price for which you can buy the item. We purchased a enormous beautiful bowl for K125 that had an initial asking price of K150. On the other hand, we also purchased a small piece of sculpture for K6 that had an initial asking price of K50!

• **When heading out to beat the bush, carry an adequate supply of drinking water and any food or snacks you think you might want.** Since you will not find refreshments along the way, take whatever you need with you.

In Search of the "Good Stuff"

We arrived in the Trobriand Islands aboard a 50 foot Danish sailing ketch "Feen". "Feen" is the base ship for the Danish film company UV-FIlm and Video ApS headed by Leif Stubkjaer. Mr. Stubkjaer was kind enough to transport us from Madang after Melanesian Tourist Services cancelled their Trobriand Island Cruise due to lack of passengers.

Since "Feen" draws 8 feet of water, we were forced to anchor a mile from the Losuia dock. On the way in we passed the largest of the regular "coasters" that normally calls in the Trobriands with freight and passengers. It was

hard aground.   As we were leaving the Trobriands, it
remained in the same position.   The crew fished to pass
the time as they awaited a storm to generate an unusually
high tide.   Patience is often more than a virtue when
traveling in this section of the world -- it is a necessity.

Once ashore we hired a mini-bus and driver from the
Kiriwina Lodge.   The Government Administrator helped us
to arrange our guide who was in general an excellent
guide.   Although the overall experience was positive, it
was not without incident.

You must resolve yourself to the expense of renting the
car.   We paid approximately $1.25 per mile for the vehi-
cle, plus the expenses for the driver and guide.   At first we
thought this to be excessive, but later saw some of the
reasoning behind the high charges.   There are no repair
facilities on the island.   At the airport we got a lesson in
tire repair, Trobriand style.   The first step after getting a
flat is to take the tire off and then transport it to the airport, where it must be air freighted to Port Moresby.   In
the meantime, someone must go to the police station to use
their shortwave radio to contact a garage in Port Moresby
which will pick up the tire, repair it, and return it by air
freight back.   Our $1.25 per mile seems cheap now.   We're
still wondering about the procedure for getting a tune-up!

After resolving yourself to the expense, care still needs
to be taken not to get ripped off.   At lunch time one day
our vehicle disappeared for several hours, apparently out to
the driver's home and to run some errands for the owner.
Late that evening, when time came to settle the bill, that
milage had not been deducted.   Since both our driver and
guide were now drunk, resolution of this issue almost
turned into a very ugly incident.   We were finally able to
get them to agree to settle the issue in the morning.   The
next day they were both pussycats, and the bill was adjust-
ed with no problem whatsoever.

Once on the road the villages were all very interesting.
While not all the villages produce "goods" for market,
those that do tend to specialize in a particular type of carving.   One village, for example, would only make bowls,
another would produce stools, while another would concentrate on walking sticks.

Villages we found particularly interesting include:

> ● **Yalumugwa:**   This village is not a major
> producer of carvings but it is home to Vala-
> wosi, one of the most creative and talented
> carvers on the island.   As with all of the
> carvers on the island, he has his own field of
> expertise.   Valawosi carves a beautiful styl-

ized fish in Kerosene or Quela wood.

- **Kabwaku:** With luck, you will find some beautiful walking sticks and stacked figures in this village. We were unfortunate to arrive several days behind a major buyer who had left us only a few scattered pieces.

- **Okaiboma:** What a delight! These wonderful people produce simply fantastic bowls. The entire village seems to be involved in the production of these works of art. Most are made out of Kerosene wood but you will also find an occasional piece of Ebony, and even more remarkable were the pieces of mottled ebony. Just gorgeous! Several ocean going canoes used in the Kula Ring trading rituals are stored in huts on a beach near this village. We asked the chief to see them and he allowed us to open up the huts and photograph these beautiful vessels.

- **Boitalu:** This village produces some beautiful tables.

Another good source for carvings is Bill Rudd. Mr. Rudd was managing the Kiriwina Lodge during our stay. He acts as a middleman for one of the large shops in Port Moresby. Depending on what stage he is in the assembling a shipment, you may find he has a storehouse of excellent quality goods. We dealt with him on a small scale and on a fixed price basis. The quality of his carvings and his prices were excellent. We had hoped he could have been more helpful in identifying the various villages that produce some of his wonderful carvings, but we also recognized that he had his business interests to preserve.

Mr. Rudd is also in the business of exporting Ulysesies butterflies (ornithoptera priamus demophanes). The islands are an excellent source for this and other species.

While the main island of Kiriwina offers the tourist or dealer the easiest access and the widest selection of goods, there are four major islands in the Trobriand group and many islets. These islands are rarely visited. They may offer the chance to discover some "special finds".

Also on this short list of areas to explore in this region is **Woodlark Island**. Woodlark is the source for the Ebony wood used in many Trobriand carvings. However, don't expect to buy many good quality Ebony pieces, be-

cause the locals tend to keep the best for themselves. This
island is even less touristed than the Trobriands; it is
renowned for its own beautiful carvings. If you are looking for something special, this may be the place to visit.

Chapter Fifteen

SHIPPING WITH CONFIDENCE

Before you begin purchasing large items, especially along the Sepik River, you should consider the shipping situation and the various shipping options available in PNG. With the exception of parcel post shipments, shipping from PNG can be expensive; it can be exceedingly expensive if you meet the wrong people!

OPTIONS AND COSTS

Shipping by **air freight** from PNG is just as expensive as air freight shipments from other countries. But sea shipments tend to be more expensive because few companies ship directly from PNG to other countries. If you live in the United States, for example, shipments are usually transhipped via Australia, Hong Kong, or Japan. This means your shipment has to be off-loaded in these other countries and consolidated with larger shipments. The cost of doing this, of course, is higher than if your shipment was sent directly from port to port.

Shipping costs vary depending on the methods and procedures you choose when arranging a shipment. **Sea freight** charges, for example, are usually figured by volume -- either by the cubic meter or a container. **Air freight** charges are based on a combination of size and weight. Sea shipments involve a minimum charge for volume -- usually one cubic meter -- that you will pay even though your shipment is of lesser volume. There are also **port fees** to be paid, a **broker** to get the shipment through customs, and unless your hometown is a major seaport that handles freighters, you will also pay **trucking fees** to transport your shipment from the port of entry to your home.

On **air freight** you only pay for the actual amount you ship by weight -- there is no minimum charge. You can usually have it flown to the international airport nearest your home and avoid port fees altogether. However, there will be a small Customs fee.

If you buy any items that are less than three feet in length and you don't wish to hand-carry them home, consider sending them by **parcel post**. This is the cheapest way to ship. Parcel post from PNG tends to be reliable, although it may take four to six months for final delivery. Most shops will take care of the packing and shipping for parcel post.

If you have items that are too large for parcel post, but nonetheless are small and relatively lightweight, **air freight** may be a viable option. Consider air freight if the package is too large to be sent parcel post, but much smaller than the minimum of one cubic meter, and does not weigh an excessive amount relative to its size. Air freight is the transportation of choice if you must have your purchase arrive right away. **Sea freight** is the better choice if your purchase is large and heavy and you are willing to wait several weeks for its arrival. When using air freight, contact a well established and reliable airline. It will be most cost effective if you can select one airline, i.e., the same carrier flies between your point of shipping and your hometown airport. For air freight from PNG one airline would not be possible, but the shipment could be made nevertheless and the additional cost should be minimal. One airline may be viable for air shipments from Australia depending on the city where you live.

CONSIDER CONSOLIDATION

All international shipments will leave from the docks in Port Moresby. If, for example, you want to ship from Wewak or Madang, the shipment will first go to Port Moresby where it is then put on another carrier for transhipment through Australia, Hong Kong, or Japan. Knowing this, you should treat Port Moresby as the central point to where all of your shipments should be sent and consolidated into a single shipment. You may, for example, buy some large items at PNG Art and Hanuacraft in Port Moresby. However, rather than have each shop arrange to ship your goods separately, have them hold your shipment for consolidation. After all, they both use the same shipping company -- Robert Laurie -- and this same shipping company can assist you with shipping items you purchase in other towns as well as along the Sepik River. If you don't think in terms of consolidation through a single shipping company based in Port Moresby, you may end up sending two or three separate shipments from PNG at a much higher cost than a single consolidated shipment.

POTENTIAL PROBLEMS AND A SOLUTION

A case in point is one problem we encountered in Madang. After completing the Ambunti to Madang Sepik River tour organized through the Melanesian Tourist Services, we were met on board the ship by a representative of a local shipping company. The representative gave us what we knew was a very high quote (K900 per cubic meter) for packing and shipping to the East Coast United States. Believing this was the only game in town, feeling stranded in a small and unfamiliar town, being in a hurry to fly out of Madang the next day for Port Moresby, and not knowing where else to turn, we felt we had no alternative than to go with this company. We were assured this was nothing more than the normal shipping rate which was acknowledged to be high in PNG in comparison to other countries.

Once we arrived back in Port Moresby we investigated the shipping charges and learned more about how to handle such a shipping situation. In so doing, we quickly discovered that K900 per cubic meter was indeed outrageous and that we had other shipping options. We worked with **Robert Laurie Company** in Port Moresby to take the shipment from Madang and bring it to Port Moresby where we consolidated it with several items we purchased at PNG Arts. Robert Laurie was able to quickly arrange for this transfer through its offices in Madang and Lae. The result of doing this was a savings of a few thousand dollars. Our seven cubic meters at K900 per cubic meter quickly dropped to the going rate -- K350 per cubic meter -- which was a savings of approximately K4250 or nearly US$4000.

The Melanesian Tourist Service has assured us that they are looking into the problems that we encountered and reported to them. We fully hope and expect that they have taken steps to correct any problems with overcharging for shipping by the shipping firm(s) they allow to come aboard their boat at the end of the Sepik or Trobriand cruises. Indeed, this was the only major sour note on what was otherwise an interesting tour of the Sepik River through this well established and reputable firm. However, if you expect you may be making several or large purchases, take time to check with a reputable shipping firm such as Robert Laurie Company before you leave Port Moresby for other areas in PNG.

RECOMMENDED ALTERNATIVES

You will find several shipping companies in PNG, we recommend one for its prices, service, and reliability -- **Robert Laurie Pty. Ltd.** on Varahe Street (Tel. 21-4053); ask for Ann Burgess. This firm is based in Port Moresby, works regularly with the two largest artifact shops (PNG Art and Hanuacraft), and has branch offices throughout the country. If, for example, you are in Lae and need shipping services, contact the local Robert Laurie office on Malaita Street (Tel. 42-3811). In Madang, their office is located on Kasagten Street (Tel. 82-2157). They also have offices in Popondetta, Kimbe, Wewak, Rabaul, Kieta, Goroka, and Mt. Hagen. These offices can arrange to ship your items to their Port Moresby warehouse where they can be consolidated with other things you buy in Port Moresby. For example, if you purchase a number of items along the Sepik River and your final stop is Madang, you can call the local Robert Laurie office in Madang (Tel. 82-2157) to arrange to have your purchases shipped to their office in Lae where they, in turn, will be sent on to Port Moresby to be consolidated with any other purchases you made there or in other towns.

Chapter Sixteen

ENJOYING YOUR STAY

In addition to shopping, PNG has a great deal to offer those who wish to experience exotic cultures, beautiful beaches, white water rafting, cave exploring, trekking and climbing, flora and fauna, scuba diving, and sailing.

While PNG's tourist infrastructure is not the same as in many other countries, especially for do-it-yourself traveling, it does have several reputable tour companies that organize tours to the Highlands, rivers, and islands. Better still, several of the companies offer special interest tours and attempt to custom design itineraries to the interests of individuals and groups. You can, for example, spend several days in Highland and river lodges visiting some of the world's most unique tribes or enjoy beautiful beaches and scuba diving in some of the world's most beautiful coral reefs as well as explore hundreds of ship wrecks from World War II.

TOURING PORT MORESBY

While in Port Moresby you may want to see the major sights in and around this city. These include the National Museum, Parliament House, markets, the Bomana War

317

Cemetery and Memorial, and Variarata National Park. **Tolu Tours** on Spring Garden Road in Hohola (Tel. 25-2847) offers daily tours to these and other sights in the Port Moresby metropolitan area. If you visit other areas in PNG and wish to take a half or full-day tour of the area, it's best to contact a local tour company for assistance. In many cases the company will offer you an individualized special interest tour.

MAJOR TOUR OPTIONS

The best way to enjoy PNG is to book one or two of the major tours operating throughout the country. Many visitors report the following destinations and activities to be major highlights of their visit to PNG:

- **Sepik River:** Tours of villages along the Upper, Middle, and Lower Sepik conducted by Melanesian Tourist Services, Trans Niugini Tours, and Pacific Expeditions.

- **Karawari Lodge:** tours of Karawari River and Sepik River villages operated by Trans Niugini Tours.

- **Ambua Lodge:** Southern Highlands lodge at 7,000 feet elevation and near Tari. Offers spectacular views, rich flora and fauna, and opportunities to meet and learn about the Highland tribes. Operated by Trans Niugini Tours.

- **Trobriand Islands:** Tours operated by the Melanesian Tourist Services and Pacific Adventures.

- **Scuba Diving:** Diving adventures off the coasts of Madang, Milne Bay, and Rabaul for World War II ship wrecks and coral reefs. Offered by Jais Aben, Melanesian Dive Centre, Tropical Diving Adventures, Walindi Diving, Aquarius/Dive Travel, and Sea New Guinea.

- **Adventure Tours:** Four-wheel drive tours through the Western and Southern Highlands; trekking programs to PNGs highest mountain (14,800 foot Mt. Giluwe), into the Southern Highlands, and the great Kokoda Trail; motorized dugout canoe trips on the Sepik River; white water rafting trips in the wilds of PNG; village stays; and sailing trips. Offered by Trans Niugini Tours, Pacific Expeditions, and Tribal World New Guinea.

- **Special Interest Tours:** Most tour companies offer special interest tours for individuals and groups. If, for example, you want to see PNG's unique flora and fauna, tour groups will custom design a tour to match your interests. Trans Niugini Tours is especially good at organizing such tours, although other tour companies have the same capabilities.

TRAVEL INFORMATION

Before deciding what to do and where to go in PNG, we recommend that you contact your travel agent for information. If your travel agent has limited resources on PNG, it's best to write directly for information and brochures on traveling in PNG. While the government does have a national tourist organization -- the Papua New Guinea Tourist Office (P.O. Box 7144, Boroko, Tel. 25-1269) -- as well as provincial tourist offices in the towns of Lorengau, Rabaul, Kimbe, and Alotau -- these offices are not particularly active since the government has yet to decide if it really wants to promote tourism to PNG.

In the meantime, the best sources of information on traveling in PNG are Air Niugini offices and private tour companies. **Air Niugini** offices function as a tourist information contact point for the government tourist office. If you write or call one of their offices, they will send you an overview brochure entitled *Papua New Guinea: Land of the Unexpected.* You can contact these offices at the following locations and numbers:

> **AIR NIUGINI** -- Head Office in PNG
> P.O. Box 7186
> Boroko
> Papua New Guinea
> Tel. 273-200

> **AIR NIUGINI** -- U.S.A.
> 5000 Birch Street
> Suite 3000, West Tower
> Newport Beach, CA 92660
> Tel. 714/752-5440

AIR NIUGINI -- West Germany
Bockenheimer
Landstrasse 33
6000 Frankfurt 1
West Germany
Tel. (069) 71400348

AIR NIUGINI -- Hong Kong
Room 1625, 16/F
Princes Building, Chater Road
Central, Hong Kong
Tel. 5-242151

AIR NIUGINI -- Japan
Imperial Hotel
1-1-1 Uchiasaiwaicho
Chiyoda-Ku, Tokyo 100
Tel. 504-1111

AIR NIUGINI -- Singapore
#17-405 Goldhill Square
101 Thomson Road
Singapore 1130
Tel. 2504868

AIR NIUGINI -- The Philippines
6776 Ayala Avenue
Makati, Manila
The Philippines
Tel. 864713

AIR NIUGINI -- Australia
100 Clarence Street
Sydney, NSW 2000
Tel. (02) 232-3100

AIR NIUGINI -- Australia
127 Creek Street
Brisbane, Qld. 4000
Tel. (07) 229-5844

AIR NIUGINI -- Australia
Shop 2, Tropical Arcade
4-6 Shields Street
Cairns, Qld. 4870
Tel. (070) 51-4177

AIR NIUGINI -- The Solomons
P.O. Box 677
Honiara
Tel. 22895

RELIABLE TOUR OPERATORS

The major tour operators within Papua New Guinea offering a variety of tours to the Highlands, Sepik River, and islands include:

MELANESIAN TOURIST SERVICES PTY.
P.O. Box 707
Madang
Papua New Guinea
Tel. 822-766

TRANS NIUGINI TOURS
P.O. Box 371
Mount Hagen
Papua New Guinea
Tel. 52-1490

TRIBAL WORLD NEW GUINEA
P.O. Box 86
Mount Hagen
Papua New Guinea
Tel. 551-555

PACIFIC EXPEDITIONS
P.O. Box 132
Port Moresby
Papua New Guinea
Tel. 257-803

Some of these tour companies also have branch offices in the United States, Australia, Japan, Germany, United Kingdom, and Hong Kong. The **Melanesian Tourist Services**, for example, has branch offices in the following locations:

MELANESIAN TOURIST SERVICES -- U.S.A.
Suite 105, 850 Colorado Blvd.
Los Angeles, CA 90041
Tel. 213/256-1991

MELANESIAN TOURIST SERVICES --
Australia
G.P.O. Box 5316

Sydney, NSW
Tel. 296063

MELANESIAN TOURIST SERVICES --
West Germany
Alt-Schwanheim 50
6000 Frankfurt am/Main 71
Tel. 35-6667

ABERCROMBIE & KENT LTD. -- United
Kingdom
Sloane Square House
Holbein Place, London SW1W 8NS
Tel. (44) 1-960-7300

ABERCROMBIE & KENT LTD. -- Hong Kong
10/F Siberian Fur Store Building
29 Des Voeux Road, Central
Tel. (852) 5-216657

VIVRE INTERNATIONAL INC. -- Japan
Arai Bld., 7-7 Monshio-Cho
Shinjuku, Tokyo 160
Tel. (03) 358-6391

Trans Niugini Tours has representatives at the following locations:

TRANS NIUGINI TOURS -- U.S.A.
408 East Islay
Santa Barbara, CA 93101
Tel. (805) 569-0558

MARKETING SERVICES (T & T) -- United
Kingdom
Suite 433, 52-54 High Holborn
London, WC1V 6RL
Tel. (01) 242-3131

NEW GUINEA ADVENTURE CENTRE --
Australia
P.O. Box 1827
Cairns, Qld. 4870
Tel. (070) 52-1127

ABERCROMBIE & KENT -- Hong Kong
10/F Siberian Fur Store Building
29 Des Voeux Road, Central
Tel. 5-216657

UNITED TOURING INTERNATIONAL --
Japan
Taiyo Building
3F/1-10 Wakaba
Shinjuku-ku, Tokyo
Tel. (03) 355-2391

SCUBA DIVING

Scuba diving in the waters of PNG is one of the great discoveries of any visit to this country. PNG offers some of the world's finest coral reefs and ship wrecks for scuba divers. Several companies offer a variety of exciting diving opportunities around Madang, Milne Bay, Rabaul, and several islands. The major scuba diving operators within Papua New Guinea include:

> **JAIS ABEN**
> P.O. Box 105
> Madang
> Tel. 823-311
>
> **MELANESIAN DIVE CENTRE**
> P.O. Box 111
> Madang
> Tel. 822-665
>
> **TROPICAL DIVING ADVENTURES**
> P.O. Box 1644
> Boroko
> Tel. 257-429
>
> **WALINDI DIVING**
> P.O. Box 4
> Kimbe
> Tel. 935441

If you are in Australia, you might want to contact these companies for information and reservations:

> **AQUARIUS/DIVE TRAVEL** - Australia
> 40-42 Taylor Street
> Ashburton, Vic. 3147
>
> **SEA NEW GUINEA** - Australia
> Lower Ground Floor
> 100 Clarence Street
> Sydney, NSW 2000
> Tel. (02) 267-5563

PLAN AHEAD

Again, it's important to emphasize that you plan your visit to PNG well ahead of your departure date. We do not -- nor does the PNG government -- encourage you to travel on your own in PNG. This is a very special place requiring a very special approach to discovering its many delights. Get as much information on the various tour options, make your reservations six months to a year ahead of time, and put yourself in the hands of PNG's experienced tour operators who are organized to deal with groups as well as special individual requests.

If you prefer not traveling in a group, just write to the tour companies and let them know where and how you would like to travel. They will make special arrangements and ensure that you have a safe and informative trip.

But if this is your first trip to PNG, start it right by visiting the Sepik River and touring the Highlands based at one of PNG's delightful jungle resorts. To attempt to visit this exotic country on your own may be simply foolish -- both a waste of time and money. If you approach this country right, you will experience some of the most exotic shopping, sights, and sounds of a lifetime!

INDEX

AUSTRALIA

PAPUA NEW GUINEA

ORDER FORM

The following *Shopping in Exotic Places* titles can be ordered directly from the publisher. Complete the following form (or list the titles), include your name and mailing address, enclose payment, and send your order to:

IMPACT PUBLICATIONS
10655 Big Oak Circle
Manassas, VA 22111 (USA)
Tel. 703/361-7300

All prices are in US dollars. Orders from individuals should be prepaid by check, moneyorder, or Visa or MasterCard number. If your order must be shipped outside the U.S., please include an additional US$1.50 per title for surface mail or the appropriate air mail rate for books weighting 24 ounces each. We accept telephone orders (credit cards), and orders are shipped within 48 hours.

Qty.	TITLES	Price	TOTAL
__	*Shopping in Exciting Australia and Papua New Guinea*	$13.95	_____
__	*Shopping in Exotic Hong Kong*	$10.95	_____
__	*Shopping in Exotic India and Nepal*	$13.95	_____
__	*Shopping in Exotic Indonesia and the Philippines*	$13.95	_____
__	*Shopping in Exotic Places: Your Passport to Exciting Hong Kong, Korea, Thailand, Indonesia, and Singapore*	$14.95	_____
__	*Shopping in Exotic Singapore and Malaysia*	$12.95	_____
__	*Shopping in Exotic Thailand*	$10.95	_____
__	*Shopping the Exotic Caribbean*	$12.95	_____
__	*Shopping the Exotic South Pacific: Your Passport to Exciting Australia, New Zealand, Papua New Guinea, Fiji, and Tahiti*	$15.95	_____

SUBTOTAL $ _____

- Virginia residents add 4.5% sales tax $ _____
- Shipping/handling ($2.00 for the first title and $.50 for each additional book) $ _____

Ansett does more than h^op around Australia.

ANSETT. We are a lot more than just Australia's most popular domestic carrier. We are Ansett, a group of companies providing the finest travel services in the South Pacific.

ANSETT AIRLINES. Ansett in the air is Ansett Airlines of Australia, Ansett W.A., Air N.S.W., Ansett N.T., Ansett New Zealand, Polynesian Airlines, Cook Islands International and now representing East-West Airlines.

ANSETT RESORTS. Located in the Whitsundays, near the Great Barrier Reef area, Ansett offers world class resorts. Hayman Island, Hamilton Island and South Molle Island.

SPECIAL AIRFARES. Overseas visitors can enjoy special discounted airfares and airpasses. For further information call your travel agent or Ansett. 800-366-1300.

Ansett.

award-winning
More than just a great Airline.

Papua New Guinea
The most Exotic Shop in the world

With arts and artifacts eminating from cultures more than 8,000 years old, Papua New Guinea offers a multitude of unique purchase opportunities.

Traditional carvings, pottery, basket weaving, jewellery, printed tapa cloth, colourful billim bags and stone age weapons abound in commercial outlets throughout the country. You can also enjoy the memorable experience of buying direct from the artists or artisans in their villages.

Contact Air Niugini for information on our gateway to exotic shopping through Sydney, Brisbane, Cairns and Townsville in Australia, or Jayapury, Honiara, Manilla, Port Vila and Singapore.